# Animal Welfare in World Rel

This unique and readable book examines the relationship between religion and animal welfare, taking a detailed dive into the teachings and practices of the major world religions.

While there are many books expounding the beliefs of the major religions and many about the rights and welfare of animals, there are few linking the two. With each chapter focusing on one of the five major religions – Judaism, Christianity, Islam, Hinduism and Buddhism – the book explores the beliefs and practices which drive our relationship with and treatment of animals. The book draws on the scriptures of the major faiths and includes the voices of leading historical religious figures and contemporary faith leaders. In doing so, it compares the teachings of old with contemporary practices and showcases the impact of the major religions on both the protection and exploitation of animals, from running animal sanctuaries, to participating in or condoning cruel sports and factory farming. Importantly, the book also includes a chapter looking beyond the major world religions, where it examines a wider range of beliefs and practices, including Indigenous peoples from the USA and Australia, Jainism, Sikhism and Rastafarianism, to provide fascinating insights into another range of beliefs and views on the human-animal relationship. Overall, this book challenges and encourages religious leaders and followers to re-examine their teachings and to prioritise the well-being of animals.

This book is essential reading for those interested in the role of religion in animal welfare, human-animal studies, and animal welfare and ethics more broadly.

**Joyce D'Silva** is Ambassador Emeritus for Compassion in World Farming, the leading charity advancing the welfare of farm animals worldwide. She is co-editor of *The Meat Crisis: Developing More Sustainable and Ethical Production and Consumption* (Routledge, 2017) and *Farming, Food and Nature: Respecting Animals, People and the Environment* (Routledge, 2018). She has been awarded honorary doctorates by the University of Winchester and the University of Keele, UK, and is a patron of the Animal Interfaith Alliance.

of the livestock industry both for human welfare as well as for animal life, all religions should be advocating for a plant-based diet, which is more available than ever before, thus promoting greater health as well as greater compassion and harmony in our world."

**Rabbi David Rosen**, *CBE, former Chief Rabbi of Ireland*
*and a President of Religions for Peace*

"Joyce D'Silva's book is a valuable contribution to the study of religion and animal ethics. The book skillfully combines a scholarly exploration of the ways that animals are understood and treated in the world's major religious traditions with an inspirational message about the sacredness of all sentient beings. D'Silva presents the diversity of views on animals that exist within every tradition, often leading to tensions and conflict within religions, while also underscoring the way that each tradition provides resources for promoting compassion for and better treatment of animals. The book, which provides passages about animals from the scriptures of the world's religions along with profiles of great Saints and thinkers, can serve as an excellent resource for scholars and activists alike. D'Silva applies the teachings found in the various traditions to contemporary issues in animal ethics, including factory farming, vivisection and biodiversity. She shows how in most cultures and traditions, people fall short of their tradition's highest teachings, but she demonstrates how religious texts and exemplars can still inspire us to be guided by their noblest ideals."

**Professor Mark Berkson**, *Professor and Chair in the*
*Department of Religion at Hamline University*

"Scientific studies of non-human animals, from apes and whales to birds, rats and octopuses, have increasingly highlighted the fact that they are both sentient and sapient. This makes the cruelty towards animals used for food, clothing, entertainment, pets, trophy hunting and so on particularly shocking and heart breaking. In this meticulously researched book, Joyce D'Silva points out that, in view of our new understanding, the leaders of the world's religions could, and should, play a major role in stressing to their millions of followers the importance of treating all animals with kindness and respect. *Animal Welfare in World Religion* should be in all libraries and university curricula – you should read it whether or not you have a faith."

**Jane Goodall**, *PhD, DBE, Founder – the Jane Goodall*
*Institute & UN Messenger of Peace*

"This book comes at a very appropriate time a few months after the adoption of a historic United Nations Resolution on Animal Welfare (UNEP/EA.5/Res.1). The resolution on animal welfare, environment and sustainable development calls on Member States to recognise that protecting animals and their welfare is an important contribution to the global objectives of protecting the environment, reducing the risks of emerging zoonoses, improving food systems and achieving sustainable development.

This book is an important contribution to understanding the ethical and moral aspects of animal welfare as described in the teachings and practices of religions. Joyce, while not a theologian, has, masterfully, not only told us stories we didn't know derived from religions, but has also showed us that we need to work on our practices that do not often match our beliefs and religious teachings.

Religion is about creation, purpose, destiny, life, and love. People's beliefs about the creator and the creation affect all aspects of their being and behaviour. The book will have a critical influence on how people look to animals. The language of the book is just suitable for everyone, decision makers, faith leaders and the public. This is an important factor in influencing readers. Covering a wide range of religions and addressing many aspects is a highly commendable effort that I hope will promote stronger engagement of religious actors in respecting the welfare of animals who are, to some religions, other communities created by God."

**Dr Iyad Abumoghli**, *Director of Faith for Earth, United Nations Environment Programme (UNEP)*

"This is a profoundly affecting and thought-provoking work. When were we taught that mankind is more important than the rest of creation? Was it through religion, or indifference or greed? Can we return to true compassion and find the way back to respecting all sentient beings? Can we live without inflicting cruelty? I urge you read this book, whether you have a faith or not: it may change your life for the better."

**Dame Joanna Lumley**, *Actor and Campaigner*

"Joyce D'Silva has spent a lifetime working, with considerable success, to improve the lives of farm animals. And yet there remains much to be done. Around the world, most people have a religious faith and, in this book, Joyce D'Silva looks at how the world's religions see animals and how these religions maintain we should live with them. The result is a book full of optimism and with many surprises. We desperately need everyone to work together to improve the lot of farm animals, which will also benefit wildlife, the environment more generally, and ourselves. This excellent book will help achieve that end."

**Rev Professor Michael J. Reiss**, *University College London*

"For those with some biological or medical training, humans are animals and it is normal to think of other sentient beings as similar to humans and very different from inanimate objects. The message in Joyce D'Silva's book is of the 'beautiful teaching' of all of the world's major faiths emphasising the value of non-human individuals and the obligation of people to care for them and consider their needs. For example, the Qur'an refers to non-human communities as like human communities and the Prophet Muhammad equates acts of kindness to humans and to other animals. Indeed, the book emphasises that such an attitude is important for everyone who lives an ethical and compassionate life. A major problem with the world at present is too much emphasis on humans and not enough emphasis on the rest of life."

**Donald M. Broom**, *Emeritus Professor of Animal Welfare, Department of Veterinary Medicine, University of Cambridge*

"This is a very timely and important work. It comes at a time when recognition of the interconnectedness of life is so significant for the future of all life and the planet. Readable and authoritative, it is essential reading for those of all faiths and none."

**Professor Joy Carter**, *CBE DL Cgeol FGS, Emeritus Professor of Geochemistry and Health, University of Winchester*

"Religious faiths are afflicted by a striking paradox: they preach kindness to others, yet rarely speak out against the harms we do to animals – in our farming systems, laboratories, for entertainment, and other purposes. With animals increasingly affected by our actions, it has never been more important that people of faith speak, and act, with kindness toward animals. The majority of humanity follow religious teachings, which have enormous potential to help bring about a better world. By providing key examples from major and lesser-known religions, D'Silva reminds us of the fundamental commitments of faith communities to values such as kindness and compassion for animals. *Animal Welfare in World Religion* provides the keys to unlocking the potential of religion to bring about a better, kinder world for animals. It should be essential reading for all who care about animals and about living a life consistent with core religious values."

**Andrew Knight**, *Professor of Animal Welfare and Ethics, University of Winchester Centre for Animal Welfare*

"Today we stand on the shore of a great ocean of human spiritual evolution, where we extend the Golden Rule – to treat others as we would wish to be treated ourselves – to our non-human, sentient sisters and brothers. Guided by the teachings and practices of the world religions, we set sail on this wondrous journey, and Joyce D'Silva's *Animal Welfare in World Religion: Teaching and Practice* is the perfect guidebook to steer us on our course. It is such a privilege to share this exciting adventure with someone as insightful as Joyce. I encourage everyone to pick up this guide and set sail."

**Barbara Gardner**, *founder and CEO of the Animal Interfaith Alliance (AIA)*

"This book provides a timely and comprehensive look at the major religions and their historical and indeed contemporary approach to animals and animal welfare. The authority of the work is underpinned by the fact that it is written by an individual who has actively made an actual real, measurable, and beneficial improvement in animals' lives over many years.

This is a book which demands attention and deserves to be widely read."
**Chris Fegan**, *Chief Executive,*
*Catholic Concern for Animals*

"Clearly written and beautifully argued book...

The author takes great pains to explain the suffering of fellow animals... complex details that even theologians and scholars of religion overlooked and neglected. It is deep and bold thinking on our responsibilities to animals and what religious teachings of the major global faiths and some Indigenous beliefs can help us to develop an ethics of compassion and moral responsibility towards all creatures."
**Ibrahim Özdemir**, *Professor of Philosophy, Uskudar*
*University, Istanbul, President, Uskudar University Forum*
*on Environmental Ethics, core member of al-Mizan:*
*A Covenant for the Earth*

"Roman Catholic Cardinal Manning in Britain was a major figure in the early 19th century animal protection movement despite the teaching of St Thomas Aquinas who held that humans have no 'direct' duties to animals. Faith leaders have mostly followed Thomist teachings and have been largely absent from discussions on animal protection and the reinvigoration of global animal protection starting in 1950. However, Joyce D'Silva demonstrates in this very accessible discussion of a variety of global faiths that concern for animals is found in the teachings of all the major world religions. Her very timely, accessible and necessary book appears a little more than seven years after Pope Francis' Laudato Si encyclical – a powerful plea to the world to change its approach to protecting the global environment and the other creatures who share the world with humans."
**Andrew Rowan**, *President of WellBeing International*

"The first thing to say is that Joyce D'Silva, the author of this book, is one of the three or four outstanding political campaigners for animal rights of the last fifty years. So she knows a great deal about what she is writing. I happen to agree with every word I have read.

Nearly all the great faiths have said wonderful things about the other animals (the Golden Rule applies). Yet too often they have forgotten this in practice. Why has no modern Pope, nor Archbishop, for example, ever made Animal Rights or Compassion for Animals the central subject for a leading Christian campaign? (Today's Pope Francis gets the nearest.)

Modern Christianity has failed miserably and ought to feel ashamed. This failure was one reason why I lost my Christian faith. (I am sure I am not alone in this.) The founders of faiths have nearly all shown their passionate concern for animals, as have the Saints. Yet their followers – the self-important second raters and bureaucrats have, however, let us all down.

I happen to believe that Jesus too was passionately concerned about the animals being cruelly sacrificed in the Temple. It was a money-making scam and it made him furious. He chucked out the cruel animal exploiters. That is one reason why he was crucified."

**Richard Dudley Ryder**, *MA DCP PhD (Cantab) AFBPsS*
*FZS, President, Animal Interfaith Alliance,*
*Past Chair, RSPCA*

"Joyce D'Silva has assembled an inspiring collection of 'beautiful words' coined by the fathers of the faiths, humbly aware that when God saw that it was good, he was referring to all life, not just us. Today, these words are largely unknown, forgotten or ignored, and not just by the secular. At a time when compassion for life is not just a moral duty but essential to our common survival, she challenges the current crop of faith leaders to take heed and give a lead."

**Professor John Webster**, *Professor Emeritus,*
*University of Bristol, 'Father of the Five Freedoms'*

"In this illuminating book, Joyce D'Silva very clearly makes the case for animal care and welfare in all the great religious traditions of the world. If we are to return any kind of dignity to the animal world – and save the planet from the perils of climate change and biodiversity loss – then we need to urgently align our world with these teachings."

**Gopal D. Patel**, *Co-Founder & Director Bhumi Global*

# Animal Welfare in World Religion

Teaching and Practice

Joyce D'Silva

*To Rachel,
changing the
food industry!*

*Joyce D'Silva*

Routledge
Taylor & Francis Group
LONDON AND NEW YORK

from Routledge

Designed cover image: Sam Brown Art – www.ceruleansam.com

First published 2023
by Routledge
4 Park Square, Milton Park, Abingdon, Oxon OX14 4RN

and by Routledge
605 Third Avenue, New York, NY 10158

*Routledge is an imprint of the Taylor & Francis Group, an informa business*

© 2023 Joyce D'Silva

*British Library Cataloguing-in-Publication Data*
A catalogue record for this book is available from the British Library

ISBN: 978-1-032-27407-2 (hbk)
ISBN: 978-1-032-27399-0 (pbk)
ISBN: 978-1-003-29255-5 (ebk)

DOI: 10.4324/9781003292555

Typeset in Goudy
by codeMantra

To the two most important and caring teachers in my life: my late husband, guitarist Amancio D'Silva, and the founder of Compassion in World Farming, the late Peter Roberts MBE.

# Contents

# Acknowledgements

I wanted to write this book because its subject fascinates me. But I could never have done it without generous support and critique from others. Firstly, I am so grateful to Philip Lymbery, Global CEO of Compassion in World Farming International, for his support and advice on the practicalities of writing a book. With three terrific books to his credit, he knows exactly how time- and energy-consuming writing can be.

I have run each chapter past a respected individual in that particular faith. I am very grateful to them for their critique and suggestions: Fazlun Khalid, Dr Richard Schwartz, Reverend Professor David Clough, Professor Mark Berkson, Robert Gussman, Wu Hung, Bhikkhu Bodhi, Professor Nanditha Krishna, Charanjit Aijit Singh, Nitin Mehta and Dr Othman Llewellyn and Doug Sam (biographies below).

I am also grateful to those who allowed me to interview them and incorporate their comments in the relevant chapter: Rabbi David Rosen CBE, Fazlun Khalid, Professor Ibrahim Özdemir, Reverend Professor David Clough, Professor Nanditha Krishna and Charanjit Aijit Singh (biographies below).

Of course, I am exceedingly grateful to all those whose published works I have been able to study and quote in places. And to the countless authors lost in history who authored some of the beautiful sacred texts from which I could draw inspiration and where I could find the relevant teachings.

I am hugely grateful to my colleague Wendy Smith for her highly efficient work in formatting the chapters and pointing out my errors! Thanks also to Patricia de Rada, Sally Richards and Carole de Fraga for specific information. Thanks also to the many wonderful and supportive colleagues whom I know through Compassion in World Farming, especially Peter Stevenson, Phil Brooke, Dr Jacky Turner, Carol McKenna and others past and present, especially Compassion's late founder, Peter Roberts, who inspired me to work in animal welfare.

Finally, a thank you to my family and friends for their moral support.

Joyce D'Silva

Royalties from the sale of this book will go to Compassion in World Farming International – UK Charity No. 1095050

## Biographies

**Dr Mark Berkson** is Professor and Chair in the Department of Religion at Hamline University. He teaches a seminar: "Resources or Relatives: The Ethical Status of Non-Human Animals".

**Ven. Bhikkhu Bodhi** is the author of "Noble Truths, Noble Path", Chair, Buddhist Global Relief.

**Reverend Professor David Clough** is Chair in Theology & Applied Sciences at the University of Aberdeen. He is co-founder of CreatureKind and led a project on the Christian ethics of farmed animal welfare in partnership with UK churches.

**Robert Gussman** served as an Anglican parish priest for nearly 30 years and is an Honorary Canon of Winchester Cathedral. He has a deep interest in furthering understanding and mutual acceptance between people of every faith.

**Fazlun Khalid** is the founder of the Islamic Foundation for Ecology and Environmental Sciences (IFEES), a leading author of Al-Mizan and author of "Signs on the Earth – Islam, Modernity and the Climate Crisis" (Kube Publishing Ltd. 2019). He was on the drafting team of the Islamic Declaration for Global Climate Change (2015) and for Al-Mizan.

**Professor Nanditha Krishna** is a Professor at the University of Madras. She is the Director of the C. P. Ramaswami Aiyar Foundation and CPR Environmental Education Centre. She is the Editor of the *Indian Journal of Environmental Education* and publisher of the *Journal of Indian History and Culture*.

**Dr Othman Llewellyn** is an Environmental Planner at the Saudi Wildlife Authority and a member of the International Union for the Conservation of Nature's World Commission on Protected Areas and World Commission on Environmental Law.

**Nitin Mehta** received an MBE in 1999 for his services to the community and has received the Ahimsa award from the Institute of Jainology.

**Dr Ibrahim Özdemir** is Professor of Philosophy and the Founding President of Hasan Kalyoncu University in Turkey. He is Professor of Islamic Philosophy at Abo Akademi University, Finland. He was on the drafting team of the Islamic Declaration for Global Climate Change (2015) and for Al-Mizan.

**Rabbi David Rosen CBE** is the former Chief Rabbi of Ireland and is an International President of the World Conference on Religion and Peace (www.religionsforpeace.org). He has a knighthood from the Pope.

**Doug Sam** studies Indigenous History at the University of Oregon.

**Dr Richard Schwartz** is President Emeritus of Jewish Vegetarians of North America (JVNA) and President of the Society of Ethical and Religious Vegetarians

(SERV). He is associate producer of the documentary "A Sacred Duty: Applying Jewish Values to Help Heal the World".

**Charanjit Aijit Singh** is a Sikh patron of the Animal Interfaith Alliance, Chair of the International Interfaith Centre in Oxford, a Vice President of the World Congress of Faiths and a member of the Peace Commission of the International Association of Religious Freedom.

**Wu Hung** was formerly a Buddhist monk and is Executive Director of the Environment and Animal Society of Taiwan (EAST).

# Introduction

We start with a huge anomaly, a three-part anomaly. Over 80% of the world's people declare that they belong to a religious faith, the majority to one of the major faiths.[1] These faiths all teach that animals should be treated with respect and kindness. Some faiths say that the divine dwells in each animal as in each human or even that animals praise God. Yet humans are responsible for a huge and growing amount of suffering being experienced by animals, be they animals imprisoned in factory farms and laboratories, or wild animals trapped, hunted or "broken in" for our entertainment. How can those of faith justify this anomaly? What can they do to right these wrongs?

This is not a book on theology nor a book about animal rights. I have written in a spirit of enquiry and have concluded with something of a challenge!

In doing my research, I have been awed by some of the beautiful writing about animals contained in the scriptures of diverse faiths. Where scriptures are lacking, I have found inspiring concepts such as "Country" in the beliefs of the First Nations of Australia (see Chapter 6).

I did not know that Allah had given cattle to the people not just for food and clothing but so that "you find beauty in them when you bring them home to rest and when you drive them out to pasture".[2]

I was unaware that one of the reasons why Moses was chosen to lead his people was that he showed compassion to a thirsty lamb who had strayed from the flock.[3]

I did not know of the 20th-century Islamic theologian, Said Nursi, who, whilst imprisoned for his beliefs, wrote a Treatise on flies, his "little birds"![4]

I was heartened by the lovely Buddhist metta (loving-kindness) prayer: "May all beings everywhere be happy. May they be healthy. May they be at peace. May they be free".

I love the story in the Hindu scriptures of Yudisthira, who was prepared to give up his place in heaven to that of a faithful dog.[5]

What of the beautiful words of Saint Isaac the Syrian who described a merciful heart as "a heart on fire for the whole of creation, for humanity, for the birds, for the animals … and for all that exists"?[6]

How about the primacy of compassion over pilgrimage, as recorded in the Sikh's revered book, the Guru Granth Sahib: "The merit of pilgrimages to the

DOI: 10.4324/9781003292555-1

sixty-eight holy places, and that of other virtues besides, do not equal having compassion for other living beings".[7]

There really is an abundance of inspiration to be found in the sacred scriptures of the faiths.

Yet we can look at the world of animals of all types and see the suffering they are enduring at the hand of humanity (inhumanity?). We can ponder the lives of the 80 billion land animals farmed for our food every year,[8] the majority of whom live in industrial "factory" farms.

I have been advised to use the term "factory farm" with caution, but truly what else are these so-called farms but factories? Like other factories, they take in "stock", process it in various ways and sell it for profit after a certain amount of time. Minimal account is taken of the fact that the "stock" in this case is composed of living, sentient creatures, who can feel not just physical pain, but emotional and mental suffering. The animals are normally deprived of their mothers and those mothers of their offspring as soon as viable after birth, so the natural maternal bond is shredded, sometimes after just 24 hours (or in the case of chickens, it never occurs at all). Instead of indulging in play, as young creatures love to do, they are crowded together in cramped conditions and the desire to play can get degraded into aggressive behaviour like tail-biting. Even walking or running or flying will be severely restricted if not impossible. Opportunities to graze or forage for food will be replaced by carefully selected rations to facilitate speedy growth or high milk yield.

Perhaps saddest of all, their own bodies may have been genetically altered by the hands of the breeding companies, in order to maximise profitable characteristics, and many may suffer lameness and other painful or uncomfortable conditions as a result. If that is not treating animals as if they were inanimate objects on a factory production line, then what is?

We all love to watch animals play. Yet over the centuries and around the globe we have forced many creatures to play for us, rather than for their own enjoyment – the tigers in the circuses, the chimpanzee tea parties, the performing bears at the roadside, the "fights" between dogs or cockerels or between human and bull (sometimes "blessed" by the clergy).

Over 100 million animals are used in research and product testing each year.[9] Some endure horrendous suffering. This is a tricky area to write about as most readers will have benefitted from medicinal products which have inevitably been tried out on animals first – the author included.

In each chapter, I have looked at the situation of animals in a country where that particular faith is predominant. Has the faith of these people affected how they treat animals, be they wild, farmed or used in other ways? The answers are sometimes surprising!

But this does perhaps take us to the heart of the matter. We humans are intrinsically self-centred; we put our own wellbeing first, both our individual wellbeing and that of our species. Let's suppose I am driving my car along a busy street. A child runs into the road on one side and a dog on the other. I have to decide which one I will hit as there's no time to stop. I know I will hit the dog and save the child. I make this point as I am not trying to be "holier than thou" in this book. I too am speciesist. I may share my home with family members or good friends, but not with rats, spiders and mosquitoes if I can help it. Out they go – gently, if possible.

The teachings of the main faiths about the human relationship with animals perhaps inevitably reflect this human-centredness. They may acknowledge that animals have been created by God or even that divinity is somehow within each being. They may teach that we have a duty of care and compassion towards them, but, in the end, it does seem that humans always come at the apex of consideration. Even non-theistic faiths like Buddhism place the animal "world" as lower than the human world.

The history of humanity's relationships with other animals is a mixture of the beautiful and the cruel. We have loved the beings closest to us, the animals we take into our homes to live with us, often dogs, cats or exotic birds. We may pay out fortunes to keep them in good health or to prolong their lives. If we leave our homes for work or pleasure, we will employ dog-sitters, cat-feeders or kennels to keep them going until our return (although we know in our hearts that they will miss us).

At the other extreme we may poison so-called "pests", hunt innocent creatures for the fun of the chase or the satisfaction of the "good shot", and of course we may wear their skins or sometimes their furs, we may sleep on pillows made from their feathers, and – ah yes – we eat them too!

Perhaps we are just honestly conflicted beings.

Can the great faith traditions help us to resolve these conflicts?

I think that perhaps they can.

All of the faiths covered in this book contain inspiring teaching about animals, about their relationships with their deity or with us. Where there are faith-founders, they too have spoken or acted in compassionate ways. Each faith has wonderful examples from history, like the medieval Saint Francis or, from more recent times, leaders like Mahatma Gandhi and many others, some of whom I have mentioned in their respective chapters.

So, the inspiration is there. If you are a person of faith, I hope this book may encourage you to find out even more from your own tradition or to look with more interest at other traditions. If you are an atheist or agnostic (truth-seeker?) then please also read on to find inspiration for your own life. Just because a teaching or a story comes from a spiritual tradition does not nullify its truth.

We are all in this together. For the Buddhists, there is no permanence, everything changes all the time. That's a hard belief to take on board as we are so sure of our own self, our own status in the world. Yet we know we are born, we mature, we age and we die. Where is the permanence?

It's the same for the animals. We are all in this together. If we are just these tiny specks of vitality in the history and geography of this earth (itself ultimately impermanent too), then perhaps we can make each speck count for something.

If caring for other sentient beings and extending a gentle spirit of fraternity towards them is something we can do, then let's do it!

We are all in this together.

## Notes

1 Religion by Country 2022. https://worldpopulationreview.com/country-rankings/religion-by-country.
2 Qur'an 16:6.
3 Exodus Rabbah 2:2.
4 S. Vahide, 1998. *The Author of the Risale-i Nur, Bediüzzaman Said Nursî* (2nd ed.). Istanbul: Sözler Publications.
5 Swaha International, 2017. Yudhisthir and The Dog, based on K.M. Ganguli, (1883–1896) "Mahaprasthanika Parva" in The Mahabharata of Krishna-Dwaipayana Vyasa (12 Volumes). Calcutta. www.swahainternational.org/yudhisthir-and-the-dog/.
6 Fr. S. Freeman, 2006. Words from St. Isaac of Syria. Homily 81. https://blogs.ancientfaith.com/glory2godforallthings/2006/11/01/words-from-st-isaac-of-syria/.
7 Guru Granth Sahib, p136.
8 Based on figures from FAOstat, www.fao.org.
9 RSPCA, 2022. Animals in Science. https://tinyurl.com/5x5vbbvy.

# 1 Judaism

## Teaching and Practice regarding Humanity's Relationship with Animals

## Introduction

As the oldest of the three main monotheistic faiths, Judaism could be said to have set the scene for both Islam and Christianity in terms of our relationship with animals. To the modern reader, this relationship may seem beset by contradictions and different interpretations of the Hebrew Bible (the Tanakh).

For all Jewish believers, one thing is certain and that is that the one God created the world and all the creatures in it. Humanity has a special role in relation to the other creatures, and although very much "in charge", is meant to exercise that role with compassion.

Looking at ancient practices such as animal sacrifice, we need to see them in their historical context. Perhaps it is more relevant to contrast practices such as industrial chicken farming with the practice of vegetarianism among a significant proportion of Jews today.

## Teaching

The Genesis (Bereishit) creation story declares that man is made in God's own image:

> And God said, 'Let us make man in our image, after our likeness, and they shall rule over the fish of the sea and over the fowl of the heaven and over the animals and over all the earth and over all the creeping things that creep upon the earth'.[1]

As God created all the creatures of the earth, the fish, the creeping things and the cattle and other animals, He "saw that it was good".[2] So, although man is given the power to rule over these creatures, they are also part of God's creation and therefore must be treated with respect.

There is an interesting comment on the order of creation in the Talmud reflecting that human beings were not created until the "sixth day so that if our minds become too proud, we could be reminded, 'Even the gnats preceded you in creation.'"![3]

DOI: 10.4324/9781003292555-2

There is another reason for this distinction between man and animal. In Genesis (2:7), humans are seen as distinct from animals as only humans have a "neshama", a spiritual soul, which seeks fulfilment in God. Both humans and animals also have a "nefesh" which is our life force, our urge for survival. When humans die, their neshama lives on. When humans or animals die, their nefesh ceases to exist.[4] There are other viewpoints in Judaism including the idea of reincarnation traversing boundaries between human and animal.[5]

Adam, the first human according to the book of Genesis, gives names to all the animals. But it appears he cannot find fruitful communication with them, so a female human companion is created for him.[6]

The serpent, accused by Eve of encouraging her to eat the forbidden fruit, is cursed by God "above all cattle and above every beast of the field".[7] Here the serpent, one of God's own creatures, is seen as guilty of initiating Eve's sin. (Many cultures portray the snake family in negative terms apart from Chinese astrology, which says that to be born in the Year of the Snake is a positive happening as such people are said to be calm, thoughtful and wise.)

Genesis tells us that God was so distressed by the way people were living that He decided to destroy his whole creation. Only Noah and his family were saved in the Ark. This too turns into a conservation story as Noah saved at least two (one male, one female) of each of the "impure" species (likely meaning non-domesticated), and seven each of the "pure" species so that when the terrible Flood was over, they could begin again to populate the earth.[8]

After the Flood, God declares that His new covenant with mankind shall also be "with every living creature that is with you, of the fowl, of the cattle, and of every beast of the earth with you".[9] Yet at the same time, God makes a concession, saying that humans can now eat meat, as "Every moving thing that liveth shall be meat for you".[10]

Many of the Psalms see a beneficence in God's relationship with animals. One Psalm declares that God provides food not only for land animals but also for birds.[11] Another Psalm, praising God for all His power and loving kindness, refers to God preserving both man and beast.[12]

One Psalm declares that animals of all kinds, from "sea monsters" to "beasts and all cattle, creeping things and winged fowl", also praise God.[13] (This concept is seen later in Islam.) God cares for the animals too: "The Lord is good to all, and His tender mercies are over all His works".[14]

A passage in Ecclesiastes declares that people and animals share the common fate of mortality and it perhaps questions the concept of a common animal soul and a special human soul:

> For that which befalls the sons of men befalls beasts; even one thing befalls them; as the one dies, so dies the other; yea, they all have one breath; so that man has no pre-eminence above a beast; for all is vanity. All go to one place; all are of the dust. Who knows the spirit of men whether it goes upward; and the spirit of the beast whether it goes downward to the earth?[15]

Looking at the prophetic works included in the Hebrew Bible, Isaiah's vision foresees an idyllic time when carnivores and herbivores alike will live in harmony:

> The wolf shall dwell with the lamb, and the leopard shall lie down with the kid; and the calf and the young lion and the fatling together; and a little child shall lead them. And the cow and the bear shall feed; their young ones shall lie down together; and the lion shall eat straw like the ox.[16]

This truly extraordinary vision turns nature on its head and must have seemed very far removed from the daily lives of the people, who would naturally fear large carnivores like lions, bears or wolves. Perhaps it is a vision of a world we would all like to see.

The Book of Isaiah contains a lovely allegory of the Lord as a caring shepherd: "Even as a shepherd that feedeth his flock, that gathereth the lambs in his arm, and carrieth them in his bosom, and gently leadeth those that give suck..."[17]

## The Role of Humanity

God's covenant is now with man but also with the animals. Yet the initial Genesis declaration that man rules over the animals has not been set aside. The concept of dominion is nowadays sometimes interpreted as stewardship, which combines both authority and care. But there is no doubt that humans are seen as beings on a different level to other creatures.

Yet animals are part of God's creation and should be treated with compassion. A fundamental Jewish teaching is that human beings must avoid tsa'ar ba-alei chayim – causing pain to any living creature. Why? Perhaps because they too are created by God and because "The righteous person regards the life of his animal".[18]

The Union for Reform Judaism clarifies this famous saying:

> One of the most touching expressions in the Jewish lexicon is tsa'ar ba-alei chayim, literally, 'pain of living things.' In the Jewish view, animals are just as much creatures of God as is humankind; and humankind has the responsibility, not only of respecting their needs and their feelings, but also of treating them with compassion. Animals suffer tsa'ar, pain, sorrow, and Jews are therefore prohibited from inflicting pain upon them.[19]

The renowned medieval rabbi and scholar Maimonides (Rabbi Moses ben Maimon, often called Rambam, 1135–1204) promoted kindness to animals. Considered by many to be the greatest of all rabbinic scholars and authorities on Jewish law, he writes in his famous book *Guide for the Perplexed*:

> It should not be believed that all the beings exist for the sake of the existence of humanity. On the contrary, all the other beings too have been intended for their own sakes, and not for the sake of something else.[20]

This is a really radical statement and could have been penned – in modern idiom – as a basic belief in the rights of animals.

Scholars have noted that several Biblical stories demonstrate that kindness to animals is a desirable quality in humans.

A later Jewish text goes into detail as to how Moses was tested by God through his shepherding: "While our teacher Moses was tending the sheep of Jethro in the wilderness a lamb ran away from him. He ran after her until she reached Hasuah. Upon reaching Hasuah she came upon a pool of water [whereupon] the lamb stopped to drink. When Moses reached her, he said, 'I did not know that you were running because [you were] thirsty. You must be tired'. He placed her on his shoulder and began to walk. The Holy One, blessed be He, said, 'You are compassionate in leading flocks belonging to mortals; I swear you will similarly shepherd my flock, Israel'".[21]

This implies that Moses, the most revered prophet, was found worthy to lead his people *because* of his compassion for animals.

Rebecca was chosen as the ideal wife for Isaac perhaps partly because of the kindness she showed to animals. Eliezer, Abraham's servant, asked Rebecca for water for himself. She not only gave him water, but also drew water from the well for his camels. This shows that Rebecca had compassion for animals too. Was this why Eliezer deemed Rebecca fit to be chosen as a suitable wife for Isaac, Abraham's son?[22]

The Bible tells us that when Jacob lay dying and called his 12 sons together, representing the 12 tribes of Israel, Simeon and Levi were chastised by him, not only for killing a man, but for ill-treating their oxen.[23]

This more modern Jewish prayer sums up the way humans should relate to animals:

> Blessed is the One who spoke and the world came to be. Blessed is the One! Blessed is the One who continually authors creation. Blessed is the One whose word is deed; blessed is the One who decrees and fulfills. Blessed is the One who is compassionate towards the world; blessed is the one who is compassionate towards all creatures.[24]

Rabbi David Rosen says, "Care for the wellbeing of our eco-system and especially for sentient beings should be the moral imperative that flows from the affirmation that the world is a Divine Creation. As the 16th-century Rabbi Judah Loewe of Prague stated 'One cannot love the Creator if one does not love His creatures'".[25]

## Caring for Animals

Kindness to animals is stressed throughout the Hebrew Bible and is even required in the most sacred laws, the Ten Commandments. Not only should people observe a day of rest on the Sabbath, but God also forbids making farm animals work on the Sabbath; they too need a day of rest.[26] Is it possible that this is the first law requiring consideration of animal welfare?

The book of Jonah describes how the Lord decides to spare the city of Nineveh from destruction, saying, "... should not I have pity on Nineveh ... wherein are more than six score thousand persons ... and also much cattle?"[27] Moreover, Psalm 36 states, "...Thy righteousness is like the mighty mountains; Thy judgments are like the great deep; man and beast Thou preservest, O Lord".[28]

There is even a suggestion that practicing conservation and compassion toward animals may assure one of a long life. In a passage that is remarkable for an ancient agricultural society that gathered all it could from nature, in Deuteronomy God says that if one comes across a bird's nest containing eggs or fledglings, the mother should not be taken.[29]

The same chapter exhorts everybody to care for domestic animals who have strayed or had an accident, even if these animals belong to someone else.[30] The motivation here may be brotherly love for one's fellow humans, but the passage also recognises how important these animals are to their owners and may hint at a concern for the creatures themselves.

The book of Numbers relates the story of Balaam and his donkey. Because the donkey could see the angel of the Lord in front and, at first, Balaam could not, the donkey kept moving aside and Balaam hit her three times. For this he was rebuked, the angel of the Lord saying,

> Wherefore hast thou smitten thine ass these three times? Behold, I am come forth for an adversary, because thy way is contrary unto me; and the ass saw me and turned aside before me these three times; unless she had turned aside from me, surely now I had even slain thee, and saved her alive.[31]

The Talmud sets forth a moral tale of why compassion to animals is an essential quality in a human: "Once a calf being led to slaughter thrust its head into the skirts of Rabbi [Yehudah HaNasi]'s robe and began to bleat plaintively. 'Go', he said, 'for this is why you were created'. Because he spoke without compassion, he was afflicted [at the hand of Heaven]. Then one day, his maidservant was cleaning his house and came upon some young weasels. She was about to chase them away with a broom, when Rabbi Yehudah said to her, 'Let them be for it is written: 'His tender mercies are upon all His works'[32] They said [in Heaven], 'Since he is merciful, let him be treated with mercy'".[33] So, the rabbi's painful condition was caused by his lack of compassion and relieved later when he showed compassion to other animals.

While sacrificial offering of an animal is understood to please God, in a passage in Exodus God declares that newborn calves or lambs should remain with their mothers for seven days before being sacrificed.[34] This is seen as an act of mercy, although in reality both mother and offspring would suffer distress by being separated. The same instruction is recorded in Leviticus, with the additional declaration that the mother cow or ewe should not be killed on the same day as her offspring.[35]

The medieval Hebrew work, *Sefer Hasidim: The Book of the Pious*, states:

> Be kind and compassionate to all creatures that the Holy One, blessed be He, created in this world. Never beat nor inflict pain on any animal, beast, or bird, or insect. Do not throw stones at a dog or a cat.[36]

The 16th-century Code of Jewish Law (Schulchan Aruch) clearly states that

> it is forbidden, according to the law of the Torah, to inflict pain upon any living creature. On the contrary, it is our duty to relieve the pain of any creature, even if it is ownerless or belongs to a non-Jew.[37]

The Talmud also states that one should not have an animal unless one can properly feed and care for it.[38] Another teaching is that "a good man does not sell his beast to a cruel person".[39]

Rabbi Yonassan Gershon tells a lovely story about the revered 16th-century teacher, Isaac Luria, who was known as "The Holy Ari" (Lion). One day the Rabbi Luria dismissed one of his students from his class. When the student asked why he had been dismissed, the Rabbi told him it was because he had not fed his chickens for three days. Because of this, the gates of Heaven would be shut to him and only opened again if he fed his chickens every morning, even before he said his prayers.[40]

The Gates of Repentance prayer book service for the Day of Atonement states, "The Lord is good to all; His compassion shelters all His Creatures". Observant Jews recite this verse, which is found in all siddurs (daily prayer books), three times a day.[41]

We can see that kindness to animals becomes a constant theme within Judaism. This was recognised by the renowned Irish historian W.E.H. Lecky (1838–1903) who wrote in his monumental work *History of European Morals, from Augustus to Charlemagne* (1869) that "the rabbinical writers have been remarkable for the great emphasis with which they inculcated the duty of kindness to animals".[42]

Dr Richard Schwarz, who has written widely on the subject of Judaism and compassion for animals, says:

> Jews are mandated to be rachmanim b'nei rachmanim, compassionate children of compassionate ancestors (Beitzah 32b), emulating a compassionate God. God is referred to in daily Jewish prayers as Ha-rachaman (the compassionate One) and as Av harachamim (Father of compassion). Since Judaism teaches that human beings, uniquely created in God's image (Genesis 1:27; 5:1), are to imitate God's positive attributes, we should surely strive to be exemplars of compassion.[43]

## Farming Methods

As with so many major faiths, early teachings and writings which deal specifically with farm animals are scarce. The early Prophets, writers and Rabbis could not have envisaged the kinds of industrial animal farming we see globally today. Contemporary voices within the Jewish community are beginning to take positions on the issue and are not unanimous.

One specific rule is found in Deuteronomy: "Thou shalt not muzzle the ox when he treadeth out the corn".[44] Presumably it was a common practice to muzzle oxen when they were threshing, in order to speed up the process. However, here it seems it is seen as more important to allow the animals the opportunity to have a munch while they are working, a welfare-oriented instruction. Today, of course, threshing is often a machine-operated business, with no oxen or horses involved.

Deuteronomy also forbids harnessing an ox and ass together,[45] presumably out of concern for the smaller, weaker animal.

In a long list of "do's and don't's" in Proverbs, we find the important command: "A righteous man regardeth the life of his beast".[46] This sits neatly alongside mentions of the virtue of being a good shepherd. There is no doubt that a small-scale herder or farmer with a few cattle, goats or chickens is able to regard the lives of their animals and has the potential to take care of them. But how can this regard be fulfilled in the world of factory farming? How can one "regard" the lives of 20,000 chickens in an intensive broiler chicken shed?

So, what kind of farming is approved of in the Hebrew Bible? The Lord says: "And I will give grass in thy fields for thy cattle".[47] This clearly implies that cattle should be allowed to graze on grass. We know from science that the physiology of ruminants like cattle is designed to deal with digestion of highly fibrous foods like grass.[48]

Modern behavioural science also demonstrates that cattle love being out on grass. Contemporary film of cows being let out on grass for the first time in springtime, after a winter indoors, shows the animals leaping about in an apparent state of joy, but then getting their heads down and munching on the lovely green grass before them.[49]

Rabbi Shlomo Yitzchaki, known as Rashi, was a revered medieval French-Jewish scholar of the Torah and the Talmud, whose teachings are still followed widely. He declared that the duty to let animals rest on the Sabbath means they must be free to roam in the fields on this day. There are no fields in factory farms.

One particularly horrendous form of factory farming is the taking of (male) calves from their dairy cow mothers within a day of being born and raising them in narrow veal crates for the rest of their four to six month lives. They soon grow too big to be able to turn around in the crates, where they have no bedding and stand on a wooden, slatted floor and are fed a liquid-only diet of reconstituted milk powder. Being ruminants, calves need to eat fibrous food like grass after a week or so, but this they are never allowed to do. Moreover, the iron content of the milk is kept low, so that they produce white, anaemic flesh, the so-called, prized, "white veal".

The widely respected 20th-century scholar, Rabbi Moshe Feinstein, declared that raising calves for veal in such a way would qualify as tsa'ar ba'alei chayim, and therefore the meat would be unacceptable.[50] Many Jews have avoided veal because of this.

More recently, such systems have been banned in the UK and the European Union as well as in several US states. Rabbi Feinstein's son, Rabbi Dr Moshe Dovid Tendler, has said that if the crate system was banned, then more humanely raised veal might be acceptable.[51]

In the USA, in 2007 the Committee on Jewish Law and Standards ruled that raising calves in narrow crates was wrong and that only veal from animals raised under humane standards can be sold, purchased or consumed. Humane standards for the raising of veal calves include sufficient space for calves to lie down, stand up, turn around and groom themselves, and proper nutrition in a mixed diet appropriate for young calves, with sufficient iron, dry, clean bedding, and limited isolation of calves.[52]

It is reasonable to look at the farming of animals for food in Israel, which has a predominantly (73.9%) Jewish population. Of Israeli Jews over age 20 in 2020, 43% self-identify as secular, 22% as traditional but not very religious, 13% as traditional-religious, 11% as religious and 10% as ultra-Orthodox.[53]

Kibbutzim are communal agricultural settlements. Kibbutz farmers and their families pool resources and share in the wealth that is produced as a result of their work. The majority of kibbutzim now identify as secular, but some still identify as religiously based. About 2% of the Israeli population live in kibbutzim. Large-scale intensive farming is a feature of many kibbutzim, while smaller farmer village-based co-operatives are called moshavim.

Many kibbutzim farm intensively. Hens are kept in cages, broiler chicken units are intensive and even beef and dairy cattle, sheep and goats are usually reared indoors. In fact, the Israeli government forbids grazing on cattle farms, so Israel's very high-yielding, mostly Holstein breed, dairy cows are zero-grazed.[54]

Although Israel's climate varies from region to region, much of the weather is hot and dry, with some regions in the south having little rainfall at all. Even the regions with a rainy winter season receive much less than half the annual rainfall of, for example, the UK. Such conditions do not encourage the growth of grass on a scale suitable for pasture-based farming.

An example of an Israeli company involved in building intensive farms is Agrotop. A recent project involved designing two sheds which will hold around 110,000 hens in cages. The cages will meet EU cage standards (as of 2021), i.e. 750 cm$^2$ per bird.[55] But respected voices within Israel are calling for a different view on eggs.

Rabbi Yonatan Neril, founder and director of The Interfaith Center for Sustainable Development in Israel, writes,

> We try to be ethical, moral, and spiritually-aware. The incredible, edible egg is incredible for the person who eats it and bound up in so much suffering for the chicken that produces it. There is a major gap between what is happening to tens of billions of chickens, the mainstream consumption of eggs, and manifesting ethical, moral, and God-resonant living on earth. The time has come to make a change. We can start by reducing or eliminating our personal consumption of eggs.[56]

Good news came in June 2022 when a Knesset (Israeli Parliament) committee approved new regulations that will end the use of cages for laying hens. Existing cages will be banned immediately, but the newer cages with slightly more space per hen will not be banned until 2038.[57]

In the book of Exodus, God describes Israel as a land "flowing with milk and honey".[58] This is certainly an accurate description today as dairy farming in Israel is now predominantly intensive and high-tech. The cows are mostly of the Holstein breed. These cows have been bred to yield high quantities of milk. Unfortunately, they are prone to suffer from lameness, partly related to their breeding but also to the high-protein diets they are fed.

In 2009, the European Commission's European Food Safety Authority (EFSA) asked its learned Panel on Animal Health and Animal Welfare (AHAW) to report on the wellbeing of dairy cows. These dairy cow experts produced several reports on the health and welfare of dairy cows. They declared that:

> the selection for high milk production has produced a cow that is dependent on a high level of management in order to maintain its health, and which requires certain management practices to maintain its high milk output, which may themselves reduce animal welfare e.g. high-starch grain-based diets, and minimal grazing.[59]

These grain-based diets are fed to the cows, who are unable to go out to graze on grass, their natural food. Many cows now produce around 3,000 gallons of milk a year (3,000 gallons is well over 13,000 litres – a very high yield – Ed). This figure is "among the highest productions in the world, if not the highest", says Dr Ephraim Maltz, a senior researcher emeritus at the Volcani Center, the Israeli Ministry of Agriculture's research arm.[60]

The EFSA Panel made it clear:

> Long term genetic selection for high milk yield is the major factor causing poor welfare, in particular health problems, in dairy cows... The genetic component underlying milk yield has also been found to be positively correlated with the incidence of lameness, mastitis, reproductive disorders and metabolic disorders.[61]

Perhaps the most telling aspect of the lives of these high-yielding Holstein-type cows is that they are commonly sent for slaughter after just two or three lactations, at less than a quarter of the normal life span of a cow. Due to failure to get pregnant, ill-health or repeated bouts of lameness, they become no longer economically viable. It is a condemnation of this type of farming that the cows' own genetic make-up, combined with their unnatural feeding regime and often poor housing, makes their longevity superfluous to the dairy industry. Wherever such systems are used – and they are widespread in the US, Europe and elsewhere – they are not in the best interests of the cows themselves.[62]

Rabbi Rosen is outspoken about the harms cause by this kind of selective breeding for productivity: "Regarding animals it is clear that making them grow unnaturally fast and especially making them unnaturally large and 'productive', involves cruelty that cannot be justified".[63]

It is not just the cows who are zero-grazed. Due to the lack of pasture in Israel, most sheep and goat farmers are using zero-grazing systems, with a full supplement feeding regime.[64]

Sadly, we see that feedlots – barren open mud yards – are growing in number in Israel, and are stocked with imported calves being reared for beef.[65]

However, extensive farming methods are used by Bedouin farmers in the southern part of the country. They raise their herds traditionally and nomadically but account for only about 20,000 goats.[66]

Perhaps it is not surprising that Israel has gone down the intensive farming route. However even if God's "tender mercies" are over all these intensively farmed animals,[67] it is not so obvious that the farmers' mercies are to be seen. Neither am I assured that the intensive farmers are observing the "tsa'ar ba'alei chayim" teaching.

It is also obvious that animals in intensive farms do not get a Sabbath day of rest and recuperation. The cows still get milked, the broiler chickens still struggle to get to their feed and watering points, the laying hens still endure the cramped conditions in their cages. Factory farms are intense in every sense of the word.

Can the owner of a factory farm really be "righteous" and "regardeth the life of his beast"?[68] If there are 20,000 broiler chickens in a shed, it is simply not possible to give each one the care that they deserve, whether on theological grounds or welfare grounds.

Several modern Jewish teachers have condemned factory farming. Rabbi Aryeh Carmell, a modern Torah scholar and teacher in Jerusalem states: "It seems doubtful from all that has been said whether the Torah would sanction 'factory farming', which treats animals as machines, with apparent insensitivity to their natural needs and instincts. This is a matter for decision by halachic authorities".[69]

Jewish author Richard H. Schwartz notes that "the condition under which [factory farm] animals are raised today are completely contrary" to the Biblical principle of the Sabbath. For:

> instead of animals being free to graze on the Sabbath day to enjoy the beauties of creation, they are confined for all of their lives to darkened, crowded stalls and cages without air, natural light, or the room in which to exercise.[70]

Rabbi David Rosen is adamant on the subject of factory farming:

> I do not see how anyone familiar with Jewish teaching in relation to animals and with the abhorrent cruelties involved in animal factory farming can justify the latter. For me it is obvious that Jewish teaching explicitly condemns such conduct.[71]

Peter Roberts, the founder of the international farm animal welfare group, Compassion in World Farming, defined factory farming in these words: "Factory farming begins where the individuality of the animal ends".[72]

## Slaughter

Prior to the Jewish laws, it was a common practice for meat to be torn from a live animal. With no refrigeration available, this was one way to obtain a little meat but have some left for the ensuing days, no matter the agony that the animals must have suffered. The Bible specifically forbids this. Severing a limb from a live animal and eating it is forbidden.[73]

Religiously observant Jews are only allowed to eat meat that has been slaughtered according to the shechita method. They believe that this is the most humane way to kill animals for food.

Most animal welfare and veterinary organisations believe that animals should be stunned before their throats are cut. The stun should render the animal unconscious and insensible to pain or terror. Stunning is done by firing a retractable metal bolt into the brain (usually used for cattle) which causes instant unconsciousness or by using electricity to stun the animal (usually used for sheep and poultry) and render it unconscious for long enough for the actual slaughter to be carried out. More recently gas stunning has been introduced, especially for poultry.

Shechita slaughter is opposed to stunning. Jewish law does not permit pre-slaughter stunning because it requires the animal to be uninjured at the time of the actual slaughter, and all pre-stunning methods are seen as involving an injury to the animal. There is also concern that the pre-stunning might kill the animal, so it would be dead already when the knife was used in the act of slaughter. This would render the meat unfit to eat. Many Jews believe that shechita produces instant loss of consciousness, so stunning is not necessary.

There is also a concern that stunning an animal before slaughter makes the ensuing bleed-out less effective. This would conflict with the Divine instruction that no blood is to be consumed.[74] This belief has been contradicted by several modern experiments, which demonstrate little difference in the amount of blood loss after stunned or un-stunned slaughter.[75]

The reason for avoiding blood is explained as follows: "The Talmud explains that the "animal soul" resides in their blood, and since the animal soul is essentially coarse and unrefined, eating blood internalizes that trait. The Torah's message is "Don't take the animal instinct, the animal life force, and increase its prominence within your personality. Minimize that part of you and maximize the aspect of you which is spiritual".[76]

Shechita requires the act of slaughter to be done by a fully trained shochet. In fact, shochetim are likely to be better trained in animal physiology than most other slaughter operatives. The animal must be killed by cutting the throat with a single stroke from a very sharp instrument called a chalaf. The cut must sever the trachea, oesophagus, carotid arteries and jugular veins. The animal must then be allowed to fully bleed out and the shochet must check the animal to see that it was correctly slaughtered, and that the animal was in a fit condition to be declared kosher or fit to be eaten.

A group of leading scientists, brought together by the European Commission, viewed all the research on stunning and slaughter and concluded:

> Without stunning, the time between cutting through the major blood vessels and insensibility [unconsciousness], as deduced from behavioural and brain response, is up to 20 seconds in sheep … up to 2 minutes in cattle, up to 2½ or more minutes in poultry, and sometimes 15 minutes or more in fish.[77]

As science indicates that animals do not lose consciousness instantaneously when their throats are cut, they must endure a period of possible pain and certainly confusion and distress as they bleed to death. Some argue that the pain from the cut is not immediately felt. It can happen (in humans too) that a very traumatic wound can sometimes induce temporary analgesia. Be that as it may, the experience of bleeding out must surely cause suffering and distress until unconsciousness is achieved.

Temple Grandin is a highly respected expert on slaughter. She has worked with Jewish communities in the US and elsewhere to change any aspects of shechita which she sees as causing unnecessary suffering. For example, some Jewish slaughterhouses were inverting the animals before slaughter. Being upside down is very stressful for the animals – even if it facilitated easier slaughter. She has now persuaded most slaughterhouses to restrain the animal in an upright position, making sure that the head is held steady in an upright position to facilitate the use of the slaughter knife. Maimonides (Rambam) explicitly permitted upright slaughter.[78] Now, in the US, the Orthodox Union and all other major kosher certifiers in the United States accept upright slaughter.[79]

We know from much evidence that, globally, slaughtering animals is often done in a cruel way and that animals are handled roughly. Grandin thinks that the religious aspect of shechita may engender more careful handling. She says:

> It is the religious belief of the rabbis in the kosher plants that helps prevent bad behavior. In most kosher slaughter plants, the rabbis are absolutely sincere and believe that their work is sacred. The rabbi in a kosher plant is a specially trained religious slaughterer called a shochet, who must lead a blameless life and be moral. Leading a blameless life prevents him from being degraded by his work.[80]

These conflicting views on slaughter are a subject of concern to Jews and non-Jews alike. In the world right now, Orthodox Jews will only eat meat which has been killed by the shechita method. The views of secular Jews are more relaxed, and many will eat meat not necessarily of shechita origin. Those whose priority is the welfare of animals will continue to press for all animals to be stunned before slaughter – as well as for slaughterhouse practices and inspections to be upgraded in *all* slaughterhouses.

The act of slaughter has always been a subject for debate within Judaism. Even that great medieval scholar of the Torah, Maimonides, writes of a particular aspect of killing:

> It is prohibited to kill an animal with its young on the same day, in order that people should be restrained and prevented from killing the two together in such a manner that the young is slain in the sight of the mother; for the pain of animals under such circumstances is very great. There is no difference in this case between the pain of people and the pain of other living beings, since the love and the tenderness of the mother for her young ones is not

produced by reasoning but by imagination, and this faculty exists not only in people but in most living creatures.[81]

Rabbi David Rosen is aware of the incredibly fast speeds at which animals are slaughtered in today's large slaughterhouses and says:

> One of my concerns about "stunning" is that it facilitates very rapid killing of animals (to meet the modern demand for meat) and as a result it is not always done effectively. Ritual slaughter at least ensures that the animal is given "personal attention" and the immediate severance of the trachea and oesophagus means that the cessation of pain is more effective than stunning. Nevertheless, I would of course far prefer that animals were not killed at all.[82]

## Eating Animals

The original Biblical creation story makes it clear that humans were to follow a vegan diet:

> And God said: 'Behold, I have given you every herb yielding seed, which is upon the face of all the earth, and every tree, in which is the fruit of a tree yielding seed-to you it shall be for food;

and He prescribed a similar diet for other creatures: "and to every beast of the earth, and to every fowl of the air, and to every thing that creepeth upon the earth, wherein there is a living soul, [I have given] every green herb for food".[83]

It is not until the fourth chapter of Genesis, when Adam and Eve have been cast out of the Garden of Eden, do we hear that their son Abel was a shepherd.[84] Although Abel is seen as offering a lamb to God, it seems reasonable to presume that the meat from his sheep were also being killed for food.

It is only after the Flood that the Divine permission to eat meat is given, as God declares that humans can now eat meat: "Every moving thing that liveth shall be food for you".[85]

However, not all living creatures are allowed as food for Jews. Based on Biblical rulings, Jewish dietary rules or Kashrut say that the only animals who are kosher (allowed, fit,) are those that have cloven hooves and chew the cud, such as cows, sheep, goats and deer. Pigs have split hooves but do not chew the cud, so pig-meat is forbidden as is camel-meat as camels chew the cud but do not have partially split hooves.[86] For seafood to be kosher, the animal must have fins and scales. Certain types of seafood, such as shellfish, crustaceans, and eels, are therefore considered non-kosher. Both chickens and turkeys are permitted in most Jewish communities. Other types of animals, such as amphibians, reptiles, and most insects, are prohibited altogether.

Traditionally, Jews have eaten meat and it has formed an important part both of the weekly Sabbath meal and of certain festivals. Other festivals focus on dairy foods. Dairy and meat are not eaten together at the same meal. Specifically, the Bible says that one should not stew a goat kid in its mother's milk.[87]

After the original Genesis command to eat plant foods, there are further allusions to eating such a diet, for example, in Deuteronomy, the Lord talks of the bounteous land he has given: "a land of wheat and barley, and vines and fig-trees and pomegranates; a land of olive-trees and honey; a land wherein thou shalt eat bread without scarceness, thou shalt not lack any thing in it".[88] However, this chapter goes on to refer to "thy herds and thy flocks",[89] so we must presume that animals were being eaten. A few chapters later the Lord refers to cattle "And I will give grass in thy fields for thy cattle, and thou shalt eat and be satisfied".[90]

Many modern Rabbis are now questioning not only factory farming, but meat consumption itself. One of the most respected of these rabbis is the Orthodox rabbi, David Rosen, former Chief Rabbi of Ireland and an International President of the World Conference on Religion and Peace (www.religionsforpeace.org). Regarding farming methods, he writes: "the current treatment of animals in the livestock trade definitely renders the consumption of meat as halachically[91] unacceptable as the product of illegitimate means…"; he goes on to declare such practices as a "flagrant violation" of the principle of not causing tsa'ar ba'alei chayim.[92]

Rabbi Rosen believes his vision is rooted in Jewish teaching:

> Aside from the fact that both the original Garden of Eden and the Messianic vision of the future reflect the vegetarian ideal in Judaism, it is of course such a dietary lifestyle that is most consonant with the goal and purpose of Torah to maximize our awareness, appreciation, and sensitivity to the Divine Presence in the world. It is therefore only natural for us to affirm as did Rav Kuk (Kook, Rav Kook, 1865–1935), the first Ashkenazi Chief Rabbi in Israel, that a redeemed world must perforce be a vegetarian world.[93]

Rabbi Rosen urges Jews not to eat meat at all: "As it is halachically prohibited to harm oneself and as healthy, nutritious vegetarian alternatives are easily available, meat consumption has become halachically unjustifiable".[94]

In a film shown on the website of JewishVeg, he says:

> Judaism's way of life, its dietary practices, are designed to ennoble the human spirit. It is therefore a contradiction in terms to claim that products that come through a process that involves inordinate cruelty and barbarity toward animal life can truly be considered kosher in our world. In our world today, it is precisely a plant-based diet that is truly consonant with the most sublime teachings of Judaism and of the highest aspirations of our heritage.[95]

Rabbi Rosen points out:

> A plant based diet is the Biblical ideal (in the Garden of Eden, and in the Messianic vision) and in today's world where animal products (not just meat, but eggs and dairy products as well) on the market, result from much cruelty; and where fruits and vegetables and plant based products are freely available;

I believe that truly religious Jews (and indeed all people of moral sensibility) should avoid animal products as much as possible.[96]

In 2017, 74 rabbis signed the following statement:

We, the undersigned rabbis, encourage our fellow Jews to transition toward animal-free, plant-based diets. This approach to sustenance is an expression of our shared Jewish values of compassion for animals, protection of the environment, and concern for our physical and spiritual well-being.

The rabbis come from all kinds of Jewish traditions: 13 Orthodox rabbis, 24 Conservative rabbis, 25 Reform rabbis, 8 Reconstructionist rabbis, 3 transdenominational rabbis, 1 Renewal rabbi and 1 Secular Humanist rabbi, as well as by 2 rabbinic students and 1 cantorial student.[97]

With so many Jewish people turning to vegetarianism and veganism, it is interesting to note the plethora of vegan Jewish websites offering for example, vegan versions of the Shabbat meal.[98]

Five percent of Israel's population is now reckoned to be vegan, and the world's largest vegan festival was hosted in Tel Aviv in 2014.[99]

## Sacrifice

As with so many other faiths, sacrificial offering, usually of an animal, to God was an important part of the faith in the early days. There are numerous Biblical references where God calls for a sacrificial offering to be made, or when people decide to make an offering themselves.[100]

Usually, sacrifices were undertaken as either a thanks offering, a votive offering or a spontaneous free-will offering. Slaughter offerings were also made at times of the ratification of solemn covenants, treaties and alliances. In fact, the book of Deuteronomy makes it clear that God required sacrifices to be made at certain times.[101]

Eventually sacrificial offerings became focussed on the great temple in Jerusalem. According to Maimonides, these offerings were a concession to the conditions in Biblical times. Since sacrifices were the universal expression of religion in that period, if Moses had tried to eliminate them, his mission would probably have failed, and Judaism would have disappeared. Offerings of animals were supposed to be accompanied by good deeds. After the destruction of the Temple, the rabbis stated that sacrifices should be replaced by prayer and good deeds.

In Hosea, we find that God declares "For I desire mercy, and not sacrifice, and the knowledge of God rather than burnt-offerings".[102]

In Isaiah, God appears to reject continued animal offerings:

To what purpose is the multitude of your sacrifices unto Me? saith the LORD; I am full of the burnt-offerings of rams, and the fat of fed beasts; and I delight not in the blood of bullocks, or of lambs, or of he-goats.[103]

Maimonides said that the people learned that "the sacrificial service is not the primary objective of the commandments, but that prayer is a better means of obtaining nearness to God". Agreeing with the early rabbis, Maimonides emphasized that the superiority of prayer is that "it can be offered everywhere and by every person".[104]

It is interesting to note that the Ten Commandments do not mention sacrifice.

Modern voices within the Jewish community are also querying whether animal sacrifices are necessary. Nathan Lopes Cardozo, an Orthodox rabbi in Jerusalem, writes:

> Does Judaism really need animal sacrifices? Would it not be better off without them? After all, the sacrificial cult compromises Judaism. What does a highly ethical religion have to do with the collection of blood in vessels and the burning of animal limbs on an altar?[105]

The Union of Reformed Judaism says:

> Whether we have sinned or not, whether we have done so intentionally or unintentionally, we still have the desire to move closer to God, to offer our own korbanot (sacrifice). To do so, we must put forth the effort to show kindness, compassion, generosity, and goodwill even if that is not easy. At the same time, we must put forth the effort to study Torah and attend worship services...the more good we do, the more good we do. This is really a model for life. Sacrifices are alive and well: They just have to be slightly redefined.[106]

## Hunting

Generally, Jews are opposed to hunting, although it did take place in Biblical times. One passage declares that the blood from a hunted animal should be buried in the earth.[107] Some modern commentators see this as meaning that hunting is shameful in the sight of God. It is clear that hunting was happening at that time.

The kind of hunting is important. If people hunt for food for themselves and their families, this is permissible, but should be done in a way that causes the least suffering. Hunting just for sport is different in its goals and is regarded as wrong.

A query was addressed to Rabbi Ezekiel Landau (1713–1793) by a man wishing to know if he could hunt in his large estate, which included forests and fields. The response stated:

> In the Torah the sport of hunting is imputed only to fierce characters like Nimrod and Esau, never to any of the patriarchs and their descendants.... I cannot comprehend how a Jew could even dream of killing animals merely for the pleasure of hunting.... When the act of killing is prompted by that of sport, it is downright cruelty.[108]

## Vivisection

Obviously, the issue of animal experimentation was not addressed in the Hebrew Bible nor in many other historical books and teachings of the Jewish faith. Any decision on whether it is permissible, must call on the accepted criteria of tsa'ar ba'alei chayim, not causing suffering and bal tashchit (wastefulness). In view of the many millions of animals subjected to experiments every year, one must ask – are not some of these experiments not only cruel, but very wasteful of animal life?

The Central Conference of American Rabbis has published on this topic. While upholding the human right to use animals, they refer constantly to the need to cause as little suffering as possible, saying: "Human life must be saved if it is at all possible…When dealing with experimental animals we should be quite certain that they are not subjected to pain or used for frivolous reasons as for example cosmetic experimentation.

> A mouse engineered genetically for a specific set of experiments, which will eventually help human beings, lies within the boundaries of utilizing animals for the benefit of human beings. Naturally the humane treatment of the animals in accordance with our tradition must be observed. It would be appropriate for Jews to be involved in this kind of genetic engineering and to use the animals that they themselves have genetically changed.[109]

Rabbi Rosen has a similar view:

> From a Jewish perspective, human life has a sanctity above that of animals (Of course that does not justify the exploitation of the latter, on the contrary.) Thus, if the use of animals in science can help advance human health, then it is justified. Nevertheless, this still has to be done in a manner that causes as little pain and suffering as possible. Such sensitivity appears to be lacking in many scientific contexts. Happily, new developments in AI appear to enable testing and analysis to be done without needing to resort to animal experimentation.[110]

Many anti-vivisectionists point out that evidence from experiments on animals does not always translate similarly in humans. There is no doubt that reconciling human need with not causing suffering to experimental animals is a difficult issue, both for Jews and for non-Jews alike.

## Wildlife and Biodiversity

The Hebrew Bible contains several passages full of praise for the world created by God and for the wild creatures who inhabit it alongside humanity: "For the earth shall be filled with the knowledge of the glory of the LORD, as the waters cover the sea".[111]

In the book of Proverbs, certain creatures are singled out for praise:

> There are four things which are little upon the earth, but they are exceeding wise: The ants are a people not strong, yet they provide their food in the summer; the rock-badgers are but a feeble folk, yet make they their houses in the crags; the locusts have no king, yet go they forth all of them by bands; the spider thou canst take with the hands, yet is she in kings' palaces.[112]

Job himself declares:

> But ask now the beasts, and they shall teach thee; and the fowls of the air, and they shall tell thee; Or speak to the earth, and it shall teach thee; and the fishes of the sea shall declare unto thee; Who knoweth not among all these, that the hand of the LORD hath wrought this? In whose hand is the soul of every living thing, and the breath of all mankind.[113]

The Psalms too, full of praise and joy, declare:

> The trees of the LORD have their fill, the cedars of Lebanon, which He hath planted; Wherein the birds make their nests; as for the stork, the fir-trees are her house. The high mountains are for the wild goats; the rocks are a refuge for the conies. Who appointedst the moon for seasons; the sun knoweth his going down. Thou makest darkness, and it is night, wherein all the beasts of the forest do creep forth... How manifold are Thy works, O LORD! In wisdom hast Thou made them all; the earth is full of Thy creatures. Yonder sea, great and wide, therein are creeping things innumerable, living creatures, both small and great.[114]

This kind of ecstatic writing displays a real reverence for wildlife and the environment, always within the context of the Divine Creation.

Today, in Israel, there are organisations which aim to protect wildlife and biodiversity. The Society for the Protection of Nature in Israel (SPNI) points out:

> Israel is blessed with a wide array of biodiversity. It is home to some 2,800 species of plants, more than 500 species of birds and 100 species of mammals. Located along the African-Eurasian flyway, Israel hosts over 500 million migrating birds twice each year. Israel is designated as a biodiversity hotspot where focused international conservation efforts will have the greatest effect.[115]

The SPNI's website says that their International Ornithological Center (IOC) operates "a network of birding centres that monitors migration patterns of 500 million birds on behalf of the international community, provides safe haven for birdlife and makes Israel a world centre for bird watchers".[116]

There is still one use of wild animals that is contentious among modern Jews and that is the wearing of fur. Jewish authorities are divided on the subject, though always paying at least lip service to avoiding tsa'ar ba'alei chayim. Historically, there was an association between the fur trade and Jews, especially in Eastern Europe.[117]

Every year, globally, over 100 million animals are killed for their fur, 90% of them raised in cages on fur farms, where they cannot fulfil their natural behaviours and often suffer greatly.[118] (The author has spent a day on a mink farm in the UK. She still remembers that day with feelings of horror and sadness.)

Several countries have now banned fur farming, including the UK, many European Union countries and Japan.[119]

Based on the prohibition of tsa'ar ba'alei chayim, the late Rabbi Haim Dovid Halevy, Sephardic Chief Rabbi of Tel Aviv, issued a p'sak (rabbinic ruling) in March 1992, prohibiting the manufacturing and wearing of fur. He based his decision on extensive research of the Torah, the Talmud, and other authoritative texts.[120]

Rabbi Rosen is also outspoken on this issue:

> I do not see the wearing of animal products in itself as illegitimate – for example in a case where an animal died naturally, and its fur is then used by humans (this would also be good environmentally responsible recycling.) However, to kill, let alone breed to kill animals for their fur is abhorrent, and far greater Jewish authorities than me have condemned such as being in contravention of Jewish teaching.[121]

It was not until June 2021, after many years of campaigning, that the Israeli government banned the sale of fur with a few exemptions for religious reasons, such as the sale of Shtreimels – fur hats traditionally worn on Shabbat and holidays by ultra-Orthodox men. The ban came into force six months later.[122]

## Conclusion

Judaism embraces the world created by God. It views humans as the most important beings in this world but recognises that animals have a rightful place in the Divine scheme. The Hebrew Bible admonishes people to be kind and to "regard" the lives of animals entrusted to their care.

The criterion for the human relationship with animals, both wild and domestic, is that one should avoid causing them pain and suffering – tsa'ar ba'alei chayim. That is surely a wonderful criterion.

There is a huge variety of opinions within Judaism about how to implement that instruction. But that variety of views perhaps only reflects the views within wider society about our relationship with animals.

Since finishing this chapter, I have come across an interesting proposal made by Dr Richard Schwartz. Writing in The Times of Israel, he proposes:

> I, along with other Jewish activists, am championing an initiative to restore the ancient Rosh Hashanah L'ma'aser Beheimah, a day initially for tithing

animals for sacrifices, and to transform it into a Rosh Hashanah LaBeheimot (a New Year for Animals), a day devoted to increasing awareness of Judaism's powerful teachings on compassion for animals and to considering a tikkun (healing) for the horrible ways that animals are treated today on factory farms and in other settings.

He goes on to give several good reasons for abandoning factory farming and other inhumane and environmentally harmful practices. He concludes:

Renewing an ancient, almost completely forgotten Jewish holiday may seem audacious. But it is essential to help revitalize Judaism, improve the health of Jews, sharply reduce the current massive mistreatment of animals, and help move our precious but imperilled planet to a sustainable path.[123]

With such a strong foundation, it would be good to see even more Jewish leaders and lay people advancing arguments for animal welfare and even for recognising the rights of animals and moving towards more plant-based diets.

## Notes

1 Genesis 1:26.
2 Genesis 1:21, 25.
3 Talmud Sanhedrin 38a.
4 Aish.com, 04/08/11. Animal Souls. www.aish.com/atr/Animal_Souls.html.
5 Rabbi David Rosen, 15/12/21. Personal communication.
6 Genesis 2:20,21.
7 Genesis 3:14.
8 Genesis 7:3.
9 Genesis 9:10.
10 Genesis 9:3.
11 Psalm 147:9.
12 Psalm 36:7.
13 Psalm 148:7–10.
14 Psalm 145:9.
15 Ecclesiastes 3:19–21.
16 Isaiah 11:6,7.
17 Isaiah 40:11.
18 Proverbs 12:10.
19 Union for Reform Judaism, u.d. "10 Minutes of Torah: Pity for the Living" in Humane Society. *Reform Judaism.* www.humanesociety.org/sites/default/files/archive/assets/pdfs/faith/reform_judaism_2.pdf.
20 D. Davies, 2011. *Method and Metaphysics in Maimonides' Guide for the Perplexed.* Oxford: Oxford University Press.
21 Exodus Rabbah 2:2.
22 Genesis 24:11–20.
23 Genesis 49:6–7.
24 Central Conference of American Rabbis, 2007. Mishkan T'filah: A Reform Siddur: Weekdays, Shabbat and Festivals Non-transliterated. https://www.google.co.uk/books/edition/Mishkan_T_filah/kx7la8tjDpYC?hl=en&gbpv=0

25 Rabbi D. Rosen, 15/12/21. Personal communication.

26 Exodus 20:10, 23:12; Deuteronomy 5:11–13.

27 Jonah 4:11.

28 Psalm 36:7.

29 Deuteronomy 22:6–7.

30 Deuteronomy 22:1–2, 4.

31 Numbers 22:32,33.

32 Psalm 145:9.

33 Talmud: Bava Metzia 85a. Translation by Rabbi Dovid Sears, in Benjamin Perla, u.d. Compassion Toward Animals and Tza'ar Ba'alei Chaim. Hebrew/English Source Sheet. www.sefaria.org/sheets/72303?lang=bi.

34 Exodus 22:29.

35 Leviticus 22:28.

36 Judah ben Samuel. Sefer Hasidim (Book of the Pious): A Translation with Notes and Introduction. Dissertation: University of Chicago, 1962. Translated by Sholom A. Singer.

37 Solomon Ganzfried, 2010. Code of Jewish Law (Kitzur Schulchan Aruch): A Compilation of Jewish Laws and Customs. Gorgias Press.

38 Yerushalmi Keturot 4:8, 29a; Yevanot 15.

39 Judah ben Samuel. Sefer Hasidim (Book of the Pious): A Translation with Notes and Introduction. Dissertation: University of Chicago, 1962. Translated by Sholom A. Singer.

40 Rabbi Gershom, 02/10/22. The Holy Ari and the Hungry Chickens: A Lesson for Yom Kippur. www.youtube.com/watch?v=dScQaoECecw.

41 Central Conference of American Rabbis, 1922. The Union Prayerbook for Jewish Worship. www.emanuelnyc.org/wp-content/uploads/2020/04/unionprayerbookf00 centiala.pdf.

42 W.E.H. Lecky, 1921. *History of European Morals from Augustus to Charlemagne* (3rd ed., revised), New York: D. Appleton, 2 vols. https://oll.libertyfund.org//title/lecky-history-of-european-morals-from-augustus-to-charlemagne-2-vols.

43 R.H. Schwartz, 2020. *Vegan Revolution: Saving Our World, Revitalizing Judaism.* Brooklyn, NY: Lantern Publishing & Media.

44 Deuteronomy 25:4.

45 Deuteronomy 22:10.

46 Proverbs 12:10.

47 Deuteronomy 11:15.

48 A.I. Orr, Ph.D., PAS, 07/01/22. Exploring Cow Digestion. www.fda.gov/animal-veterinary/animal-health-literacy/how-cows-eat-grass.

49 J. Webb, 19/04/18. Cows Jump for Joy at Being Let Outside for the First Time in Months. *The Independent.* www.independent.co.uk/video/news/cow-jumping-joy-grass-first-time-long-winter-funny-a8312231.html.

50 M. Yodeya, 2014. Is Eating Veal Permissible? https://judaism.stackexchange.com/q/37393.

51 VIN News, 22/04/15. New York - Rav Moshe's Veal Ban to Be Lifted in the Future? https://vinnews.com/2015/04/22/new-york-rav-moshes-veal-ban-to-be-lifted-in-the-future/.

52 Committee on Jewish Law and Standards, 12/12/07. Veal Calves. https://tinyurl.com/7je9je6a.

53 Jewish Virtual Library, 2022. Latest Population Statistics for Israel. www.jewishvirtuallibrary.org/latest-population-statistics-for-israel.

54 R. Mandel, H.R. Whay, E. Klement and C.J. Nicol, 2016. Environmental enrichment of dairy cows and calves in indoor housing. *Journal of Dairy Science*, **99**:3, pp1695–1715.https://doi.org/10.3168/jds.2015-9875.

55  Agrotop, 2020. Emek Ha'ela Project Illustrates Agrotop's Vision for Future Poultry Houses. https://agrotop.co.il/emek-haela-project-illustrates-agrotops-vision-for-future-poultry-houses/.

56  Y. Neril, 18/04/18. What Does God Have to Do with Eggs? https://blogs.timesofisrael.com/what-does-god-have-to-do-with-eggs/.

57  S. Surkes, 20/06/22. Cages for Laying Hens Banned from New Coops, to Be Phased Out in Existing Ones. *Times of Israel*. www.timesofisrael.com/cages-for-laying-hens-banned-from-new-coops-to-be-phased-out-in-existing-ones/.

58  Exodus 33:1–3.

59  EFSA, 2009. Scientific Report on the Effects of Farming Systems on Dairy Cow Welfare and Disease. www.efsa.europa.eu/en/efsajournal/pub/rn-1143.

60  A.D. Sharon, 09/05/17. 'Startup Nation' Meets Shavuot: The Story of Israel's Efficient, High-tech Dairy Industry. www.jns.org/start-up-nation-meets-shavuot-the-story-of-israels-efficient-high-tech-dairy-industry/#.WPcgAtKGPIU=.

61  EFSA, 2009. Scientific Report on the Effects of Farming Systems on Dairy Cow Welfare and Disease. www.efsa.europa.eu/en/efsajournal/pub/rn-1143.

62  For more information, see J. Webster, 2017. Beef and Dairy, in J. D'Silva and J. Webster (Eds). *The Meat Crisis – Developing More Sustainable and Ethical Production and Consumption.* Abingdon: Earthscan and Routledge,pp121–126.

63  Rabbi D. Rosen, 15/12/21. Personal communication.

64  H. Leibovich, u.d. The Sheep and Goat Industry in Israel. www.dairyschool.co.il/the-sheep-and-goat-industry-in-israel/.

65  D. Dvoskin and S.J. Cohen, 2019. The Beef Industry in Israel. www.longhornproject.org/problems/industry/.

66  H. Leibovich, u.d. The Sheep and Goat Industry in Israel. www.dairyschool.co.il/the-sheep-and-goat-industry-in-israel/.

67  Psalm 145:9.

68  Proverbs 12:10.

69  A. Carmell, 1991. *Masterplan: Its Programs, Meanings, Goals.* Jerusalem and Spring Valley, NY: Feldheim Pub, p69.

70  R.H. Schwartz, 2001. *Judaism and Vegetarianism.* New York: Lantern Books, p38.

71  Rabbi D. Rosen, 15/12/21. Personal communication.

72  Peter Roberts, 1986. Personal communication.

73  Genesis 9:4 and Leviticus 17:19.

74  Leviticus 7:26–27.

75  R. Khalid, T.G. Knowles and S.B. Wotton, 2015. A comparison of blood loss during the halal slaughter of lambs following traditional religious slaughter without stunning, electric head-only stunning and post-cut electric head-only stunning. *Meat Science*, 110, pp15–23. https://doi.org/10.1016/j.meatsci.2015.06.008.

76  Aish.com, 04/08/11. Animal Souls. https://www.aish.com/atr/Animal_Souls.html.

77  EFSA, 2004. Opinion of the Scientific Panel on Animal Health and Welfare (AHAW) on a Request from the Commission Related to Welfare Aspects of the Main Systems of Stunning and Killing the Main Commercial Species of Animals. www.efsa.europa.eu/en/efsajournal/pub/45.

78  Mishneh Torah, Ritual Slaughter 2:7. https://www.sefaria.org/Mishneh_Torah%2C_Ritual_Slaughter.1.1?lang=bi.

79  M.T. Schuchman, 2012. A Cut Above: Shechita in the Crosshairs, Again. https://www.star-k.org/articles/kashrus-kurrents/548/a-cut-above-shechita-in-the-crosshairs-again/.

80  B. Wolfman, 1998. Kosher Slaughter. Mishpahah:364. https://www.grandin.com/ritual/kosher.slaughter.html.

81  D. Davies, 2011. *Method and Metaphysics in Maimonides' Guide for the Perplexed.* Oxford: Oxford University Press, USA.

82  Rabbi D. Rosen, 15/12/21. Personal communication.

83  Genesis 1:29–30.

84  Genesis 4:2–4.

85  Genesis 9:3.

86  Leviticus Chapter 11.

87  Deuteronomy 14:21 and Exodus 23:19.

88  Deuteronomy 8:8,9.

89  Deuteronomy 8:13.

90  Deuteronomy 11:15.

91  Halacha is often translated as "Jewish law", although a more literal translation might be "the way to behave" or "the way of walking".

92  R. Kalechofsky (Ed), 1995. *Rabbis and Vegetarianism*. Marblehead, MA: Micah Publications, pp53–60. www.jewishvirtuallibrary.org/rabbinic-teachings-on-vegetarianism.

93  R. Kalechofsky (Ed), 1995. *Rabbis and Vegetarianism*. Marblehead, MA: Micah Publications pp53–60.

94  R. Kalechofsky (Ed), 1995. *Rabbis and Vegetarianism*. Marblehead, MA: Micah Publications pp53–60.

95  Jewish Veg - Rabbinic Statement. https://www.jewishveg.org/rabbinic-statement.

96  Rabbi D. Rosen, 15/12/21. Personal communication.

97  Jewish Veg - Rabbinic Statement. https://www.jewishveg.org/rabbinic-statement.

98  Kosher.com. Shabbat Menu – Vegan. https://www.kosher.com/lifestyle/shabbat-menu-vegan-1644.

99  R. Frazin, 2019. The Jewish State Was Uniquely Situated to Become the World's Most Vegan Country. A Viral Video Was the Tipping Point. www.thetower.org/article/how-israel-became-the-global-center-of-veganism/ and www.exceedinglyvegan.com/eating-out/vegan-israel-most-vegan-friendly-country-world.

100 Leviticus 22:18–24.

101 Deuteronomy, Chapters 12 and 16.

102 Hosea 6:6.

103 Isaiah 1:11.

104 H.J. Fields and C. Giora, 1990. *A Torah Commentary for Our Times*, New York, NY: UAHC Press, p100.

105 N.L. Cardozo, 2018. *Jewish Law as Rebellion: A Plea for Religious Authenticity and Halachic Courage*. Jerusalem: Urim Publications, p219.

106 My Jewish Learning, u.d. 'Sacrifices Are Alive And Well!'. www.myjewishlearning.com/article/sacrifices-are-alive-and-well/.

107 Leviticus 17:13.

108 Yoraah De'ah, 2nd Series, 10.

109 Jewish Involvement in Archives, u.d. Central Conference of American Rabbis. www.ccarnet.org/responsa-topics/jewish-involvement-in/.

110 Rabbi D. Rosen, 15/12/21. Personal communication.

111 Habakkuk 2:14.

112 Proverbs 30:24–28.

113 Job 12:7–10.

114 Psalm 104:16–20, 24,25.

115 Society for the Protection of Nature in Israel (SPNI), u.d. Who We Are. https://natureisrael.org/Who-We-Are.

116 Society for the Protection of Nature in Israel (SPNI), u.d. What We Do. https://natureisrael.org/What-We-Do.

117 M. Ingall, 04/04/14. 'Tznius' in Furs: What Judaism Has to Say About My Mink Coat. www.tabletmag.com/sections/community/articles/fur-coats.

118 Fur Free Alliance, u.d. Fur Farming – Animal Welfare Problems'. www.furfreealliance.com/fur-farming/.

119 Fur Free Alliance, u.d. Fur Bans. https://www.furfreealliance.com/fur-bans/.

120 *Lilith Magazine*, Winter 1992–1993. 'Inheriting Fur'. https://lilith.org/articles/inheriting-fur/.
121 Rabbi D. Rosen, 15/12/21. Personal communication.
122 Fur Free Alliance, 2021. Israel Becomes World's First Country to Ban Fur Sales. www.furfreealliance.com/israel-becomes-worlds-first-country-to-ban-fur-sales/.
123 R.H. Schwartz, 16/8/22. Restoring and Transforming the Ancient Jewish New Year for Animals: An Idea Whose Time Has Come. *The Times of Israel.* https://tinyurl.com/33m4zub8.

## Reference

Note: This chapter uses for its scripture references the Hebrew Bible (Tanakh) provided by Mechon Mamre at https://mechon-mamre.org/.

# 2 Christianity

## Teaching and Practice regarding Humanity's Relationship with Animals

### Introduction

Christians see themselves as inheritors of the Old Testament and its teaching as well as being believers in the teaching of Jesus, and of his early followers such as St Paul, as recorded in the New Testament. These two books make up the Christian Bible. Jesus is understood to be both human and Divine, the incarnation of the second aspect of the Holy Trinity of Father, Son and Holy Spirit in one God. Christians base their faith on this revealed wisdom and teaching.

From being persecuted as a cult in its early days, all changed for Christians when the Emperor Constantine embraced their minority faith. As the Franciscan theologian Fr. Richard Rohr puts it:

> It's possible to trace the movement of Christianity from its earliest days until now. In Israel, Jesus and the early "church" offered people an experience; it moved to Greece, and it became a philosophy. When it moved to Rome and Constantinople, it became organized religion. Then it spread to Europe, and it became a culture. Finally, it moved to North America and became a business... The original desire or need for a "Jesus" experience was lost, and not even possible for most people.[1]

So, from Jesus being a revolutionary campaigner, crucified by the local Roman ruler, and with early Christians being fed to the lions in Rome, suddenly Christianity became the established religion of the Roman Empire. Even though the Empire itself fell away, the Church was by now a strong moral force in much of Europe and its blessing and authority were sought by kings and commoners alike for many centuries.

Christianity became absorbed in the rightness of its official teaching (and the wrongness of the teaching of others) and in encouraging or disciplining its followers to follow that teaching, as only in this way could people ensure their eternal salvation in heaven. It became a very anthropocentric, perhaps theocentric, set of teachings. Animals did not feature to any great extent in the core, established teaching.

As Professor Charles Camosy reflects, Christianity is "an imperfect tradition with respect to animals".[2]

DOI: 10.4324/9781003292555-3

That prolific author of books on Christianity and the status of animals, Dr Andrew Linzey, also ruefully confesses, "It has, I think, to be sadly recognised that Christians, Catholic or otherwise, have failed to construct a satisfactory moral theology of animal treatment".[3] Linzey himself believes in the theos-rights (God-rights) of animals; in other words, they have rights based on the right of the Creator to have His creation treated with respect.

Over the centuries, there seem to be at least two strands of thought and practice within Christianity regarding animals, strands that seem irreconcilable. One strand sees animals on earth solely within our power and with the human right to use them for our own purposes in any way we want. Catholic theologian Deborah Jones describes this well: "Christianity has erected a barrier between human beings and animals which can seem insuperable".[4]

The other strand sees animals as God's creatures, capable of suffering, and believes that humans have a responsibility to care for them.

It is perhaps an anomaly that the Christian faith, so associated with the gospel teachings on love and mercy, should be so mute on our fellow creatures, their place in the Divine plan and how we should relate to them.

## Symbolic Animals

Although Christianity professes only one God, particular animals have been associated, often within art, as symbols of Christ and of the four evangelists who wrote the gospel accounts of the life and teaching of Jesus. Christians perhaps "appropriated" the lion symbol for Jesus Christ, as the Lion of Judah originally represented the Israelite tribe of Judah. We first meet this Christianised lion in the book of Revelation: "Then one of the elders said to me, 'Do not weep. See, the Lion of the tribe of Judah, the Root of David, has conquered, so that he can open the scroll and its seven seals.'"[5] Some interpret this as referring to the second coming of Christ (and see the piece on Rastafarianism in the final chapter of this book).

The Holy Spirit is often depicted as a dove, bringing grace "down" from heaven, which was still seen as "up there". The dove was mentioned in the Old Testament, but its inaugural reference in the New Testament was when Jesus was baptised by John the Baptist: "At that moment heaven was opened, and he saw the Spirit of God descending like a dove and alighting on him".[6]

The animal symbols of the four evangelists are derived from the four living creatures seen in Ezekiel's vision in the Book of Ezekiel, chapter one. Later they are identified as cherubim, angels, in chapter ten. Applied much later to the evangelists, they are ascribed as follows: Matthew the man, Mark the lion, Luke the ox, and John the eagle. When the symbols of the four evangelists appear together, it is called a Tetramorph and is common in the medieval art of Europe. Various writers have ascribed particular characteristics of each of the four creatures to each particular evangelist.

The use of these creatures is not viewed as idolatry, but it is interesting to see how close an association has been made between humans and animals. As we shall see later, some theologians view the Incarnation of Jesus as the Divine becoming "flesh", all flesh, not just human flesh.

## The Teaching

Christians incorporate the Genesis teachings into their belief system. So, God creates the world and all the creatures in it, including humanity, and He sees that it is "very good".[7] God goes on to make humanity in His own image, the "imago Dei" as the Latin world came to call it. Theologians have long argued as to what exactly this means – perhaps most ending up with the view that only humans have the capacity to relate to God and are thus made in His image.

This view would be supported by the highly influential St Thomas Aquinas (1225–1274) who adopted the Aristotelian view of the divisions of the "soul": inanimate, vegetative, sensitive (animals) and reasoning (only humans). Aristotle wrote that "if nature makes nothing incomplete, and nothing in vain, the inference must be that she has made all animals for the sake of man".[8]

Humanity came to be seen as at the apex of the Divine creation, apart from the angels. Everything else in the created world is there to serve humanity, although Aquinas concedes that ultimately everything in creation "exists for the sake of the universe" which "is ordained towards God as its end...thus it is plain that Divine goodness is the end of all corporeal beings".[9] Aquinas is the master of this strand of Christian thought, the Aristotelian-Thomistic strand.

Many other important historical figures within Christianity have taken a similar or even more limited view. Martin Luther (1483–1546), regarded as a founding figure of Protestantism, wrote: "The beasts of the field and the birds of the heaven were created for mankind; these are the wealth and possessions of men".[10] Luther rebelled against much traditional Church teaching, but his view of animals mimics that of Aquinas.

Rev Dr David Clough, Chair in Theology & Applied Sciences at the University of Aberdeen, believes that there are some positive points in the Aristotelian/Thomistic view:

> There is much in Aristotelian and Thomistic accounts of animals that is valuable for contemporary Christian animal ethics. Both value the diversity of creaturely life. Both affirm the importance of appreciating the particular mode of life of all creatures and the goods that they pursue in their flourishing. Both were wrong to believe in hierarchy between different kinds of humans and to understand the role of animals as serving human needs. Aquinas was wrong to exclude animals from Christian ethical concern. Modern scientific understandings of animals are helpful in providing grounds for revising their views about the uniquely rational nature of humans. Christian animal ethics should draw on core elements in Aristotelian and Thomistic thought while offering correction at appropriate points.[11]

With animals usually relegated to a lower status than human animals, there exists a fairly horrendous history of human exploitation and abuse of animals, often seemingly sanctioned by Christian authorities. In medieval times, animals were sometimes put "on trial" for their apparently devilish actions, such as attacks on humans.[12]

Some Catholic writers, such as the French Jesuit Père Bougeant, suggested that animals were, in fact, evil spirits and should be treated harshly, as befitted such creatures.[13]

In more modern times, bishops have apparently attended and sanctioned bull-fights, monastic abbeys and convents have owned and run factory farms, where the animals are caged or confined, and some of the clergy have participated in hunting for sport.

One contemporary example of this first strand can be found in the fundamentalist Christian website, Gospelway, which declares:

> So the Bible teaches that men have dominion over animals, including the right to control them, confine them, and require them to obey us. We have the right to possess them as property, use them, and make them work for us. They are required to serve our purposes to meet our needs. God did not "liberate" them as if they have the "right" to act as they please.[14]

Another very conservative Catholic voice is that of the writer Joseph Sobran (1946–2010), who wrote: "Broadly speaking…animals are violent, predatory … and lacking in compassion. We owe them no apologies. Besides, many of them taste good".[15]

Could it be that centuries of teaching and practice have ignored the actual teaching of the Christian saviour, Jesus Christ? What does the New Testament tell us about his teaching and relationships with animals?

Although traditional Nativity scenes of the birth of Jesus depict an ox and an ass, there is no mention of their presence in the gospels. Some theologians think that the ox represents Israel and the Jewish people and the ass represents the Gentiles, or non-Jewish people, with the implication that Jesus brings the two together.[16] While the Nativity stories include visits by the wise men from the East[17] they also include the visit of the shepherds.[18] If these stories imply that the Christian teaching is for the high and the lowly in society, including the "foreigner", could the addition of the ox and ass imply that the birth of Jesus is also important for our relationship with animals?

The gospel of Mark tells us that as the public work of Jesus is about to begin, he is baptised by Saint John the Baptist in the river Jordan. After the Holy Spirit speaks to him, he then spends 40 days in the wilderness "with the wild beasts".[19] Does this suggest that the wild creatures left Jesus alone or that he had some kind of influence or control over them? Did they comfort him in his isolation? We just do not know. Some think that this period of peace with wild animals is meant to foreshadow the future peaceable kingdom described by the prophet Isaiah.[20]

In the recorded teaching of Jesus, he does give status to animals, particularly birds. However, his analogies end up with his saying that people are more important than such creatures. For example, in Luke's gospel he says: "Are not five sparrows sold for two pennies? Yet not one of them is forgotten by God. Indeed the very hairs of your head are all counted. Don't be afraid; you are worth more than many sparrows"[21] and: "Consider the ravens: they do not sow or reap, they do not have storeroom or barn; yet God feeds them. And how much more valuable you are than birds!"[22]

Perhaps it is comforting to hear that each tiny sparrow has a place in the Divine consciousness and that the ravens are cared for by God.

On one occasion when Jesus finds a man with a withered hand, his disciples ask if it is permissible to heal on the Sabbath rest day. He replies: "He said to them, 'If any of you has a sheep and it falls into a pit on the Sabbath, will you not take hold of it and lift it out? How much more valuable is a person than a sheep! Therefore it is lawful to do good on the sabbath'" and he heals the man.[23]

Jesus gives a similar answer to another question about the Sabbath: "You hypocrites! Doesn't each of you on the Sabbath untie your ox or donkey from the stall and lead it out to give it water?"[24]

While these references to the animal world are somewhat inconclusive and disappointing to those who seek support for their view of animals as our fellow beings, some of the analogies used by Jesus show an appreciation for the beauty and wholeness of nature: "Again he said, 'What shall we say the kingdom of God is like, or what parable shall we use to describe it? It is like a mustard seed, which is the smallest of all seeds on earth. Yet when planted, it grows and becomes the largest of all garden plants, with such big branches that the birds can perch in its shade'".[25]

Then there is the rather lovely analogy, which Jesus uses, of the mother hen protecting her chicks: "Jerusalem, Jerusalem, you who kill the prophets and stone those sent to you, how often I have longed to gather your children together, as a hen gathers her chicks under her wings, and you were not willing!"[26]

In his teaching to his disciples, Jesus makes repeated use of the analogy of the good shepherd who cares for his flock. He engages with Simon Peter: "When they had finished eating, Jesus said to Simon Peter, 'Simon son of John, do you love me more than these?' 'Yes, Lord', he said, 'you know that I love you'. Jesus said, 'Feed my lambs'. Again Jesus said, 'Simon son of John, do you love me?' He answered, 'Yes, Lord, you know that I love you'. Jesus said, 'Take care of my sheep'. The third time he said to him, 'Simon son of John, do you love me?' Peter was hurt because Jesus asked him the third time, 'Do you love me?' He said, 'Lord, you know all things; you know that I love you'. Jesus said, 'Feed my sheep.'"[27]

Yet again:

> I am the good shepherd; I know my sheep and my sheep know me - just as the Father knows me and I know the Father - and I lay down my life for the sheep. I have other sheep that are not of this sheep pen. I must bring them also. They too will listen to my voice, and there shall be one flock and one shepherd.[28]

These shepherd references are perhaps based on similar verses in the Book of Isaiah.[29] The shepherd analogy would make sense to those listening to Jesus. They would appreciate the importance of the shepherd watching over and caring for his flock.

John's gospel also records how Jesus went to Jerusalem and became angry when he witnessed the lively trade in sacrificial animals attached to the Temple. Cattle, sheep and doves were being sold for sacrifice, as well as money-changing taking place: "So he made a whip out of cords, and drove all from the temple courts, both sheep and cattle; he scattered the coins of the money changers and overturned their tables. To those who sold doves, he said, 'Get these out of here! Stop turning my Father's house into a market!'".[30] Was his anger due to the captivity and sacrifice of the animals or was it the nature of the trading so close to the venerated Temple? Perhaps both? We do not know for sure.

The most problematic passage in the New Testament is in Mark's gospel, where Jesus tells the bad spirits to leave a man who is being tortured by them. Whereas it is often said that Jesus ordered the bad spirits to enter into the large herd of pigs nearby, in fact the text says that it is the spirits who ask to enter instead into the pigs, who then dash down the hillside into the lake and drown. Jesus simply acquiesces in the request of the spirits.[31]

Some see the whole story as metaphorical. The spirits are called "Legion". Could they simply be symbolic of the Roman legions who kept the country under control? Or did Jesus really have no concern for the pigs themselves? An agriculturalist might ask: How could the supposed 2,000 pigs sustain themselves on the comparatively barren soils of the area? A historian might ask: Why would a predominantly Jewish community be keeping pigs anyway, when they were not allowed to be eaten?

It is important to note that Jesus did make clear that God values animals, including the birds, each one of them. The New Testament writers saw the mission of Jesus as directed towards humanity, so it is not surprising that they record how he emphasises the importance of humans and how God cares especially for them.

Dr Andrew Linzey suggests that whereas the canonical gospels, the official ones recognised by most Churches, contain little about Jesus and his relations with animals or his teaching on animals, the many apocryphal accounts of Jesus, which were not accepted into the official New Testament, show a different picture. One such "Coptic fragment" records how Jesus comes upon an overloaded mule, who had fallen on a steep hill. Jesus upbraids the animal's owner "Man, why do you beat your animal? Do you not see that it is too weak for its burden, and do you not know that it suffers pains?" When the man denies this, Jesus calls out "Woe to you, that you do not hear how it complains to the Creator in heaven and cries out for mercy". He then heals the mule and tells the man, "From now on do not beat it any more, so that you too may find mercy".[32]

Even the limited official gospel accounts do portray Jesus as having respect and sympathy for others. He says, "Blessed are the merciful"[33] and in many instances refers to helping those who are worse off than oneself. This could be understood as helping not only fellow humans but fellow creatures who are suffering on the earth.

Several Christian theologians have given deeper meaning to the belief in the Incarnation of Jesus, the Divine made man, the cornerstone of Christian belief. David Clough explains that the incarnation was not just that God became human, but that God became a fleshly creature, like all other creatures, and he quotes John's gospel: "the Word became flesh".[34,35]

Father Richard Rohr, the respected Franciscan teacher, expresses it thus: "The early Church theologians saw incarnation and divine indwelling as occurring as a metaphysical union with nature as a whole, not just in one human being (Jesus)".[36]

Fr. Rohr is also blunt about God's relationship with animals: "Either God is for everybody, and the divine DNA is somehow in all creatures, or this God is not God by any common definition, or even much of a god at all".[37]

Archbishop Bartholomew, the Ecumenical Patriarch, wrote in 2012: "We cannot undermine the crucial importance of animals, too, for the orderly function of the world...Man's relationship with animals has been very close...It is characteristic that God reserves special care for the preservation of the animal kingdom".[38]

Back in 1986, Pope John Paul II issued an encyclical which includes the roots of the same concept, that by the Incarnation of God the Son, not only was human nature united with God, but "the whole of humanity, the entire visible and material world...with all "flesh", with the whole of creation".[39]

Theologian Sallie McFague (1933–2019) described creation as "the body of God" and the place of salvation. She wrote, "Creation as the place of salvation means that the health and well-being of all creatures and parts of creation is what salvation is all about—it is God's place and our place, the one and only place".[40]

Indeed, there seems to be Biblical justification for this wider view. When Jesus speaks to his 11 remaining disciples after his resurrection, he tells them: "Go into all the world and preach the gospel to all creation".[41] Not just to humans, then.

St Paul's Letter to the Romans seems to imply that all creation, not just humanity, will be "saved":

> I consider that our present sufferings are not worth comparing with the glory that will be revealed in us. For the creation waits in eager expectation for the children of God to be revealed. For the creation was subjected to frustration, not by its own choice, but by the will of the one who subjected it, in hope that the creation itself will be liberated from its bondage to decay and brought into the freedom and glory of the children of God.[42]

This view of the Divine incarnation being with all flesh, not just in one human being, can raise further thoughts, such as: Why was a human body chosen? Might the incarnation have happened in another kind of intelligent sentient being, a whale perhaps or an elephant? If that sounds incongruous, then perhaps the answer is to see the incarnation in the form of a human, Jesus, as simply representing all creatures, all "flesh".

Way back in medieval times, the controversial Dominican friar known as Meister Eckhart (c. 1260–c. 1328) wrote: "A person who knew nothing but creatures would never need to attend to any sermons, for every creature is full of God and is a book".[43]

The founder of the Methodist movement, John Wesley, spoke passionately about the place of animals in creation. He abhorred that they have to live under "the bondage of corruption" but believed that they will share in the resurrection, alongside humanity, and then "they shall enjoy happiness, suited to their state, without alloy, without interruption and without end".[44]

## The Role of Humanity

Christian teacher Brian McLaren describes how we all need to see ourselves in a context, a "framing story". He writes:

> But if our framing story tells us that we are free and responsible creatures in a creation made by a good, wise, and loving God, and that our Creator wants us to pursue virtue, collaboration, peace, and mutual care for one another and all living creatures, and that our lives can have profound meaning if we align ourselves with God's wisdom, character, and dreams for us… then our society will take a radically different direction, and our world will become a very different place. As Christians, we have the opportunity to live the story that was given to us at the very beginning (Genesis 1), that creation is "good," even "very good," and that it is our vocation to nurture and grow such goodness wherever we can.[45]

The old Genesis story of humans being given the power of dominion over all the other creatures is perhaps better seen in its more modern interpretation of steward-ship, rather than dominion. Or is stewardship still a paternalistic concept? Is stewardship simply dominion without its rough edges? Is it a kinder type of dominion?

Would we relate better to other creatures if we viewed them as fellow beings, almost as brothers and sisters on our shared planetary home?

David Clough puts it this way: "Humans and other animals are fellow crea-tures of God. Each of God's creatures has a unique vocation to glorify God in their particular mode way of being a creature. Part of the human vocation is to promote the flourishing of their fellow creatures, both human and more-than-human. In relation to animals that means avoiding practices that inflict harm or suffering unnecessarily, only keeping domesticated animals in ways that are compatible with their flourishing and protecting the environments wild animals need to flourish".[46]

## Caring for Animals

Away from the power centre of Rome, early Christian mystics and saints would often retreat to the wilderness to pray and develop their own personal relationship with God. Tales abound of their close relationships with the surrounding wild animals and their harmonious and simple living. As Fr. Richard Rohr points out: "These issues were still taken seriously by those who fled to the deserts of Egypt, Syria, Palestine, and Cappadocia. Their practices grew into what we now call 'religious life' as observed by monks, nuns, hermits, and anchorites who held onto the radical Gospel in so many ways".[47]

Most of their stories were translated from Greek into Latin between the 5th and 6th centuries. The few following examples are based mainly on the wonderful book *Beasts and Saints* by the scholar, Helen Waddell, originally published in 1934.[48] One such tale tells us of St Gerasimus (d. 475) (sometimes confused with St Jerome), an abbot living near the river Jordan. Coming upon a lion in extreme pain with a thorn in his foot, Gerasimus removed the thorn. From then on, the lion followed the saint everywhere and was told to guard the donkey who fetched water every day. When the donkey was stolen the lion stood accused of eating him, but years later, the lion came upon the same donkey and rescued it, bringing it back to the monastery. When Gerasimus died, the lion searched everywhere for him, roaring his sorrow. Finally, the new abbot took him to where Gerasimus had been buried and explained that he had died. The lion lay down on the grave, beat his head on the earth and died.

Saint Isaac the Syrian (613–700) was a scholarly monastic who was at one time Bishop of Nineveh. He wrote one of the most beautiful descriptions about love and compassion: "What is a merciful heart? It is a heart on fire for the whole of creation, for humanity, for the birds, for the animals … and for all that exists. By the recollection of them the eyes of a merciful person pour forth tears in abundance. By the strong and vehement mercy that grips such a person's heart, and by such great compassion, the heart is humbled and one cannot bear to hear or to see any injury or slight sorrow in any in creation".[49]

Saint Cuthbert was a famous early English saint who became Prior of Lindisfarne on the coast of Northumberland. Most nights he spent standing in the sea, praying and chanting. An inquisitive fellow monk followed him one night and described how when Cuthbert finally returned to the shore, a couple of sea otters would follow him and rub their fur on his feet to dry them and warm them. After ten busy years he retired to the Inner Farne island and lived as a hermit. It is said that he would sing and play his lute-type instrument to the seals, who would come up on the rocks to listen to him. He died in 687 CE, and his remains are interred in Durham Cathedral. St Cuthbert is also credited with establishing the first animal welfare rule in England. He forbade the killing and eating of the many Eider ducks who lived close to his island hermitage.[50]

The story of the Irish Saint Kevin (d.618) was recorded by the 12th-century chronicler Giraldus Cambrensis. St Kevin was another monk who favoured the life of a hermit and settled by a beautiful lake in the Wicklow mountains, now called Glendalough. Of the many tales of his affinity with animals, perhaps the most beautiful, is the story of the blackbird. While Kevin was praying in his tiny cell he stretched one arm out through the window recess, with his hand palm upwards in prayer. A blackbird came and laid her eggs in his hand. The story says that Kevin waited until all her eggs had hatched and her fledgelings had flown before he retracted his hand.

The Irish Nobel Laureate poet Seamus Heaney wrote a lovely poem based on this story of "St Kevin and the Blackbird".[51]

These and many other stories of the early saints show how a remarkable affinity can develop between animals and the saintly men and women who posed no threat to the creatures themselves. It is as if the animals could recognise the goodness in the saints' hearts. Perhaps, in recording these stories, the writers were foreshadowing the future as prophesied in the Book of Isaiah, "the wolf shall dwell with the lamb, and the leopard shall lie down with the kid;" and so on.[52]

The Greek Orthodox theologian, Rev Dr John Chryssavgis, writes of these early desert fathers and other mystics and hermits: "In God's eyes, the wild animals and the sand dunes are of sacred importance and have their unique place alongside humanity. In their understanding of heaven, birds and trees could never be eliminated or excluded".[53]

Moving forward in time we come to the best-known saint to develop close relationships with a variety of animals, Saint Francis of Assisi (1181–1226). As Saint Bonaventure wrote, just 25 years after he died, Francis would call creatures, no matter how small, by the name of "brother" or "sister", because he knew they shared with him the same beginning. He had an "all-embracing love for every creature" and often bought back lambs who were being taken to slaughter. When other animals – or even a fish – were brought to him, he would greet them and set them free, even returning the fish to the lake. When a wolf was threatening the local town of Gubbio, Francis is said to have done a deal – the townsfolk promised to feed the wolf and the wolf promised not to attack any more. "For of a truth it is this piety which, allying all creatures unto itself, is profitable unto all things, having promise of the life that now is, and of that which is to come".[54] Francis also was known for his love of the poor and the sick and he lived a life of absolute simplicity and devotion. His love and compassion seemed to embrace all beings.

St Bonaventure himself appears to have shared the Franciscan outlook, writing: "For every creature is by its nature a kind of effigy and likeness of the eternal Wisdom. Therefore, open your eyes, alert the ears of your spirit, open your lips and apply your heart so that in all creatures you may see, hear, praise, love and worship, glorify and honour your God".[55]

One other saint whose life mirrors that of Francis in many ways is Saint Martin de Porres (1579–1639) who lived in Peru. The son of a Spanish nobleman and a freed slave of African and native Peruvian origin, he served as a lay brother in the Dominican order of friars, doing menial work. Although he is famed for his care of the sick and dying, his intense devotion and his associated healing miracles, he was known to avoid eating meat and to care for all stray animals. When the monastery was plagued by mice, who were about to be exterminated, Martin asked them to leave, promising that he would feed them at the kitchen door every night. The mice left. Pope John XXIII canonised him in 1962.[56]

As the well-known philosopher Lynn White wrote:

> Francis tried to depose man from his monarchy over creation and set up a democracy of all God's creatures. With him the ant is no longer simply a homily for the lazy, flames a sign of the thrust of the soul toward union with God; now they are Brother Ant and Sister Fire, praising the Creator in their own ways as Brother Man does in his.[57]

The Christian mystic, Thomas A' Kempis (1380–1471), wrote that the soul desiring communion with God must learn from all of God's creatures, including the non-humans: "…and if thy heart be straight with God", he wrote, "then every creature shall be to thee a mirror of life and a book of holy doctrine, for there is no creature so little or vile, but that showeth and representeth the goodness of God".[58]

An outstanding Christian advocate for animals was the Quaker Benjamin Lay (1682–1759), who moved from England to America and became an outspoken campaigner against slavery. He also adopted a vegetarian diet, refusing to eat or wear anything that had caused loss of animal life or had involved slave labour.[59]

We can conclude that although there are no recorded words of Jesus about how we should care for animals, it became an important theme in the lives of many saintly Christians. In fact, their affinity and care for animals seemed to signify their high level of holiness. These theologians and holy folk demonstrate the other strand of Christian thinking about our relationship with animals. We could call it the Franciscan school of thought – animals are our fellow creatures, our brothers and sisters on the earth. They are creatures of God, as we humans are, and should be treated with respect and love.

In the early years of the 19th century, we find Christians such as the evangelical William Wilberforce (1759–1833) leading the fight in Britain against the slave trade, and later, slavery itself, but also known for promoting animal welfare. Inspired by their faith, in 1824 he and Rev Arthur Broome, an Anglican clergyman, helped found the first modern animal welfare society, now known as the RSPCA. Again, we find people who care deeply about the suffering of humanity, but who can extend their circle of compassion to embrace animal welfare as well. The Society adopted a resolution in 1832 that "the proceedings of the Society were entirely based on the Christian faith and Christian principles".[60] This resolution was dropped in 1932 when the Society became a different legal entity.

As the 20th century moved on, more Christian voices spoke out about our relationship with animals. The Benedictine scholar Dom Ambrose Agius, who was later appointed Apostolic Delegate to the Philippines by Pope Pius X in 1904, wrote:

> The Bible…tells us that cruelty to animals is wicked and that it is opposed to God's will and intention…The duty of all Christians (is) to emulate God's attributes, especially that of mercy, in regard to animals. To be kind to animals is to emulate the loving kindness of God.[61]

Dom Ambrose goes further: "If our ambition is to be able to say with St Paul, 'I live, now not I; but Christ liveth in me' (Gal. 2: 20), consideration for animals will be one sign of the indwelling Christ".[62]

The Christian theologian and missionary Albert Schweitzer (1875–1965) developed a philosophy which he called "Reverence for Life", for which he received the 1952 Nobel Peace Prize. He wrote:

> Only by means of reverence for life can we establish a spiritual and humane relationship with both people and all living creatures within our reach. Only

in this fashion can we avoid harming others, and, within the limits of our capacity, go to their aid whenever they need us.[63]

The famous environmentalist Rachel Carson dedicated her ground-breaking book, *Silent Spring*, to Albert Schweitzer.

Also in 1915, the year in which Schweitzer's book was published, and in the midst of the First World War, Pope Benedict XV wrote to the Italian Society for the Protection of Animals, saying that he favoured everything that may "foster respect for these other creatures of God, which Providence forbids us to exploit without concern and enjoins us to show wisdom in our use of them...". He went on to encourage the clergy to: "train souls in sentiments of enlightened gentleness and fostering care and guidance so that they may offer to the animals refuge from every suspicion of roughness, cruelty or barbarism...".[64]

The first Catholic Society devoted to animal welfare was formed in England in 1935 and still goes strong today, with over 50 branches and links to similar societies worldwide. Now a registered charity called Catholic Concern for Animals, its regular publication is "The Ark".[65] Other denominations have since formed their own societies, such as the Anglican Society for Animal Welfare, begun in 1970[66] and more recently SARX – For All God's Creatures, another, perhaps more evangelical, Christian charity.[67] These are great examples of Christians who believe that promoting care for animals is a fundamental part of a good Christian life.

Leading Lutheran theologian, Professor Jurgen Moltmann, says: "Nature is not our property...All living beings must be respected by humans as God's partners in the Covenant...Whoever injures the dignity of animals, injures God".[68] Moltmann has also called for a Universal Declaration of Animal Rights which "should be part of the constitutions of modern states and international agreements".[69] These rights would include a prohibition on factory farming and genetic modification of animals.

Pope John Paul II (Pope from 1978 to 2005) wrote in his encyclical *Gospel of Life*: "Human beings may be merciful to their neighbours, but the compassion of the Lord extends to every living creature".[70] These are beautiful sentiments, but there is a lack of detail as to how to interpret them. (This Pope was canonised by Pope Francis I in 2014 and is now also known as Saint John Paul the Great.)

The newest Catechism of the Catholic Church declares: "Animals are God's creatures. He surrounds them with his providential care. By their mere existence they bless him and give him glory. Thus men owe them kindness". But it goes on to say: "it is legitimate to use animals for food and clothing" and:

> It is contrary to human dignity to cause animals to suffer or die needlessly. It is likewise unworthy to spend money on them that should as a priority go to the relief of human misery. One can love animals; one should not direct to them the affection due only to persons.[71]

So, we can kill animals for food and clothing, but we must be kind to them – just not too loving! If this sounds like a passage written by a group of theologians with widely differing views, that is probably correct!

In June 2015, Pope Francis 1 issued a radical encyclical, "Laudato Si' – on care for our common home", in which he proposes an "ecological conversion", which is based on "attitudes which together foster a spirit of generous care, full of tenderness" and which "entails a loving awareness that we are not disconnected from the rest of creatures but joined in a splendid universal communion".[72]

The encyclical lists the actions which individuals can take in their own lives, from avoiding waste and using less water to "showing care for other living beings". The issue of our relationship with the other creatures in the world is constantly referred to in the encyclical. The Pope quotes from the most recent edition of the Catechism which he says,

> clearly and forcefully criticizes a distorted anthropocentrism: 'Each creature possesses its own particular goodness and perfection... Each of the various creatures, willed in its own being, reflects in its own way a ray of God's infinite wisdom and goodness. Man must therefore respect the particular goodness of every creature, to avoid any disordered use of things'.[73]

This encyclical has been hugely influential and is being studied and discussed by Christians and others all over the world.

## Farming Methods

In 1984, Peter Roberts, a highly spiritual person and the founder of Compassion in World Farming, took an intensive veal farm to court. These calves were owned by the Norbertine friars in Sussex in southern England. The case generated huge publicity. Many Catholics were outraged that the friars sustained themselves by subjecting calves to being chained by the neck throughout their lives in narrow crates, unable to turn round.[74] Peter lost the case and lost again on Appeal, but just a few years later, the UK government banned the keeping of calves in narrow crates.[75]

The friars who ran the Sussex veal crate farm were not the only religious order to own a factory farm. The Sisters of Our Lady of the Passion ran a battery hen farm near Daventry in Northamptonshire in England in the 1980s. The convent strongly defended its farm on the grounds that the caged hens were happy, but the place became the subject of much animal rights protest. In a strange turn of events a large outbreak of salmonella in the UK egg industry in the late 1980s led to the hens being slaughtered and this factory farm coming to an end.[76]

David Clough sums up the case against industrial farming of animals:

> Industrialised animal agriculture prioritises productive efficiency above what farmed animals need to flourish. It subjects farmed animals to impoverished environments that disallow their preferred behaviours, prevents maternal care and the establishment of family and social groups, and frequently involves painful and disabling bodily mutilations. It cannot be defended as necessary for human wellbeing because it threatens human food and water security and creates serious threats to human health. It subjects farm and

slaughterhouse workers – who are disproportionately migrant and members of ethnic minorities – to dangerous working conditions.[77]

One can only wonder how the fine sentiment expressed in Pope John Paul II's encyclical could be applied to farm animals – could the "compassion of the Lord" ('Evangelium Vitae', 1995) possibly be compatible with factory farming? Almost certainly not! Factory farming seems obviously incompatible with true "reverence for life" as evinced by Dr Schweitzer.[78]

When the future Pope Benedict XVI was interviewed (while still Cardinal Ratzinger) he spoke out against force feeding geese for foie gras and battery cages for hens, describing these practices as an "industrial use of creatures" which seemed to him "to contradict the relationship of mutuality that comes across in the Bible".[79]

The contemporary theologian Dr Andrew Linzey is one of the few outspoken voices within the Christian community (Anglican in his case) speaking out clearly about the horrors of factory farming:

> Does the Church really see the suffering of farm animals? Does it have any appreciation of what they have to endure in intensive farming – debeaking, castration, tail-docking without anaesthetics, battery cages – to take only a few examples?… Has it really grasped that now, as never before, we have turned God's creatures into meat machines?[80]

The Rt Rev John Austin Baker, former Bishop of Salisbury (UK), who died in 2014, spoke out against factory farming from the pulpit. He said that when taken around some local farms he was "disgusted" with the farrowing pens for pigs and found the battery hen unit "harrowing". He described the breeding and factory farming of turkeys for Christmas as "absolutely scandalous". He said: "it is wrong to exploit animals or be cruel to them in order to feed ourselves".[81]

After a conference in 1988, the World Council of Churches issued a non-official report which recommended: "Avoid meat and animal products that have been produced on factory farms. Instead purchase meat and animal products from sources where the animals have been treated with respect or abstain from these products altogether".[82] Sadly, this report has not been officially adopted.

Theologian Charles Camosy declares, "Christians should refuse to serve factory-farmed meat in their homes".[83]

David Clough writes:

> Given the unprecedented cruelties we are currently inflicting on farmed animals in intensive systems, it seems to me urgent for Christians to reclaim the connection between concern for animals and Christian faith, and be in the vanguard of campaigns to resist production systems that have no regard for the flourishing of animals.[84]

Dr Clough has started an organisation aimed at Christian churches and institutions, called CreatureKind. It calls on Christians to sign up to a triple commitment:

1 Reduce our consumption of animal products, such as meat, fish, dairy, and eggs, by consuming more plant-based foods that are less resource-intensive.

2 Source animal products we do consume from farms or fisheries where we are confident animals are able to flourish in a good life as creatures of God.

3 Continue to consider how our Christian faith should be put into practice in relation to other ways we treat our fellow animal creatures.[85]

Dr Clough has also produced a Policy Framework for Churches and Christian organisations, devised in cooperation with representatives of several Christian churches and animal welfare groups and academics. He writes:

Farmed animals glorify God by fully living out their particular abilities, activities, relationships, and characteristics. Their flourishing is threatened when they are subjected to impoverished environments and painful mutilations, deprived of social and familial relationships, killed after severely shortened lives and selectively bred to prioritize productivity over welfare.

The Framework's theme is that farmed animals should be able to flourish. In their flourishing, the animals give glory to God. Clough fondly describes how that flourishing of farmed animals may manifest: "By gathering in social groups, dust-bathing, rooting, grazing, swimming, caring for their young, teaching and learning, and growing to maturity. All as created by God in their species-specific particularity". The common methods used in industrial "factory" farming are condemned as they obstruct flourishing. In fact, such methods amount to "systemic sin". He calls them no more than "product management, which seriously impairs their ability to flourish as animal creatures". He calls on Christians to "promote the highest level of welfare possible, both for each species of farmed animal and for each individual within species".[86]

This most helpful document then examines each of the species commonly farmed and gives details about good or poor welfare. It is truly a spiritual and very practical guide for Christians of every denomination – and indeed for those outside the Christian community.

## Teaching and Global Practice

It is interesting to see if belief in Christianity has had any effect on how various majority Christian countries treat their animals in law and general practice.

Brazil is a secular country, but nearly 80% of its population identify as Christian, with Catholicism being the main religion, a legacy of the Portuguese heritage. Brazilian governments have produced documentation on farm animal welfare but, at the time of writing, no legislation has been passed to ban some of the most inhumane systems, such as sow stalls (gestation crates).

Breeding sows are kept in these narrow sow stalls throughout their 16.5-week pregnancies, unable to turn round and take more than a step or two forwards or backwards. The floor is usually concrete, with a slatted area at the back for drainage. The system makes it easy to keep huge numbers of sows together in a small area. As they cannot exercise, they can be given less feed. However, the system totally flouts the animals' needs.[87] Keeping pigs almost immobile on a hard floor is inherently inhumane. Research shows that pigs like to spend most of their daytime rooting in the soil with their sensitive snouts, searching for roots or insects to eat.[88]

This system has been banned in several European countries such as Sweden and the UK and it is partially banned in all 27 EU countries.[89] Many US states such as California have also banned the system. It is surely time for Brazil to enact similar legislation.[90]

Brazil has become the world's largest beef exporter, exporting 2 million tons in bovine carcass weight each year, approximately one-fifth of its production, a trade worth more than $5.4 billion per year (in freight-on-board value).[91] Many of these cattle have to undergo long and stressful journeys to slaughterhouses within Brazil.

In addition, Brazil exports around half a million live cattle a year, some to destinations as far away as Lebanon, Angola and Egypt.[92] Such long journeys subject the cattle to the vagaries of sea and wind conditions and may cause immense stress and suffering. Although we have no data on particular Brazilian tragedies, a similar export ship, carrying thousands of live sheep and cattle from Uruguay to Syria in 2009 capsized in the Mediterranean Sea. All the animals drowned as well as about half the 80-plus crew.[93] With beef exports being so large, it does seem unnecessary to export live animals on such very long journeys.

Sadly there is still recent evidence of workers in the Brazilian beef industry being treated as slave labourers.[94]

So, these workers suffer, the animals suffer and of course, we know that much of the Amazonian forest has been cut down to facilitate cattle rearing or the growing of soya for export for animal feed. Satellite data shows that destruction of the Brazilian rainforest surged by 22% in the 12 months to July 2021, the fastest rate recorded in 15 years.[95]

Many of the owners, managers and farmers involved in rearing, marketing, slaughtering and exporting cattle in Brazil must, statistically, be Christian. It is perhaps a sad reflection on Christianity's failure to preach and practice the "mercy" required by Jesus, that they maintain these activities and benefit from them.

Perhaps the one piece of better news from Brazil is that organic farming is also on the increase, with over 17,000 producers in 2018, up from around 7,000 in 2013.[96]

The United States of America is another predominantly Christian country, with Protestants of various kinds being the majority.[97]

Although change is on its way there, the general treatment of all kinds of animals has been among the worst globally. There is no federal (national) law protecting the welfare of farm animals on farm, and poultry are excluded from slaughter laws incorporating welfare. Purpose-bred rats, mice and birds, fish, amphibians, reptiles and invertebrates who make up 90% of the animals used in laboratories, are not covered by legislation on animal experimentation.[98]

If you wonder why this is so, then you need to understand the strength and wealth of the groups lobbying on behalf of agribusiness and the pharmaceutical industry, many of whose members are presumably adherents of the Christian faith in one form or other.

Nationally, pig farming is highly industrialised. Pigs just don't go out, and the majority of sows are kept in the narrow stalls described above throughout their pregnancies.

When they are ready to farrow (give birth) they will be moved into farrowing crates. Yet again these are narrow crates in which the sow can only stand up and lie down or take a step or two backwards or forwards. Here the sow farrows and feeds her piglets for three to four weeks. There will be an extra restriction to prevent the sow from lying on her piglets. The piglets are removed long before their natural weaning (which would be at 11 or 12 weeks old), as they are to be fattened up for slaughter. The sow is then impregnated again and is returned to her narrow gestation crate for another long, miserable pregnancy.

With the failure of federal laws, animal welfare groups in the US have shown ingenuity and campaign energy in getting some reform at state level, with the first successful ban on gestation crates taking place in Florida in 2002, coming into force in 2008.[99]

A big campaign in Arizona led to the phasing out of both gestation crates and veal crates for calves in 2006, coming into force in 2012. Some other states followed.[100] The biggest change of all came in California in 2008 when a large majority of citizens voted to ban gestation crates, veal crates and cages for laying hens.[101]

Although some industry bodies have tried – and are still trying – to overthrow these successes, many agribusiness companies have seen how the public is becoming more welfare-conscious and they are setting their own phase-out dates for the abysmal confinement systems they have been using for so long.[102]

Statistically, some factory farmers, agribusiness company executives and animal welfare campaigners must have professed Christianity in their personal lives. Perhaps this anomaly demonstrates very clearly the two strands of Christian thinking about the place of animals in the world in relation to humans.

David Clough is clear: "Christians should avoid supporting the operation of industrialized animal agriculture as consumers, workers, and investors wherever possible and support legal and regulatory reform aimed at bringing it to an end".[103]

Anecdotally, the author recalls a discussion with animal welfare colleagues from different US groups after a busy conference day in San Francisco. Of the eight of us around the table, seven had been brought up as Catholics!

## Eating Animals

We cannot be sure that Jesus ate meat, although it is likely that he partook of the Jewish Sabbath and other festivals of the time, where meat-eating was involved. There is a Biblical record that he ate fish, as when he came upon his disciples after his resurrection from the dead:

> And while they still did not believe it because of joy and amazement, he asked them, "Do you have anything here to eat?" They gave him a piece of broiled fish, and he took it and ate it in their presence.[104]

Matthew's gospel records the "miracle of the loaves and fishes" when the hungry crowd needed to eat and the disciples said to Jesus: "We have here only five loaves of bread and two fish" and he said

> Bring them here to me. And he directed the people to sit down on the grass. Taking the five loaves and the two fish and looking up to heaven, he gave thanks and broke the loaves. Then he gave them to the disciples, and the disciples gave them to the people. They all ate and were satisfied, and the disciples picked up twelve basketfuls of broken pieces that were left over.[105]

It would be likely that Jesus himself would also have eaten of this food, but we do not know. It could be argued that by miraculously multiplying the two dead fish, he spared more fish being caught and killed!

John's gospel records how, again after the Resurrection, Jesus joined some of his disciples who were fishing. They had fished all night without catch, but when Jesus ordered them to try again, they caught a massive number of fish. Some fish were grilled over the charcoal fire for breakfast and Jesus handed the food out to them. We can only presume that he also ate this food.[106]

When Jesus partook of the Last Supper, it was not lamb or goatmeat that he distributed to his disciples, but bread and wine, basic vegan food and drink. To this day the Communion Service or Mass continues to use this simple meal as a symbol of his body and blood or in the case of Catholics, as transformed into his body and blood. (Nowadays wine may be clarified with animal-based ingredients such as egg white or the swim bladders of certain fish, but it is unlikely that these additions were used at the time of Jesus.)

One passage which has proved troubling to Christian vegetarians is the vision which Saint Peter had, which showed all kinds of edible animals jumbled together in a large sheet, accompanied by a voice from heaven saying: "Get up Peter. Kill and eat".[107] Peter is shocked to learn that he can eat animals which are forbidden in Jewish teaching. The voice is heard again: "Do not call anything impure that God has made clean".[108]

Rather than seeing this as a dietary lesson, it is important to see this story in its context. Peter is immediately invited to the home of a Roman centurion who wants to accept the Christian faith. Peter comes to understand his vision as meaning that faith in Jesus is open to all kinds of Gentile people, not just to Jewish people.

Christians believe that when Jesus was crucified on the cross, his sacrifice replaced the sacrifice of a lamb at the Jewish Passover festival. It was the ultimate and final sacrifice. Jesus is sometimes referred to or depicted as the Paschal Lamb, who takes away the sins of humanity.

Although some of those early Christian saints probably followed a vegetarian or vegan diet and many Christians today will adopt such diets, there is no standard Christian teaching on the issue. For centuries, Catholics were forbidden to eat meat on Fridays. Orthodox Christians follow many meatless fast days during the year. However, abstinence from meat was usually undertaken as a penance for oneself in honour of God, rather than out of a belief that slaughtering animals for food was wrong.

The formidable early theologian, Saint Augustine, declared that the command "Thou shalt not kill" obviously only refers to not killing another human and does not apply to the killing of "irrational animals, because they have no fellowship with us".[109]

Vegetarian diets were condemned by the Protestant reforming theologian John Calvin as "unsupportable tyranny", causing injury to God.[110]

Ellen White, founder of the Seventh Day Adventist Church believed that kindness to animals was a Christian duty. She urged her followers to: "Think of the cruelty that meat eating involves, and its effect on those who inflict and those who behold it. How it destroys the tenderness with which we should regard these creatures of God!"[111]

In the mid-20th century, Rev Basil Wrighton wrote:

> Our minds are in compartments and to preserve our comfort we see to it that the contents of different compartments do not get mixed. May I remind you that 'holiness' carries the meaning of 'wholeness', so that he who aspires must needs see about breaking down these compartments. I hold that because of our kinship we have a clear ethical duty to protect animals from cruelty and sudden death, and not to eat them.[112]

More recently the Christian philosopher Stephen Clark wrote: "But vegetarianism is now as necessary a pledge of moral devotion as was the refusal of emperor-worship in the early church...Those who still eat flesh when they could do otherwise have no claim to be serious moralists".[113]

Kenneth Rose believed that as the first diet recommended for humanity was a plant-based one, then, in order to prepare for the Kingdom to come, Christians should follow a vegetarian diet: "To live in this way must be considered as part of God's ultimate intention for humanity, for how else can one account for the fact that the Bible both begins and ends in a kingdom where the sound of slaughter is unknown?"[114]

Theologian Brian McClaren says:

> If Christians were to join God in God's concern for creation...especially sentient creation, animal life, I think it would ... make us more concerned about

the conditions in which our food is grown, it might make us much more willing to eat more of a plant-based diet than an animal-based diet....[115]

David Clough also leans towards the plant-based diet but is realistic about where the average Christian might place themselves on a meat-to-vegan scale:

> There are strong faith-based reasons for Christians to adopt a plant-based diet. Reducing the global consumption of animals is crucial to address issues of human welfare, such as food and water security, the growth of antibiotic resistance, the risk of zoonotic disease pandemics, and to improve human dietary health. It is essential in order to reduce global carbon emissions and reverse the changes in land use currently contributing to a global loss of biodiversity and the sixth mass extinction event of animals. It would also reduce the numbers of animals being drawn into industrial animal agriculture. All Christians should recognize that industrial animal agriculture is incompatible with their responsibilities towards fellow animal creatures. All Christians should recognize that a significant reduction in the global consumption of animals is necessary. Christians may continue to disagree as to whether it is justifiable to kill animals for food if they have been farmed to high welfare standards, or whether it is impermissible to kill animals for food where there are adequate alternative sources of nutrition.[116]

In July 2022, perhaps for the first time, Pope Francis urged young people to consider their meat consumption:

> May you aspire to a life of dignity and sobriety, without luxury and waste, so that everyone in our world can enjoy a dignified existence. There is an urgent need to reduce the consumption not only of fossil fuels but also of so many superfluous things. In certain areas of the world, too, it would be appropriate to consume less meat: this too can help save the environment.[117]

## Slaughter

There is no "Christian" way to slaughter, as there is in Judaism and Islam. Methods to stun animals before the cut have been developed in predominantly Christian countries, so they might be associated with a Christian desire to spare animals the agony of slaughter. There is nothing fundamentally Christian about these developments.

## Hunting and Sport

Bullfighting was condemned by Pope Pius V in 1567,[118] although this prohibition was later relaxed by other popes. Pope Benedict XV, who seems to have had genuine concern for animals (see above), condemned the "human savagery" of bull fights and declared that the Church continues to "condemn these shameful and bloody spectacles".[119]

In the 1930s, Pope Pius XI forbade priests from attending bullfights in Spain.[120] This cruel sport still continues in much of Spain, although the province of Catalonia has voted to stop it and the last bullfight in Barcelona's huge bullring took place in 2011.[121]

Today there are still priests in Spain who act as chaplains for the bullrings and support the bullfighters.[122]

In medieval times it was common for bishops to go hunting, but in the 21st century, it is more unusual. However, the occasional vicar can be seen joining their local hunt.[123]

## Vivisection

In 19th-century England, there seems to have been an increase in debates about our relationship with animals. As scientific investigation into how our bodies worked and how sicknesses could perhaps be healed, experimenting on animals became more common. Cardinal John Henry Newman (1801–1890) held the traditional view of animals as being here for our own ends, but he was outspoken in his opposition to vivisection: "Cruelty to animals is as if man did not love God... There is something so very dreadful, so Satanic, in tormenting those who have never harmed us, who cannot defend themselves, who are utterly in our power".[124]

Another Cardinal, Henry Edward Manning (1808–1892), also spoke out against cruelty to animals, especially experimentation upon animals. He wrote: "We owe ourselves the duty not to be brutal or cruel; and we owe to God the duty of treating all His creatures according to His own perfections of love and mercy".[125]

Of course, strong arguments can be made for experimenting on animals to ensure our medications are safe and effective. Experimenting for human vanity such as cosmetics is hard to justify and thankfully, more and more countries and companies are abandoning this type of testing.

Globally it is calculated that around 192 million animals are used in experiments every year.[126]

If we apply Clough's concept of "flourishing" to the lives of animals kept in laboratories for experiments, we can see at once that true flourishing must be absolutely impossible for them.

For many Christians who believe in the more Franciscan approach, using medication tested on animals is a genuine dilemma and one that only each individual can answer for themselves.

David Clough sums up a modern, humane viewpoint:

> Most experiments on animals require them to be kept in impoverished environments, subjected to suffering, and end in their being killed. Imposing these kinds of costs on animals should only be done in situations of grave urgency. The vast majority of experiments currently carried out do not meet this criterion. Many experiments are performed for regulatory reasons where other measures to assess safety would provide results that are as good or better. Others are used to increase scientific knowledge that could be pursued

using other methods that do not require animal experiments. Many animals are still unnecessarily subjected to suffering and death for the purposes of education. Christians in nineteenth century Britain campaigned for the abolition of vivisection against the scientific and medical establishment of their day, arguing that the strong should not exploit the weak for their own ends. An appropriate Christian regard for the flourishing of animals as fellow creatures would result in the ending of virtually all experimentation on animals.[127]

## Wildlife and Biodiversity

In 2021 researchers at Texas Tech University found that land areas dedicated to growing soy in South America had more than doubled over the past two decades – from 264,000 to 551,000 square kilometres. It now covers an area larger than the state of California or the Iberian Peninsula. Most of the land encroachment for soy has been through taking over pasture previously used for raising cattle. As the pasture is depleted, ranchers move to new areas, which means destroying the rainforest. They also found that the largest expansion of soy came in Brazil, with an increase of 160%, nearly half located in the Brazilian Cerrado.[128] As the forest and biodiversity-rich areas like the Cerrado are cut down or dug up for soy or cattle, millions of wild creatures lose their homes and habitat. Indigenous peoples may also find their traditional homes devastated. There are few winners in this situation, except perhaps the big agribusiness companies that deal in soy-based animal feed or beef cattle.

Again, if we apply the "flourishing" concept to the creatures living in the areas being deforested, it is obvious that flourishing may be a state in which they have previously lived but which becomes impossible, unless they are able to flee with speed to a different area. Not all creatures are able to move with speed, so they will be doomed.

On 21 July 2022, Pope Francis gave a strong message on the World Day of Prayer for the Care of Creation, saying:

> In the first place, it is our sister, mother earth, who cries out. Prey to our consumerist excesses, she weeps and implores us to put an end to our abuses and to her destruction. Then too, there are all those different creatures who cry out. At the mercy of a "tyrannical anthropocentrism" (Laudato Si', 68), completely at odds with Christ's centrality in the work of creation, countless species are dying out and their hymns of praise silenced.[129]

## Sacrifice

Christians believe that the crucifixion of Jesus was the ultimate and final sacrifice, that he gave his life so that our sins may be forgiven by God. Animal sacrifice may continue in a few isolated churches, but it is not part of any formal church belief.[130]

## Christianity and Animal Use

All over the world believing Christians farm animals, sometimes in dire conditions, they may experiment on them, hunt them for sport or even go "trophy hunting" to shoot lions or elephants, subject animals to stressful "entertainments", confine them in zoos and, of course, eat them regularly and as part of the celebrations at major Christian festivals such as Christmas and Easter. Some keep dogs, cats and other species as companion animals or so-called "pets". Many have a sincere love for these animals and take great care of them. They are all surely following the Aristotelean-Thomistic tradition.

More and more may begin to see the anomaly of loving dogs and eating pigs and chickens.

A minority of Christians follow the more Franciscan strand. They may rescue abandoned animals, donate to animal charities, avoid factory-farmed animal products and are likely to move towards plant-based diets, or even go entirely vegan. They will choose products not tested on animals and possibly campaign against animal exploitation such as in hunting or animal circuses.

Which "way" is closer to Christian teaching and to the qualities that Jesus proclaimed?

## Conclusion

What a dilemma for the believing Christian! Should they follow the Thomist way, so clearly expressed in that Gospelway website (see above)? Should they see animals just as here for our own purposes, as food, clothing, experimental creatures etc?

As Dr Christina Nellist, Eastern Orthodox theologian, explains:

> Unfortunately for the non-human beings and the environment, this compassionate tradition has too often been hidden under a tradition that focused on the role and superiority of the human being, rather than on our unique role as icon of God. Thus, the rest of the created world was forgotten, abused and exploited to the detriment of us all.[131]

Personally, I think that the modern Christian now has so much more scientific knowledge about the cognitive and emotional capacities of other animals, that adopting the more Franciscan strand of Christian thought is the way to go. Pope Francis has thrown out the challenge in "Laudato Si".

The Rt Rev John Arnold, Roman Catholic Bishop of Salford, explains this more compassionate way of living:

> We all need to grow in an understanding that we share a common home for which we need to care and that care must encompass the environment, the reality of climate change, the consumption of unsustainable resources, the detrimental impact of industry and consumerism on people who have

done least to damage our world – and a care for the animal kingdom with its delicate balance and dependence. Animals have their own dignity as part of God's creation.[132]

In 1989, Ecumenical Patriarch Dimitrios I of the Eastern Orthodox Church proclaimed the 1st of September as a day of prayer for creation. The World Council of Churches has adopted the idea and Pope Francis welcomed it to the Catholic Church in 2015. The original Day of Prayer for Creation now lasts over a month, until 4 October, the Feast of St. Francis of Assisi.[133] This is truly encouraging.

Rev Fletcher Harper who founded and runs the environmental organisation GreenFaith has proposed three possible actions which Christians can adopt to reduce their impact on the climate. One of these is "reduce your meat consumption or go vegetarian or vegan".[134]

If the fraternal relationship with our fellow creatures, as lived so vividly by St Francis, can become the inspiration and the standard teaching and practice of the world's 2 billion plus Christians, then there is no doubt that much suffering could be avoided and much goodness achieved.

## Notes

1  R. Rohr, 18/10/21. Jesus and the Empire. Daily Meditation.
2  C. Camosy, 2013. *For Love of Animals: Christian Ethics, Consistent Action*. Cincinnati: Franciscan Media.
3  A. Linzey and P.A.B. Clarke, 1990. *Animal Rights. A Historical Anthology*. New York: Columbia University Press.
4  D. Jones, 2009. *The School of Compassion: A Roman Catholic Theology of Animals*. Leominster: Gracewing.
5  Revelation 5:5.
6  Matthew 3:16.
7  Genesis 1:31.
8  J. Barnes (Ed), 1995. *Politics 1.8. The Complete Works of Aristotle*. Princeton, NJ: Bollingen.
9  Summa Theologica 1.65.2, quoted in D. Jones, 2009. *The School of Compassion: A Roman Catholic Theology of Animals*, Leominster: Gracewing.
10  Martin Luther, Luther's Works, 1.58–9.
11  D. Clough, 03/03/22. Personal communication.
12  Sky History, u.d. The Law Is an Ass: 8 Famous Animal Trials from History. www.history.co.uk/articles/the-law-is-an-ass-8-famous-animal-trials-from-history.
13  G.-H. Bougeant, 1739. *Amusement Philosophique sur le langage des bestes et des oiseaux*. Paris: Chez Gissey.
14  Gospelway. www.gospelway.com/religiousgroups/animal_liberation.php.
15  J. Sobran, October 2006. The Dark Side of Dolphins. *Christian Order* magazine 47, quoted in D. Jones, 2009. *The School of Compassion*. Leominster: Gracewing.
16  J. Pageau, 24/112/12. *Orthodox Arts Journal*. https://orthodoxartsjournal.org/why-an-ass-and-an-ox-in-the-nativity-icon/.
17  Matthew 2:1–2 & 9–11.
18  Luke 2:8–20.
19  Mark 1:9–13.
20  Isaiah 11:6–9.
21  Luke 12: 6–7.
22  Luke 12:24.

23 Matthew 12:11–12.
24 Luke 13:15.
25 Mark 4:30–32.
26 Luke 13:34.
27 John 21:15–17.
28 John 10: 14–16.
29 Isaiah 40:11.
30 John 2:15–16.
31 Mark 5:1–13
32 Translation of .Coptic text by Richard Bauckham, quoted in A. Linzey, 2007. *Creatures of the Same God*. Winchester: Winchester University Press.
33 Matthew 5:7.
34 John1:14.
35 D. Clough, 2012. *On Animals. Volume 1: Systematic Theology*. London: Bloomsbury.
36 Adapted from R. Rohr, 2016. *A Spring Within Us: A Book of Daily Meditations*, Wyoming: CAC Publishing, pp314–315; in Daily Meditation 15/08/21.
37 R. Rohr, 29/05/22. Ever-Widening Circles. Richard Rohr's Daily Meditations.
38 Greeting to a conference organised by Compassion in World Farming and the Food and Agriculture Organization of the United Nations, 20/03/12.
39 Dominum et Vivificantem: Encyclical Letter on the Holy Spirit in the Life of the Church and the World, 1986. www.vatican.va/content/john-paul-ii/en/encyclicals/documents/hf_jp-ii_enc_18051986_dominum-et-vivificantem.html.
40 S. McFague, 1993. *The Body of God: An Ecological Theology*. Minneapolis, MN: Fortress Press, p182.
41 Mark 16:15.
42 Romans 8: 18–21.
43 Meister Eckhart, Sermon on Sirach 50:6–7.
44 John Wesley, Sermons, 129, quoted in D. Clough, 2012. *On Animals*, Vol 1. London: Bloomsbury.
45 B.D. McLaren, 2007. *Everything Must Change: Jesus, Global Crises, and a Revolution of Hope*. Thomas Nelson, pp5–6.
46 D. Clough, 03/03/22. Personal communication.
47 R. Rohr, 28/9/20. Mystics on the Margins. Daily Meditation. https://cac.org/daily-meditations/a-church-on-the-margins-2020–09–28/.
48 H. Waddell, 1934. *Beasts and Saints*. London: Constable and Company.
49 Fr. S. Freeman, 2006. Words from St. Isaac of Syria. Homily 81. https://blogs.ancientfaith.com/glory2godforallthings/2006/11/01/words-from-st-isaac-of-syria/.
50 Rose's Rambles, 01/08/16. The Song of the Seals. https://rosesislandramble.wordpress.com/2016/08/01/the-song-of-the-seals/.
51 S. Heaney, 1996. St Kevin and the Blackbird. www.poetrybyheart.org.uk/poems/st-kevin-and-the-blackbird/.
52 Isaiah 11:6.
53 Rev Dr J. Chryssavgis, 2020. The Desert Tradition and the Natural Environment. https://sarx.org.uk/articles/the-natural-world/the-desert-tradition-and-the-natural-environment-john-chryssavgis/.
54 Saint Bonaventure. The Life of Saint Francis of Assisi, translated by E. Gurney Salter, 1904. www.ecatholic2000.com/bonaventure/assisi/francis.shtml.
55 Saint Bonaventure. The Soul's Journey into God.
56 St Martin Apostolate, 2021. Life of St Martin de Porres. www.stmartin.ie/life-st-martin/.
57 L. White, 1967. The historical roots of our ecological crisis. *Science*, **155**, pp1203–1207.
58 T.À. Kempis, The Imitation of Christ.
59 Wikipedia, u.d. BenjaminLay.https://en.wikipedia.org/wiki/Benjamin_Lay#Biography.
60 W. Fairholme and E.G. Pain, 1924. *A Century of Work for Animals: The History of the RSPCA 1824–1924*. London: John Murray.

61 Rev Dom Ambrose Agius, 1970. God's Animals. Catholic Study Circle for Animal Welfare.

62 Rev Dom Ambrose Agius, 1958. Cruelty to Animals: Catholic Truth Society Tract. www.ecatholic2000.com/cts/untitled-115.shtml.

63 A. Schweizer, 1915. Reverence for Life. Referenced in www.reverenceforlife.org.uk.

64 Rev Dom Ambrose Agius. The Popes and Animal Welfare.

65 Catholic Concern for Animals. https://catholic-animals.com/.

66 Anglican Society for the Welfare of Animals. www.aswa.org.uk/.

67 Sarx. https://sarx.org.uk/.

68 J. Moltmann, 1990. At the North American Council for Religious Education (NACRE) Conference, Caring for Creation.

69 J. Moltmann, 2012. *Ethics of Hope*, M. Kohl, trans. Minneapolis, MN: Fortress Press.

70 Evangelium Vitae, 1995.

71 Catholic Catechism, 2003.

72 His Holiness Pope Francis, 2015. Encyclical Letter Laudato si' of the Holy Father Francis on Care for Our Common Home. www.vatican.va/content/francesco/en/encyclicals/documents/papa-francesco_20150524_enciclica-laudato-si.html.

73 His Holiness Pope Francis, 2015. Encyclical Letter Laudato si' of the Holy Father Francis on Care for Our Common Home. www.vatican.va/content/francesco/en/encyclicals/documents/papa-francesco_20150524_enciclica-laudato-si.html.

74 AgScene, Sep/Oct 1983. Priory Veal? Reproduced on the website of the Fellowship of Life. www.all-creatures.org/fol/art-20120917-04.html.

75 Compassion in World Farming, 2001. The Case against the Veal Crate. www.ciwf.org.uk/media/3818635/case-against-the-veal-crate.pdf.

76 The Fellowship of Life, u.d. Interviews: "Sacred factory farms". www.all-creatures.org/fol/interview-20090406.html.

77 D. Clough, 03/03/22. Personal Communication.

78 A. Schweizer, 1915. Reverence for Life. Referenced in www.reverenceforlife.org.uk.

79 J. Ratzinger and P. Seewald, 2002. *God and the World: A Conversation with Peter Seewald*, San Francisco: Ignatius Press.

80 A. Linzey, 2007. *Creatures of the Same God*. Winchester: Winchester University Press.

81 Philip Lymbery, 11/06/2014. Wonderful Champion of Animal Welfare Dies. www.ciwf.org.uk/philip-lymbery/blog/2014/06/wonderful-champion-of-animal-welfare-dies.

82 World Council of Churches, September 1988. Liberation of Life. Excerpt from report from meeting at Annecy, France, referenced in The Fellowship of Life, 1990s edition, Calling All Christians and People of Goodwill. www.all-creatures.org/fol/lit-calling.html.

83 C. Camosy, 2013. *For Love of Animals*. Cincinnati: Franciscan Press.

84 D. Clough, 2017. Animals: Who Cares? https://sarx.org.uk/articles/christianity-and-animals/animals-who-cares/.

85 Creature Kind. Sign the Creature Kind Commitment. www.becreaturekind.org/creaturekind-commitment.

86 D. Clough, M.B. Adam, D. Grumett and S. Mullan, 2020. The Christian Ethics of Farmed Animal Welfare. http://www1.chester.ac.uk/cefaw.

87 EFSA, 2007. Scientific report on animal health and welfare aspects of different housing and husbandry systems for adult breeding boars, pregnant, farrowing sows and unweaned piglets. Question no. EFSA-Q-2006–028. European Food Safety Authority. *Annex to the EFSA Journal*, **572**, pp1–13.

88 A. Stolba and D. Wood-Gush, 1989. The behaviour of pigs in a semi-natural environment. *Animal Science*, **48**:2, pp419–425. https://doi.org/10.1017/S0003356100040411.

89 Council Directive 2008/120/EC laying down minimum standards for the protection of pigs.

90 Animal Protection Index, 2020. Brazil. https://api.worldanimalprotection.org/country/brazil.

91 Erasmus K.H.J. Zu Ermgassen, et al., 2020. The origin, supply chain, and deforestation risk of Brazil's beef exports. *Proceedings of the National Academy of Sciences*, **117**:50, pp31770–31779. https://doi.org/10.1073/pnas.2003270117.

92 M.E. Pinheiro de Sa et al., 2018. Data on network of live cattle exports from Brazil. *Data in Brief*, **19**, pp1963–1969. www.sciencedirect.com/science/article/pii/S2352340918307108.

93 The Wreck site.org. MV Danny F. II. www.wrecksite.eu/wreck.aspx?169777.

94 Repórter Brasil, 2021. Slave Labor in Brazil's Meat Industry. https://reporterbrasil.org.br/wp-content/uploads/2021/01/Monitor-8-Slave-labor-in-Brazils-meat-industry.pdf.

95 M. Pooler and C. Ingizza, 01/03/22. Brazil's Beef Industry Starts to Tackle Methane Emissions. *FT*. https://www.ft.com/content/ab9ceb79-0777-499e-a04a-beb412039159.

96 C. Boehm, 30/08/18. Organic Farming on the Rise in Brazil. https://agenciabrasil.ebc.com.br/en/economia/noticia/2018-08/organic-production-rise-brazil.

97 Pew Research Center, 2021. Measuring Religion in Pew Research Center's American Trends Panel.

98 HSI Global, 2022. About Animal Testing. https://tinyurl.com/59pncv85.

99 ASPCA, 2022. Farm Animal Confinement Bans by State. www.aspca.org/improving-laws-animals/public-policy/farm-animal-confinement-bans.

100 Compassion in World Farming, 2022. Welfare Issues for Pigs. www.ciwf.com/farmed-animals/pigs/welfare-issues/.

101 ASPCA, 2022. Farm Animal Confinement Bans by State. www.aspca.org/improving-laws-animals/public-policy/farm-animal-confinement-bans.

102 ASPCA, 2022. Farm Animal Confinement Bans by State. www.aspca.org/improving-laws-animals/public-policy/farm-animal-confinement-bans.

103 D. Clough, M.B. Adam, D. Grumett and S. Mullan, 2020. The Christian Ethics of Farmed Animal Welfare. www1.chester.ac.uk/cefaw.

104 Luke 24:41–43.

105 Matthew 14:17–20.

106 John 21:1–13.

107 Acts 10:13.

108 Acts 10:13.

109 Augustine of Hippo, The City of God 1,20, c. 420 C.E.

110 J. Calvin. Commentaries on the first book of Moses, cited in A. Linzey and T. Regan (Eds), 2007. *Animals and Christianity*. Eugene: Wipf and Stock Publishers.

111 E. White. *The Ministry of Healing*, first published 1905 by Pacific Press Publishing Association.

112 Justice and the Animals, The Ark, January 1952 reprinted in Catholic Study Circle for Animal Welfare, 1987. Reason, Religion and the Animals.

113 S.R.L. Clark, 1977. *The Moral Status of Animals*. Oxford: OUP.

114 K. Rose, 1984. The Lion Shall Eat Straw Like the Ox: The Bible and Vegetarianism. www.backtogodhead.in/the-lion-shall-eat-straw-like-the-ox-by-kenneth-rose/.

115 Sarx, 2017. Are Animal Issues Christian Issues? – Brian McLaren. www.youtube.com/watch?v=lxe-qnGmdxM.

116 D. Clough, 03/03/22. Personal communication.

117 Message of His Holiness Pope Francis to the Participants in the EU Youth Conference, Prague, 11–13 July 2022.

118 Compiled by Luis Gilpérez Fraile, u.d. Of Interest to Bullfighting Catholics. https://asanda.org/descargas/documentos/taurinos/de-interes/bula.PDF.

119 Letter to the Toulon Society for the Protection of Animals. *The Ark*, **49**, 1953.

120 J. Thaler, November 1997. No Bull: Pius V and Bullfighting. *Satya*. https://sharkonline.org/index.php/animal-cruelty/bullfighting/80-animal-cruelty/bullfighting/other-bullfighting-articles/814-no-bull-pius-v-and-bullfighting.

121 K. Hounsell-Robert, 07/04/17. Spain's Big City Rivals Go Head to Head over Bullfights. *The Tablet*. www.thetablet.co.uk/blogs/1/984/spain-s-big-city-rivals-go-head-to-head-over-bullfights.

122 M. Malavia, 14/05/18. Las Ventas, the Largest Church in Madrid. www.vidanuevadig-ital.com/2018/05/14/las-ventas-la-iglesia-mas-grande-de-madrid/.

123 R. Mile, 05/09/16. Petition Calls for Herefordshire Vicar to Be Sacked for Taking Part in Fox Hunting. *Hereford Times.* www.herefordtimes.com/news/14723470. petition-calls-for-herefordshire-vicar-to-be-sacked-for-taking-part-in-fox-hunting/.

124 J.H. Newman, 1868. *Parochial and Plain Sermons.* San Francisco: Ignatius Press.

125 Letter, July 13, 1891.

126 Cruelty Free International, u.d. Facts and Figures on Animal Testing. https://tinyurl. com/4kp972xu.

127 D. Clough, 03/03/22. Personal communication.

128 X.P. Song, M.C. Hansen, P. Potapov, et al., 2021. Massive soybean expansion in South America since 2000 and implications for conservation. *Nature Sustainability*, **4**: 784–792 https://doi.org/10.1038/s41893-021-00729-z.

129 Laudato Si' Movement, 21/07/22. Message of His Holiness Pope Francis for the Celebration of the World Day of Prayer for the Care of Creation. https://laudatosi-movement.org/news/message-of-his-holiness-pope-francis-for-the-celebration-of-the-world-day-of-prayer-for-the-care-of-creation/.

130 Jill Hamilton, 15/12/11. There is no role for animal sacrifice in Christianity. www.the-guardian.com/commentisfree/belief/2011/dec/15/no-role-animal-sacrifice-christianity

131 C. Nellist, 2020. Orthodoxy and Care of Creation. https://sarx.org.uk/articles/ christianity-and-animals/orthodoxy-and-care-of-creation-christina-nellist/.

132 Bishop J. Arnold, 27/08/21. How Can We Live Laudato Si? https://sarx.org.uk/articles/ the-natural-world/see-judge-act-living-laudato-si/.

133 Season of Creation, 2022. What Is the Season of Creation? https://seasonofcreation. org/2021/08/27/what-is-the-season-of-creation/.

134 Climate Justice, Your First Steps,16/12/21, received via email.

# 3 Islam
## Teaching and Practice regarding Humanity's Relationship with Animals

## Introduction

Many people in the West have negative ideas about Muslim concern for animal welfare. If you asked the average European or American which religion they most associated with poor animal welfare, I suspect they might well choose Islam.

As I researched this chapter, I have found that Islamic teaching contains a wealth of concern for animals. The Qur'an refers to them as communities like our own communities and it declares that they praise God. The Prophet Muhammad is on record as equating acts of kindness to animals with acts of kindness to humans.

Travellers to predominantly Muslim countries often return with tales of having seen donkeys overworked and beaten, of scarecrow-thin ponies pulling tourist vehicles and of markets selling caged wildlife. I believe them. I have seen them too. What these stories really tell us is that many Muslims may be unaware of the teaching of their own faith with respect to animals.

In this chapter, I shall show the wealth of teaching within the Islamic holy books as well as positive examples of good practice by individual Muslims or Muslim-owned companies. I shall not shy away from recounting the negative examples as well.

Having discovered the teaching, I shall end with a call to Muslims individually and collectively, to take action to rediscover the teaching of their own holy books and to put this into practice, becoming leaders in the movement for better animal welfare globally.

## The Teaching

Allah is the Creator and Originator, the one God; although He has many names (99 are known), there is no other than Him. He is the Almighty. He is Great. Yet He is also the Compassionate, the Merciful and the Source of Peace.[1]

The word "Islam" means "submission" and to be a Muslim is to submit oneself to this one and only Allah ("God" in Arabic). Allah is the Regulator and so Muslims often say *insha allah* (God willing). Islam also means peace, in the sense that by submitting fully to Allah, one finds peace within oneself.

DOI: 10.4324/9781003292555-4

Islam is one of the three major monotheistic, Abrahamic religions. Islam recognises the Biblical prophets such as Abraham (Ibrahim), Moses (Musa) etc. – and, indeed, Jesus (Isa).[2]

The Prophet Muhammad is regarded as the last of the prophets and the Qur'an is believed to have been transmitted to him by the angel Gabriel (Gibril). The Prophet Muhammad then dictated the verses, which he had received, to his scribes – over a period of 23 years.

As the Qur'an makes clear: "Prophet Muhammad is only a messenger before whom many messengers have been and gone".[3]

Allah created the world and everything in it, but for whom did He create it? The Qur'an tells us "He set down the earth for his creatures".[4] Indeed, the animals are on earth to enjoy its benefits, just as humans do: "...and the earth too He spread out, bringing waters and pastures out of it, and setting firm mountains (in it) for you and your animals to enjoy".[5]

This is a really important point: the pastures are for humans and animals to enjoy. As we shall discuss, many farmed animals never get to "enjoy" pastures.

The Qur'an makes it clear that not only did Allah create the animals, but that they actually praise Him: "Do you not see that all those who are in the heavens and earth praise God as do the birds with wings outstretched?"[6] Another verse makes clear that animals prostrate or submit before God: "Do you not realize that everything in the heavens and earth submits to God: The sun, the moon, the stars, the mountains, the trees, and the animals?"[7]

Moreover, Allah cares for all creatures: "There is not a creature that moves on earth whose provision is not His concern. He knows where it lives and its final resting place".[8]

Although the earth has been created for all His creatures, there is no doubt that, in Islam, humanity is regarded as the pinnacle of His creation. In fact, there is a strong understanding that the earth and its bounty have been created primarily for humanity: "It was He who has created all that is on the earth for you".[9] Only humanity has a spiritual awareness of closeness to Allah and fear of Him (sometimes referred to as Taqwa). Only a human has the capacity to use her reason and to choose between good and evil.

Yet the animals resemble humans in so many ways: "All the creatures that crawl on the earth and those that fly with their wings are communities like yourselves".[10] This last reference is followed in the Qur'an by an interesting allusion which implies that on the Last Day, not only will humans experience a resurrection, but also the animals: "We have missed nothing out of the Record and in the end they will be gathered to their Lord".[11]

As theologian İbrahim Özdemir, Dean, Faculty of Humanities and Social Sciences, Uskudar University, Istanbul declares: "We must understand that animals are like our fellow men, at least in some respects. Contrary to the prevailing modern views, there is no clear-cut distinction between humans and non-humans; they are creatures of the same Creator".[12]

Over the centuries, some noted Islamic scholars, such as the 20th-century Islamic theologian Said Nursi, have believed that "animal souls are eternal".[13]

Without getting into the details of Sharia law, it is worth quoting the respected Islamic scholar and environmentalist, Othman Abd-ar-Rahman Llewellyn:

> Masālih al-khalq: the universal common good – The ultimate objective of the sharī'ah is defined as the welfare of God's creatures (masālih al-khalq or masālih al-'ibād), encompassing both our immediate welfare in the present and our ultimate welfare in the hereafter. It also encompasses the universal common good, the welfare of the entire creation (masālih al-khalqi kāffah). This is a distinctive characteristic of Islamic law. It means, first, that both material and nonmaterial dimensions must be taken into account, and second, that the welfare of humans and of non-human sentient beings must be considered in the course of planning and administration.[14]

## The Role of Humanity

Islam teaches that humans have a duty to act as *Khalifah* for the earth and all within it.[15] The word Khalifah is variously translated as "vice-regent", "trustee", "agent" (of God), or "having a sacred duty".

The Islamic scholar and environmentalist Fazlun Khalid explains the concept well:

> We are required to care for and manage the earth in a way that conforms to God's intention in creation: it should be used for our benefit without causing damage to the other inhabitants of planet Earth, who are communities like ourselves….[16]

For centuries, much of humanity has used and abused the earth itself and the creatures who inhabit it – all for their own ends, often for their own power and profit. New technologies have expedited both the exploitation of the earth and its forests for fuels, minerals, food and animal feed. We have ravaged the earth and also poisoned it with an array of chemical fertilisers, pesticides and herbicides in order to increase productivity/profits. Pollution of the soil, the waterways, the ocean and the air itself are the result. This is not in accord with Islamic teaching.

Although humanity is accepted as having exceptional qualities and capacities, the Qur'an also firmly puts the creation of the earth itself as even more precious: "The creation of the heavens and earth is greater by far than the creation of mankind, though most people do not know it".[17]

Fazlun Khalid clarifies this verse: "The human community is but an infinitesimal part of the natural world, but we have now lost sight of this through our proclivity for dominating it".[18]

Indeed, humanity is told "Do not strut arrogantly about the earth…".[19] When we face up to the current climate crisis, the pollution, the loss of biodiversity and extinction of species, we have to admit that we humans have indeed been strutting arrogantly on the earth for many decades.

So, what kind of person should a khalifah be? The Qur'an describes them: "The servants of the Lord of Mercy are those who walk humbly on the earth, and who, when aggressive people address them, reply with words of peace".[20]

The Qur'an gives special mention to the animals we farm: "And livestock He created them too. You derive warmth and other benefits from them: you get food from them".[21] In fact, these benefits are mentioned several times: "It is God who provides livestock for you, some for riding and some for food, you have other benefits in them too. You can reach any destination you wish on them".[22] Other verses refer to the use of animal skins for shelter, to the drinking of milk and the use of honey "in which there is healing for people".[23]

This is a utilitarian view of these animals – but the Qur'an goes further: "You find beauty in them when you bring them home to rest and when you drive them out to pasture".[24] So, these animals not only may be used to feed one's hunger, but, through their intrinsic beauty, they can feed the soul, as it were, as well.

It seems obvious that although the Qur'an allows the use of animals for food and as a means of transport, the duty of guardianship and care is not to be forgotten.

Fazlun Khalid sums it up:

> The Quran helps us by describing animals as "communities like us" and they "shall be gathered to their Lord in the end" like we shall be. What separates us is our superior intelligence, our capacity for invention and our penchant for modifying the environment. As we encroach on the spaces of other sentient beings to meet the demands of our exaggerated needs, loss of biodiversity has now become an issue. We are now beginning to realise that we depend on them, from the tiniest microbe upwards, for our survival.[25]

Islamic scholar, Professor Seyyed Hossein Nasr, writes;

> A central concept of Islam cited often in the Qur'an is haqq (plural huquq), which means at once truth, reality, right, law, and due… According to Islam, each being exists by virtue of the truth (haqq) and is also owed its due (haqq) according to its nature. The trees have their due, as do animals or even rivers and mountains. In dealing with nature, human beings must respect and pay what is due to each creature, and each creature has its rights accordingly. Islam stands totally against the idea that we human beings have all the rights and other creatures have none except what we decide to give them. The rights of creatures were given by God and not by us, to be taken away when we decide to do so….We cannot take away the haqq of various creatures given to them by God, but must pay each being its due (haqq) in accordance with the nature of that creature.[26]

In the new Islamic document, Al-Mizan (the Balance), leading Islamic authors write about how animals should be treated: "As they are sentient beings and communities like us, we are obliged to treat them with reverence and care (taqwā), compassion (rahmah), and striving to do the utmost good (ihsān)".[27]

The authors go on to state:

> The most essential ethical implication of God's oneness is to serve the one God – the Lord of all beings – by doing the greatest good we can to all His creatures. If we recognise that God is the one and only Lord of every created being, then we must know that devotion to Him requires utmost goodness toward His entire creation – and that we must treat every single creature with taqwā, or reverence toward its Creator. God is the Lord of every species, every generation, and every individual created being.[28]

Our understanding of the Islamic view of our relationship with animals can be deepened by referring to the Hadith literature which contains accounts of what the Prophet Muhammad said and did, recounted by his followers. Often a Hadith can add an extra dimension to a Qur'anic teaching.

## Caring for Animals

Several Hadiths refer to the merit of being kind to animals: "The Prophet was asked if acts of charity even to the animals were rewarded by God. He replied: 'Yes, there is a reward for acts of charity to every beast alive'".[29]

One Hadith refers to the use of animals for riding from one place to another. In it, the Prophet is recorded as saying: "Do not use the backs of your beasts as pulpits, for God has only made them subject to you in order that they may bring you to a town you could only otherwise reach by fatigue of the body".[30]

Another Hadith declares: "Do not clip the forelocks of your horses, not their manes nor their tails, for the tail is their fly-whisk, their mane is their covering and the forelock has good fortune bound within it".[31]

One of the Hadiths records that the Prophet Muhammad came across a camel in a very poor state. When he discovered the owner of the camel he said: "Don't you fear God with regard to this animal, whom God has given to you? For the camel complained to me that you starve him and work him endlessly".[32] This is particularly interesting as the passage declares that the camel "complained" to the Prophet. Does this imply that camels can speak, or that they can convey their feelings to humans, or does it suggest that perhaps the Prophet had special powers to understand how animals are feeling?

Another Hadith recounts how a thirsty man dipped his shoe into a well to get water for a dog who was dying of thirst. For this act of kindness to an animal, his sins were forgiven.[33]

Another Hadith recounts how making animals fight each other, as in cock-fights or dog-fights, is unlawful.[34]

Hunting for food is permitted but not for sport/targets.

> Whoever kills a sparrow in jest, it will come on the day of Judgement chirruping to God, saying: 'O Lord, this man killed me in jest and took no benefit from me and did not leave me to eat the fruits of the earth'.[35]

Any kind of hunting is forbidden when one is on the pilgrimage to Mecca.[36]

The Al-Mizan authors remind us that "On the march from Al-Madinah to Makkah with an army of 10,000 men, he came across a mother dog and her litter of new-born pups, and he posted a guard over her to ensure that no one disturbed her".[37]

It is known that hunting for pleasure has been a widespread activity of some Muslim rulers, such as the Mughal rulers of India. Emperor Jahangir reportedly killed over 17,000 animals, including 86 tigers and lions.[38] This type of so-called "sport" hunting cannot be compared to the hunting for survival of the poor and hungry in society.

One Islamic legal expert says that committing a crime against an animal is a double crime – against that creature and against God. It requires that one beg the pardon of God and make restitution to the harmed creature. As the author says: "All creatures are considered an integral part of the inhabitants of our global life".[39]

It is obvious from the references in the Qur'an and Hadiths that Islam teaches that animals are indeed creatures of God and should be treated with compassion. Kindness to them will be rewarded – simply because they are creatures of Divine origin and destiny.

In the past, various schemes have existed within Muslim countries to protect the environment, wildlife or stray animals. There was at one time a charity for stray dogs in the holy pilgrimage city of Mecca. Much of the land around Mecca is also subject to various rules on environmental and wildlife protection.

Scholar Richard Foltz refers to the writings of the French traveller of the 16th century, Michel de Montaigne, who visited Turkey and wrote that "The Turks have alms and hospitals for animals".[40]

Foltz also refers to the 14th-century Indian Sufi Shaykh Ahmad of Ahmedabad, who used to pay for injured birds so that he could nurse them back to health.[41]

Alphonse de Lamartine (1790–1869), a French statesman, diplomat, and traveller visited Istanbul, reporting:

> Muslims have good relations with all creatures, animate and inanimate: trees, birds, dogs, in short, they respect all the things God has created. They extend their compassion and kindness to all the species of wretched animals which in our countries are abandoned or ill-treated.[42]

Dr İbrahim Özdemir has drawn my attention to two of Islam's early saints and animal lovers, Rabi'a al-'Adawiyya and Bayazid Bistami as well as the wonderful Said Nursi.

Rabi'a al-'Adawiyya (714/717–801) was a mystic, inspired by ardent love of God. She viewed the whole creation with compassion and was rewarded with the friendship of animals. We are told: "One day Rabia had gone to the mountain, and herds of wild animals gathered around her. Hasan appeared and the animals ran away. He was angry and asked Rabi'a, 'Why did they run from me but had friendship with you?' Rabi'a asked him what he had eaten that day, to which he replied onions fried in fat. 'You have eaten their fat,' she remarked, 'How should they not run away from you?'"[43]

One of the first Sufi thinkers, Bayazid Bistami (d. 875), one day purchased some cardamom seed in the city of Hamadhân, and before departing put a small quantity which was left over into his gaberdine. On reaching his native town, Bistâm, and recollecting what he had done, he took out the seed and found that it contained a number of ants. Saying, "I have carried the poor creatures away from their home," he immediately set off and journeyed back to Hamadhân—a distance of several hundred miles—to return the ants. What stimulated Bayazid was compassion for all creatures based on the love and respect for God.[44]

Dr Özdemir writes of the Islamic theologian Said Nursi (1877–1960) that he

> is said to have shared food with ants, cats, mice, and pigeons, and to have reprimanded a student for killing a lizard, asking him "Did you create it?" When arriving at Barla, his place of exile for seven years, he prevented a gamekeeper who was accompanying him from shooting the partridges, reminding him that it was their nesting time.[45]

Said Nursi was imprisoned for many years as he was out of favour with the new secular regime in Turkey. While imprisoned he wrote a short treatise on flies! He referred to them as "little birds". Earlier, while on a study retreat, Nursi recalled that "in the evening those miniature birds would be lined up in most orderly fashion on the washing line". However, when one of his students needed the washing-line to hang up the washing and tried to move the flies, Nursi immediately reproved him, saying: "Don't disturb those little birds; hang it somewhere else".[46]

In more recent times, the "Daily Sabah" newspaper in Turkey contains reports about Kartepe, a popular ski resort in the northwestern province of Kocaeli. Before the cold winter weather sets in, the town's municipality builds houses for stray cats, with feeding and watering facilities. The town's mayor, Mustafa Kocaman (in October 2021), said that they are also working on the construction of a rehabilitation and treatment centre for stray animals.[47]

It would seem that there is an ongoing line of extraordinarily compassionate people in the history of Islam – and probably many others whom we have not heard about. These exceptional individuals tried to display in their lives the divine compassion of Allah. Nursi quoted Imam Shafi'i (767–820 CE), one of the four great Imams, who said: "'In the Name of God, the Merciful, the Compassionate' is only one verse, yet it was revealed one hundred and fourteen times in the Qur'an".[48]

## Farming Methods

It is clear that the Qur'an permits the eating of meat, the drinking of milk and the use of honey. Equally obvious is the fact that 20th-century developments such as keeping animals in industrial factory farms could not have been envisaged in Prophet Muhammad's lifetime or the lifetime of the Hadith writers. If one had crowded animals together in darkened sheds in the scorching temperatures of the Middle East, they would quickly have died of suffocation or heat stress, as there would have been no air conditioning, or even the huge electric fans which one sometimes sees today in the chicken sheds of south-east Asia. Neither would there have been antibiotics to treat the likely infections arising from such crowded conditions.

There is no *explicit* disapproval of factory farming within the Islamic holy books, but there is certainly an *implicit* condemnation.

Fazlun Khalid comments: "There is absolutely no evidence in the sacred texts that would in any way support factory farming. The exemplary behaviour of the prophet points to care, concern and compassion. These qualities are palpably absent in factory farming".[49]

Factory farming methods do not allow animals to live in "communities".[50] They are either kept in solitary confinement or in such large groups that natural grouping of families or a "pecking order" is impossible. They are, in effect, imprisoned. Yet one respected Hadith states clearly: "It is a great sin for a man to imprison the animals which are in his power".[51]

If Allah is concerned for each animal and knows "where it lives",[52] then He would surely condemn the zero-grazing dairy farms, where cows are never allowed outside to graze, or the broiler (meat) chicken sheds, where 20–30,000 young birds, bred for fast growth, struggle to keep alive for their short, six-week lives, with many going lame, crippled from their sheer body-weight and others dropping dead from the aptly named Sudden Death Syndrome. What would He think of the laying hens cooped up in cages for most of their lives, never able to fully stretch their wings, never able to fly?

No one could find "beauty"[53] in these poor creatures, nor could their lives allow them to praise God "with wings outstretched".[54] Nor can the animals themselves "enjoy" the pastures, waters and mountains which God has created for both them and for humanity.[55]

Some farm animals have their bodies mutilated to fit them to the system in which they are reared. For example, laying hens often have the tip of their beaks cut off, although the beak is a highly sensitive organ. This mutilation means they can be kept in cages without damaging each other or be kept in massive farms, where, again, the natural pecking order has long broken down and the frustrated and confused animals may attack each other. Mutilating the beak limits the damage they can inflict on each other.

Yet there are two verses in the Qur'an which explicitly condemn the then common practice of slitting the ears of aging female animals and turning them loose. In fact, one verse compares this mutilating of the animals to the work of the Devil.[56]

Sheep often have their tails docked, either by a cut or by application of a tight rubber ring, which deprives the tail of blood, forcing it to wither. The Hadith condemns the cutting off of the tails of horses, so one would assume this applies to other animals too.

Perhaps worse still is the selective breeding of farm animals to increase their productivity and, thereby, the profitability of the enterprise. The modern dairy cow, whose original milk production was sufficient to feed her suckling calf, has now been bred to produce many times as much milk as her calf would ever have suckled from her. Her calf is taken away from her at a day old and she is then milked to capacity until shortly before her next calf is due a year later (so for six to seven months each year she is both pregnant and being milked). After two to four years of this stressful lifestyle, often interspersed with bouts of lameness or mastitis, she will be culled, worn out with the strains of production.

Such a cow can certainly find little to "enjoy"[57] in her life. Nor can those meat chickens, bred to grow so fast and meaty that their age at slaughter has been more than halved in the last 50 years. At just five to six weeks old, many will already have been "despatched" or have died from metabolic failure or from lameness which renders them unable to get to their food and water outlets. There is no enjoyment in such a life.

Caring pastoralist herding and small-scale farming of chickens etc are being overwhelmed by large-scale factory farming of animals. The world's agriculture has moved from 20 chickens in the backyard, seeking their nourishment from the soil and from household crumbs, to 20,000 chickens in a shed, fed to company order and often reliant on antibiotics for their very survival. God may care for these exploited creatures – it is obvious that humanity does not.

Othman Abd-ar-Rahman Llewellyn writes:

> And taqwa is the attitude of reverence toward the Lord of all beings, coupled with utmost care in our treatment of all His creatures. In this context, the highest manifestation of taqwa in our deeds is ihsan: we are morally obliged to serve the Lord of all beings by doing utmost good to all His creatures. Most destructive, most wasteful by far are industrial farms, industrial live-stock production, industrial fisheries that efface the diversity of life on Earth: Industrial farms that bulldoze the natural landscape, poison the soil, air, and water, that replace the diversity of native plants with sterile monocultures; industrial chicken farms, feedlots, slaughterhouses, and dairies; Industrial fisheries – trawlers with vast nets that scrape the seabed; industrial agriculture, as practiced today, is perhaps the single greatest cause of the loss of biodiversity on Earth, and the gravest agent of global climate change.[58]

Llewellyn also writes that if the rights of animals are accepted, there will need to be massive change:

> If these rights of animals are secured, the impact on modern industrial farming and fishing practices will be revolutionary. It will require major changes in the ways that biological and medical research and trade in wildlife are conducted, and in the design and management of abattoirs, livestock markets, zoos, and pet shops.[59]

## Teaching and Global Practice

One can only deduce that the Islamic teachings on God's care for His creatures and the implicit teaching that they should live natural lives and be cared for conscientiously by humans, are being transgressed widely, globally. Muslim-majority countries have adopted these industrial farming methods and many Muslims throughout the world regularly consume the flesh and products of these animals. Sadly, there seems to be a complete disconnect between the teaching and the practice.

However, there are pockets of hope. In the UK, Willowbrook Farm is run on organic farming principles, which the Muslim owners see as the best way for them to farm according to their Khalifah role. They do not produce factory-farmed chickens, but say:

> Unlike most commercial farmers, rearing large numbers of fast-growing hybrid birds, we choose to rear only traditional and natural breeds of chicken. We maintain our flocks at naturally sustainable and manageable stocking levels, providing them with plenty of access to fresh pasture, providing a non-GM diet, using no chemicals, medication or hormones, on our animals or on our land... Unlike modern breeds of chicken, which live an average of 5 weeks, ours will reach full maturity at 12 weeks and have full access to woodland & pasture all year long![60]

The first principle of their farming methods is: "To treat livestock ethically, meeting their physiological and behavioural needs".[61]

Sadly, such principles, which seem to be truly based on Islamic teaching, are totally lacking in the kind of intensive systems which are common in the west and which have been adopted and invested in by many Islamic countries.

For example, the poultry industry is a significant employer in Indonesia. Industry sources state that 3 million people are employed in the industry.[62] Indonesia is of course the world's largest Muslim-majority country. Most of the chicken farming is of the intensive methods already described.

Cobb is one of the world's two largest chicken breeders. In 2020, Cobb Asia set up a new technical school in Bali focusing on broiler chicken management. Referring to their Cobb 500 fast-growing chicken, Dr Youngho Hong, director of technical services at Cobb Asia, declared, "The Cobb 500 is selected on many different traits with an emphasis on feed conversion rate and average daily gain".[63] In other words, the chickens are bred to grow at a very fast rate.

But other, better things are happening in Indonesia too. In 2018 Humane Society International, in conjunction with the Indonesian Veterinary Medical Association, hosted Southeast Asia's first technical workshop on cage-free egg production in Surabaya, Indonesia.[64] In 2020, the multinational consulting firm Global Food Partners (GFP) and Aeres University of Applied Sciences (Aeres) announced a partnership to establish an Indonesia-based training centre and model cage-free egg farm focused on management and production for Asian farmers.[65]

Intensive poultry production is also well-established in Egypt. For example, an Egyptian distributor hosted a Wadi Poultry Academy meeting in March 2020 with around 100 participants, all of whom are involved in using the Ross breed of chicken – one of the other major broiler breed brands in the world.[66] Wadi has had investment loans from the International Finance Corporation, the private lending arm of the World Bank.[67]

The largest dairy producer in Egypt is Dina Farms, with around 17,000 high-yielding Holstein cattle.[68] Although, from their promotional video, it looks as though the cows do get to go outdoors into mud yards, the calves appear to be in individual outdoor cages and the whole process is highly intensive.[69]

There are pockets of more holistic farming within Egypt, such as the SEKEM farms, which operate on the biodynamic model. Their SEKEM website proclaims that "it treats soil fertility, plant growth, and livestock care as ecologically inter-related tasks".[70] Claiming to respect life, they say that animals "are capable of different patterns of behavior and even show emotional life in their higher stages of development. Like human beings, they are sensitive to pain. Treating animals in a species-appropriate way means to respectfully deal with life itself".[71]

The founder of SEKEM farms saw its methods as combining Islamic teaching with biodynamic methods. After much discussion, the association of Muslim sheiks in Egypt gave the community a plaque verifying that SEKEM is an Islamic initiative.[72]

Even in Saudi Arabia, the homeland of the Prophet Muhammad, intensive poultry production is growing. Just one hatchery, Arab Takamul, produces up to 11 million broiler chickens per year, and we read of involved companies with names like Farming Business Arab Company for Livestock Development (ACOLID).[73] The objectives of ACOLID are to develop and promote livestock resources in the Arab countries and the industries associated with them. ACOLID has established 38 projects, affiliated companies and different shareholdings distributed geographically in 11 Arab States.

It is good to know that there is a Department of Organic Production within the Saudi Ministry of Environment, Water and Agriculture (MEWA), although the number of animals being raised to organic standards is still small.[74]

In 2018, the Saudi government launched an enormous (USD$200 million) Organic Action Plan, aiming to increase the country's organic production by 300% within 13 years. The investment in organic farming is partly to conserve water, as organic farming enriches soils, helping them to retain moisture.[75]

In addition to chickens, there has been a huge growth in intensive zero-grazing dairy farming in the Middle East. In Saudi Arabia, one company alone has 105,000 cows in five different farms. They are fed four times a day and milked four times a day. This must put a huge metabolic strain on the animals, and it is not surprising that the cows average only 3.5 lactations before they are culled. Male calves go for veal production.[76] A film showing the scale of the dairy operation is available.[77]

It is unlikely that one would find "beauty"[78] in looking at these animals, who can never graze for themselves but who have to have all their feed brought to them.

A few years ago, the Alliance of Religions and Conservation (ARC) in liaison with Global One, and with support from Abdalla Mohamed Kamwana, Vice Chairman of the Supreme Council of Kenyan Muslims (SUPKEM) and the Ethiopian Islamic Affairs Supreme Council (EIASC) launched "Islamic Farming:

A Manual for Conservation Agriculture", as "a new curriculum that integrates Qur'anic scriptures and teachings about caring for the Earth as a religious responsibility with practical training in conservation agriculture".[79] It gives detailed instructions on how to care for the land and soil, grow crops and rear farm animals. It says: "It is important that we look after the livestock that Allah blesses us with. As we provide the care and resources that our animals require, we will be following Allah's commands".[80]

Perhaps that short statement could inform the future of animal farming in Muslim communities and countries.

## Eating Animals

"Halal" literally means "acceptable" "permitted" or "sanctified" and applies widely to a multitude of products and actions, not just to food, although that is the narrow interpretation of halal often taken up in the West. In fact, today Muslims debate whether nuclear energy is halal or the use of plastics.[81]

The concept of halal food goes further than the literal meaning and is used in the Quran in conjunction with the word "tayyib", meaning pure, healthy, good or natural. The Qur'an explicitly says: "People, eat what is good (tayyib) and lawful (halal) from the Earth …".[82]

Some animal foods are explicitly forbidden (haram), such as pig-meat, carrion and some other, usually wild, creatures. Flowing blood is also forbidden.[83]

Let us focus on those animal foods which are widely eaten in the global Muslim community: beef cattle, lambs, goats, chickens, camels (mainly in the Middle East), most kinds of fishes, dairy products and eggs.

These foods are definitely halal in themselves, but do they fulfil the requirement to be good (tayyib)? If we consider the short and miserable life of the broiler (meat) chicken, as described earlier, it is hard to argue that there is anything pure, healthy, good or natural in the origin of that meat. The same argument would apply to eggs from laying hens kept for most of their lives in cages.

Another aspect of tayyib is that the Qur'an urges consumers not to be extravagant or to waste food: "…eat and drink but do not be extravagant: God does not like extravagant people"[84] and a similar exhortation: "You who believe, do not forbid the good things God has made lawful to you – do not exceed the limits: God does not love those who exceed the limits".[85] Fazlun Khalid says Muslims haven't given serious consideration to this issue up to the present time.[86]

Prior to the COP 21 UN Climate Change Conference in Paris in 2015 at which the Paris Climate Change Agreement was signed by 195 countries, several learned Muslims wrote and submitted the Islamic Declaration on Global Climate Change. It refers to many of the Qur'anic verses quoted in this chapter, but also adds some descriptions of the Prophet Muhammad, including that he "ate simple, healthy food, which only occasionally included meat".[87] (In fact, this excellent document calls for divestment from fossil fuels, protection of biodiversity, and a circular economy and is well worth reading.)

Sheikh Hamza Yusuf, a leading US-based Muslim academic, argues that historically Muslims ate so little meat they were almost vegetarian. "Meat is not a necessity in sharia, and in the old days most Muslims used to eat meat – if they were wealthy, like middle class – once a week on Friday. If they were poor – on the Eids".[88]

Several individual Muslims have told me that Muslims should eat lightly and should never continue eating until they feel full. They have also told me that eating meat should be moderate and that they feel appalled by the amount of meat consumed by many Muslims today.

This seems to be based on a Hadith which quotes the Prophet Muhammad as saying:

> The human being does not fill any vessel worse than his stomach. It is sufficient for the son of Adam to eat a few mouthfuls, to keep him going. If he must do that (fill his stomach), then let him fill one third with food, one third with drink and one third with air.[89]

Fazlun Khalid agrees with the concept of moderation, pointing out that: "Prophet Muhammad very rarely ate meat. He lived on dates and barley. Excessive meat production is now one of the causes of global warming".[90]

Muslim author Reza Shah-Kazemi corroborates this, writing:

> Let us note that the Prophet and his companions were virtually vegetarians, eating meat most probably not more than a few times each month. In this regard, the following saying of Imam Ali is of great practical import for our times: 'Do not make your stomachs graveyards of animals (maqābir al-ḥayawān)'.[91]

The Islamic teachings would therefore seem to encourage Muslims to eat animal products only in moderation and to eat only those from animals who have been able to "enjoy" their lives. Eating the products originating in industrial factory farms would plainly appear to violate the "tayyib" (good) principle.

To date, in the UK and probably elsewhere, tayyib has been viewed as a food safety standard from the point of slaughter to the processing of the meat products afterwards.[92]

It is surely time for a more ethical and wider understanding of what "tayyib" really means.

## Slaughter

The issue of halal slaughter has become extremely contentious, both within the Muslim world but also in the non-Muslim world. In most of the "western" world, the general view is that animals should be stunned (rendered unconscious) before their throats are cut and they bleed to death. In this way they are not aware of the cut and the gradual loss of consciousness that follows. Many Muslims believe that stunning harms and hurts the animal and that it should not be used. Others say that as the Qur'an does not mention stunning, it should not be used.

It is an important point to note that legislation on the slaughter of animals has been evolving for nearly a hundred years and is still evolving as new and more humane methods become available.

In the European Union (EU), the Regulations for non-religious slaughter require animals to be stunned before the cut or to be killed by a method, such as gas, which causes unconsciousness followed by death.[93]

One of the most common methods of stunning is the use of the captive bolt pistol which fires a retractable bolt into the brain, causing immediate loss of consciousness. This is used for cattle and sometimes for calves and sheep. Many sheep and goats may be stunned by the use of electric tongs placed on either side of the head, which should cause instantaneous unconsciousness when done properly. This kind of stunning is reversible and makes the animals unconscious for a short period of time, long enough for them to be slaughtered and bled to death. However, they should be able to regain consciousness if they are not slaughtered. This is important for Muslims as they believe that animals should still be alive when they are actually slaughtered with the knife.

Poultry have often been stunned by being hung upside down on a conveyor belt which dipped their heads in an electrified water bath, causing a stun. Today most poultry in wealthier countries are stunned using a gas mixture which causes them to lose consciousness.

Once unconscious, all animals should be quickly killed. This is done either by cutting the throat, in the case of birds or, in the case of large animals such as cattle, more often by cutting the chest and severing all the blood vessels leading from the heart.

Animals die from blood loss, whether stunned first or not. It is the cut to the throat or chest which causes the blood to gush out. After some time, lacking oxygen, the brain loses consciousness. There are ways to check that the animal is unconscious before butchering of the carcase begins.

The EU Regulation on slaughter gives a derogation to Muslim and Jewish communities on the requirement to stun but now leaves it up to EU Member States to interpret this as a ban on non-stun slaughter or maintaining the derogation. In the UK, Jewish and Muslim communities are exempt from the legal requirement to stun animals before slaughter. However, there are strict procedures regarding the handling of animals about to be slaughtered, in order to minimise the time of stress and suffering which the animal may suffer.[94]

Several European countries do not allow derogations from the general requirement of prior stunning. These include Sweden, Norway, Iceland, Denmark, Slovenia and two administrative regions of Belgium.[95]

New Zealand banned slaughter without stunning in 2010 and made reversible stunning mandatory.[96] Sheep are stunned with electricity and then slaughtered by Muslim slaughtermen. The meat produced is certified as halal by religious communities within New Zealand, and much of the meat is exported to over 100 countries, including Malaysia, India and countries in the Middle East.[97]

Halal slaughter traditionally involves cutting the animal's throat without stunning the animal first, but also saying a prayer, *Bismillah* (in the name of God), in acknowledgement that one is taking away a God-given life. However, some Muslims accept stunning before slaughter, so it is interesting to note that the Food Standards Agency (FSA) report on slaughter methods in England and Wales 2018 showed that 58% of certified halal meat is from animals stunned before slaughter.[98]

In 2019, Ismailağa Cemaati, the largest Islamic group in Turkey, publicly announced that stunning animals prior to killing them is acceptable and halal.[99]

There is no doubt that slaughtering any animal is an unpleasant business. From the animal's point of view, it usually entails a journey in a truck first, which is undoubtedly stressful, may involve feelings of hunger, thirst and fear and may sometimes cause injury. This is followed by unloading at the slaughterhouse, a strange place with its unfamiliar sounds and smells.

In the UK, the law implementing the 2015 EU Regulations permits a Muslim person to slaughter without stunning if, in the case of bovines, "the animal is individually restrained in an upright position in a restraining pen" and in the case of all large animals, "ensure it is killed by the severance of both its carotid arteries and jugular veins by rapid, uninterrupted movements of a hand-held knife". Once the cut has been made, the law says the animal must not be moved or hoisted for "in the case of a sheep or a goat, a period of not less than 20 seconds; and in the case of a bovine animal, a period of not less than 30 seconds".[100] This time-lapse period is to allow the animal to become unconscious.

In the case of poultry, both carotid arteries must be cut and the time lapse before any further action must be in the case of a turkey or goose, a period of not less than 2 minutes; and in the case of any other bird, a period of not less than 90 seconds.

Some of these time periods seem too short, as research has shown that the time between the cut and unconsciousness can be long. A group of leading scientists, brought together by the European Commission, viewed all the research and concluded:

> Without stunning, the time between cutting through the major blood vessels and insensibility [unconsciousness], as deduced from behavioural and brain response, is up to 20 seconds in sheep, up to 25 seconds in pigs, up to 2 minutes in cattle, up to 2½ or more minutes in poultry, and sometimes 15 minutes or more in fish.[101]

As the science indicates that animals do not lose consciousness instantaneously when their throats are cut, they must endure a period of possible pain and certainly confusion and distress as they bleed to death. Some argue that the pain from the cut is not immediately felt. It can happen (in humans too) that a very traumatic experience can sometimes induce temporary analgesia. Be that as it may, the experience of bleeding out must surely cause suffering.

Is this not incompatible with the recorded words of the Prophet Muhammad? Shaddid b. Aus said: "Two are the things which I remember Allah's Messenger (pbuh) having said: 'Verily Allah has enjoined goodness to everything; so when you kill, kill in a good way and when you slaughter, slaughter in a good way'".[102]

This reference goes on to enlarge on killing, "So every one of you should sharpen his knife and let the slaughtered animal die comfortably".[103]

In those days, centuries before stunning methods had been developed or used, sharpening the knife for a quick and effective cut was undoubtedly the most compassionate way to slaughter. Can we not deduce that the intention of killing in "a good way" so that the animal can "die comfortably" means that today the best stunning methods should be used – or even better methods developed?

Some Muslims have argued that if the animal is stunned first, then the blood does not drain out so abundantly. Islamic scholar Al-Hafiz Basheer Masri points to the Qur'an, which prohibits "flowing blood".[104] Firstly, it is obvious that any piece of fresh meat will contain residual blood, not flowing blood. Secondly several experiments have taken place to show that blood loss is similar in stunned and non-stunned animals.[105]

Sadly, much evidence has come to light of very cruel practices being used in slaughterhouses in countries such as Egypt, Indonesia and the Lebanon where the meat is being sold on the halal market. Film has been taken, either by veterinary surgeons working in slaughterhouses, or by animal welfare groups.[106] In some cases, cattle had their tendons cut in order to make them fall to the floor, where they would then be held down by a couple of workers while a third worker would perform the cut. Others were winched up by one leg so that the slaughterman could access the throat or chest. This painful injuring and mistreatment of the animal prior to slaughter would surely make the meat unfit to be labelled halal.[107]

Clearly there is a huge need for the authorities to carry out regular unannounced inspections in all slaughterhouses and to insist on proper training, facilities and care for workers.

It seems to me that New Zealand may be leading the way forward for the future. Slaughter for the halal market is performed by Muslim slaughtermen, the prayer is said, and the animal is stunned before the slaughter cut is made. This agreement appears to satisfy both the welfare authorities and the religious requirements of the Muslim communities.

## Vivisection

This subject is a matter of real concern to animal welfarists globally. Experimenting on animals is another "use" which was obviously not practised in the days of the Prophet Muhammad.

Today millions of animals spend their lives in laboratories being used to test new medicines and medical or surgical procedures, while others are used for testing of cosmetics, toiletries and household products.

Figures from the anti-vivisection group Cruelty Free International say that 192.1 million animals were used for scientific purposes worldwide in 2015 of which 79.9 million were used in actual experiments, with others used for breeding of genetically modified animals, or killed for their tissues.[108]

Countries vary in the legislation they have (or do not have) regarding vivisection. Some countries keep experimental animals in moderately comfortable, but confined, conditions, while others do not. In the UK, experiments come under the Animals (Scientific Procedures) Act of 1986.[109] All those conducting experiments must apply for a licence to the government (the Home Office).

Although huge numbers of animals are used by pharmaceutical companies, many experiments globally take place in universities and some universities have Ethics Committees which decide if an experiment is justified.

Obviously for Muslims to decide if they feel experiments are justified, they can turn to the many Qur'anic references to the place of animals in creation and our human responsibilities towards them, as outlined in earlier paragraphs.

In his excellent book *Animal Welfare in Islam*, Al-Hafiz Basheer Masri devotes much thought to the issue of experiments. His conclusion is that if the experiment is truly going to help humans or animals, then it is justifiable, but only if pain relief is used. Trivial experiments for toiletries are not justified.[110]

Nowadays more and more alternatives to animal experiments are being developed. However, some countries still require animals to be used before new products are released on the market. Fortunately, there are an increasing number of companies developing cosmetics which are not tested on animals and which are also halal and tayyib and can be bought by Muslims as well as others who care about animal wellbeing.

Some Muslim-majority countries have taken action in this area. In 2018, Saudi Arabia's Ministry of Environment, Water and Agriculture (MEWA) prohibited several practices that constitute cruelty toward animals in accordance with the GCC Animal Welfare Law which was approved by the Royal Decree No. (M/44) dated 26/7/1434 H. Some of these practices are prohibited except for medical justification, while others are forbidden for any reason whatsoever.[111]

The list of practices that are banned except for medical necessity includes tail docking and ear cropping, declawing, debarking, dehorning and chemical castration. Other practices that are forbidden for any reason whatsoever are dyeing animals, using injectable cosmetic fillers on animals, especially camels, and using animal-growth stimulants or stimulant drugs in racing.

In Indonesia, Law No. 18 of 2009 (Husbandry and Animal Health) defines animal welfare as "all matters relating to animal physical and mental conditions". This is a positive recognition that animals can suffer mentally as well as physically. The law goes on to mention "reasonable treatment and tender care" – the latter not a term usually found in legislation.[112]

In Egypt, the State carries responsibility for animal welfare and while the Agriculture Law (1966) provides some minimal protection for farm animals, there is no law covering scientific procedures.[113]

Perhaps I can do no better than quote the words of a respected Muslim thoracic surgeon, Dr Moneim A. Fadali, who writes:

Animal models differ from their human counterparts. Conclusions drawn from animal research, when applied to human disease are likely to delay progress, mislead and do harm to the patient. The claim that we owe most, if not all of our advances in medicine to animal research is not only untrue, but also preposterous and absurd - an outright lie.[114]

## Wildlife and Biodiversity

Knowing of the current dire global situation regarding wildlife and the current onslaught on biodiversity, it is important to see if Islam has anything to contribute to the debate.

Islam teaches that wild animals have their own "communities".[115] Perhaps more than animals kept in farms or laboratories, they have an opportunity to experience "joy" in their lives. The unity of all creatures under one God is known as Tawhid.

Of course, the Qur'anic spirit of care and compassion extends to wild creatures. One Hadith is related by a disciple of the Prophet Muhammad. When they were travelling, the Prophet left the others, who took two young birds away from their mother in the nest. The mother bird hovered above with fluttering wings and when the Prophet returned, he said, "Who has injured this bird by taking its young? Return them to her".[116]

This Hadith makes it clear that people should not interfere in the lives of wild animals but should respect them.

Looking at the modern world and how that principle is being implemented, we see that Indonesia has a Wildlife Crime Unit and acknowledges the Five Freedoms principles of animal welfare. The country participates in regional animal welfare meetings, but regulations are left to regional or local offices to enforce, and this is open to interpretation.[117]

In addition, the Indonesian Council of Ulema issued a fatwa (Muslim religious decree) declaring the illegal wildlife trade forbidden under Islamic law. The fatwa requires the country's Muslims to take an active role in protecting threatened species including tigers, rhinos, elephants and orangutans. Although not binding under Indonesian law, the fatwa is an effective deterrent in a country that is 87% Muslim.[118]

In Saudi Arabia, there is an area called Jabal Aja, which has the greatest concentration of biological diversity in the interior of the Arabian Cape.[119] It is managed by the National Commission for Wildlife Conservation and Development (NCWCD). This initiative aims at applying the provisions of Islamic law to protect this area and to set an example to all Muslim countries for the regeneration of wildlife habitats, as well as safeguarding the main existing wildlife types (e.g., Nubian Ibex, Arabian Wolf, Idmi Gazelle), and dispersion of native plants and animals into the surrounding region.[120]

Aishah Abdallah, Wilderness Leader, IUCN Commission on Education and Communication, questions:

> Should we not expect Muslim ethicists, imbued with the teaching that all created beings are unique signs that glorify the Creator, and that each is

created in truth and for right, to be foremost in striving to protect the earth's remaining wildlands?[121]

There are pockets of concern for wildlife and preservation of biodiversity within the Muslim world. In view of the teachings within the holy books, it is sad not to see more such projects.

## Islam and Animal Use

This whole area of animal use and abuse is understandably a problematic one for Muslims today. If a practice is not mentioned in the Qur'an or the Hadiths, then how should they make their decision?

Respected Islamic scholar Professor Abdullah Saeed writes:

> Contextualists are led by the work of scholars such as Fazlur Rahman. They represent an important step in relating the Qur'anic text to the contemporary needs of Muslim societies. Rahman relies heavily on understanding the historical context of the revelation at the macro level, and then relating it to a particular need of the modern period. In this, he draws on the idea of the 'prophetic spirit' or, in other words, how the Prophet might act were he living today.[122]

That sounds like a pragmatic and sensible way forward. Would the Prophet really have approved of animals kept in laboratory conditions and subject to painful experiments? Would he have approved of massive industrial farms where the animals are unable to experience any joy in their lives? Would he have approved of any of the myriad ways in which animals are abused in so-called entertainment, animal-to-animal fights, sport hunting etc.?

The whole question of the relationship between humans and animals is coming under discussion within the Muslim community. Richard Foltz records the Egyptian animal welfare conference of 2004 hosted by the prestigious Islamic University, Al-Azhar, in Cairo.[123]

The author has also attended and spoken at two other animal welfare conferences held in Egypt in recent years, organised by local animal activists, many of them Muslim, and attended by government representatives and scholars from Al-Azhar University.

There was a very important case in the High Court in Islamabad, Pakistan in 2020. The judge was asked to rule on two cases involving an elephant and a bear and another case involving stray dogs. Justice Athar Minallah, Chief Justice of the Islamabad High Court, said:

> Do the animals have legal rights? The answer to this question, without any hesitation, is in the affirmative.... Like humans, animals also have natural rights which ought to be recognized. It is a right of each animal...to live in an environment that meets the latter's behavioral, social and physiological needs.[124]

These wonderfully strong words will hopefully influence judges around the world, both Muslim and non-Muslim.

In citing verses from the Qur'an, the judge went on to say: "It is inconceivable that, in a society where the majority follow the religion of Islam, that an animal could be harmed or treated in a cruel manner".[125]

## Sacrifice

Sacrifice appears to be a truly fundamental part of most faiths and Islam is no exception. Sacrificing something precious to oneself is seen to please or placate the deity.

The main Islamic sacrifice is performed at the festival of Eid ul Adha, which comes at the end of the pilgrimage to Mecca (the Hajj). It commemorates the sacrifice of Ibrahim (Abraham) who was prepared to sacrifice his son but was allowed by God to sacrifice an animal instead. At this time, Muslims around the world sacrifice an animal, not just those taking part in the actual pilgrimage.

An essential aspect of the sacrifice is that the meat of the sacrificial animal should be shared, not just with one's family, but with the poor.

A sacrifice of an animal may also be made when a child (of either gender) is born into a family or an animal may be sacrificed purely for charitable purposes, to feed the hungry.

The Qur'an makes it clear "It is neither their meat nor their blood that reaches God, but your piety".[126]

In the past the mass sacrificial slaughter during the Hajj often resulted in dead animals being left to rot on the ground. In recent years the authorities have acted to organise the slaughter and even to fly much of the sacrificial meat to poor countries nearby.[127]

Some Muslims believe that the slaughter of the animal is unnecessary and that a financial donation will suffice. Al-Hafiz Basheer Masri was one such person. He believed that the prime purpose of the Hajj sacrifice was to feed the hungry. In his book he writes: "the Qur'anic approach is not meant to take animal sacrifice as an end in itself; it is meant to be used as a means to serve a social need".[128]

## Conclusion

With so many references to the place of animals in creation and so many injunctions to treat them well and not cause them suffering, Islam could be the ideal major faith to lead the way on animal welfare. Looking at current practice in the Muslim world we see the opposite in many cases. There may be huge social or cultural issues as to why this is so. This chapter is not about developing a blame culture stigmatising Islam. On the contrary, what I propose is a challenge to the Muslim community and its leaders.

It is undoubtedly time for a new Masri as it were, for a respected Muslim (or Muslims) to make the theological case for Islam to promote animal welfare. Is it not time for Imams to devote at least one Friday sermon a year to the issue of respect and care for animals? It is perhaps time for Muslims to forge new Muslim-based organisations which promote and campaign for animal welfare either nationally or internationally. It is surely time for Muslim policymakers and politicians, wherever they may live, to propose and support new animal welfare laws.

The teaching on animals within the Qur'an and Hadiths seems to have been overlooked or neglected. But the important thing is that it is there. Any Muslim wishing to take up the challenge of promoting animal welfare can surely do so in the knowledge that he or she is doing work blessed by God, for, after all, "There is not a creature that moves on earth whose provision is not His concern".[129]

# Notes

1 Qur'an 59:22–24.
2 Qur'an 19:16–34, 5:109–118.
3 Qur'an 3:144.
4 Qur'an 55:10.
5 Qur'an 79:30–33.
6 Qur'an 24:41.
7 Qur'an 22:18.
8 Qur'an 11:6.
9 Qur'an 2:29.
10 Qur'an 6:38.
11 Qur'an 6:38.
12 İ. Özdemir, 2003. Towards an Understanding of Environmental Ethics from a Qur'anic Perspective, in R.C. Foltz, F.M. Denny and A. Baharuddin (Eds). *Islam and Ecology: A Bestowed Trust.* Cambridge, MA: Harvard University Press, p26.
13 R.C. Foltz, 2006. *Animals in Islamic Tradition and Muslim Cultures.* London: Oneworld Publications.
14 Othman Abd-ar-Rahman Llewellyn, 2003. The Basis for a Discipline of Islamic Environmental Law, in ch 2 of R.C. Foltz, F.M. Denny and A. Baharuddin (Eds). *Islam and Ecology: A Bestowed Trust.* Cambridge, MA: Harvard University Press.
15 Qur'an 6:165, 38:26.
16 F.M. Khalid, 2019. *Signs on the Earth.* Kube Publishing.
17 Qur'an 40:57.
18 F.M. Khalid, 2019. *Signs on the Earth.* Kube Publishing.
19 Qur'an 17:37.
20 Quran 25:63.
21 Qur'an 16:5.
22 Qur'an 40:79,80.
23 Qur'an 16:66, 16:69, 16:80.
24 Qur'an 16:6.
25 F. Khalid, 08/02/22. Personal communication.
26 S.H. Nasr, 2003. Islam, the Contemporary World, and the Environmental Crisis, in R.C. Foltz, F.M. Denny and A. Baharuddin (Eds). *Islam and Ecology: A Bestowed Trust.* Cambridge, MA: Harvard University Press, p97.
27 UNEP Faith for Earth, IFEES, F. Khalid, O. Abd-ar-Rahman Llewellyn, et al., 2022. Al Mizan: A Covenant for the Earth. www.unep.org/al-mizan-covenant-earth.
28 UNEP Faith for Earth, IFEES, F. Khalid, O. Abd-ar-Rahman Llewellyn, et al., 2022. Al Mizan: A Covenant for the Earth. www.unep.org/al-mizan-covenant-earth.
29 Bukhari 322; also Muslim vol. 4 Hadith 2244, also Mishkat, bk 6, ch 7, 8:178.
30 Awn, 7:235 Hadith 2550.

31  In Alfred Guillaume, 1924. The traditions of Islam. An Introduction to the Study of the hadith literature. Narrated by Abdullah-al-Salami, Abu Dawud, also Awn, 7:216,217, Hadith 2525.
32  Sunan Abu Dawud 2186. Musnad Ahmad 1654 and 1662 (similar).
33  Sahih Bukhari 557, Anbiya' 54.
34  Abu Daud, Jihad 51; Tirnidki Jihad 30.
35  Sahih Bukhari, Adhan 90.
36  Qur'an 5:96.
37  Muhammad ibn 'Umar Al-Wāqidī, *Kitāb al-Maghāzī*. See Abdal Hamid [Fitzwilliam-Hall], *Islamic Environmental Ethics*, 63.
38  P. Krishna, 29/06/20. Tiger Hunting in Colonial India. *Journal of Indian History and Culture*, 26, pp29–42.
39  F. Malekian, 2011. *Principles of Islamic International Criminal Law: A Comparative Search*. Leiden: Koninklijke Brill NV.
40  R.C. Foltz, 2006. *Animals in Islamic Traditions and Cultures*. London: Oneworld Academic.
41  R.C. Foltz, 2006. *Animals in Islamic Traditions and Cultures*. London: Oneworld Academic.
42  Quoted in İ. Özdemir, 2021. Review of Kim Fortuny, 2021. Animals and the environment in Turkish culture: Ecocriticism and transnational culture. *Journal of Islamic Ethics*. https://doi.org/10.1163/24685542-12340076.
43  A. Schimmel, 2011. *Mystical Dimensions of Islam*. Chapel Hill: University of North Carolina Press, and B.L. Helms, 1993. *Al-Rabawiyah - As Mystic, Muslim and Woman*. Montreal: Institute of Islamic Studies, McGill University.
44  R.A. Nicholson, 1999, first published 1914. *The Mystics of Islam*. Abingdon: Routledge.
45  İ. Özdemir, 2020. A common care for creation: Said Nursi and Pope Francis on environment. *International Journal of the Asian Philosophical Association*, 13:1. www.asianpa.net/assets/upload/discussions/zEV47hBzmlLRgfok.pdf.
46  S. Vahide, 1998. *The Author of the Risale-i Nur, Bediüzzaman Said Nursî* (2nd ed.). Istanbul: Sözler Publications.
47  Daily Sabah, 08/10/21. Turkish Town Gives Cozy Homes to Cats Ahead of Winter. https://tinyurl.com/y6jcwrch.
48  İ. Özdemir, A new ethics of compassion to animals: Said nursi on the rights of flies. *Brill's Journal of Islamic Ethics*, 6, pp53–80. https://doi.org/10.1163/24685542-12340083.
49  F. Khalid, 08/02/2022. Personal communication.
50  Qur'an 6:38.
51  Sahih Muslim, Zakat 48.
52  Qur'an 11:6.
53  Qur'an 16:6.
54  Qur'an 24:41.
55  Qur'an 79:30–33.
56  Qur'an 4:119.
57  Qur'an 79:33.
58  O. Abd-ar-Rahman Llewellyn, 8–9/03/19. Reverence and Utmost Good: Merciful Harvests. Presentation at "Halal and Tayyib: Rethinking the Ethical" at the Zaytuna College Center for Ethical Living.
59  O. Abd-ar-Rahman Llewellyn, 2003. The Basis for a Discipline of Islamic Environmental Law, in ch 2 of R.C. Foltz, F.M. Denny and A. Baharuddin (Eds). *Islam and Ecology: A Bestowed Trust*. Cambridge, MA: Harvard University Press.
60  Willowbrook Farm. www.willowbrookfarm.co.uk/farming.
61  Willowbrook Farm. www.willowbrookfarm.co.uk/farming.
62  US AID, 2013. Indonesia's Poultry Value Chain. https://pdf.usaid.gov/pdf_docs/pbaaa047.pdf.

63 The Poultry Site, 04/03/20. Cobb Asia Debuts New Module-based Technical School. www.thepoultrysite.com/news/2020/03/cobb-asia-debuts-new-module-based-technical-school.

64 The Poultry Site, 09/10/19. Southeast Asia's First Workshop on Cage-free Egg Production a Success. www.thepoultrysite.com/news/2018/10/southeast-asias-first-workshop-on-cagefree-egg-production-a-success.

65 The Poultry Site, 21/05/20. GFP and Aeres Team Up to Promote Cage-free Eggs in Asia. www.thepoultrysite.com/news/2020/05/gfp-and-aeres-team-up-to-promote-cage-free-eggs-in-asia.

66 The Poultry Site, 30/05/19. Fifth Wadi Academy Offers Knowledge to Advance a Growing Market. https://thepoultrysite.com/news/2019/05/fifth-wadi-academy-offers-knowledge-to-advance-a-growing-market.

67 https://disclosures.ifc.org/project-detail/SII/39716/wadi-iv.

68 R. Whitehead, 17/07/19. Egypt's Biggest Dairy Farm to Get Even Bigger. https://tinyurl.com/4jrdwtpz.

69 Dina Farms. www.dinafarms.com/.

70 Sekem Agriculture, u.d. Agriculture in the Desert – Quite a Task. www.sekem.com/en/ecology/sekem-agriculture/.

71 Sekem Agriculture, u.d. Agriculture in the Desert – Quite a Task. www.sekem.com/en/ecology/sekem-agriculture/.

72 K.J. Ims and L. Zsolnai, 2015. Social Innovation and Social Development in Latin America, Egypt and India, in G. Enderle and P.E. Murphy (Eds). *Ethical Innovation in Business and the Economy*. Cheltenham, UK and Northampton, MA: Edward Elgar, pp197–213.

73 The Poultry Site, 12/06/20.Turnkey Hatchery of First Stage in ACOLID's New Integrated Poultry Project Up and Running. https://thepoultrysite.com/news/2020/06/turnkey-hatchery-of-first-stage-in-acolids-new-integrated-poultry-project-up-and-running.

74 S. Salama, 06/06/21. 28% Increase in Organic Farms in Saudi Arabia. https://gulfnews.com/world/gulf/saudi/28-increase-in-organic-farms-in-saudi-arabia-1.79712830.

75 *Arab News*, 06/07/18. $200m Organic Farming Plan Unveiled by Saudi Arabia. www.arabnews.com/node/1334096/saudi-arabia; FAO, u.d. Organic Agriculture. www.fao.org/organicag/oa-faq/oa-faq6/en/.

76 A. Forde, 28/02/17. Pics: Milking 22,500 Cows in the Saudi Arabian Desert. www.agriland.ie/farming-news/pics-milking-22500-cows-in-the-saudi-arabian-desert/.

77 *Irish Farmers Journal*, u.d. Almarai Al Badiah Farm in Saudi Arabia. www.youtube.com/watch?time_continue=214&v=dhP6r2grhGk&feature=emb_title.

78 Qur'an16:6.

79 ARC, 2014. Islamic Farming. www.arcworld.org/projects02bd.html?projectID=634.

80 ARC, 2014. Islamic Farming. www.arcworld.org/projects02bd.html?projectID=634.

81 F. Khalid, 2020. Personal communication.

82 Qur'an 2:168.

83 Qur'an 6:145.

84 Qur'an 7:31.

85 Qur'an 5:87.

86 F. Khalid, November 2020. Personal communication.

87 Islamic Declaration on Climate Change. http://ifees.org.uk/wp-content/uploads/2020/01/climate_declarationmmwb.pdf.

88 J. Mayton, 26/05/16. Eating Less Meat Is More Islamic. www.theguardian.com/commentisfree/belief/2010/aug/26/meat-islam-vegetarianism-ramadan.

89 Narrated by al-Tirmidhi and classed as saheeh by al-Albaani in Saheeh al-Tirmidhi. https://islamqa.info/en/answers/71317/why-does-islam-not-tell-us-to-eat-less-red-meat.

90 F. Khalid, 08/02/22. Personal communication.

91  R. Shah-Kazemi, 2021. Seeing God Everywhere: Qur'anic Perspectives on the Sanctity of Virgin Nature.

92  J. Alzeer, U. Rieder and K.A. Hadeed, 2018. Rational and practical aspects of halal and tayyib in the context of food safety. *Trends in Food Science & Technology*, 71, pp264–267. https://doi.org/10.1016/j.tifs.2017.10.020.

93  Council Regulation (EC) N° 1099/2009 on the Protection of Animals at the Time of Killing. https://eur-lex.europa.eu/legal-content/EN/TXT/HTML/?uri=CELEX:32009R1099&from=EN.

94  Defra, 2015. Halal and Kosher Slaughter. https://www.gov.uk/guidance/halal-and-kosher-slaughter.

95  The Law Library of Congress, 2018. Legal Restrictions on Religious Slaughter in Europe. www.loc.gov/law/help/religious-slaughter/europe.php.

96  *The Guardian*, 09/10/20. Nine Out of 10 EU Citizens Oppose Animal Slaughter without Stunning, Poll Finds.

97  MIA, u.d. Halal. www.mia.co.nz/what-we-do/trade/halal/.

98  Results of the 2018 FSA Survey into Slaughter Methods in England and Wales, February 2019. https://assets.publishing.service.gov.uk/government/uploads/system/uploads/attachment_data/file/778588/slaughter-method-survey-2018.pdf.

99  Eyes on Animals. https://m.facebook.com/story.php?story_fbid=576980396441766&id=300794950003003.

100  The Welfare of Animals at the Time of Killing (England) Regulations 2015. www.legislation.gov.uk/uksi/2015/1782/schedule/3/made.

101  AHAW, 2004. Opinion of the Scientific Panel on Animal Health and Welfare on a Request from the Commission Related to Welfare Aspects of the Main Systems of Stunning and Killing the Main Commercial Species of Animals. https://www.efsa.europa.eu/en/efsajournal/pub/45

102  Sahih Muslim 1955 a, Book 34, Hadith 84.

103  Sahih Muslim 1955 a, Book 34, Hadith 84.

104  Qur'an 6:145.

105  R. Khalid, T.G. Knowles and S.B. Wotton. 2015. A comparison of blood loss during the halal slaughter of lambs following traditional religious slaughter without stunning, electric head-only stunning and post-cut electric head-only stunning. *Meat Science*, 110, pp15–23. https://doi.org/10.1016/j.meatsci.2015.06.008.

106  Compassion in World Farming. The EU's Cruel Live Animal Export Trade. http://youtu.be/iH60V-IvBC4.

107  P. Stevenson, 2014. Note on Welfare at Slaughter Conditions in Certain Countries. Compassion in World Farming. www.ciwf.org.

108  Cruelty Free International, u.d. Facts and Figures on Animal Testing. https://tinyurl.com/4kp972xu.

109  Animals (Scientific Procedures) Act 1986. www.legislation.gov.uk/ukpga/1986/14/contents.

110  Al' Hafiz B.A. Masri, 2007. Animal Welfare in Islam. The Islamic Foundation.

111  Royal Decree No. M/44 dated 26/7/1434 AH. https://gulflegislation.com/default.aspx?Action=DispalyAllLegs&&CatID=2628&id=2606&type=3.

112  Law No. 18/2009 on Husbandry and Animal Health. www.fao.org/faolex/results/details/en/c/LEX-FAOC098701/.

113  Animal Protection Index Egypt. https://api.worldanimalprotection.org/country/egypt.

114  M.A. Fadali, 1997. *Animal Experimentation - A Harvest of Shame*. Santa Monica: Hidden Springs Press.

115  Qur'an 6:38.

116  Muslim, also Awn, Hadith 2658.

117  Animal Protection Index Indonesia. https://api.worldanimalprotection.org/country/indonesia.

118 Bhumi Global, The Parliament of the World's Religions, UNEP Faith for Earth & United Religions Initiative, 2020. Faith Action on the UN Sustainable Development Goals: Progress and Outlook.

119 Wikipedia, u.d. Jabal Aja Protected Area. https://en.wikipedia.org/wiki/Jabal_Aja_Protected_Area.

120 D.M. Abdelzaher, A. Kotb and A. Helfaya, 2017. Eco-Islam: Beyond the principles of why and what, and into the principles of how. *Journal of Business Ethics*. https://doi.org/10.1007/s10551-017-3518-2.

121 Islamic Values, Relating to Wildlands and Wildlife, & Wilderness Leadership. Presentation by Aishah Abdallah, Wilderness Leader, IUCN Commission on Education and Communication. Rosales 2017.

122 A. Saeed, 2006. *Islamic Thought: An Introduction*. Abingdon: Routledge.

123 R. Foltz, 2006. *Animals in Islamic Traditions and Cultures*. London: Oneworld Academic.

124 N. Pallotta, 02/10/20. Islamabad High Court Holds that Animals Have Legal Rights. Animal Legal Defense Fund. https://aldf.org/article/islamabad-high-court-holds-that-animals-have-legal-rights/.

125 N. Pallotta, 02/10/20. Islamabad High Court Holds that Animals Have Legal Rights. Animal Legal Defense Fund. https://aldf.org/article/islamabad-high-court-holds-that-animals-have-legal-rights/.

126 Qur'an 22:37.

127 *Arab News*, 13/05/19. KSA Delivers Sacrificial Meat to Needy People in Gaza. www.arabnews.com/node/1496256/corporate-news.

128 Al' Hafiz B.A. Masri, 2007. *Animal Welfare in Islam*. Leicester: The Islamic Foundation.

129 Qur'an 11:6.

## Further Reading

Al'Hafiz B.A. Masri, 2007. *Animal Welfare in Islam*. Leicester: The Islamic Foundation.

F.M. Khalid, 2019. *Signs on the Earth. Islam, Modernity and the Climate Crisis*. Leicester: Kube Publishing.

H.A. Haleem (Ed), 1998. *Islam and the Environment*. London: Ta'Ha Publishers.

R.C. Foltz, 2017. *Animals in Islamic Tradition and Muslim Cultures*. London: Oneworld Academic.

## Reference

The Translation of the Qur'an used is that by M.A.S Abdul Haleem, (Professor of Islamic Studies, at the School of Oriental and African Studies, University of London,) Oxford University Press, first published 2005, reprinted 2016.

# 4   Hinduism

Teaching and Practice regarding
Humanity's Relationship with
Animals

## Introduction

The name Hindu appears to be geographical in origin and was the name given by
the Persians, Greeks and others who lived beyond the Indus, who came from the
north-west, to those peoples and cultures that existed east of the Indus river. One
particular group, the Aryans, entered the north-west of the Indian subcontinent
thousands of years ago, probably in the second millennium BCE. No one can put an
exact date on it, but it seems they came gradually and assimilated over the centuries.

Already existing in the north-west was a different culture, the Indus Valley
civilisation, centred on cities like Harappa and Mohenjo-Daro. Whether by conquest or communication, it seems that the cultures began to mix. Over the centuries, distinctive features became prominent and are now fundamental to what
we call Hinduism. It is said that in more recent times, the British rulers of India
helped to establish the term Hinduism to apply specifically to a set of religious
beliefs and practices. Many Hindus prefer to call their faith Sanatana Dharma
(the Eternal Law of Righteousness). With respect and for ease of understanding,
I shall use the terms Hinduism and Hindu in this chapter.

Bovines emerge early on in both cultures. Emblems depicting bulls have been
found in the Indus Valley excavations, with one seal depicting a godlike figure
surrounded by many animals, including elephants, tigers and antelopes. As the
script of this civilisation has not yet been deciphered, our knowledge of their
beliefs is somewhat limited.

To the Aryans, cows were a source of wealth. Horses were also vital as the
Aryans were charioteers as well as horse-riders. Not surprisingly, horses became
associated with military might, conquest and power.

It seems that the division of society into four main caste groups also came from
Aryan sources. Although not crucial to this chapter, it is useful to understand
that the two upper castes, the priests (known as brahmans or brahmins) and
the warriors (the kshatriyas) were considered more "advanced" than the traders and farmers (the vaishyas) or the workers (the shudras). Historians generally
attribute the beginnings of the caste system to a type of colour prejudice. The
invading Aryans had a lighter skin tone than the inhabitants of the Indus Valley areas or other people already living in the Indian subcontinent. Outside the

DOI: 10.4324/9781003292555-5

caste system were the untouchables, whose very name reveals the very low status they had in society. They performed the jobs that caste Hindus did not want to do, such as making animal skins into leather and dealing with sanitation (read, human excrement). Different names have been attached to these people, such as Dalits (scattered ones), Harijans or children of God, a term favoured by Mahatma Gandhi, and the official term used by the government, Scheduled Castes. Although the Indian Constitution has forbidden discrimination against the Scheduled Castes, and further laws have been enacted to protect them, there is still considerable active discrimination against them, especially in rural areas.

## Holy Books

To understand the status of Hindu beliefs regarding animals, it is helpful to know a little about the source texts on which beliefs are based or where they became formulated.

The Aryans developed a large set of materials, later written down in Sanskrit and known as the Vedas or the Knowledge. The earliest is the Rig Veda, followed by the Sama Veda, the Yajur Veda and finally the Atharva Veda. All are regarded as divine revelation or "sruti". In this way, they would hold the same status as the Qur'an for Muslims or the Bible for Christians.

The Upanishads were written later, probably around 500–800 BCE and are called the Vedanta or culmination/conclusion of the Veda. They form the essence of Hindu philosophy. They are also usually recognised as "sruti".

Important Hindu literature also includes two major epic tales, the Ramayana and the Mahabharata. The much-loved Bhagavad Gita forms part of the Mahabharata. Technically the epics are "smriti" (that which is remembered) and they were written down by a person or persons. Most Hindus probably relate more easily to these epic tales than to the rather inscrutable Vedas.

All these revered books, plus several others, are important in forming the principles and practices of Hindus today.

## How Many Gods Are There?

Some say that there are 330 million gods in Hinduism, others that there is but one. There are many local deities within Hinduism, often recognised only in that one area and often associated with an historical event or person or with a mountain, a river or a tree. It is not unusual for every local mountain, river or forest to be identified with a deity. This means that much of the natural world is seen as sacred.

As that wonderful philosopher and theologian – and later President of India (1962–1967) – Dr Sarvepalli Radhakrishnan wrote: "If popular deities are worshipped, it must be understood that they are only varied manifestations of the One Supreme".[1]

Most Hindus would recognise about eight main gods/goddesses: Brahma, the creator, with his consort Saraswati, Vishnu the preserver with his consort Lakshmi and Shiva the destroyer (one has to destroy in order for new creation) and his consort Parvati, who is sometimes revealed as the mighty Durga or the ferocious Kali, who likes blood sacrifice.

Some Hindus are specifically followers of a particular god, such as Shiva for the Shaivites, or Vishnu for the Vaishnavas. They see their own god as the one and ultimate god who created the world and sustains it. Shiva is often portrayed as an ascetic, but wearing a tiger or elephant skin, carrying a human skull as an alms bowl and with his hair tied up with snakes and a snake around his neck. This could be seen as a crude depiction of animals, but each animal represents a legend or a belief. For example, the snake is seen as representing the cycle of birth and death.

To make it more complicated, these main gods are often incarnated in other gods. For example, the very popular god Krishna is seen as an incarnation of Vishnu.

Gods are often associated with animals or are depicted riding on special animal vehicles or vahanas. Shiva's vahana is Nandi, the white bull.

A very popular Hindu god is the elephant-headed Ganesha, son of Shiva. Born of Parvati, Shiva decapitated him in a case of mistaken identity, so an elephant was beheaded and his head was attached to the youngster. Not surprisingly, Ganesha is the god of removing obstacles. During his annual festival, clay statues of him are paraded through crowds in the streets and are finally immersed in the sea or a nearby lake or river. He is much loved.

Hanuman, the monkey god, played a vital role in helping Rama (another incarnation of Vishnu) regain his kidnapped wife, Radha, as recorded in the Ramayana epic. For this reason, monkeys are said to be sacred throughout India and Hanuman is revered.

For some Hindus, the cow is divine in herself and they pray to gau-mata, cow mother. She is both mother and goddess of the earth. Some believe that all the gods live within the cow, which is why she is so revered and has her own festival.

In many of the Upanishads, Brahman is revered as the ultimate reality and power in the whole universe. Brahman is the one god above all the more colourful gods of Hinduism. The respected Hindu scholar Eknath Easwaran (1910–1999) explains the concept of Brahman: "This Reality is the essence of every created thing, and the same Reality is our real Self".[2] Dr Radhakrishnan puts it thus: "Brahman is the supra-cosmic Reality".[3]

## Sacrifice

The Vedas reveal to us that sacrifice was an important part of the Aryan belief system. A special drink "soma" was critical to most sacrifices. It may have been juice from a hallucinogenic plant. It was offered to the god, and drunk by the brahmans or priests, who performed the sacrifices and were seen as connecting the ordinary people with the divine.

Sacrifice was seen as essential to appeasing the god and maintaining social order. There were benefits too for the person who sponsored the sacrifice. As only the brahmans could access the Vedic knowledge and perform the sacrificial rituals, they held extraordinary power.

Animal sacrifice, often of a bull or a goat, was common. The Ashvamedha or "horse sacrifice", was an elaborate variant of the soma sacrifice. The chosen horse would be allowed to roam free, but guarded, for a year and then caught and sacrificed.

A much-revered book, the Bhagavata Purana, dating from the 8th to 9th centuries CE, expresses real understanding of animal feeling, saying: "Seeing someone about to sacrifice with material offerings, beings are filled with dread, fearing 'This self-indulgent (human), having no compassion, will slay me'".[4]

Over centuries, different gods became the recipients of the sacrifice, including the terrifying goddess Kali, who was described in the later epic story, the Mahabharata, as enjoying wine, flesh and animal sacrifice.[5] Until recently, hundreds of animals, usually goats, would be sacrificed to Kali at the Kalighat temple in Kolkata. In 2006, the Kolkata High court banned the practice, perhaps mainly because it upset tourists.[6]

Some Hindus are devotees of the mother goddess, who emanates power as Shakti. Shakti manifests in many other female deities and was often offered animal sacrifice, usually a buffalo. In one of her manifestations as Durga, she defeated the buffalo demon.

Animal sacrifice still persists in some parts of India, often linked to the festival of a local deity. There are occasional voices raised in protest, but they are usually outnumbered.[7]

One particular mass sacrifice which has persisted into the 21st century is the five-yearly sacrifice at the Gadhimai temple in Nepal. Gadhimai is a manifestation of the goddess Kali.

Devotees come from all over Nepal and northern India to bring their animals, usually buffalo, for sacrifice, or just to watch the bloody spectacle – and bloody it is. In 2014, it is estimated that over 200,000 buffalo were cut to death in the open-air massacre.

Many Hindus would agree with Swami Agnivesh, president of the Hindu reform movement, the World Council of Arya Samaj, who said, at the 2014 Gadhimai festival: "India was a pioneer in introducing the principle of ahimsa to the entire world. Rituals like Gadhimai where scores of animals are mercilessly sacrificed only corrode our values of compassion".[8]

In spite of legal action and advice from the Nepalese Supreme Court to end all animal sacrifices in the country and in spite of the actions of Nepalese and Indian animal activists, the slaughter did still occur in the latest festival in 2019. However, the number of animals killed was greatly reduced.

## The Teaching

The Vedas must have had many authors over many years. Although sacrifice was so important at that time, there is an interesting verse in the Rig Veda, which says:

> The yatudhana who fills himself with the flesh of man,
> He who fills himself with the flesh of horses or of other animals,
> And he who steals the milk of the cow,
> Lord, cut off their heads with your flame.[9]

A yatudhana was someone regarded as having magical powers or perhaps a sorcerer. It is not clear if this passage applied to ordinary mortals.

Many of the religious books of the Hindu tradition give a very different view of the spiritual life from the sacrificial, ritualistic Vedas.

As the Mundaka Upanishad declares:

> The rituals and the sacrifices described
> In the Vedas deal with lower knowledge.
> The sages ignored these rituals
> And went in search of higher knowledge.[10]

The name "Upanishad" translates roughly as "sitting down near (to a teacher)" and the word conjures up images of a wise person surrounded by disciples, one or more of whom is writing down what the teacher says. Around 700–500 BCE was a time of upheaval in the Indian subcontinent and many sages may have retreated to the forest, living with their followers.

From a theological viewpoint the Upanishads are crucial, as well as being the foundation of Hindu philosophy. The one divine essence behind and within every being, Brahman, is also the Self or Atman. Brahman is "attributeless" and "omnipresent".[11] The Atman or perhaps what we might call the higher Self is distinct from the lower self, which dictates most of our daily thoughts and actions – the "me-mine" self.

The Chandogya Upanishad explains the concept of Brahman:

> This universe comes forth from Brahman, exists in Brahman, and will return to Brahman. Verily, all is Brahman.[12]

The Katha Upanishad explains that Brahman and the Self, Atman, are one:

> As the same fire assumes different shapes,
> When it consumes objects differing in shape,
> So does the one Self take the shape
> Of every creature in whom he is present.[13]

It is only when someone has realised the unity of Brahman/Atman that one can be released from the cycle of birth, death and rebirth, samsara.

> If one fails to realise Brahman in this life
> Before the physical sheath is shed,
> He must again put on a body
> In the world of embodied creatures.[14]

One important aspect of seeing not the ego self but the real Self is to see the connection with all beings.

> The Self is hidden in the lotus of the heart. Those who see themselves in all creatures go day by day into the world of Brahman hidden in the heart.[15]

The Isha Upanishad also emphasises the unity of the individual person with all beings:

> Those who see all creatures in themselves
> And themselves in all creatures know no fear.
> Those who see all creatures in themselves
> And themselves in all creatures know no grief.
> How can the multiplicity of life
> Delude the one who sees its unity?[16]

Some of the later Upanishads tend to a more devotional relationship with the Divine, sometimes described as the Lord of Love. This is seen especially in the Shvetashvatara Upanishad:

> On this ever-revolving wheel of life
> The individual self goes round and round
> Through life after life, believing itself
> To be a separate creature, until
> It sees its identity with the Lord of Love
> And attains immortality in the indivisible whole.
> He is the eternal reality, sing
> The scriptures, and the ground of existence.
> Those who perceive him in every creature
> Merge in him and are released from the wheel
> Of birth and death.[17]

So, unless one can realise that the divine permeates all creatures, is immanent in all, one cannot escape being reborn again.

This particular Upanishad is beautifully poetic:

> The Lord dwells in the womb of the cosmos,
> The Creator who is in all creatures...
> The Lord of Love, omnipresent, dwelling
> In the heart of every living creature.[18]

Even more poetically:

> He is the blue bird; he is the green bird
> With red eyes; he is the thundercloud,
> And he is the seasons and the seas.[19]

But what does this realisation of unity mean for a person's daily life? The Mundaka Upanishad provides an answer:

> The Lord of Love shines in the hearts of all.
> Seeing him in all creatures, the wise
> Forget themselves in the service of all...[20]

Here we see the concept of karma or action. Knowledge on its own is not enough, although it is one important way to achieve release from the cycle of rebirth – but one must put one's belief into action, karma. This teaching is attributed to the theologian Yajnavalkya, and it is vital when we come to consider Hindu practice in relation to animals today.

Gradually the old Vedic rituals, performed in obeisance to the mighty gods, began to be replaced by the gentler, more mystical teachings of the Upanishads. By the 6th century BCE, the related concepts of rebirth, karma and moksha (release from the rebirth cycle, samsara) replaced or enriched the teachings of the older Vedic period.

Not everyone could live by the mystical concepts of the Upanishads. Over time, books of law and practice began to be written down and these books still govern the lives of most Hindus. The Laws of Manu or Manusmriti were written down, probably around 100 CE, and elucidated the morality of daily life, marriage and funeral rites, pollution and purification, dietary law and the punishments of hell for the transgressor. The Laws tell believers how to live their lives, how to fulfil their dharma or right living. The concept of concern for other creatures is also elucidated:

> He who injures innocent beings with a desire to give himself pleasure never finds happiness neither in life nor in death.[21]

There are so many rules about daily living, many of which may seem to us outdated, that it is good to reveal the laws pertaining to our relationship with other creatures. Here the Laws of Manu can be very clear regarding the duties of a Brahmin caste householder. Agriculture is declared to be Pramrita, that is, it causes many deaths.[22]

This is explained further. The top two castes, the Brahmin priests and the Kshatriya (warriors), "shall carefully avoid (the pursuit of) agriculture, (which causes) injury to many beings and depends on others.

"(Some) declare that agriculture is something excellent, (but) that means of subsistence is blamed by the virtuous; (for) the wooden (implement) with iron point injures the earth and (the beings) living in the earth".[23] So, even to prevent a wooden spike from inadvertently injuring an earthworm, Brahmins should not be farmers.

One must be generous to the hungry, be they fellow humans or animals: "A householder must give (as much food) as he is able (to spare) to those who do not cook for themselves, and to all beings one must distribute (food) without detriment (to one's own interest)".[24]

In view of the modern dairy industry, it is interesting to note the rule: "Let him not interrupt a cow who is suckling (her calf)".[25]

Looking at the long journeys inflicted on animals in modern-day transport, it is good to note: "Let him not travel with untrained beasts of burden, nor with (animals) that are tormented by hunger or disease, or whose horns, eyes, and hoofs have been injured, or whose tails have been disfigured".[26]

The laws of Manu demonstrate the special place of cows in Hindu society: "Dying, without the expectation of a reward, for the sake of Brahmans and of cows, or in the defence of women and children, secures beatitude to those excluded (from the Aryan community, vahya)".[27]

There are two great epic tales, known to virtually every Hindu, the Ramayana and the Mahabharata. The Ramayana or story of Prince Rama tells of how his wife Sita is kidnapped by the demon king Ravana of Lanka (modern-day Sri Lanka). Rama is only able to get her back with the help of a troop of monkeys, led by their king Hanuman. The monkeys build a bridge across the sea to Lanka, to enable Rama and his allies to retrieve Sita. (In fact, this legend of the monkey army may be based on a real forest-dwelling tribe of people, who perhaps already worshipped monkeys and who were induced to support Rama in his battle in Lanka.) Hanuman is recorded as having amazing abilities, such as flight.

Because of this story, monkeys are still regarded as sacred and roam freely in the countryside and cities throughout India. Many temples are surrounded by troops of monkeys. Worshippers give them food to earn good karma. Re-enactments of the Ramayana, often translated from the original Sanskrit into the local language, are staged frequently throughout India and in countries in south-east Asia where substantial Hindu populations have migrated and settled.

The Mahabharata is an epic tale of a family feud. The story is full of battles and animal sacrifices.

At one point there is a long conversation between Yudhisthira and his dying grandfather Bhisma. The old king tells his grandson:

> The life-breaths of other creatures are as dear to them as one's own breaths are to one's own self. Men endued with intelligence and cleansed souls should always behave towards other creatures after the manner of that behaviour which they like others to observe towards themselves.[28]

This incredibly long epic ends with a wonderful story of a human-animal relationship. King Yudisthira, his wife and brothers set out to climb Mount Meru in northern India, at the summit of which they would enter the celestial world. A dog began to follow them.

During the climb, one after the other, in the cold and snow, his wife and all four brothers dropped down and died. Alone, Yudisthira advanced onward. Looking behind, he saw the faithful dog was still following him. And so the king and the dog went on, through snow and ice, climbing higher and higher, till they reached the summit of Mount Meru; and there they began to hear the chimes of heaven, and celestial flowers were showered upon the virtuous king by the gods. Then the chariot of the gods descended, and the mighty god Indra told Yudisthira, "Ascend in this chariot, greatest of mortals: thou that alone art given to enter heaven without changing the mortal body".

And Yudhishthira looked around and said to the dog, "Get into the chariot, little one". The god stood aghast. "What! the dog?" he cried. "Do thou cast off this dog! The dog goeth not to heaven! Great King, what dost thou mean? Art thou mad? Thou, the most virtuous of the human race, thou only canst go to heaven in thy body".

"But he has been my devoted companion through snow and ice. When all my brothers were dead, my queen dead, he alone never left me. How can I leave him now?"

"There is no place in heaven for men with dogs. He has to be left behind. There is nothing unrighteous in this".

"I do not go to heaven", replied the king, "without the dog. I shall never give up such a one who has taken refuge with me, until my own life is at an end. I shall never swerve from righteousness, nay, not even for the joys of heaven or the urging of a god."

"Then", said Indra, "on one condition the dog goes to heaven. You have been the most virtuous of mortals and he has been a dog, killing and eating animals; he is sinful, hunting, and taking other lives. You can exchange heaven with him."

"Agreed", says Yudisthira. "Let the dog go to heaven".

At once, the scene changed. Hearing these noble words of Yudhishthira, the dog revealed himself as Dharma; the dog was no other than Yama, the Lord of Death and Justice. And Dharma exclaimed,

> Behold, O King, no man was ever so unselfish as thou, willing to exchange heaven with a little dog, and for his sake disclaiming all his virtues and ready to go to hell even for him. Thou art well born, O King of kings. Thou hast compassion for all creatures, of which this is a bright example. Hence, regions of undying happiness are thine.[29]

This is a real tale of morality and compassion and sets a high standard for Hindus and all of us to follow!

The most famous and much-loved part of the Mahabharata is the Bhagavad Gita, in which Prince Arjuna, who is hesitant about killing his cousins in battle, is instructed to do his duty by his charioteer, who turns out to be the god Krishna, an incarnation of Vishnu. Krishna gives much spiritual teaching to Arjuna, pointing out that it is Arjuna's caste duty to wage the war. Krishna tells him not to be attached to the outcomes of his actions, for only the physical body is slain. The eternal Self lives on:

> As a man casts off his worn-out clothes
> And takes on other new ones
> So does the embodied soul cast off his worn-out bodies
> And enters others new.[30]

So, one should not grieve, because:

> For sure is the death of all that comes to birth
> Sure is the birth of all that dies
> So in a matter that no one can prevent
> Thou hast no cause to grieve.[31]

Krishna carries on teaching Arjuna about the fact that the divine exists in all beings:

> Wise ones see the self-same thing
> In a brahmin wise and courteous,
> As in a cow or elephant,
> Nay, as in a dog or an outcaste.[32]

As the distinguished theologian Dr S. Radhakrishnan explains: "The Eternal is the same in all, in animals, as in men, in learned Brahmins as in despised outcastes. The light of Brahman shines in all bodies and is not affected by the differences in the bodies it illumines".[33]

Krishna teaches Arjuna about the three paths of Yoga, the paths of knowledge, action and devotion. He explains again that the Yoga practitioner sees "the Self in all beings standing" and "All beings in the Self".[34]

Krishna reiterates the Upanishadic teaching on Brahman, the ultimate reality:

> When once a man can see that the diversity
> Of contingent beings abides in One (alone),
> And from that alone they radiate,
> Then to Brahman he attains.[35]

The Bhagavad Gita firmly aligns with the concept of caste and the duty to behave as one's caste requires. It mentions the importance of sacrifice. But its teaching on the same ultimate reality, Brahman, existing in all beings, relates more to the teaching of the Upanishads. If Hindus follow this teaching, then they must surely be compassionate, realising that Brahman exists also in all animals.

## Hindu Teachers

Over the centuries there have been many famous Hindu spiritual teachers, such as Adi Shankara, in the 9th century. Shankara based his advaita, (non-dual) teaching on the Upanishads, and while he always paid respect to the Vedas, he ignored sacrifice and the caste system and was against animal sacrifice. He taught that only knowledge of the truth as revealed by the Upanishads can grant liberation from rebirth. Many Hindus still study and follow his teachings.

Mirabai was a 16th-century teacher who wrote bhajans (devotional songs) about her huge love for the god Krishna, and Sant Dariya Saheb (1674–1780) preached non-violence to all beings. In fact, Hinduism has a multitude of holy people who have been influential in its history.

Looking nearer to our own time it seems that Swami Vivekananda (1863–1902) was highly influential in putting Hinduism on the map of world religions. He was invited to speak at the Parliament of the World's Religions in Chicago in 1893. He created a sensation there and, in the end, spoke several times. He established a Vedanta Society in New York and over the years many more such societies have been set up in the US.

Back in India he developed a huge following. Speaking in Jaffna in 1897, he said:

> In every man and in every animal, however weak or wicked, great or small, resides the same Omnipresent, Omniscient soul. The difference is not in the soul, but in the manifestation. Between me and the smallest animal, the difference is only in manifestation, but as a principle he is the same as I am, he is my brother, he has the same soul as I have. This is the greatest principle that India has preached. The talk of the brotherhood of man becomes in India the brotherhood of universal life, of animals, and of all life down to the little ants — all these are our bodies.[36]

This is an interesting speech, especially as it is said that the Swami continued to eat the traditional Bengali foods of his childhood, such as fish and mutton. In fact, it appears as an anomaly!

Swami Vivekananda is still a legend and regarded as a saint by many Hindus. He took monastic vows and followed the teachings of the Upanishads and the Bhagavad Gita. The Gita and *The Imitation of Christ*, a 15th-century devotional book probably written by Thomas à Kempis, were said to be his favourite books. He worked to help the poor, he opposed the caste system and he favoured education for all.

Sri Aurobindo (1872–1950) led a fascinating life before he undertook serious spiritual practice. After education in both India and England, he worked for the Indian Civil Service, but began to organise opposition to British Rule in India and was imprisoned for his efforts.

During his second imprisonment, he underwent a spiritual experience and said that he felt Swami Vivekananda talking to him. This was just a few years after Swami Vivekananda had died.

Being threatened further by the authorities he moved to Pondicherry in south India, then still a French colony. Gradually followers were drawn to his teaching and practice and in 1926 he established his ashram, which still exists today. Handing over practical matters to his spiritual partner, "The Mother", he devoted himself to writing, teaching and spiritual practice.

He wrote prose, poetry and spiritual guidance on his own system of Integral Yoga, such as in his book, *The Life Divine*, published in 1919. Based largely on the Upanishads and the Gita, but with western philosophical influences too, Aurobindo believed that the so-called supermind mediated between the infinite and the finite world.[37]

Sri Aurobindo's writings are said to have inspired a range of other artists and philosophers, from the composer Karlheinz Stockhausen to the modern American writer Ken Wilber. Sri Aurobindo ensured that only vegetarian food was served at the ashram.

Sri Aurobindo explained: "Life is life – whether in a cat, or dog or man. There is no difference there between a cat or a man. The idea of difference is a human conception for man's own advantage".[38]

Bhagavan Ramana Maharshi (1879–1950) was a famous yogi who drew thousands of people to come to see him at his ashram on the Arunachala hill in Tiruvannamalai in Tamil Nadu, in southern India. He lived very simply and was credited with saying: "Vegetable food contains all that is necessary for maintaining the body".[39] He was interested only in the spiritual life and lived in almost constant meditation. However, he broke various food taboos as he insisted that beggars should not be given hand-outs but should be invited into the ashram to eat with others. The same welcoming treatment was given to outcastes, causing dismay to some of his higher caste followers. He also abhorred food waste and insisted that leftovers be heated up for breakfast, another taboo broken!

A. C. Bhaktivedanta Swami Prabhupada (1896–1977) was a Vaishnavite Hindu, who only took up teaching and preaching at the age of 50. He translated many Sanskrit texts but is best known for founding ISKCON, the International Society for Krishna Consciousness, known as the Hare Krishna movement. His teaching is in the tradition of bhakti yoga, the way of love and devotion. He taught that by the practice of bhakti yoga, we can develop pure love for all living beings. This in turn creates a peaceful and harmonious society

He wrote: "One should treat animals such as deer, camels, asses, monkeys, mice, snakes, birds and flies exactly like one's own son. How little difference there actually is between children and these innocent animals".[40]

However, ISKCON belief still places humans on a very different level to animals, as this extract from their website makes clear:

> Animals are largely controlled by natural instincts, arising from impulses born of the modes of nature. Due to the fact that their consciousness is less evolved than the soul occupying a human form of life, animals are not held responsible karmically for these actions; they do not incur any new karma. Humans on the other hand have received their life form as a result of naturally occurring evolution of consciousness, including the ability of rational thinking, thus making choices of behaviour beyond the level of animalistic impulse. With this facility of higher consciousness comes responsibility for their actions, thus resulting in karma. By design, human life is ultimately meant for reviving our lost relationship with God by following the instructions of God contained in religious books like the Bhagavad-Gita, Srimad-Bhagavatam, etc. Animals do not have the capacity or developed intelligence by which they can understand the process of self-realization and God realization (including understanding why are we suffering, who am "I", what is the goal of my life, etc.). These are some of the major differences between the animal and the human form of life.[41]

Sadly, in Hinduism pigs are often portrayed as filthy creatures who eat excrement. It is true that in some areas of India such as Goa, one form of sanitation was for a basic lavatory seat to be situated at the edge of the house. Excrement would drop down onto the earth and pigs would indeed come and eat it. From an animal welfare point of view, we know that in hot conditions, pigs will roll in wet mud to

cool themselves, as they do not sweat. This may have contributed to their reputation as dirty animals. Yet we know that in natural conditions, pigs will defecate
away from their sleeping quarters, so they are already "house-trained" in the way
we teach our "pet" dogs to be.

Swami Prabhupada bought into this description of pigs as revealed in one of his
filmed sermons.[42]

At the ISKCON temple near London, Bhaktivedanta Manor, there is a working dairy farm. The cows are known by name and are milked by hand and remain
on the farm throughout their lives. Male calves are not sent to slaughter (the usual
practice on dairy farms). Bulls are put to work on the farm, pulling carts, although
from an animal welfare point of view, their harness looks uncomfortable.[43] The
milk is labelled as "slaughter-free" from the "Ahimsa Dairy".

Sri Chinmoy (1931–2007) lost both his parents by the age of 13 and grew up
in the ashram set up by Sri Aurobindo in Pondicherry and learned meditation
from an early age. He felt drawn to working in the west and moved to the US
in his thirties, giving talks and leading meditation groups. He advocated self-
transcendence, going beyond what one felt capable of and gained many celebrity
followers from music and sport, both areas in which he was himself talented. The
heart of his teaching was bhakti yoga, the way of devotion.

Based in New York, for many years he regularly led meditation sessions at the
United Nations for UN delegates, staff, and NGO representatives. Over the years,
he gained many thousands of followers all over the world.

Personally, he loved animals and kept many companion animals. He wrote:

> There are many, many ways animals can help us in our evolution. Again, in
> the process of evolution, we are higher because we are conscious of God. The
> poor animals are not conscious of God. Either we pray to God or meditate on
> God; it is up to us. But we are conscious that there is somebody in Heaven or
> inside us who is watching us, while animals are not.[44]

This common attitude to animals seems based on the belief in reincarnation. If
one leads a bad life as a human, one may be reborn as an animal. Some Hindus
believe that one needs to be reborn into the Brahmin priestly caste to be able
to proceed to moksha, liberation from rebirth. Others believe that anyone, even
someone without the caste system altogether, can achieve moksha. As Professor
Nanditha Krishna explained to me: "We have examples of saints such as, Nan-
danar, Namdev, Ravidas, Arunagirinathar, etc., who belonged to the so-called
'untouchable' caste, yet because of their total devotion to God, they merged with
the divine and achieved moksha".[45]

Mahatma (great soul) Gandhi (1869–1948) is surely one of the greatest teachers
of the essence of Hinduism. The word Ahimsa or non-violence will always be
associated with him. This was a principle he applied to all aspects of his life, politics, campaigning and relations with animals. He based it firmly on the teachings
of the holy books of Hinduism, although he may well have been influenced by
Jainism (see Chapter 6).

His theory is wonderfully summed up by Nibedita Priyadarshini Jena:

> Mahatma Gandhi's profound theory of Ahimsa or non-violence takes into account both human beings and animals. His fundamental thought on the subject of protecting animals is the outcome of a cluster of theories, including the non-violence of Jainism, the teachings of the Gītā, Sānkhya, Christianity, and Tolstoy...He suggests that non-violence does not merely imply non-hurting in thought and deed, but that it entails an extension of love and compassion... Gandhi demands protection of their lives (rights) and also enhancement of their welfare.[46]

In his inspiring autobiography, Gandhi spends much time on the issue of food. But the teaching is clear:

> To my mind, the life of a lamb is not less precious than that of a human being. I should be unwilling to take the life of a lamb for the sake of the human body. I hold that, the more helpless a creature, the more entitled it is to protection by man from the cruelty of man.[47]

He goes on to castigate the Hindus of Bengal, many of whom (as we have seen with Aurobindo and Vivekananda) continue to eat fish and sometimes meat: "How is it that Bengal with all its knowledge, intelligence, sacrifice and emotion tolerates this slaughter?"[48]

Gandhi's autobiography ends in the 1920s (although he lived to 1948), long before the powerful events leading up to the independence of India and Pakistan from British rule and the dreadful violence that followed, as Hindus, Muslims and Sikhs left their homes to seek residence in another country, violence which Gandhi tried hard to prevent.

In spite of Gandhi's lifelong involvement in politics, workers' rights and seeking independence, his personal spiritual journey was never far from his mind – and his practice. An ardent believer in Ahimsa, non-violence, he felt he must apply this principle in every area of his life. At the end of his autobiography, he declares:

> Identification with everything that lives is impossible without self-purification: without self-purification the observance of the law of *Ahimsa* must remain an empty dream; God can never be realised by one who is not pure of heart... So long as a man does not of his own free will put himself last among his fellow creatures, there is no salvation for him. *Ahimsa* is the farthest limit of humility.[49]

## The Role of Humanity

The Sanatana Dharma is deeply concerned with how an individual can achieve moksha or liberation from the cycle of birth and rebirth. Most of its teachings are about the nature of the divine and of the material world and how one should behave in this world (which may or may not be "real"), in order to achieve oneness with the divine, be that expressed as Brahman or as one of the gods like Vishnu.

The sacred books we have looked at imply that Hindus should live a good life, perform their duties, and act with compassion. Living the good life in this way is aligning with one's dharma, the right way for one to live.

Apart from fulfilling the duties of one's dharma, The Laws of Manu require people to avoid causing harm to other creatures:

> He who injures innoxious beings from a wish to (give) himself pleasure, never finds happiness, neither living nor dead. He who does not seek to cause the sufferings of bonds and death to living creatures, (but) desires the good of all (beings), obtains endless bliss. He who does not injure any (creature), attains without an effort what he thinks of, what he undertakes, and what he fixes his mind on.[50]

In summarising the laws for all believers, the Laws of Manu include: "Abstention from injuring (creatures)".[51]

As Krishna teaches in the Bhagavad Gita:

> Let a man feel hatred for no contingent being
> Let him be friendly, compassionate,
> Let him be done with thoughts of "I" and "mine",
> The same in pleasure as in pain, long-suffering.[52]

Apart from not injuring or harming other creatures, the sacred books do not elucidate in detail how one should relate in practical ways with animals – apart from not eating them.

It is only in relation to cows that there seems to be a duty of active care required. There is a long history of veneration of the cow, who represents the ideal of motherhood. The cow is believed to produce milk and its derivative products like yoghurt and ghee in order to feed people, her urine is used for medicinal products and her dung is dried for use as fuel or for plastering floors and walls. The god Krishna is said to have been a cowherd in his early years. He is seen as the protector of cows. The mother earth goddess Bhumi is often portrayed as a cow.

Do Hindus worship the cow? Some surely do, but more modern Hindus reject this claim:

> Hindus don't worship cows. We respect, honour and adore the cow. By honouring this gentle animal, who gives more than she takes, we honour all creatures. Hindus regard all living creatures as sacred – mammals, fishes, birds and more. We acknowledge this reverence for life in our special affection for the cow. At festivals we decorate and honour her, but we do not worship her in the sense that we worship the Deity.[53]

There is an annual festival of cows, Gaupastami. Cows will be painted and decorated and given extra tasty foods.

In the Vedas, cows represent wealth and happiness. From the Rig Veda, we read

> The cows have come and have brought us good fortune. In our stalls, contented, may they stay! May they bring forth calves for us, many-coloured, giving milk for Indra each day. You make, O cows, the thin man sleek; to the unlovely you bring beauty. Rejoice our homestead with pleasant lowing. In our assemblies we laud your vigour.[54]

Both Sri Prabhupada and Gandhi believed that care for cows is fundamental to a good life.

Killing a cow would be the worst thing a Hindu could do, apart from human murder. As we shall see, this can create a conflict of interest between a believer and a veterinarian, whose job is solely to alleviate suffering in the present moment.

## Farming Methods

Over the years, since the time of the Vedas, milking cows has been a part of rural life in India. Most farmers had small herds of cows, producing milk for the family and maybe some left over for sale locally. The poor were lucky if they had just one cow.

India today is not only the leading global milk producer, but it has also become the world's largest consumer of milk. India's 2022 milk production is forecast at 700,000 metric tons.[55]

Around half of India's milk comes from buffaloes. They are not venerated – the goddess Durga fought the buffalo demon. Much buffalo milk is turned into milk powder.

In 1970 the Indian government launched Operation Flood to modernise and increase dairy production in India. This was done with good intent and it helped establish many dairy co-operatives throughout the country.

In 2017, the main Indian animal protection organisation FIAPO (the Federation of Indian Animal Protection Organisations) carried out a survey of dairy farming in ten states in India. *Cattle-ogue: Unveiling the Truth of the Indian Dairy Industry* makes worrying reading.

In 78.8% of the dairies, the cows were tethered, often by short tethers. There was no bedding or soft ground for them to lie on. In over 63% of the dairy farms, the cows were tied by their hind legs. Injuries to the animals were seen in over 64% of the dairies.

Oxytocin is a hormone that assists in "let-down" of milk. Injections of oxytocin have become common in Indian dairies. Its use was banned in 2018, but 46.9% of the dairies used oxytocin illegally.

Male calves were often neglected or sold to beef traders. Of those kept on at the dairies, 25% had died after one month.

The worst farms were not the very small smallholder farms, not even the big modern dairies, but the medium-sized dairies near the cities and towns.

As the report concludes: "This first-of-its-kind investigation in India's largest milk producing states as well as in the national capital has revealed the dark underbelly of the mushrooming and unregulated milk production industry".[56]

With around 80% of the population of India being Hindu, this is surely an unacceptable state of affairs. While FIAPO, with its 80 members and 200 supporter organisations in India can do so much, it is up to the national and state governments to enforce existing laws and implement reforms.

This unsatisfactory state of the dairy industry, coupled with the peripatetic wandering of cows living loose on the land and in the urban streets, often ingesting plastic rubbish, cows who receive no care or veterinary attention, amounts to an animal welfare horror story. If India wants to protect its cows, then it must surely do better.

As Professor Nanditha Krishna explains:

> Today, the dairy industry has become a big business…With the introduction of tractor farming, the male calf which would have been used on the farms is either abandoned or killed. Only the female calf is permitted to live for future milk production. If Hindus want to protect the cow, they must cut down milk production by cows and stop the export of milk and milk products.[57]

What of other farmed animals in India? Broiler (meat) chicken production is the fourth largest in the world, behind the US, Brazil and China. Around 20% of production is small scale, but 80% is the usual indoor housing and use of fast growth genetics, as is common throughout the world. This raises health questions regarding the use of antimicrobials in broiler farms and the spread of antibiotic resistance in the human population.[58]

India raises 460 million egg-laying hens every year, making it the world's third largest egg producer.[59] Until recently, 80% of the hens were kept in battery cages. As this article in Mongabay explains

> These cages pack 8–10 birds per cage, do not allow the hens to even stand up straight, turn around or even spread their wings. They prohibit the hens from expressing any of their natural behaviours, such as perching, nesting, laying their eggs privately in a nest box, roosting, among others.[60]

Fortunately, India seems to be moving towards cage-free systems, which is encouraging.

In 2013, the Animal Welfare Board of India concluded that battery cages were in violation of Section 11 (1)(e) of the 1960 Prevention of Cruelty to Animals Act and issued an advisory to all state governments stating that battery cages should not be used and existing ones should be phased out by 2017.[61]

This advisory seems to have been largely ignored. In 2019, the organisation Animal Equality carried out an investigation into hen farms in several states in India. This is what they found:

"Four to eight hens crammed in a cage no bigger than two letter size (8.5" × 11") sheets of paper, unable to comfortably move".

"Hens with sore, cracked and deformed feet, injured from the wire floor of cages".

"Overcrowded cages stacked on top of each other, causing urine and faeces to fall onto birds in the lower cages".

"Hens missing their feathers and suffering from abrasions and skin irritations".

"Sick hens left to die slow agonising deaths with little to no veterinary care".

"Litter collected in huge piles underneath the stacked cages, only disposed of once every few weeks, creating high concentrations of ammonia".[62]

If Hindus sincerely follow the teaching in the Upanishads, if they believe that Brahman exists in all creatures, that "the one Self" takes the shape "of every creature in whom he is present"[63] then how can such cruel factory farming systems be allowed to exist in India?

If some Hindus follow a bhakti yoga journey of devotion, how do they equate "The Lord of Love, omnipresent, dwelling in the heart of every living creature"[64] with the hen in the cage?

If the Lord of Love

> is the blue bird; he is the green bird
> With red eyes; he is the thundercloud,
> And he is the seasons and the seas,[65]

is he not also the hen in the cage?

Recently, several state governments, Goa, Himachal Pradesh, Karnataka, Madhya Pradesh, and Rajasthan, have prohibited the use of gestation and farrowing crates for sows. In June 2022, the Delhi government also banned the use of gestation crates (sow stalls) and farrowing crates for pigs.[66] These are very welcome moves and one can only hope that the national government will follow suit.

Professor Nanditha Krishna is clear that Hinduism and factory farming are incompatible:

> I believe Hindu teaching is not consistent with factory farming of animals… Factory farming means ill-treatment of animals as greed and financial benefits become all-important, whereas Hindu teachings are based on Dharma or the law of righteousness. There is no dharma in factory farming.[67]

## Wildlife and Biodiversity

With the elephant-headed god Ganesha being so loved by Hindus everywhere, it is interesting to look at the situation of elephants in India. Asian elephants are smaller than African elephants and only the males bear tusks. Prior to recent and rapid population growth and the expansion of agriculture, Asian elephants roamed the forests of India. Now, as their habitat is being decimated, elephants frequently find themselves in opposition to local farmers whose crops they can destroy.

As Professor Nanditha Krishna explains in her lovely book *Sacred Animals of India*, elephants live in groups of females, led by a matriarch, and have an important role to play in forest ecosystems. They clear old vegetation and create space for new growth and light to get through.[68] Males may live on their own or in small groups.

The elephants' gentle nature has resulted in them being forced into labour of all kinds, from giving repetitive tourist rides to working with loggers shifting the trees that have been cut down. Mostly these highly social animals are housed alone, which must cause them deep distress. Training methods are also painful and distressing.

Perhaps most ironic of all, many Hindu temples keep elephants, a practice especially common in Kerala, which is said to hold about one fifth of India's 2,500 captive elephants.[69] Often, they are kept chained by one leg, resulting in sores and infections. On festival days they will be painted, decorated and forced to carry weighty images of gods or musicians such as drummers. As elephants dislike sudden loud noises, this must be a torturous experience for them.

Professor Nanditha Krishna is strongly opposed to temple elephants:

> Elephants belong to the forest...They were never meant to be tamed and used in temples. Taming elephants is probably the cruellest way to treat any animal. The young elephants are kept in kraals and beaten black and blue till their spirit is broken. They are chained all their lives, sometimes even with spikes. I strongly support the banning of elephants from temples and hope this will happen soon.[70]

In an interview with the BBC in 2020, documentary maker Sangita Iyer told the reporter: "So many elephants had ghastly wounds on their hips, massive tumours and blood oozing out of their ankles, because chains had cut into their flesh and many of them were blind".[71]

In 2009 an investigation into temple elephants in India was undertaken by the Indian animal welfare organisation CUPA (Compassion Unlimited Plus Action) and ANCF (Asian Nature Conservation Foundation). They studied 153 temple elephants. Fifty-six percent were chained using spikes or were hobbled by their forelegs and the mean chaining duration was 17.5 hrs. The report declared:

> The physical space provided to elephants in temples is completely alien to the biology of the animal. All temples have stone flooring on which these elephants stand for long durations, never getting a chance to walk on natural substrates. Due to such unsuitable flooring, over 50% of the elephants suffer from foot rot. The practice of chaining elephants in temples is universal.[72]

In some contrast to this, a veterinary surgeon in India told me how he had been called to the post-mortem of an elephant who had dropped dead in the courtyard of her owner's house. The knackermen who had been called to dismember the elephant and remove her body were all Dalit Hindus, regarded as the lowest of the low by society. Before they began their unpleasant work, they held a short ceremony. Garlands were placed on the elephant, prayers and hymns were said and sung, incense was lit and purifying fire was swung about. Only when they had done this did the dismemberment begin.[73] These men felt they must revere this elephant before they cut up her body.

There are still over 27,000 wild elephants in India, but that is a huge drop from the million or so who lived there just a decade ago. Since 1986, the Asian elephant has been listed as Endangered on the IUCN Red List, as the wild population has declined by at least 50% since the 1930s to 1940s. 60% of Asian elephants live in India.[74]

It is ironic and distressing to see that the symbol of elephants everywhere, the much-loved god Ganesha, continues to be worshipped, his image in many Hindu homes, while his blood and flesh siblings are treated so badly – and especially at temples!

If, as the Bhagavad Gita teaches:

> Wise ones see the self-same thing
> In a brahmin wise and courteous,
> As in a cow or elephant,
> Nay, as in a dog or outcaste, [75]

then how can cows be tethered on dairy farms and temple elephants be chained by the leg?

India is rich in biodiversity of all kinds and successive governments have taken action to preserve this. Details can be read on the website of the Convention on Biological Diversity.[76]

More positive news is that in 2013 India made it illegal to use captive dolphins for public entertainment. The Ministry of Forests and Environment announced this policy, referring to dolphins as "highly intelligent and sensitive" creatures.[77]

While the Indian government banned the use of most wild animals in circuses in 1998, the use of elephants was only banned in 2013.[78]

Another positive development is the Bhumi Global organisation. Their mission is "to engage, educate, and empower people and communities to address the triple crisis of climate change, biodiversity loss, and pollution" and their work "is based on Hindu principles of environmental care".[79] They are active around the world including at the United Nations, seeking to promote care and concern for the environment, including animals.

## Hunting and Sport

Other wild animals are also suffering in India. Tigers and wild boar were always hunted by maharajas and other royal figures. During the era of the British Raj, it became good sport for the conquerors to continue indulging in such pastimes, with pig-sticking and tiger hunting particular favourites. Robert Baden-Powell, founder of the Scouting movement, loved pig-sticking so much that he wrote a book on it, declaring: "Yes, hog-hunting is a brutal sport – and yet I loved it, as I loved also the fine old fellow I fought against".[80]

Tiger hunting was also a popular "sport" of the ruling classes and the British Raj. After ascending the throne in 1911, King George V and his retinue travelled north to Nepal, slaying 39 tigers in 10 days.[81] Hunting tigers for sport was only banned in India under the Wildlife (Protection) Act in 1972. Tigers continue to be poached for their skins and have also lost much wild habitat. According to the National Tiger Conservation Authority, there were an estimated 2967 tigers left in India in 2021.[82]

The tiger reserves of India were set up in 1973 and are governed by Project Tiger, which is administrated by the National Tiger Conservation Authority. At the time of writing, 53 protected areas have been designated tiger reserves in India. India is home to 80% of tigers in the world and there are hopes that their numbers will increase due to these reserved areas.[83]

## Caring for Animals

There are an estimated 35 million "street" dogs living in India. Keeping dogs as "pets" is still not a very common practice, and these "indie" dogs live on scraps and the occasional hand-out. People are often scared of them, as rabies still kills around 20,000 people every year in India.[84] There are a growing number of shelters and veterinary centres which capture the dogs, neuter them and vaccinate them against rabies before releasing them back into their familiar territory. Sensibly, they make a notch in the dog's ear under anaesthesia, so when they are released, the local people know that the dogs no longer pose a rabies risk.

One such campaign is still being carried out by Help in Suffering Veterinary Centre in Jaipur. Over a few years of the programme the number of rabies infected people locally fell to zero.[85] A similar programme is being carried out in the huge city of Chennai by the Blue Cross.[86] These centres are financially supported by Hindus living locally but also by people, Hindu or non-Hindu, from all over the world.

One way in which Hindus practice cow care is by supporting gaushalas, which are sanctuaries for cows. Most of the cows in gaushalas have been set loose in the streets by farmers, or they may have been victims of road accidents or have eaten rubbish such as plastic bags lying in the road. It is estimated that India has about 5,000 stray cattle.[87] According to a 2014 reply in the Parliament, India has about 3,030 gaushalas.[88]

Because most Indian states forbid cow slaughter, poor farmers cannot afford to keep their worn-out animals and feel it is kinder to let them roam on their own rather than sell them to a trader who may transport them hundreds of miles to states like Kerala or West Bengal, where cow slaughter is allowed.

India has officially banned single-use plastics from July 2022. With poor quality rubbish collection in many areas, plastic bottles and shopping bags tend to get thrown on the streets and it is here that those wandering cows may ingest them. This causes blockages in their digestive system and extreme pain. Often such cows are taken to gaushalas or veterinary centres. Occasionally operations may be able to save them but often the damage is fatal. The cows are not allowed to be killed, so they can only be treated with medication to ease their dying.

Gaushalas may be financially supported by philanthropists or by small donations or even by governments at the state level. For the last few years India's national government has set aside considerable funds to support them.[89]

One veterinary surgeon, working in an Indian city, told me how she was called by an elderly Hindu couple to see to a cow which had been lying down unable to stand for three weeks on the pavement outside their home. Throughout this time the couple had provided the cow with water and fodder, but they were starting to realise that this unfortunate animal would never walk again. They allowed the cow to be removed to the veterinary centre and continued to turn up every day to feed it. The vets did what they could for the cow, but they knew she was doomed. They also knew that the couple would never give permission for her to be put out of her misery, so they quietly euthanised her when the couple were not present.[90]

So, there can be a conflict between caring for animals in the best interests of their welfare, the dharma of a veterinary surgeon perhaps, and fulfilling one's perceived religious duty.

One contemporary example of a Hindu living a life of service to animals is that of Chinny Krishna. As a schoolboy he was expelled from his school for refusing to dissect a frog in his biology class, as to him biology meant the study of life and he felt it wrong to study life by killing something. Many years later Chinny's engineering company developed computer programmes to replace dissection in schools. He went on to play vital roles in the Animal Welfare Board of India, the Blue Cross and in the Committee for the Purpose of Control and Supervision of Experiments on Animals (CPCSEA).[91]

There is a Hindu sect called the Bishnois, who exhibit exceptional care for animals. Their founder Guru Jambheshwar (also known as Guru Jambhoji) (1451–1536) taught his followers to protect animals, trees and their local environment. There are estimates of between 600,00 and 1 million Bishnois, mostly based in north-western India in the state of Rajasthan.

In 1730, Maharaja Abhay Singh of Jodhpur decided to build a new wooden palace. He sent his men to cut down the Khejri trees from the Khejari village to build his palace. As Bishnois believe in protecting trees, Amrita Devi Bishnoi and three of her daughters hugged the first tree and stood in protest. The soldiers beheaded all four of them and went on to kill over 350 other villagers. The story goes that when the Maharaja heard this he was upset, apologised to the local people and promised to leave their trees undisturbed.[92]

Bishnois take practical action to protect local wildlife, run animal sanctuaries and clinics, feed migratory birds and many join the local wildlife service in order to work for something they believe in.

Swami Vishudhananda, head priest at a Bishnoi temple in Rajasthan, explains:

> We believe in Vasudhaiva Kutumbakam or 'the world is one family.' As God makes all life, animals and plants are also part of this family. Hence, we must

take care of them. We must also keep our needs within limits to check the wanton destruction of nature. To stay happy and healthy, we must spend more time in natural settings.[93]

A short piece of film about the Bishnois can be seen on a BBC site.[94]

## Eating Animals

The Laws of Manu, while allowing the slaughter of animals for sacrifice, are outspoken about meat-eating:

> Meat can never be obtained without injury to living creatures, and injury to sentient beings is detrimental to (the attainment of) heavenly bliss; let him therefore shun (the use of) meat. Having well considered the (disgusting) origin of flesh and the (cruelty of) fettering and slaying corporeal beings, let him entirely abstain from eating flesh.[95]

The text goes further to implicate all those involved in the meat trade, right up to the consumer:

> He who permits (the slaughter of an animal), he who cuts it up, he who kills it, he who buys or sells (meat), he who cooks it, he who serves it up, and he who eats it, (must all be considered as) the slayers (of the animal).[96]

In the Mahabharata, there is a conversation between Yudhisthira (of the dog story) and his grandfather Bhisma about meat-eating. Bhisma declares:

> O monarch, know that the discarding of meat is the highest refuge of religion, of heaven, and of happiness. Abstention from injury is the highest religion. It is, again, the highest penance. It is also the highest truth from which all duty proceeds.[97]

Most of the many gurus and sages of Hinduism have advocated vegetarianism.

Sri Aurobindo said that vegetarian foods bring peace and clarity to the mind. "Vegetarianism is another question altogether; it stands, as you say, on a will not to do harm to the more conscious forms of life for the satisfaction of the belly".[98]

Swami Prabhupada advocated vegetarianism, saying "We do not give the chance to the animals to live properly, rather we are trying to eat the animals... Why should we eat animals?" He advocated keeping cows for their milk, but not eating them.[99] All ISKCON temples and centres serve only vegetarian food.

Sri Chinmoy advocated vegetarianism, but not to spare the animals *per se*, saying:

> If you want to lead a better life, a disciplined life, a pure life, I feel that a vegetarian diet is necessary. Those who eat meat, unconsciously are taking in the

consciousness of an animal. In addition to their hostile and other undivine qualities, animals have tremendous restlessness… when we eat meat, we take in the restless, destructive consciousness of animals.[100]

So, his view was based more on the concept of physical and psychic purity, rather than concern for animals being slaughtered.

At one time Mahatma Gandhi adopted and continued to advocate a strict vegan diet of "sunbaked fruits and nuts". However, when he later fell ill, he began to drink goat's milk, much as he longed for "a vegetable substitute for milk" (of which we now have many types).

Following his principle of Ahimsa, non-violence, he continued to be a strong advocate of vegetarianism, telling a London audience in 1931: "I have found from my own experience, and the experience of thousands of friends and companions, that they find satisfaction, so far as vegetarianism is concerned, from the moral basis they have chosen for sustaining vegetarianism".[101]

Professor Nanditha Krishna explains: "Hinduism is a very liberal religion. It tells you what is the best way to liberate yourself from your karmas, from birth, death and rebirth. Vegetarianism heads the list and is therefore the highest form of living".[102]

With the holy books teaching so much about human one-ness with other creatures, it is safe to say that if Hindus take these books seriously, then they will avoid eating meat. Perhaps because some parents have forced their children to be vegetarian "because that is what we do", many younger urban Hindus have rejected vegetarianism as old-fashioned, and they have taken to savouring meat and frequenting fast-food outlets. The most-ordered dish on a major Indian food delivery platform in 2021 was chicken biryani.[103]

It is ironic that while this is occurring in India, at the same time in the western urban world there is a big growth in veganism, more interest in reducing meat consumption and much wider availability of vegetarian and vegan products in supermarkets and restaurants.

Other Hindus are promoting the vegetarian diet for both traditional reasons and teachings but also in view of today's concerns about climate change, pollution of the earth and loss of biodiversity. The Hindu Declaration on Climate Change, published prior to the Paris Climate Agreement in 2015, made it clear that dietary change is an important part of the climate debate, saying:

> Adopting a plant-based diet is one of the single most powerful acts that a person can take in reducing environmental impact. In doing all of this, we help maintain the ecological and cosmic order, an order that allows life and existence to flourish.[104]

## Slaughter

Slaughter, especially of cows, is a controversial topic in India. So, it is perhaps surprising to discover that, according to a 2016 United States Department of

Agriculture review, India has rapidly grown to become the world's largest beef exporter, accounting for 20% of the world's beef trade.[105]

This trade is not based on exports of beef from cows, but from the slaughter of water buffaloes, many of whom will have been part of the dairy industry.

According to a 2018 article in the *Indian Express*, India has 73 buffalo abattoirs/meat processing plants approved by the Agricultural & Processed Food Products Export Development Authority (APEDA) under the Union Commerce Ministry.[106] The animals are slaughtered by the halal, non-stun method. There are said to be also many smaller illegal slaughtering places.

Although Hindus may be involved in ownership of slaughterhouses, the actual slaughtering is generally performed by Muslims.[107]

Cow slaughter is banned in most Indian states. It is true to say that to the non-Hindu outsider it may seem an anomaly that buffaloes, so similar to cattle in physiology, can be reared by Hindu farmers and slaughtered, sometimes in abattoirs owned by Hindus, but cows may not be slaughtered. Perhaps it is also anomalous that a country identified with vegetarianism reaps a healthy income from slaughtering animals and exporting their meat.

India also has a huge leather industry, adding up to 13% of the world's total production of skins, with around 10% of the world's footwear production also from India.[108] The leather is usually from buffaloes, goats or from cows who have died of natural causes.

## Vivisection

India's first national animal welfare law, the Prevention of Cruelty to Animals Act (1960), makes cruelty to animals a criminal offence, though exceptions are made for the treatment of animals used for food and animals used in scientific experiments. The 1960 law also created the Animal Welfare Board of India to ensure the anti-cruelty provisions were enforced and to promote the cause of animal welfare.[109]

The Breeding of and Experiments on Animals (Control and Supervision) Rules, 1998, set general requirements for breeding and using animals for research. A 2013 amendment bans the use of live animal experiments in medical education.[110] In 2014, India became the first country in Asia to ban all testing of cosmetics on animals and the import of cosmetics tested on animals.[111]

As the Animal Protection Index points out, the 1998 Breeding of and Experiments on Animals (Control and Supervision) Rules mandate that any establishment carrying out experimentation has to be registered and apply for permission to the Committee for the Purpose of Control and Supervision of Experiments on Animals or Institutional Animal Ethics Committees. This Committee (CPCSEA) oversees the use of animals for scientific research and is in charge of taking all measures to ensure that animals are not subjected to unnecessary pain or suffering before, during or after the scientific experiment performed on them.[112]

In 2001 a letter published in the respected medical journal *The Lancet* highlighted the poor animal welfare standards in most Indian laboratories at the time, saying: "Although a few private laboratories and government organisations maintain their animal houses well, fewer than a dozen of the roughly 5000 laboratories in the country have been certified to conform to good laboratory practices requirements".[113]

An investigation into India's laboratories in 2003 revealed appalling conditions for the animals.[114]

We hope sincerely that there has been serious reform since these revelations.

Professor Nanditha Krishna takes a thoughtful view:

> Without animal experimentation, we could not have eliminated polio or coped with Covid-19. However, most experiments using animals are useless or repetitive. Animal experimentation at the student level is unnecessary and for items like beauty products, etc., should be banned. If they are required for human health purposes, they should be done with great compassion towards the animals. Further, random testing on animals is totally unnecessary and neurological tests even more so. When there are alternatives like the use of human cells, etc., we don't need animal experiments.[115]

## Teaching and Practice

Because of so much teaching on concern for animals in Hinduism's holy books, it is not surprising that India has a formal animal welfare body. The Animal Welfare Board of India is a statutory advisory body on Animal Welfare Laws and promotes animal welfare in the country. Established in 1962, it was started under the stewardship of the late Rukmini Devi Arundale, a well-known humanitarian and animal welfarist.

The Board aims to ensure that animal welfare laws in the country are followed and provides grants to animal welfare organisations. It also advises the Government of India on animal welfare issues and the need for new legislation. The Board consists of 28 Members, some of whom are from animal welfare organisations.[116] The Board's overarching aim is: "To prevent the infliction of unnecessary pain or suffering on animals".[117]

In 2018 the Animal Welfare Board was moved from being under the Ministry of Environment, Forest and Climate Change to now falling under the responsibility of the Ministry for Agriculture.[118]

Although Indian law has not so far officially recognised that animals are sentient beings, it is perhaps implicit. The Prevention of Cruelty to Animals Act 1960 provides a partial recognition of sentience as the purpose of this Act is to 'prevent the infliction of unnecessary pain or suffering' to animals.[119] The Act therefore recognises the capacity of animals to suffer. However, the problem with such wording is: How do you interpret "*Unnecessary* suffering"?

They say there is a 15 million strong Hindu diaspora. Around the world, people of Hindu origin or faith could be divided into those who have dropped many of their former religious habits, while others will keep a small shrine in their homes, perform daily puja (worship) and avoid eating meat. Some may belong to associations of Hindus in those countries such as the American Hindu Foundation.[120]

## Conclusion

All the sacred books of Hinduism show respect for animals, even when they also require animal sacrifice. Some identify deities with animals. The Upanishads see the one Brahman in all beings. The thread of ahimsa, non-violence, runs through much of the history of Hinduism and has been beautifully expressed by Mahatma Gandhi in fairly recent times.

Visitors to India may see skinny cows wandering the streets or working animals like camels and horses with harness-inflicted injuries. They may be scared of the many dogs living lone lives on the streets. They may feel that a country where the vast majority of people are Hindu should be doing better by its animals.

But you can't ignore poverty and there is no doubt that people struggling to cope with poverty and feed their families, may have little time or energy to devote to animal care.

The positive thing is that there are animal groups in all major urban centres in India. Some will promote animal rights and vegan or vegetarian diets, others run sanctuaries for abandoned or abused animals, the more vehement may campaign to close butchers' shops.

It is important that these groups do not exclude members because of their faith or lack of caste. It would be a shame if that were to happen. Christians and Muslims should feel welcome in these animal groups. As this book shows, their faiths too call for concern for animals. It is also important that animal groups do not identify with any particular political party. Of course, they must lobby politicians and local and national governments on behalf of the animals and call for better laws. But if they identify with one political party, then those who do not support that party will feel excluded. So, they may be "political", but it is best not to be "party political", no matter what their personal voting intentions may be.

There is undoubtedly a conflict between the genuine Hindu belief in preserving animal life (especially the life of the cow) and the welfare or veterinary view that when an animal is facing extreme, incurable injury or disease or is in terminal and miserable decline, the kindest thing to do is to euthanise the creature to end its suffering.

One can only hope that respectful dialogue and progressive legislation will help to resolve this conflict.

It is hard to see how some practices like factory farming of chickens and cows can be supported in India. It seems almost blasphemous for Hindu temples to chain their elephants and train them to perform "tricks", such as bowing to the faithful.

As Professor Nanditha Krishna sadly reflects: "I think materialism has come with globalization and, seeing the very attractive lifestyles of the West, has made modern Hindus put aside compassion and become materialistic and greedy".[121]

Could India's Hindus be awaiting the arrival of a new Gandhi, who sees the divine in all beings and who will once again lead the Hindu faith and its millions of adherents to a more compassionate, non-violent future?

# Notes

1 S. Radhakrishnan, 1948. *The Bhagavad Gita*. London: George Allen and Unwin (11th impression 1976).
2 E. Easwaran, 2007. *The Upanishads*. Tomales: Nilgiri Press.
3 S. Radhakrishnan, 1948. *The Bhagavad Gita*. London: George Allen and Unwin (11th impression 1976).
4 Bhagavata Purana, 7.15.10.
5 Mahabharata 4:7.
6 *Hindustan Times*, 21/09/06. Court Ruling on Animal Sacrifice Bolsters Activists. www.hindustantimes.com/india/court-ruling-on-animal-sacrifice-bolsters-activists/story-aOWUX1ajguzQVirmEJba0O.html.
7 *The Times of India*, 2/10/17. Why Stopping Animal Sacrifice Looks Tall Order in this Village. https://timesofindia.indiatimes.com/blogs/below-the-belt/why-stopping-animal-sacrifice-looks-tall-order-in-this-village/.
8 Gabriel Power, 05/12/19. What Is the Gadhimai Festival and Why Is It So Controversial? *The Week*. www.theweek.co.uk/the-week-unwrapped/104702/what-is-the-gadhimai-festival-and-why-is-it-so-controversial.
9 Rig Veda 10.87.16.
10 Mundaka Upanishad 1.2:1.
11 Katha Upanishad 11.3:4.
12 Chandogya Upanishad 111.14:1.
13 Katha Upanishad 11.2:9.
14 Katha Upanishad 11:4.
15 Chandogya Upanishad 8.3:3.
16 Isha Upanishad 6:7.
17 Shvetashvatara Upanishad 6:7.
18 Shvetashvatara Upanishad 2:16, 3:11.
19 Shvetashvatara Upanishad 4:4.
20 Mundaka Upanishad 3.1:4.
21 Laws of Manu 5:45.
22 Laws of Manu 4.5.
23 Laws of Manu 10:83, 84.
24 Laws of Manu 4.32.
25 Laws of Manu 4.59.
26 Laws of Manu 4.67.
27 Laws of Manu 10.62.
28 Mahabharata13:115.
29 Swaha International, 2017. Yudhisthir and The Dog, based on K.M. Ganguli, (1883–1896) "Mahaprasthanika Parva" in The Mahabharata of Krishna-Dwaipayana Vyasa (12 Volumes). Calcutta. www.swahainternational.org/yudhisthir-and-the-dog/.
30 Bhagavad Gita 11:22.
31 Bhagavad Gita 11: 27.
32 Bhagavad Gita V:18.
33 S. Radhakrishnan, 1948. *The Bhagavad Gita*. London: George Allen and Unwin (11th impression 1976).
34 Bhagavad Gita VI: 29.
35 Bhagavad Gita X111:30.
36 Swami Vivekananda, 1896. *The Complete Works of Swami Vivekananda*, Vol. 3.Kolkata:AdvaitaAshram.
37 Sri Aurobindo, 1942. *The Life Divine*. New York: Sri Aurobindo Library.
38 Supreme Master TV, 20/09/20. Sri Aurobindo (vegetarian): Integral Yoga for Divine Awakening. https://tinyurl.com/3bk6b4wp.

39  International Vegetarian Union, 15th World Vegetarian Congress 1957. Bhagavan Sri Ramana Maharshi's Views on Food. http://www.ivu.org/congress/wvc57/souvenir/ramana.html.

40  Śrīmad-Bhāgavatam, His Divine Grace A. C. Bhaktivedanta Swami Prabhupāda, Canto Seven, Chapter 14, Text 9.

41  ISKCON Desire Tree, 12/05/16. Perception of Animals. https://iskcondesiretree.com/profiles/blogs/perception-of-animals.

42  Vanipedia, 28/05/13. Why You Should Eat Animals? www.youtube.com/watch?v=LgWA4asqKcM.

43  Bhaktivedanta Manor. https://www.krishnatemple.com/manor/cows/.

44  Sri Chinmoy Centre, u.d. Animals – from the Writings of Sri Chinmoy. https://patanga.srichinmoycentre.org/animals-writings-sri-chinmoy.

45  Professor Nanditha Krishna, April 2022. Personal communication.

46  Nibedita Priyadarshini Jena, 2018. Gandhi's perspective on non-violence and animals: Ethical theory and moral practice. *Journal of Global Ethics*, **13**:3. https://doi.org/10.1080/17449626.2018.1425216.

47  Mahatma Gandhi, 1949. *Gandhi: An Autobiography*. London: Jonathan Cape. First published 1927.

48  Mahatma Gandhi, 1949. *Gandhi: An Autobiography*. London: Jonathan Cape. First published 1927.

49  Mahatma Gandhi, 1949. *Gandhi: An Autobiography*. London: Jonathan Cape. First published 1927.

50  Laws of Manu 5:45–47.

51  Laws of Manu 10.63.

52  Bhagavad Gita X1.1:13.

53  NHSF, 09/05/2007. Why Do Hindus Worship the Cow? www.nhsf.org.uk/2007/05/why-do-hindus-worship-the-cow/.

54  Rig Veda 4:28.1:6.

55  Dairy Industries International, 09/11/21. India Is Now Top Producer and Consumer Globally. https://tinyurl.com/4p9v5saj.

56  FIAPO, 2017. Cattle-ogue: Unveiling the Truth of the Indian Dairy Industry. www.fiapo.org/fiaporg/wp-content/uploads/2017/10/National-Dairy-Report-2017.pdf.

57  Professor Nanditha Krishna, 03/05/22. Personal communication.

58  One Health Poultry Hub, u.d. India. https://www.onehealthpoultry.org/where-we-work/india/.

59  One Health Poultry Hub, u.d. India. https://www.onehealthpoultry.org/where-we-work/india/.

60  Alokparna Sengupta, 03/07/19. [Commentary] Factory Farming for Eggs Impacts India's Environment. Mongabya.com. https://tinyurl.com/4v464whu.

61  HSI, 13/05/13. Hope for Hens: India Agrees That Battery Cages Are Illegal. www.hsi.org/news-media/victory_hens_india_051413/.

62  Animal Equality, 2019. Investigation: India's Egg Industry. https://animalequality.org/news/investigation-indias-egg-industry/.

63  Katha Upanishad 11.2.9.

64  Shvetashvatara Upanishad 2:16, 3:11.

65  Shvetashvatara Upanishad 4:4.

66  *Hindustan Times*, 24/06/22. Delhi Govt Bans Use of Gestation Crates in Pig Farming. www.hindustantimes.com/cities/delhi-news/delhi-govt-bans-use-of-gestation-crates-in-pig-farming-101656008910006.html.

67  Professor Nanditha Krishna, 03/05/22. Personal communication.

68  Nanditha Krishna, 2010. *Sacred Animals of India*. London: Penguin Books.

69  Swaminathan Natarajan, 07/09/20. The Woman Trying to Save India's tortured temple elephants. BBC World Service. www.bbc.co.uk/news/world-asia-india-54026294.

70 Professor Nanditha Krishna, 03/05/22. Personal communication.
71 Swaminathan Natarajan, 07/09/20. The Woman Trying to Save India's Tortured Temple Elephants. BBC World Service. www.bbc.co.uk/news/world-asia-india-54026294.
72 CUPA/ANCF, 2009. Captive Elephants of Temples of India. www.asiannature.org/sites/default/files/13.TR-Temple%20Elephants%20of%20India_P.pdf.
73 Professor Nanditha Krishna, April 2022. Personal communication.
74 Wikipedia, u.d. Indian Elephant. https://en.wikipedia.org/wiki/Indian_elephant.
75 Bhagavad Gita V:18.
76 Convention on Biological Diversity, u.d. India. www.cbd.int/countries/profile/?country=in.
77 L. Burko, 24/06/13. India Banned Dolphin Captivity on Moral Grounds. www.vice.com/en/article/wnn3vq/india-banned-dolphin-captivity-on-moral-grounds.
78 N. Brooks, u.d. Victory! India Bans the Use of Wild Animals in Circuses. www.onegreenplanet.org/news/india-bans-wild-animals-in-circuses/.
79 Bhumi Global, u.d. Our Work. www.bhumiglobal.org/our-work.
80 Africa Hunting.com, 28/06/10. Pig Sticking in India. www.africahunting.com/threads/pig-sticking-in-india-during-the-british-rule.3142/.
81 P. Krishna, 29/06/20. Tiger Hunting in Colonial India. *Journal of Indian History and Culture*, **26**, pp29–42.
82 Tiger Universe, 2021. How Many Tigers Left in India in 2021? https://tiger-universe.com/blogs/tiger-blog/how-many-tigers-left-in-india.
83 ADDA 247, 07/01/22. List of Tiger Reserves in India. www.adda247.com/upsc-exam/list-of-tiger-reserves-in-india/.
84 Deepa Lakshmin, 22/04/20. 'The new cool': Why Adopting Street Dogs Is Gaining Popularity in India. www.nationalgeographic.co.uk/animals/2020/04/the-new-cool-why-adopting-street-dogs-is-gaining-popularity-in-india.
85 J.F. Reece and S.K. Chalwa, 2006. Control of reproduction and rabies in Jaipur, India by the sterilisation and vaccination of neighbourhood dogs. *Veterinary Record*, **159**, pp379–383.
86 Blue Cross of India, 2022. A Few Steps for Man…A Giant Leap for Animalkind. https://bluecrossofindia.org/.
87 D.K. Sadana, 05/04/21. India Needs to Look beyond Gaushalas to Address Its Stray Cattle Problem. www.downtoearth.org.in/news/wildlife-biodiversity/-india-needs-to-look-beyond-gaushalas-to-address-its-stray-cattle-problem--76189.
88 Save Indian Cows.org, u.d. What Is Goshala? https://saveindiancows.org/goshala/.
89 Save Indian Cows.org, u.d. What is Goshala? https://saveindiancows.org/goshala/.
90 April 2022. Personal communication.
91 April 2022. Personal communication.
92 Oishimaya Sen Nag, 13/01/22. India's Bishnoi Community Has Fearlessly Protected Nature for over 500 Years. www.worldatlas.com/articles/india-s-bishnoi-community-have-fearlessly-protected-nature-for-over-500-years.html.
93 Oishimaya Sen Nag, 13/01/22. India's Bishnoi Community Has Fearlessly Protected Nature for over 500 Years. www.worldatlas.com/articles/india-s-bishnoi-community-have-fearlessly-protected-nature-for-over-500-years.html.
94 BBC, 2014. The Bishnoi Religion. https://www.bbc.co.uk/programmes/p029bjmj.
95 Laws of Manu 5. 48,49.
96 Laws of Manu 5.51.
97 Mahabharata 13:115.
98 Sri Aurobindo, Letters on Yoga-IV: Food. http://aurosruti.in/cwsa/31/food#p59.
99 Vanipedia, 28/05/13. Why You Should Eat Animals? www.youtube.com/watch?v=LgWA4asqKcM.
100 Sri Chinmoy Library, 1977. Question: Why Do You Recommend Vegetarianism? Is It Related to Purity? www.srichinmoylibrary.com/gmc-38.

101  M.K. Gandhi, 20/11/31. The Moral Basis of Vegetarianism. Speech Delivered by Gandhi to the London Vegetarian Society on 20 November 1931. www.sophia-project. org/uploads/1/3/9/5/13955288/gandhi_vegetarianism.pdf.

102  Personal communication. 3/5/22.

103  Aparna Alluri, 08/04/22. Meat Ban: India Isn't Vegetarian but Who'll Tell the Right-Wing? BBC News, Delhi. www.bbc.co.uk/news/world-asia-india-61020025.

104  Oxford Centre for Hindu Studies/Bhumi Project, the Hindu American Foundation, Green Faith and Our Voices, 2015. Hindu Declaration on Climate Change. https:// hinduclimatedeclaration2015.org/english.

105  M. Landes, A. Melton and S. Edwards, June 2016. From Where the Buffalo Roam: India's Beef Exports. Archived 7 May 2017 at the Wayback Machine, United States Department of Agriculture, pp1–6.

106  Harish Damodaran, 26/06/18. The Journey of a 400 kg Buffalo. *Indian Express.* https://indianexpress.com/article/india/the-journey-of-a-400-kg-buffalo-cow-slaughter-uttar-pradesh-4644146/.

107  A. Iqbal, 10/04/17. Who Is Making Millions in India Out of Beef Export? Muslims? Think Again. Sabrang India. https://sabrangindia.in/article/who-making-millions-india-out-beef-export-muslims-think-again.

108  IBEF, 2018. Leather Exports from India: Going Strong! www.ibef.org/blogs/ leather-exports-from-india-going-strong.

109  Parliament of India, 1982. The Prevention of Cruelty to Animals Act, 1960, as amended by Central Act 26 of 1982.

110  India Legislation & Animal Welfare Oversight, 25 January 2016.

111  PETA, 24/05/14. Cosmetics Testing Ban on Animals Now Permanent. www.petaindia. com/blog/cosmetics-testing-banned-on-animals/.

112  Animal Protection Index, 2020. India. https://api.worldanimalprotection.org/country/ india.

113  S. Chinny Krishna, 2001. Animal Testing in India. *The Lancet* **357**: 9259, p885. https://doi.org/10.1016/S0140-6736(05)71818-3

114  ADI and NAVS, 2003. Animal Experimentation in India. www.navs.org.uk/ downloads/animalexperimentsinindia.pdf.

115  Professor Nanditha Krishna, 03/05/22. Personal communication.

116  Animal Welfare Board of India. About AWBI. www.awbi.in/about.html.

117  Animal Welfare Board of India. Roles/Functions. www.awbi.in/roles_functions.html.

118  Animal Protection Index, 2020. India. https://api.worldanimalprotection.org/country/ india.

119  The Prevention of Cruelty to Animals Act, 1960. www.indiacode.nic.in/bitstream/ 123456789/11237/1/the_prevention_of_cruelty_to_animals_act%2C_1960.pdf.

120  Hindu American Foundation. www.hinduamerican.org/about.

121  Professor Nanditha Krishna, 03/05/22. Personal communication.

# 5    Buddhism

## Teaching and Practice regarding Humanity's Relationship with Animals

## Introduction

Many have argued that Buddhism is not a religion at all as it does not call for belief in a God. That is true, but Buddhism absolutely fills the space in many people's spiritual lives that the theistic religions inhabit. It is sometimes described as a philosophy, a code of ethics or, simply, a way of life.

A 2020 review estimated there to be 535 million Buddhists worldwide – between 8% and 10% of the world's population.[1]

The founder of historical Buddhism is Siddhartha Gautama (c. 563–483 BCE), a prince from what is now Nepal, who became deeply disturbed on discovering the depth and spread of suffering in the world. One relevant story of the young Prince Gautama's growing realisation of the reality of suffering describes how he went into the countryside and came upon some recently ploughed land. He saw all the little creatures, the worms and the insects killed by the plough, saw the hard life of the ploughmen and the exhaustion of the oxen pulling the plough. The scriptures say that he dismounted from his horse, "and walked gently and slowly over the ground, overcome with grief. He reflected on the generation and the passing of all living things, and in his distress, he said to himself: 'How pitiful all this!'" This experience led him into deep meditation on the suffering of the world and to his departure from the palace.[2]

This story shows that the Buddha's concern was not just for other humans, but also for all creatures and for the earth itself.

He set out on a spiritual quest to find an answer to suffering and it is believed that after a prolonged meditation under a Bodhi tree (tree of awakening), he found the answer and became the Buddha (the Enlightened One). He is sometimes referred to as the Buddha Shakyamuni, or the sage from the Shakya tribe. Following his enlightenment, he gathered followers and established the Sangha or monastic order, around him. The teachings were originally disseminated in India, but in later centuries they spread more widely to southeast Asia and then to China, Japan, and Korea, and northwards to Tibet and elsewhere in the Himalayas.

Did this particular fig tree, the Bodhi tree, play a role in his enlightenment? The respected writer Amitav Ghosh says that many Buddhists regard the enlightenment as being a "trans-species encounter" and that "the Buddha himself

DOI: 10.4324/9781003292555-6

believed the tree to be essential to his attaining Enlightenment, which is why millions of Buddhists consider the Bodhi tree sacred to this day".[3]

The Buddhacarita or Acts of the Buddha, written in the 1st century, say that when Siddhartha Gautama went into a state of deep meditation: "At that moment the birds uttered no sound, and, as if in trance, they sat with their bodies all relaxed". At that time too, "All living beings rejoiced and sensed that things went well".[4] So, we see that nature and all creatures seem to have sensed that something incredible was happening – a true trans-species event.

Although the Buddha has a 6th to 5th century BCE lifetime, a series of stories about his previous lifetimes also grew up, commonly known as the Jataka Tales. Many of these stories also contain what one might term "trans-species encounters". One of these tales, said to have been told by the Buddha to his personal attendant Ananda, describes how he, then living as Prince Mahasattva, and his two brothers came across a tigress in a bamboo forest. She was weak and starving and had five cubs with her. They realised she was too weak to hunt for food for herself and her cubs. Mahasattva decided to feed her with his own body, which would be "a sublime deed". He declared, "for the weal of the world I wish to win enlightenment, incomparably wonderful. From deep compassion I now give away my body, so hard to quit, unshaken in my mind". He lay down in front of the tigress, cut his throat with a bamboo shard and allowed himself to be eaten by her.[5]

This story is important as it emphasises the quality most associated with Buddhism, compassion or loving kindness, not just for other humans, but for all sentient beings.

Some of the Jataka Tales describe the Buddha as an animal in a particular past lifetime. During each of these lifetimes, whether human or animal, he perfected an important virtue, such as loving kindness or patience. Finally, he mastered the ten paramis (perfections or moral virtues), which laid the foundation for his ultimate awakening under the Bodhi tree.

The paramis are the moral virtues of giving, morality, renunciation, discerning wisdom, energy, patience, truthfulness, determination, loving kindness and equanimity. Having mastered these, Siddhartha was ready for his complete enlightenment and realisation of Buddhahood.

## Holy Books and Schools

There are different "schools" of Buddhism, the main ones being the Mahayana (Great Vehicle), found mostly in China, Tibet, Japan and Vietnam, and the Theravada (The Way of the Elders) which prevails in Sri Lanka and southeast Asia. As with the other faiths described in this book, there are many sub-divisions within the schools. I shall not dwell on these, unless there is a specific reason to mention something relevant to attitudes or practices involving animals.

The oldest form of Buddhism appears to be the Theravada school. From this school, some of the leading Buddhist forms of practice popular in the West have sprung, such as the Vipassana tradition and the Thai Forest Tradition.

The oldest Buddhist written teachings are contained in the Pali canon (which was committed to writing in the 1st c. BCE), also called Tipitaka ("Triple Basket"), the teachings of the historical Buddha, as remembered by his monks. Pali is a Middle Indian literary language closely related to the vernaculars of the Buddha's time. The Pali canon contains the popular Dhammapada, an anthology of 423 verses, assembled by the Buddha's followers soon after his death. Dhamma can mean law, discipline, justice, virtue, truth – that which holds things together. Pada means way, path, step, foot. So, The Dhammapada is the path of virtue, or the way of truth.

In one tale the Buddha's teaching is spread by the holy Lord Avolakita, who transforms himself into a cuckoo, a Great Bird, in order to communicate with the other birds, who come to him, one by one. Talking to the parrot, Great Bird, who has meditated for a year, speaks of "this ocean of samsara" (cycle of rebirth) where he has found nothing substantial: "Down to the very last, I saw the generations die, they killed for food and drink – how pitiful!" Gradually the birds spread the teaching throughout the community of birds.[6]

One aspect which differs between the two main schools is that a Theravadan Buddhist emphasises the attainment of arhantship, the attainment of nirvana and release from the cycle of rebirth in this very life itself. Choosing a monastic life is very common within the Theravadan tradition.

A Mahayana Buddhist will also follow the teaching with a huge emphasis on the cultivation of compassion (karuna), so much so that one may strive to become a bodhisattva, one who foregoes nirvana in order to be reborn and help others to achieve enlightenment.

## The Teaching

The existence of the soul or self, which is accepted in the other major faiths, is not accepted within Buddhism. But, as the Dalai Lama has pointed out, even the Buddha himself sometimes referred to our burden of the body/mind, but at other times "the Buddha refutes any objective existence at all".[7]

Anatta or an-atman is the concept of non-self and is in contrast to the Hindu concept of Atman, the permanent soul or self which reincarnates. It is linked to the concept of anicca, impermanence – everything is constantly changing.

This impermanence is shared by every other being or part of the world, from a tiger to a tortoise to a mountain or a river or a drop of water or a blade of grass. Everything changes, all the time. Therefore, there is no permanent self. By recognising our impermanence, we can, through meditation and the cultivation of wisdom and an ethical life, finally reach the state of ultimate peace or nirvana. Meanwhile we are all caught up in the cycle of birth, death and rebirth, samsara.

This impermanence may seem hard to reconcile with the idea of rebirth. If there is no permanent self, then what is reborn? One distinguished modern Buddhist scholar, Roger Jackson (author of *Rebirth: A Guide to Mind, Karma, and Cosmos in the Buddhist World*, Shambala Publications, 2022) explains it thus:

> If you light a torch at sundown and then every hour, from that torch, you
> light another torch, and an hour later, you light another torch from that, and

at the end of 12 hours, there is a final torch, the question arises: Is the flame of that final torch the same as or different from the flame of the original torch at sundown? There's not exactly an answer to that. There are some ways in which it is the same and some ways in which it's different. So, there is continuity without stasis, I suppose, would be a way of putting it.[8]

American Buddhist teacher Jack Kornfield tells a good story about this issue: "The more solidly we grasp our identity, the more solid our problems become. Once I asked a delightful old Sri Lankan meditation master to teach me the essence of Buddhism. He just laughed and said three times, 'No self, no problem'".[9]

To simplify the teaching, Buddhists have many lists of virtues to follow in daily life. Buddhist monks have many more rules to adhere to than lay people.

The Buddha's teaching is summed up in the four Noble Truths:

1. Suffering (dukkha) is real and can be seen everywhere. We all suffer.
2. There are causes of suffering, mainly our own selfishness and our attachments.
3. These causes can be transformed and our suffering terminated.
4. The way to transform and terminate the causes of suffering is through cultivating the right path.

The last Truth is divided into a system called the Noble Eightfold Path: Right View, Right Intention, Right Speech, Right Action, Right Livelihood, Right Effort, Right Mindfulness, and Right Concentration.

The Five Precepts are the basic rules by which all Buddhists should live, both lay people and monks. The precepts are:

Refrain from taking life. Not killing any living being.

Refrain from taking what is not given. Not stealing from anyone.

Refrain from sexual misconduct

Refrain from wrong speech.

Refrain from intoxicants that cloud the mind.

Buddhism recognises five Cardinal Virtues: Faith, Vigour, Mindfulness, Concentration and Wisdom. Under Vigour the teaching says: "However numerous sentient beings are, I vow to save them", presumably meaning to help them on their path towards enlightenment.[10]

The "vow to save all beings" is something specific to East Asian Mahayana Buddhism.

The monks have many other rules, listed in the Pratimoksha, some of which demonstrate concern for animals. For example, they are not allowed to build a hut if "it involves the destruction of living beings" nor are they allowed "deliberately to deprive an animal of life".[11]

Metta is loving kindness, bringing joy to others. There is a well-known Buddhist prayer, the Karaniya Metta Sutta, part of which reads:

Even as a mother protects with her life her child, her only child,
So with a boundless heart should one cherish all living beings;
Radiating kindness over the entire world.[12]

Part of this prayer is also translated as: "May all beings everywhere be happy. May they be healthy. May they be at peace. May they be free".[13]

Many Buddhists believe that humans have abilities which animals do not have. The Dalai Lama says:

> Generally speaking, human beings are superior to animals. We are equipped with the ability to judge between right and wrong and to think in terms of the future and so on. However, one could also argue that in other respects human beings are inferior to animals. For example, animals may not have the ability to judge between right and wrong in a moral sense, and they might not have the ability to see the long-term consequences of their actions, but within the animal realm there is at least a certain sense of order. If you look at the African savannah, for example, predators prey on other animals only out of necessity when they are hungry. When they are not hungry, you can see them coexisting quite peacefully.[14]

There is a kind of anomaly to overcome in Buddhism. Animals are said to live in a lower realm and, not having human capacity for spiritual learning and practice, it is hard for them to progress to a human incarnation. Buddhist scholar Reiko Ohnuma goes so far as to write

> to be an animal in a Buddhist cosmos is to live a miserable and pathetic existence, to suffer intensely, to lack the intelligence that makes spiritual progress possible, and to die in a state of abject terror, with little hope of ever attaining a higher rebirth (let alone nirvana).[15]

Buddhism generally accepts that there are five realms of existence or destiny: hell, then the animal realm, then ghosts/human spirits, moving on to human beings and then the gods.[16] It is hard for animals to move up to the human state and probably more likely that sinful humans will descend to the animal state.

Although it seems impossible for most animals to break free of their animal state, in some forms of Mahayana Buddhism, animals are seen as capable, like humans, of possessing "Buddha nature", the ability to become an enlightened being.

Human superiority does not mean that animals cannot feel and suffer as humans do, and it is clear that they must be treated with equal respect. In many of the Jataka Tales, it is the animal (usually a bodhisattva in an earlier life) who preaches the Buddhist virtues of compassion for all beings. By putting the teaching into the mouths of animals, there may be a lesson in humility for all humans.

The Dalai Lama explains: "So all beings form a single whole, for we all have in common the same suffering and happiness, and all the parts of this whole should be treated in the same way".[17]

In Mahayana Buddhism, one aims to develop bodhicitta, a mind which aspires to attain enlightenment for the benefit of all sentient beings. The arising of bodhicitta is the first step to becoming a bodhisattva, one who aspires to attain enlightenment as a Buddha in order to help others achieve enlightenment and nirvana. Bodhisattvas may have attained some levels of realisation or insight, but not yet enlightenment, which marks the attainment of Buddhahood.

## The Role of Humanity

Buddhism embraces all beings and the natural world as part of one constantly changing whole. Yet there is no doubt that humans have a special role to play during their earthly existence. Not only can they achieve enlightenment but, by practising wisdom and compassion in their lives, they can relieve the suffering of other sentient beings. So, the purpose of one's life is not to become wealthy or famous but to be of service to all other sentient beings.

Dharma (dhamma) is both the essential nature of reality and also the teachings and practices that enable the realisation of that essential nature.[18] It is the way things are and the way of living that enables one to become enlightened. In Buddhism it has a slightly different meaning to the Hindu meaning which is more associated with the concept of duty.

Karuna or compassion means the intention to relieve the suffering of others. One doesn't just send loving feelings to other beings, who are suffering, be they human or animal, but one "takes on" their suffering. This is a big challenge for ordinary people, but it appears to be a requirement for those who are aspiring to be bodhisattvas.

In the Vajrayana tradition of Tibetan Buddhism, this taking-and-sending practice is called tonglen. Through deep meditation, one vows to awaken for the benefit of all and strive to skilfully develop one's own wisdom and compassion in order to benefit all beings everywhere.[19]

The Tibetan Buddhist monk Yongey Mingyur Rinpoche explains simply that as one strives for bodhicitta, one can "send all one's happiness to all sentient beings and absorb their suffering", in other words, tonglen. He suggests that at the end of a meditation session one can dedicate the merit one may have gained by saying this prayer:

> By this power may all beings,
> Having accumulated strength and wisdom,
> Achieve the two clear states
> That arise from strength and wisdom.[20]

This practice must be really challenging. One takes on the suffering of all sentient beings and then radiates loving kindness out to them all. For most people radiating loving kindness to all may seem feasible, but to take on the world's suffering may seem too great a challenge. Yet that is what the practice requires at its deepest level. One Lama suggests that one can breathe in the suffering as darkness and breathe out lovingkindness as the healing white light.[21]

The Dalai Lama describes tonglen as: "The practice of giving and taking" and it is by means of the visualisation of giving and taking that we practice equalising and exchanging ourselves with others. "The practice of tonglen, giving and taking, encapsulates the practices of loving kindness and compassion: the practice of giving emphasizes the practice of loving kindness, whereas the practice of taking emphasizes the practice of compassion".[22]

The Dalai Lama teaches that by meditating in this way you:

> Train your mind to cultivate the altruistic aspiration to help other sentient beings. When this arises together with the aspiration to attain full enlightenment, then you have realized bodhichitta, that is, the altruistic intention to become fully enlightened for the sake of all sentient beings.[23]

In one of his books, the Dalai Lama writes "The essence of mind training is the cultivation of bodhicitta, the altruistic mind seeking to attain the full enlightenment of a Buddha in order to most effectively benefit all sentient beings".[24]

He goes on to quote the verse written by Shantideva, a revered 8th-century Mahayana monk and teacher:

> For as long as space remains
> As long as sentient beings remain
> May I too remain
> To dispel their misery.[25]

Buddhist teacher Thích Nhất Hạnh says that compassion is an energy that empowers us. "Compassion is very mighty and powerful".[26]

He also declares in the first of his Five Mindfulness Trainings:

> Aware of the suffering caused by the destruction of life, I am committed to cultivating compassion and learning ways to protect the lives of people, animals, plants, and minerals. I am determined not to kill, not to let others kill, and not to support any act of killing in the world, in my thinking, and in my way of life.[27]

## Buddhist Teachers and Leaders

One of the most extraordinary leaders of Buddhism came from an unexpected place. King Asoka lived in India around 304–233 BCE and was king of the Mauryan Empire. He was known for engaging in bloody battles with neighbouring states. It was after one of these massacres, at the battle of Kalinga, that he seems to have had a sudden conversion to Buddhist teachings. He changed his way of life, became a peace-loving person and tried to spread Buddhist teaching, the Dhamma, far and wide.

We only know most of this as he had mighty pillars erected throughout his empire and beyond. Fragments of these pillars have been found as far away as in modern Afghanistan and scholars have been able to translate them. They tell an amazing story.

Here are some examples:

> Here (in my domain) no living beings are to be slaughtered or offered in sacrifice…Twenty-six years after my coronation various animals were declared

to be protected -- parrots, mainas, ruddy geese, wild ducks, bats, queen ants, terrapins, boneless fish, fish, tortoises, porcupines, squirrels, deer, bulls, wild asses, wild pigeons, domestic pigeons and all four-footed creatures that are neither useful nor edible. Those nanny goats, ewes and sows which are with young or giving milk to their young are protected, and so are young ones less than six months old. Cocks are not to be caponized (castrated), husks hiding living beings are not to be burnt and forests are not to be burnt either without reason or to kill creatures. One animal is not to be fed to another.[28]

So, animal sacrifice is banned, many wild creatures are protected from killing and protection is given to both mother and young offspring of farmed animals. (This is much more than such animals receive today throughout the world!) Was he the first religious leader to give protection to fishes? If the teaching on not feeding one animal to another had been followed in the 20th century, we might have been spared the horrors of bovine spongiform encephalopathy (BSE), so-called mad cow disease.

All this is set within the context of Buddhist teachings: "There is no gift like the gift of the Dhamma…And it consists of this: proper behaviour towards servants and employees, respect for mother and father, generosity to friends, companions, relations, Brahmans and ascetics, and not killing living beings".[29] Yet although Asoka clearly followed the teachings of the Buddha, he did not see that as precluding respect for the Brahmans, the priests of Hinduism.

Asoka also set up medical centres for both humans and animals and

Along roads I have had banyan trees planted so that they can give shade to animals and men…I have had wells dug, rest-houses built, and in various places, I have had watering-places made for the use of animals and men.[30]

Asoka also declared that although thousands of animals used to be killed every day in his royal kitchens, now only three are to be killed, "And in time not even these three creatures will be killed".[31]

The Dalai Lamas are believed by Tibetan Buddhists to be manifestations of Avalokiteshvara or Chenrezig, the Bodhisattva of Compassion and the patron saint of Tibet. Bodhisattvas have vowed to forego the attainment of nirvana in order to be reborn in the world to help all living beings to attain enlightenment.

The Dalai Lama describes himself as follows: "I'm a practitioner of the Buddhadharma, a follower of the Nalanda tradition, and our main practice is to focus on the welfare of all sentient beings—bodhichitta", His Holiness said.

We pray for the benefit of all sentient beings… there are limitless insects, birds, and animals, but there's little we can do to teach them. In practical terms the beings we can help are human beings because we have language and we can communicate and share our experiences.[32]

The Dalai Lama says that it is helpful to recite the following verses for generating a mind ready for enlightenment:

> With a wish to free all beings
> I shall always go for refuge
> to the Buddha, Dharma and Sangha
> until I reach full enlightenment.
> Enthused by wisdom and compassion,
> today in the Buddha's presence
> I generate the Mind for Full Awakening
> for the benefit of all sentient beings.
> As long as space endures,
> as long as sentient beings remain,
> until then, may I too remain
> and dispel the miseries of the world.[33]

Matthieu Ricard is a modern Buddhist monk originally from France but attached to the Shechen Tennyi Dargyeling Monastery in Nepal. He is a vegan and a passionate advocate for animals. In his brilliant book, "A Plea for the Animals", he concludes: "Kindness, altruistic love and compassion are qualities that do not harmonize well with bias…Applying our compassion only to certain beings, human beings in this case, makes it a lesser and a poorer thing". He goes on to declare that the world "cannot pretend to uphold decent and coherent moral values and at the same time exclude from the ethical field the majority of the sentient beings who populate the earth".[34]

Thích Nhất Hạnh (1926–2022) has been a hugely influential icon of Buddhism in the western world. His early years in Vietnam were devoted to his monastic life but also to engaging with communities. In 1966 he established the Order of Interbeing, based on the traditional Buddhist bodhisattva precepts. Because of his travel to the US and his call for peace, he was exiled from his homeland for 39 years. Finally, he settled in France and his "Plum Village" in the south of the country attracts thousands of visitors every year. In the last 20 years over 100,000 people have made a commitment to follow Thích Nhất Hạnh's modernised code of universal global ethics in their daily life, known as "The Five Mindfulness Trainings". Much of his teaching is relevant to how we relate to animals.

In his beautiful book on peace, he tells us that global and personal peace are "based on respect for life, the spirit of reverence for life. Not only do we have to respect the lives of human beings, but we have to respect the lives of animals, vegetables and minerals".[35]

Bhikkhu Bodhi is a Theravada bhikkhu (monk) and President of the Buddhist Association of America. He has also founded Buddhist Global Relief, an aid and educational organisation. He strongly urges people to have empathy with all humanity and with all sentient beings.

Speaking on Vesak Day, (which marks the birth, enlightenment, and the ultimate passing away of the Buddha) in 2021, he encouraged humans to "be a light in the darkness" by "living a life of loving kindness and compassion for all sentient beings".[36]

Buddhist environmentalist Paul Hawken takes a positive attitude: "Reverence is the process of awakening to being alive. It's the realisation that life is amazing, and every living being is our sibling".[37]

## Farming Methods

With around 93% of Thailand's population claiming to be Buddhist, in the Theravada tradition, it is interesting to see if Buddhist teaching has affected how animals are farmed there.

Farming of meat chickens is both a small business and a big business in Thailand. In 2020, the production volume of chicken meat in Thailand amounted to around 1.8 million tons, slightly increasing from the previous year.[38] This equates to over 315 million actual broiler (meat) chickens raised.[39]

In 2021, Thailand exported 900,000 tonnes of chicken products, bringing in 100 billion baht (nearly $3,000,000,000) into the country.[40] This is an important business without a doubt.

Interestingly, in 2010, the RSPCA said that Thai poultry had higher welfare living conditions than chickens reared in the UK. For example, they had more space – around 13 chickens per square metre compared with 20 per square metre in basic UK production – and were allowed to grow for longer, 42 days, compared to as little as 35 days in the UK. They were also allowed more rest; six hours of continuous darkness rather than the four they have in the UK. The birds are also of a genotype that would be marketed in the UK as "slower growing".[41]

It is good to hear of a company called Hilltribe Organics, established in 2013, where people living in the remote hill country of Thailand have been encouraged to rear organic, free-range hens and make money from selling their eggs. Most of the hen's feed is also grown by local farmers.[42] The award-winning project appears to be achieving its purpose.[43]

Some of the world's big agribusiness companies now operate in Thailand. Cargill Meats Thailand produces and exports ready-to-eat chicken to more than 19 countries around the world and is one of the largest exporters of cooked chicken products in Thailand. It employs more than 14,000 people across two locations in Korat and Sarabur.[44]

In Thailand, Cargill Meats have supply chain feed mills, hatcheries, farms and processing plants as well as a poultry health centre, R&D centre and a central food safety lab. In late 2016, they announced a $50 million expansion of their operations to meet growing demand. More recently, they have introduced Sun Valley, a premium chicken consumer brand in Thailand.[45]

Although 90% of chicken farmers in Thailand are the small-scale type, 70% of actual chicken production is from the integrated commercial farms – in other words, intensive factory farms. There are also Thai-owned companies involved in large-scale chicken production, such as Charoen Pokphand Foods. One business website proclaims: "The Thai broiler industry is aggressively industrialising and moving towards more vertical integration … It is now commonplace for medium- to large-scale companies to own feed mills". In 2018, the mills produced some 8 million tonnes of feed for broilers and laying hens, comprising 4.8 million tonnes of maize and 2.2 million tonnes of soybeans.[46]

In 2021, Prasit Boondoungprasert, Chief Executive Officer of Charoen Pokphand Foods Public Company Limited (CPF) was reported in the Bangkok Post as saying:

> We need to take everything into account, from the places animals live and their well-being to manufacturing safety and standards, as well as sustainability, energy consumption, and environmental impacts…we need technology that reduces human contact with animals, to reduce possible spread of diseases.[47]

That does sound as though the company has taken some consideration for the welfare of the animals they farm. Reducing human contact with the animals might or might not be a welfare improvement and of course it might minimise disease transfer. Could CCTV really compensate for a human inspecting the 20,000 chickens in each shed every day to ensure that none are in pain or dying?

The Food and Agriculture Organization of the United Nations (FAO) says there is a separate chicken market in Thailand, with over 50% of households keeping small flocks of Thai Indigenous Chickens (TICs). Overall, around 112 million TICs were raised in 2021. They are usually kept free range and their meat and eggs are consumed by the family or sold locally. Apparently, farmers are often very attached to their chickens and treat them almost as people elsewhere might treat their companion animals.[48]

But there is another side to the raising of these colourful Thai Indigenous Chickens: Cockfighting (see the below section on Hunting and Sport).

As with chickens, so with pigs. Many rural people in Thailand used to keep a few indigenous native pigs for home or local consumption. But since the 1960s when the first commercial pig breeds were imported from the United Kingdom and the United States, pig breeding has become intensive and commercialised.

Intensive, often barren living conditions for pigs are completely unsuited to their natural way of life, which is to live in family groups and spend most of their daylight hours exploring and finding their own food in the earth. A BASF film from 2014 shows young pigs being reared on metal flooring.[49]

It is good to hear that in 2019 Charoen Pokphand Foods announced switching to group housing for gestating sows in its pig farms, driven by the global tendency to move away from gestation crates.[50] Might Buddhist teaching also have been a factor in this decision?

Another country with a large Buddhist population is Japan, with most being followers of the Mahayana tradition in one form or other. Buddhism only reached Japan in the 6th century CE, firstly from Korea and then from China. In Japan, Buddhism and its predecessor Shinto seem to exist side by side and even sometimes share temple space! There are many schools of Buddhism in Japan, the best-known one being Zen, but many others have huge followings such as Shin Buddhism – the largest Buddhist sect in Japan – which teaches the practice and realisation of the "heart of great compassion". New Buddhist schools, usually based on the teachings of one person, are still arising in the modern era. For example, Nichiren Buddhism dates from the 13th century but one of its offshoots is the 20th-century school of Soka Gakkai which now has 12 million followers globally. Both believe in instant enlightenment and in the value of chanting. Both demonstrate the values of altruism and seeking peace in the world.[51]

So, it is interesting to see if Buddhist teachings on compassion to animals have influenced farming methods in Japan. Sadly, this seems, as yet, not to be the case.

Although the traditional Japanese diet was based on rice, vegetables (including sea-vegetables) and fish, meat became popular after the Second World War and the seven-year American occupation. But the Americans did not bring small-scale or organic-type farming with them; they brought their intensive practices.

In 2020, over 743 million broiler chickens were produced in Japan, where poultry is now considered a staple meat product in Japanese food culture.[52] Japan's stocking densities for the chickens are very high and their growth rate speedy, with the birds achieving 3 kg in weight by 50 days. Although Europe and even the US are moving towards slightly higher welfare standards for their chickens, so far this has not happened in Japan.[53]

Pig farming is also common, with around 16 million pigs being slaughtered in 2021.[54] The usual intensive methods are common, with sows kept in gestation crates, piglets removed from their mothers at 22 days old, when their natural weaning time would be at several months! In 2021 the animal rights organisation PETA carried out a filmed investigation at Nippon Ham, Japan's leading pork producer. Apart from some workers inflicting unnecessary cruelty on some pigs, the situation of all the pigs was as bad as it always is in factory farms worldwide.[55] Japan also imports breeding pigs from both the European Union and the United States.

A 2021 study into the use of antimicrobials on Japanese pig farms found that "a large proportion of antimicrobials are used for prophylactic and metaphylactic purposes", which means to prevent disease rather than for treating illness.[56]

Japan has had an Act on the promotion of Organic Agriculture since 2006 and a Japanese Agricultural Standard for Organic Livestock since 2018.[57] This is encouraging but, sadly, the area of land devoted to organic farming is still less than 0.5%.[58]

One cannot speak of agriculture in Japan without mentioning Masunobu Fukuoka (1913–2008) a Japanese farmer and philosopher, who pioneered a school of farming called 'natural farming' which incorporates a lack of trust in chemical farming. Fukuoka became well known within the global sustainable farming movement, with his book "The One-Straw Revolution" selling millions of copies in various languages. The book, first published in 1978 in the US, became such a phenomenon that in June 2009, The New York Review of Books republished the English language translation to celebrate its 30th anniversary.[59]

The Permaculture Research Institute writes of the Buddhist influences which inspired him:

> Fukuoka took nature as the inspiration for his spirituality, philosophy, and practice. Nonetheless, one of the most striking features of Fukuoka's texts is the manner in which they incorporate many Buddhist elements, particularly those derived from the Taoist-inspired Zen school. With this Zen Buddhist influence, Fukuoka beautifully articulates natural farming as a form of spiritual practice that ultimately overcomes the sense of alienation, dissatisfaction and disenchantment that are characteristic of modern life.[60]

Sometimes Fukuoka referred to his way of farming as Mahayana farming, comparing it with modern scientific (chemical) farming:

> Philosophically, however, scientific farming cannot be superior to Mahāyāna natural farming because, while scientific farming is the sum of knowledge and forces extracted from nature by the human intellect, this still amounts to finite human knowledge. No matter how one totals it up, human knowledge is but a tiny, closely circumscribed fraction of the infinitude of the natural world. In contrast to the vast, boundless, perfect knowledge and power of nature, the finite knowledge of man is always limited to small pockets of time and space. Inherently imperfect as it is, human knowledge can never be collected together to form perfect knowledge.[61]

Neither organic nor "natural" farming are prevalent in Japan, although there are many farmers rearing native chickens, who are allowed to grow to 75 days old before slaughter. In 2020, a new label for humanely, sustainably produced chicken and eggs was promised by the Japanese government.[62]

Most chicken farming for meat appears to follow the western industrial model, with thousands of fast-growing birds packed into sheds, with little concern for their needs or welfare. In 2020 the Animal Rights Center in Japan filmed one such farm and placed its film on YouTube. It does not make for pleasant viewing.[63]

Despite the global shift towards abolishing battery cages, 94% of poultry farmers in Japan continue to use them to house hens, according to a 2019 report by the International Egg Commission, cited in the Japan Times. The Japanese government has opposed moves to adopting more humane systems.[64]

Not only does Japan produce its own intensively reared chicken, but since a 2021 Trade Agreement with the UK, British intensive chicken producers can also export their products to Japan! Dr Richard Irvine, UK Deputy Chief Veterinary Officer, is quoted as saying: "This is another positive step towards strengthening the UK's trade relationship with Japan, in addition to the existing agreements which enable export of pork, beef and lamb from the UK".[65]

In Japan, the Act on Welfare and Management of Animals (1973) was amended in 2014. It states in the fundamental principle of the Act that 'no person shall destroy, injure or inflict cruelty on animals' as they are living beings. However, although farm animals are included in this law, there are no specific laws for the different species of farmed animals.[66]

It does seem that Buddhist teaching has yet to have much influence on big farming business in Japan.

## Wildlife and Biodiversity

Thailand used to be largely forested. But a combination of the teak logging trade and agricultural expansion has seen a huge amount of forest destroyed over the last century. The FAO reports that Thailand's forest cover was stripped back to a mere 28% of its former size before logging was banned in 1989. Because of this, the elephants of Thailand have lost much of their territory. Today only 3,000–4,000 elephants remain in the country, with around half living in the wild and the other half domesticated. The International Union for the Conservation of Nature (IUCN) classifies Asian elephants as endangered.[67]

Yet Thai Buddhists regard the elephant as sacred as it is said that the day before his birth, the Buddha's mother had a dream where a white elephant came to her and gave her a lotus flower. The elephant is the national symbol of Thailand too.

With elephants no longer allowed to be used for logging, they have become victims of the tourist trade, with thousands of people willing to pay money for elephant rides, trekking and shows. When not working, many of these elephants are kept chained.

The captive elephants are often replaced by captured wild elephants who may have to undergo a cruel training period, called Phajaan, or elephant crushing. Young elephants are taken from their mothers and confined to a small space, then "trained" with bullhooks and bamboo sticks spiked with nails.[68]

Animal welfare and environmental campaigners ask tourists not to ride elephants and instead to visit one of the genuine elephant sanctuaries, where rides are not allowed, such as Elephant Nature Park, founded by Sangdeaun Lek Chailert. She also looks after hundreds of street dogs, and sees that they are neutered, vaccinated and given veterinary care.[69] Other sanctuaries include Phang Nga Elephant Park and the Thai Elephant Conservation Centre (TECC) near Chiang Mai.

In spite of the dire situation of the unfortunate elephants in the tourist trade, it is good to see many efforts to help distressed animals by Thai people, such as the Wildlife Friends Foundation Thailand (WFFT), founded in 2001, The Bird Conservation Society of Thailand, founded in 1953 and The Soi Dog Foundation started in Phuket in 2003 to help the stray dogs.[70] WFFT is a partner in a regional project with EIA and Education for Nature Vietnam. The WFFT has documented the 54 facilities across Thailand that between them house over 1900 tigers. When Phuket Zoo closed in 2022 the organisation stepped in to rehouse their 11 tigers.[71]

In 2022 the BBC showed a series of films made at an elephant hospital in MaeYao National Reserve in Lampang. Founded in 1993, the hospital treats over 100 elephants a year. The films show Thai vets and assistants treating the sick elephants with real care and sensitivity.[72]

In spite of these positive examples of elephant care, Thailand has had a large trade in elephant ivory tusks, with most being traded to China. However, the

2015 Elephant Ivory Tusks Act makes trading in tusks from wild elephants illegal. Tusks from captive elephants can still be traded.[73]

With the growing global popularity of coconut milk, it is reported that, in Thailand, monkeys, in this case pig-tailed macaques, are trained to climb trees to get the coconuts and that when they are not working, they are kept caged or chained in poor conditions. Some major retailers of coconut milk have withdrawn their products after protests from consumers.[74]

One interesting development in Thailand has been the growth of Buddhist "ecology monks", who teach farmers ecological methods and work to save the forest. Sometimes their work may take them into conflict with the authorities or with exploitative businesses. They appeal to the people through Buddhist teachings on ending suffering and through rituals such as "ordaining" trees.[75] Buddhist writer Christopher Ives points out that "This practice, originating in the 1980s, immediately caused backlash from developers and government officials whose profits, power, and agendas were threatened by the practice".[76]

Japan has a worrying reputation regarding some wild animals. From September to March or April each year, dolphins may be driven into small narrow coves where they are slaughtered for meat or captured for entertainment shows. The "fishermen" go out to sea where they bang on metal poles to herd the disoriented dolphins into the coves. Once enough dolphins are in the cove the exit back to the ocean is sealed off, the youngest dolphins may be captured for sale and then the killing begins. The most notorious of these cove hunts is at Taiji.

Over 500 dolphins were slaughtered in the 2021 hunt, while over 180 were taken from the sea for use in theme parks.[77]

There are activists campaigning within Japan for an end to this practice. Ren Yabuki, Director of the Life Investigation Agency (LIA), said

> We have never seen crueller treatment of dolphins than what LIA volunteers witnessed these past six months. We documented every drive, slaughter and captive selection during the 2021/22 dolphin hunting season. This documentation will be used to help educate and share the truth about what is behind these hunts.[78]

When Ren Yabuki first witnessed the dolphin killing at Taiji, he recalled:

> What I can say is I felt sadness, despair, anger and helplessness as I was unable to stop or do anything but watch at my horror as the events unfolded in front of me. At the end of the day, I was completely exhausted and drained from what I saw at the dolphin hunt.

His Association is campaigning to ban the Taiji dolphin killing.[79]

In 2009 an award-winning documentary was made about the Taiji dolphin killing, called "The Cove". It was a revelation to many Japanese citizens. Sadly, the practice continues.[80]

It is hard to see how this kind of indiscriminate killing of these sentient, intelligent creatures can be compatible with Buddhist teaching. It is encouraging to see Japanese people campaigning to end this dolphin capture and massacre.

It is only fair to note that a similar planned slaughter of dolphins takes place annually in the Faroe Islands, where the vast majority of the islanders belong to the Faroese Evangelical Lutheran Church.[81]

Japan has a history of whaling and has, up to now not wanted any restrictions on this practice. As of 2013 Japan was still permitting whaling annually under the auspices of science. In March 2014, the United Nations International Court of Justice ruled that the whaling taking place in the Antarctic was not for scientific research and that the Japanese government should withdraw existing licences for whaling in the Antarctic and refrain from issuing new ones. The Japanese government has accepted the decision but retains its whaling programme in the North Pacific.[82]

## Hunting and Sport

The Dalai Lama refers to hunting, saying: "Sometimes we engage in actions purely out of indulgence – we kill out of a sense of "sport," say, when we go hunting or fishing. So, in a sense, one could argue that human beings have proven to be inferior to animals".[83]

In one of the Jataka Tales, the bodhisattva is a deer who gets trapped in a snare.

> Thinking that he would cut himself free, he pulled, and his skin was cut. He pulled again, and his flesh was cut. He pulled a third time, and his tendon was cut, until the snare penetrated through to the bone.[84]

This graphic description corroborates what many hunters and trappers have found when they locate the creatures they have trapped and who have fought vainly to free themselves. It is not surprising that the Dalai Lama would therefore condemn such "indulgence" on the part of humans.

In Thailand, cockfighting is the national sport. It has links to the farming of Thai Indigenous Chickens as described in the Farming Methods section above. Farmers also involved in supplying cockerels for fighting pay great attention to their genetics. Often birds who lose fights are returned to the farm to be used for breeding more chickens for meat, as they will have larger, stronger, more profitable bodies than non-fighting chickens.

Cockfighting is seen as part of traditional Thai culture, having originated in a very ancient ceremony of 'faun phi', a north-eastern tradition which honours ancestral spirits and encompasses cockfighting in a religious and symbolic context. Today cockfighting may be small-scale and local or national and involve big money. Champion birds may be sold for millions of baht (the Thai currency) and all birds have to be registered and issued with an ID card. A whole industry has risen around it; from the feed supplements and hormones used to plump the birds, to the special wicker baskets they are reared in. Bangkok has the nation's biggest cockfighting arena, holding up to 5,000 spectators. Although gambling is illegal in Thailand, the 100 or so registered cockfighting venues are exempt. Local gambling still occurs even though it is known to be unlawful.[85]

Dhanin Chearavanont, the former chairman of Charoen Pokphand Foods was a huge supporter of cockfighting, sponsoring a major arena and a cockfighting research centre.[86] He is credited with bringing in legislation in 1998 to protect the birds from serious injury or death. In Thailand, the fighting cocks have their natural leg spurs covered so they cannot cause too much damage to each other. In the Philippines, cocks have blades attached to their spurs and usually fight to the death.[87]

Cockfighting seems incompatible with the Buddhist belief in compassion for all sentient beings. It is true that the Thai fighting cocks have their natural weapons covered to prevent inflicting too much pain or injury on their opponent. However, after two or three hours of fighting, both birds will be bruised, cut and exhausted.

The Buddha said that monks and nuns should not watch animal fights because they were considered a vulgar entertainment and because they involved cruelty. For monastics and lay people, participation in blood sports would seem to be against the first Precept which requires that we have 'care, kindness and compassion to all living beings'.[88]

Apparently, cockfighting takes place illegally in Japan. Gambling is illegal also. In April 2022, Director Okuda of the Ministry of the Environment said:

> Cockfighting that is socially accepted as a traditional event may be acceptable if it does not use means or methods that exceed the required limits and cause distress to the animal. Cockfighting for the purpose of entertainment is not justified and likely falls under cruelty.[89]

It is hard to understand why just because an event is "traditional", that it is legal. Cruelty and suffering are the same whatever the purpose or historical roots of the event.

## Sacrifice

Sacrificing animals, as was common in the Vedic religion of the Buddha's era, was completely condemned by Buddhist teaching. In some of the Pali suttas (discourses), the Buddha condemns animal sacrifice, pointing out that a better way to perform sacrifice is to support the Buddhist teaching, especially the Five Moral Precepts, which of course include the ban on killing.

One of the Jataka Tales records how a brahmin prepared a goat for sacrifice. The goat laughed and then wept. The brahmin asks the goat why he laughed, and then cried. The goat replies that he had been a brahmin in a previous existence and because he himself had sacrificed a goat, as a result, he had had his own head cut off in the following 499 existences. As this is his 500th existence, he knows that it will be the last time he will be sacrificed, so he laughed. But why did he cry? The goat replies: "Just as I have endured the suffering of having my head cut off in 500 existences because I killed a single goat…this brahmin, having killed me, will likewise endure the (same) suffering…And feeling pity for you, I cried".[90]

The Buddhist rejection of animal sacrifice was a notable marker in distinguishing it from Vedic (Hindu) belief and practice at that time.

## Caring for Animals

Venerable Ajahn Sumedho, a follower of the venerable Ajahn Chah from a famous forest monastery in Thailand, has written that our society is one that likes to get rid of pests, both inward and outward ones. He writes,

> I hear monks say, 'I can't meditate because there are too many mosquitos, if only we could get rid of them.' Even though you can never really like mosquitos, you can have Metta for them, respecting their right to exist and not getting caught up in resentment at their presence.[91]

Buddhist monk Matthieu Ricard declares strongly that we need to change our attitude to animals, pointing out that "we ascribe infinite value to human life but at the same time the value of animals is almost zero... We love dogs, but we eat pigs and wear cows". He adds: "It's completely clear that animals do have emotions, they feel pain – fishes feel pain a lot". In a video talk, he points out that we behave as if "eight million other species are absolutely just for us...we use our immense power to abuse other animals...we cannot defend that ethically".[92]

In another video Ricard makes a plea to everyone: "Please make your heart big enough to include all sentient beings without exception".[93]

## Life Release

One Buddhist practice which is very common, especially in south-east Asia, is Life Release. Buddhists buy a captive bird or fish – or even an animal from a slaughterhouse – and release the animal from its cage or container. This simple act of compassion is widely seen as earning one merit. The birds fly away, the fishes are dropped into a river or into the sea. Sadly, there may be downsides to this well-meaning practice.

There are some warnings from conservationists about the danger of releasing these creatures into unsuitable environments. For example, Dr Imogen Bassett, biosecurity principal advisor for Auckland Council, has pointed out to Buddhists engaging in this practice in New Zealand that: "Animals such as turtles or koi carp that are not native to New Zealand can have a devastating impact on our native species and put an additional stress on our already fragile freshwater ecosystems".[94]

In response, the Fo Guang Shan Buddhist temple in South Auckland issued a statement clarifying that acts of releasing animals were not something propagated at the temple and urging members of society to apply wisdom when desiring to act on compassion. The statement included a quote from Fo Guang Shan Buddhist Order founder, Venerable Master Hsing Yun: "Compassion and tolerance alone are not enough. They need to be supplemented by wisdom...For instance, the common practice of freeing live animals actually causes harm to more animal lives".[95]

The whole practice raises another ethical question, which does not yet seem to have been addressed by Buddhist leaders. Is it not strange to spend money purchasing a bird in a cage, to release it and then to go home and perhaps eat a meal that includes eggs from hens who have been kept in cages? Might it not be preferable to campaign for a ban on keeping all hens and all birds in cages? In this way one would be helping to release thousands, probably millions of birds from cages. Might this be not even more meritorious?

## Eating Animals

There is an expectation among many non-Buddhists that all Buddhists must be vegetarian. After all, is this not the faith that teaches compassion for all sentient beings? But the fact is that probably the majority of practising Buddhists still eat meat, fish and other animal products.

Looking back to the Jataka Tales, there is one tale which demonstrates that humans cannot be trusted as they like to eat animals. Two oxen, who are brothers, are overworked and underfed by their farming family owners. One is envious of the family's pig which is given lots of food and sleeps under the bed. The older ox is in fact a bodhisattva (enlightened being) and explains to his brother, "Don't covet his food – that pig is eating the food of death!" It turns out that the pig is being fattened for the wedding feast of the family's daughter. As the older ox says, "In a few days, the guests will come, and then you will see them grabbing the pig by the feet, dragging him, driving him out from underneath the bed, killing him, and turning him into curry for their guests". And that is exactly what happens.[96]

In the Dhammapada, it states:

> All living things fear being beaten with clubs
> all living things fear being put to death
> put oneself in the place of the other
> let no one kill nor cause another to kill.[97]

The Dhammapada also states:

> The person who has lain down violence
> Towards sentient beings
> Who neither kills nor causes to kill,
> That one I call superior.[98]

Right Livelihood is the fifth factor of the Noble Eightfold Path. Buddhists must choose work which enables them to follow Buddhist principles. Buddhists should definitely have respect for all life. Therefore, they prefer not to take part in the trading or slaughter of animals, although some are obviously involved in the rearing of animals who will ultimately be slaughtered. You will rarely find Buddhist slaughtermen; the act is performed by Muslim or Christian workers.

Life is involved in that continual cycle of birth and death known as samsara and freedom from this cycle comes through enlightenment. Buddhists believe in karma or 'intentional action'. Taking the life of an animal unnecessarily is a bad action and this will have an effect on the quality of the next life. The outcome might be rebirth in animal form where one experiences the same kind of mistreatment.[99]

In the Vinaya rules for monastic life, there is no prohibition on eating meat.[100] The Dalai Lama describes how he had discussed this subject with a monk from Sri Lanka who said Buddhist monks are neither vegetarian nor non-vegetarian. The principle is that a monk should accept whatever food he is given. He added: "But the Vinaya clearly mentions that meat which was purposely killed for you was not to be eaten, but in general was not prohibited". He pointed out that some texts like the Lankavatara Sutra prohibited any kind of meat, including fish, etc., but some other texts do not prohibit meat, so really it is up to each person to decide.

The Lankavatara Sutra, which is an important, but later, text in Mahayana Buddhism, is said to be one of the Buddha's sermons. In it he says: "Practitioners of the Way should abstain from meat, because eating it is a source of terror for beings".[101]

In the Lankavatara Sutra, the "Blessed One" speaks to Mahamati, saying that

> the Bodhisattva, whose nature is compassion, is not to eat any meat; I will explain them: Mahāmati, in this long course of transmigration here, there is not one living being that, having assumed the form of a living being, has not been your mother, or father, or brother, or sister, or son, or daughter, or the one or the other, in various degrees of kinship; and when acquiring another form of life may live as a beast, as a domestic animal, as a bird, or as a womb-born, or as something standing in some relationship to you; [this being so] how can the Bodhisattva-Mahāsattva who desires to approach all living beings as if they were himself and to practise the Buddha-truths, eat the flesh of any living being that is of the same nature as himself?... Thus, Mahāmati, wherever there is the evolution of living beings, let people cherish the thought of kinship with them, and, thinking that all beings are [to be loved as if they were] an only child, let them refrain from eating meat.[102]

It is not quite clear if refraining from meat eating is because of samsara and the possibility that one might be eating one's ancestor or relative, or because of one's kinship with all beings. Perhaps it is both?

Unlike vegetarian Hindus, who may view meat as polluted in itself, Buddhist monk Matthieu Ricard states that in principle, Buddhists "would find nothing wrong with eating the flesh of an animal that had died from natural causes".[103] Meat is not disgusting in itself. If no intentional suffering has been inflicted on the dead animal, then (provided it is hygienic – Ed) no bad karma would result from eating it.

Regarding the Dalai Lama's personal diet, his kitchen in his base in Dharamsala is vegetarian. However, during visits outside of Dharamsala, he is not necessarily vegetarian.[104]

In a recorded message for World Animal Day in 2020, the Dalai Lama urged people around the world to move toward more compassionate and sustainable ways of living that rely less on the exploitation of animals. "It is very useful to promote vegetarianism", His Holiness said. "We should pay more attention toward developing more vegetables [in our diet]".

He lamented the extreme exploitation of animals and the growing consumption of meat from industrial-scale livestock farms in countries such as the United States, which are "environmentally very harmful", although he also noted that "in modern times, some people are really showing concern about animal rights. This is very, very encouraging".

However, His Holiness said that it would be impractical to suggest that everyone become vegetarian,

> especially in cold climate regions like northern Tibet and Mongolia, whose primary source of livelihood through generations has depended on animals… Whereas countries like India have a rich supply of vegetables and is known for vegetarianism, which should be encouraged in other parts of the world.

The Dalai Lama explained that in recent years he had been actively encouraging Buddhist monasteries and Tibetan schools to serve more vegetarian meals and added that more fruits and vegetables should be cultivated for them.[105]

At another meeting in India in 2018, he said "We are consuming too much meat". He went on to underscore the need to be sensitive to the suffering of all living beings. "However small they are, they too experience pain and pleasure", he said.[106]

Thích Nhất Hạnh has said that if we want to stop animal suffering, "we should stop eating animals". In a lovely short video, he points out that in the Sutra of the Son's flesh, the Buddha says that "we should eat in such a way to preserve compassion in our hearts, otherwise you'll be eating the flesh of our own sons and daughters". That's a strong statement and he explains it by pointing out that children are dying of hunger and malnutrition and "because the amount of grain used for feeding animals and making alcohol is huge", if we eat meat and drink alcohol "it is like we are eating their flesh and blood". He advises us to eat in ways "that can preserve compassion and preserve our beautiful planet and help beings suffer less". [107]

That is an extraordinarily wise and radical teaching. Because animal farming uses so much of the world's cereals (about 40%) and so much of the world's soya – much of which could have been used for human consumption – by eating the meat from these animals, we are, in reality, taking food from the mouths of hungry humans and eating *them*!

In a further teaching film, Thích Nhất Hạnh declares "to be vegan is not perfect, but it helps reduce the suffering of animals". He has obviously seen some films about factory farming because he says that if you watch these films "you will see the suffering of the chicken, the suffering of the cows and so on. You would not like to eat chicken, drink milk or eat cheese any more".[108]

The Dharma Voices for Animals organisation was started by Buddhists in the US but now works in Sri Lanka, Thailand and Vietnam. They aim to persuade Buddhist monasteries and institutes to adopt plant-based eating. Through their Thai colleagues, they are currently working with 3,000 monastics in Thailand where most monasteries still accept meat eating.[109]

California-based Andrew Bear, a chapter leader for the Silicon Valley Chapter of Dharma Voices for Animals since 2015 and a committed vegan, explains:

> In the Buddhist traditions of China and Vietnam, for example, vegetarianism and veganism are the norm. In other Buddhist traditions, people do consume animal "products," and may not find any contradiction. This is why Dharma Voices for Animals is so important. As the only international Buddhist animal rights organization, Dharma Voices for Animals (DVA) raises awareness of the suffering of animals in the Buddhist community.[110]

The first female Bhikkuni (nun) in Thailand, Dhammananda Bikkhuni (formerly a university philosophy teacher under the name of Dr Chatsumarn Kabilsingh), says "To eat meat supports taking life. How can I live my life depending on others' lives? That would be an injustice".[111]

Consumption of beef, pork and chicken meat is increasing in Japan.[112] However, Buddhist monks in Japan still follow a shojin-ryori totally vegan diet, which is based on tofu, soya beans and seasonal vegetables, balancing flavours and colours. Apparently, this way of eating was brought to Japan from China by the monk Dogen, who founded the Soto school of Zen Buddhism.

In 675 CE, the Japanese Emperor Tenmu issued a decree banning the consumption of beef, horse, dog, chicken, and monkey during the height of the farming season from April to September. As time went on, the practice expanded into a year-round taboo against all meat eating.

Most Japanese continued to eat their traditional diet with protein coming mainly from rice and fish. Portuguese missionaries came to China in the 16th century and their presence and a more general contact with other cultures and diets may have been behind the decision of the Emperor Meiji to begin eating meat again, in this case, beef. In 1872, a group of Japanese Buddhist monks broke into the Imperial Palace to seek an audience with the emperor to beg him to desist from this practice. In the ensuing fight with the guards, half of them were killed. The monks believed the new trend of eating meat was "destroying the soul of the Japanese people".[113]

Today the Japanese are known for eating not just fish but whale and dolphin meat, as well as chicken, pork and, increasingly, beef.[114]

## Slaughter

Buddhists do not like to work in slaughterhouses, although they may eat the flesh that comes from them. Even in predominantly Buddhist countries, most workers in slaughterhouses are not Buddhists.

Many Thais enjoy eating pork as well as chicken, and there are many pig slaughterhouses. Rules regarding pig slaughter were brought in in 2006 and state that they are based on recommendations from the World Organization for Animal Health and the FAO. The rules specifically state that pigs must be rendered completely unconscious prior to slaughtering.[115]

An article in The Guardian newspaper in 2019 reports that in many small and medium-sized pig abattoirs in Thailand, the rules are ignored. Pigs are hit with bats before being cut with the slaughter knife. Sometimes home-made electrical stunning equipment is used to subdue the pigs. This may paralyse them but will not render them unconscious.[116]

It seems strange that a country so devoted to Buddhism ignores the horrendous suffering of the pigs in its slaughterhouses. Thankfully there are animal welfare groups in Thailand such as the Thai Society for the Prevention of Cruelty to Animals (TSPCA) and the Animal Activist Alliance of Thailand. Thanks to pressure from these groups the "Prevention of Animal Cruelty and Provision of Animal Welfare Act 2014" was passed. Animal owners are meant to follow the Five Freedoms principles of animal welfare, namely freedom from hunger or thirst, from discomfort, from pain, injury or disease, from fear and distress, and have freedom to express normal behaviour.[117] One can only hope they may be able to bring about slaughterhouse reform too.

## Vivisection

Animal experimentation did not exist at the time of the Buddha and Buddhism does not have specific rules about this. Buddhists can remember the first Precept, the principle of ahimsa and the idea of Right Livelihood and use these beliefs to help them to decide what is right regarding animal experiments.

If it is considered that an animal experiment is justified and there is no alternative, then Buddhists who work out the principle of ahimsa would still expect the animals involved to be treated with kindness, be harmed as little as possible and not be killed if this can be avoided.[118]

The Animals for Scientific Purposes Act BE 2558 became law in Thailand in 2015. This Act defines procedures on the use of animals for scientific purposes to bring Thai practices in line with international animal welfare standards and requires institutions to obtain licences before carrying out experiments on live animals.[119]

Cruelty Free Soul estimates that Japan ranks third in the world (behind the United States and China) in the number of animals used in experiments.[120] The Japanese government has produced many guidance documents relating to the use of animals in scientific research, such as the Guidelines for Proper Conduct of Animal Experiments (2006), which calls for minimising stress to the animals and refers to the widely approved Three Rs principles of refinement, replacement and reduction in animal experimentation.[121] However, more detailed legislation is necessary.

## Teaching and Practice

There is no doubt that animals are included in the Buddhist concern for all "sentient beings". Scientists will continue to debate where exactly sentience begins in biological terms. For ease of understanding, I think Buddhists would agree that sentience of some kind exists in all mammals, birds, fishes and insects.

Concern for sentient beings seems to be fundamental to Buddhist meditative practices and to daily living. One should be kind to all beings; one should not kill, at least not on purpose.

It seems to me that really serious Buddhist practice goes far deeper than a general ethic of care for other creatures. If one embraces the tonglen style of meditation one has to be brave enough to accept all the suffering of sentient beings everywhere – and that is possibly an overwhelming amount of suffering. It is much easier to send feelings of loving kindness to all beings than to accept their suffering.

In the Buddhist way, compassion becomes something far greater than having a general attitude of love and kindness towards other beings. Its root lies in action, in this case the action of absorbing the suffering of others – taking their burden on to your own shoulders.

There is no way of knowing how many Buddhists practice this kind of meditation. Some may not even have heard of it. But all Buddhists will be aware that one should be kind to animals.

Is that caring demonstrated in the laws and practices of mainly Buddhist countries? From my research I would say that some lip service is paid to it – the fighting cocks in Thailand have their sharp leg spurs covered, in order to limit damage to their opponent, the huge Thai chicken producer CP Foods says it takes animal welfare into account and seems to do so to a limited extent. It is still responsible for sending umpteen chickens to their deaths daily.

How can a Buddhist reconcile commercial – or even "scientific" – whaling or the dolphin capture and slaughter in Taiji with loving kindness for all sentient beings?

What of the anomaly of "Life Release" of caged birds and the keeping of hens in battery cages?

Of course, there are countless Buddhists practising care for animals, in their own way or by helping to run or support animal sanctuaries, by educating the young or their friends about the compassionate way or by campaigning for reform.

## Conclusion

The Buddhist way is a difficult one, not least as it is so difficult for us self-centred "me" beings to accept firstly that there is no "self" as such. Buddhism says there is only movement, change and impermanence. Yet one's way of life on this earth is full of meaning and implication for "your" future. Compassion and loving kindness need to be at the core of everyday living.

Buddhists are probably no better than the followers of any of the major faiths at putting its teachings into practice, as this chapter has shown.

Perhaps Buddhist monks and leaders need to be more prominent and persistent in calling for more compassionate practices, for putting the beautiful teaching into the minds of all Buddhists. That would be a really beautiful thing!

## Notes

1 Religion Media Centre, 2021. Factsheet: Buddhism. https://religionmediacentre.org. uk/factsheets/factsheet-buddhism/.
2 From the Buddhacarita Acts of the Buddha, recorded in Buddhist Scriptures, selected and translated Edward Conze, Penguin Classics 1979, first edition 1959.
3 Amitav Ghosh, 2021. Brutes: Meditations on the Myth of the Voiceless. *Orion* magazine. https://orionmagazine.org/article/brutes/.
4 Recorded in Buddhist Scriptures, selected and translated by Edward Conze, Penguin Classics 1979, first edition 1959.
5 Recorded in Buddhist Scriptures, selected and translated Edward Conze, Penguin Classics 1979, first edition 1959.
6 Recorded in Buddhist Scriptures, selected and translated by Edward Conze, Penguin Classics 1979, first edition 1959.
7 His Holiness the Dalai Lama, 2011. *The Profound Mind, Cultivating Wisdom in Everyday Life.* London: Hodder and Stoughton.
8 Tricycle Talks, 2022. A Beginner's Guide to Rebirth with Roger Jackson. Episode #74. https://cdn.tricycle.org/wp-content/uploads/2022/06/Roger-Jackson-transcript.pdf?_ga=2.186337705.1641123013.1655563960-836498520.1633426729.
9 J. Kornfield, u.d. Identity and Selflessness in Buddhism: No Self or True Self? *Tricycle* magazine. https://tinyurl.com/48barsv5.
10 Recorded in Buddhist Scriptures, selected and translated by Edward Conze, Penguin Classics 1979, first edition 1959.
11 Recorded in Buddhist Scriptures, selected and translated by Edward Conze, Penguin Classics 1979, first edition 1959.
12 Karaniya Metta Sutta translated from the Pali by The Amaravati Sangha, 1994. https://www.accesstoinsight.org/tipitaka/kn/khp/khp.9.amar.html.
13 Yogapedia, u.d. Metta Prayer of Loving Kindness. www.yogapedia.com/definition/11141/metta-prayer-of-loving-kindness.
14 Website of His Holiness the 14th Dalai Lama of Tibet, u.d. Training the Mind: Verse 2. www.dalailama.com/teachings/training-the-mind/training-the-mind-verse-2.
15 R. Ohnuma, 2017. *Unfortunate Destiny: Animals in the Indian Buddhist Imagination.* New York: Oxford University Press.
16 I. Harris, 2006. Animals and the Buddhist Cosmos, in P. Waldau and K. Patton (Eds). *A Communion of Subjects.* New York: Columbia University Press,pp207–217.
17 T. Gyatso Dalai Lama, 1992. *A Flash of Lightning in the Dark of the Night.* Paris: Albin Michel, quoted in M. Ricard, 2016. *A Plea for the Animals.* Boulder: Shambala Publications Inc.
18 Learn Religions, 2018. What Does Buddha Dharma Mean? //www.learnreligions.com/what-is-the-buddha-dharma-449710.
19 Lama P. Drolma, 2019. *Love on Every Breath: Tonglen Meditation for Transforming Pain into Joy.* Novato, CA: New World Library.
20 Yongey Mingyur Rinpoche, 2007. *The Joy of Living.* New York,NY:Three Rivers Press.
21 Lama P. Drolma, 2019. *Love on Every Breath: Tonglen Meditation for Transforming Pain into Joy.* Novato, CA: New World Library.
22 Website of His Holiness the 14th Dalai Lama of Tibet, u.d. Training the Mind: Verse 7. www.dalailama.com/teachings/training-the-mind/training-the-mind-verse-7.
23 Website of His Holiness the 14th Dalai Lama of Tibet, u.d. Training the Mind: Verse 8. - https://www.dalailama.com/teachings/training-the-mind/training-the-mind-verse-8

24  His Holiness the Dalai Lama, 2011. *A Profound Mind: Cultivating Wisdom in Everyday Life*. London: Hodder and Stoughton.

25  Quoted in: His Holiness the Dalai Lama, 2011. *A Profound Mind: Cultivating Wisdom in Everyday Life*. London: Hodder and Stoughton.

26  Plum Village, u.d. What Can I Do When I See Animals Suffer? Thich Nhat Hanh Answers Questions. www.youtube.com/watch?v=78qgek8GJ9k.

27  T.N. Hanh, 2005. *Touching Peace: Practicing the Art of Mindful Living*. Berkeley, CA: Parallax Press.

28  King Ashoka, Fourteen Rock Edicts, Minor Rock Edicts and The Seven Pillar Edicts in The Edicts of King Ashoka; An English Rendering by Ven. S. Dhammika, 1993. Buddhist Publication Society: Sri Lanka. DharmaNet Edition, 1994. buddhanet.net/pdf_file/edicts-asoka6.pdf.

29  King Ashoka, Fourteen Rock Edicts, Minor Rock Edicts and The Seven Pillar Edicts in The Edicts of King Ashoka; An English Rendering by Ven. S. Dhammika, 1993. Buddhist Publication Society: Sri Lanka. DharmaNet Edition, 1994. buddhanet.net/pdf_file/edicts-asoka6.pdf.

30  King Ashoka, Fourteen Rock Edicts, Minor Rock Edicts and The Seven Pillar Edicts in The Edicts of King Ashoka; An English Rendering by Ven. S. Dhammika, 1993. Buddhist Publication Society: Sri Lanka. DharmaNet Edition, 1994. buddhanet.net/pdf_file/edicts-asoka6.pdf.

31  King Ashoka, Fourteen Rock Edicts, Minor Rock Edicts and The Seven Pillar Edicts in The Edicts of King Ashoka; An English Rendering by Ven. S. Dhammika, 1993. Buddhist Publication Society: Sri Lanka. DharmaNet Edition, 1994. buddhanet.net/pdf_file/edicts-asoka6.pdf.

32  C.C. Lewis, 13/08/18. Dalai Lama Advocates Global Need for a More Compassion-based Diet. www.buddhistdoor.net/news/dalai-lama-advocates-global-need-for-a-more-compassion-based-diet/.

33  Website of His Holiness the 14th Dalai Lama of Tibet, u.d. Generating the Mind for Enlightenment. www.dalailama.com/teachings/training-the-mind/generating-the-mind-for-enlightenment.

34  M. Ricard, 2016. *A Plea for the Animals*. Boulder: Shambala Publications Inc.

35  Thích Nhất Hạnh, 1992. *Peace Is Every Step: The Path of Mindfulness in Everyday Life*. New York: Bantam Books.

36  Buddhist Tzu Chi Foundation BTCF, 2021. Healing the World: Prayers and Reflections for All Sentient Beings. www.youtube.com/watch?v=1fEjSE35Ruk.

37  P. Hawken, 9/4/22. "Paul Hawken on Helping Our Planet Heal Itself". *Tricycle* magazine. https://tricycle.org/article/paul-hawken-climate-crisis/.

38  www.statista.com/statistics/922823/thailand-poultry-meat-production/.

39  www.statista.com/statistics/922823/thailand-poultry-meat-production/.

40  Thai PBS, 29/03/22. Thailand Ships Chicken Products to Saudi Arabia for the First Time since 2004. www.thaipbsworld.com/thailand-ships-chicken-products-to-saudi-arabia-for-the-first-time-since-2004/.

41  M. Hickman, 04/11/10. Thai Chicken Better than Most British Production, Says RSPCA. *The Independent*. www.independent.co.uk/climate-change/news/thai-chicken-better-than-most-british-production-says-rspca-2124580.html.

42  Hilltribe Organics. https://hilltribeorganics.com/.

43  Compassion in World Farming, Food Business, 2022. Compassion Celebrates 2022 Award Winners. www.compassioninfoodbusiness.com/our-news/2022/06/compassion-celebrates-2022-award-winners.

44  Cargill, u.d. Poultry. www.cargill.co.th/en/poultry.

45  Cargill, u.d. Poultry. www.cargill.co.th/en/poultry.

46  Ipsos Consulting, 2013. Thailand's Poultry Industry. https://tinyurl.com/2tbmp5nc#.

47  Bangkok Post, 2021. CEO of the Year 2021. www.bangkokpost.com/ceo-announcement/detail/Prasit-Boondoungprasert.

48 FAO Animal Production and Health Division, 2007. www.fao.org/ag/againfo/home/events/bangkok2007/docs/part3/3_5.pdf.

49 BASF, 2014. Pig Farmer Thailand 2014. https://www.youtube.com/watch?v=0cBRs-RmcplM.

50 Animal Protection Index, 2020. Thailand. https://api.worldanimalprotection.org/country/thailand.

51 BBC, 2013. Nichiren Buddhism. https://tinyurl.com/bddwjh8u.

52 https://www.statista.com/statistics/1121846/japan-broiler-chicken-production-number/.

53 Animal Rights Center, 2020. Exposing the Reality behind Japan's Chicken Meat Production. https://arcj.org/en/issues-en/farm-animals-en/broiler-en/pressrelease_50days/.

54 Pig333.com, 2021. How Will Japan's Swine Industry Do in 2021? www.pig333.com/latest_swine_news/provisions-for-japanese-swine-production-and-pork-imports-in-2021_17235.

55 PETA, 2021. Piglets Slammed into Concrete, Left to Die at Nippon Ham Farm in Japan. https://investigations.peta.org/nippon-ham-pig-farm-japan/.

56 K. Fujimoto, M. Kawasaki, Y. Endo, T. Yokoyama, I. Yamane, H. Yamazaki, et al., 2021. Antimicrobial use on 74 Japanese pig farms in 2019: A comparison of Japanese and European defined daily doses in the field. *PLoS ONE*, **16**:8. https://doi.org/10.1371/journal.pone.0255632.

57 Ministry of Agriculture, Forestry and Fisheries, 2019. Organic Farming. https://tinyurl.com/3syybvcy.

58 Y. Miyake and R. Kohsaka, 2020. History, ethnicity, and policy analysis of organic farming in Japan: When "nature" was detached from organic. *Journal of Ethnic Food*, **7**, 20 https://doi.org/10.1186/s42779-020-00052-6.

59 DNA, 21/008/10. Masanobu Fukuoka: The Man Who Did Nothing. www.dnaindia.com/lifestyle/report-masanobu-fukuoka-the-man-who-did-nothing-1426864.

60 T. Brown, 25/07/20. The Philosophy of Masanobu Fukuoka. www.permaculturenews.org/2020/07/25/the-philosophy-of-masanobu-fukuoka/.

61 In R. Green, u.d. Farming Satori: Zen and the Naturalist Farmer Fukuoka Masanobu. https://terebess.hu/zen/mesterek/Farming_Satori.pdf.

62 Nikkei Asia, 14/01/20. Japan's Eco-friendly Chicken and Eggs Receive New Label. https://asia.nikkei.com/Business/Agriculture/Japan-s-eco-friendly-chicken-and-eggs-receive-new-label.

63 Animal Rights Center, 2020. Exposing the Reality behind Japan's Chicken Meat Production. https://www.youtube.com/watch?v=CEjhkWW8KRo.

64 J. McCurry, 16/12/20. Cash for Cages? Japan Probes Alleged Bribery from Chicken Industry. www.theguardian.com/environment/2020/dec/16/japan-cash-cages-chickens-alleged-bribery.

65 Defra, 16/06/21. UK Secures Markets Access to Japan for Exports of Poultry Meat. www.gov.uk/government/news/uk-secures-markets-access-to-japan-for-exports-of-poultry-meat.

66 Animal Protection Index, u.d. Japan. https://api.worldanimalprotection.org/country/japan.

67 Z. Domingo, 26/01/2022. How the Elephant in Thailand Became a National Symbol. www.gviusa.com/blog/how-the-elephant-in-thailand-became-a-national-symbol/.

68 World Nomads, 2019. Why Elephant Riding Should Be Removed from Your Travel Itinerary. www.worldnomads.com/responsible-travel/make-a-difference/planet/why-elephant-riding-should-be-removed-from-your-list.

69 Challenges Abroad, u.d. Wildlife Conservation in Thailand. www.challengesabroad.com.au/blog/wildlife-conservation-in-thailand/.

70 Tourism Authority of Thailand, 2019. Thai Wildlife Conservation and Animal Care Efforts Are Working. www.tatnews.org/2019/07/thai-wildlife-conservation-and-animal-care-efforts-are-working/.

71 Environmental Investigation Agency, 2022. EIA Local Partner in Thailand Nominated for the Marsh [Charitable Trust] Awards! https://eia-international.org/what-can-you-do/supporter-stories/eia-local-partner-in-thailand-nominated-for-the-marsh-awards/.

72 BBC, 2017. Inside Thailand's Elephant Hospital. www.bbc.co.uk/news/av/world-asia-39590571, accessed 26/6/22.

73 Animal Protection Index, 2020. Thailand. https://api.worldanimalprotection.org/country/thailand.

74 R. Fobar, 19/02/21. Monkeys Still Forced to Pick Coconuts in Thailand Despite Controversy. www.nationalgeographic.com/animals/article/monkey-labor-continues-in-thailands-coconut-market.

75 S.M. Darlington, 1998. The ordination of a tree: The Buddhist ecology movement in Thailand. *Ethnology*, 37:1, pp1–15. https://doi.org/10.2307/3773845.

76 C. Ives, 2017. Buddhism: A Mixed Dharmic Bag. Debates about Buddhism and Ecology, ch. 5, in W. Jenkins, M.E. Tucker and J. Grim (Eds). *Routledge Handbook of Religion and Ecology*. London and New York: Routledge/Taylor & Francis Group.

77 D. Groves, 02/03/22. Latest Taiji Slaughter Season Ends with Many Dolphins Killed. https://uk.whales.org/2022/03/02/latest-taiji-slaughter-season-ends-with-many-dolphins-killed/.

78 Dolphin Project, 01/03/22. Taiji's Dolphin Drive Hunts End for Season. www.dolphinproject.com/blog/taijis-dolphin-drive-hunts-end-for-season/.

79 Dolphin Project, 1402/22. Japanese Activists File Lawsuit against Taiji. www.dolphinproject.com/blog/japanese-activists-file-lawsuit-against-taiji/.

80 Oceanic Preservation Society, u.d. The Little Town with a Really Big Secret. www.opsociety.org/our-work/films/the-cove/.

81 Faroese Islands.fo. Religion. https://tinyurl.com/38kf3yus.

82 Animal Protection Index, u.d. Japan. https://api.worldanimalprotection.org/country/japan.

83 Website of His Holiness the 14th Dalai Lama of Tibet, u.d. Training the Mind: Verse 2. www.dalailama.com/teachings/training-the-mind/training-the-mind-verse-2.

84 Suvannamiga Jataka, recorded by R. Ohnuma, 2017. *Unfortunate Destiny: Animals in the Indian Buddhist Imagination*. New York: Oxford University Press.

85 Samui, 27/02/17. Something to Crow About! – Cock-fighting is One of Thailand's Most Popular Activities. https://tinyurl.com/33nrdmzb.

86 Nikkei Asia, 14/04/19. Thailand's Richest Man Resigns as Chairman of CP's Core Business. https://asia.nikkei.com/Business/Companies/Thailand-s-richest-man-resigns-as-chairman-of-CP-s-core-business and Forbes.com, 17/03/03. Fowl Play. www.forbes.com/forbes/2003/0317/182.html.

87 Coconuts TV, 15.12.19. Cockfighting in Thailand, Kind or Cruel. www.facebook.com/watch/?v=561744037992539.

88 Guide To Buddhism A To Z, u.d. Bloodsports. www.buddhisma2z.com/content.php?id=473.

89 Animal Rights Center, 29.04.22. Ministry of the Environment Definition: Making Animals Fight Is Illegal. https://arcj.org/en/issues-en/entertainment-en/cockfighting-is-illegal/.

90 Recorded in R. Ohnuma, 2017. *Unfortunate Destiny: Animals in the Indian Buddhist Imagination*. New York: Oxford University Press.

91 Venerable A. Sumedho, 1983. *Cittaviveka: Teachings from the Silent Mind*. Great Gaddesden: Amaravati Publications.

92 M. Ricard, u.d. A Plea for The Animals (talk). www.youtube.com/watch?v=vLwlNOFvpzM.

93 M. Ricard, 2016. A Plea for The Animals (Short film about book, M. Ricard, 2016. *A Plea for the Animals*. Shambala Publications.) https://www.youtube.com/watch?v=Gm-4Ed2FxsI.

94 C. Lewis, 21/1/19. Environmental Expert Warns that Buddhist Practice of Life Release Could Spark Ecological Crisis. www.buddhistdoor.net/news/environmental-expert-warns-that-buddhist-practice-of-life-release-could-spark-ecological-crisis/.

95 C. Lewis, 21/1/19. Environmental Expert Warns that Buddhist Practice of Life Release Could Spark Ecological Crisis. www.buddhistdoor.net/news/environmental-expert-warns-that-buddhist-practice-of-life-release-could-spark-ecological-crisis/.

96 From the Saluka and Munika Jatakas, related in R. Ohnuma, 2017. *Unfortunate Destiny: Animals in the Indian Buddhist Imagination.* New York, NY: Oxford University Press.

97 Dahammapada from Teachings of the Buddha, Thomas Byron. https://archive.org/stream/pdfy-5xsS5pSi8sQDrKnc/The%20Dhammapada_djvu.txt.

98 The Dhammapada, Verses on the Way, 23, 405, tr. Glen Wallis, 2007. New York: The Modern Library.

99 BBC, u.d. What Does Buddhism Teach about Animal Rights? www.bbc.co.uk/bitesize/guides/zc3c7ty/revision/5.

100 Middle Length Discourses, sutta no. 55, Discourse to Jīvaka.

101 BBC, u.d. What Does Buddhism Teach about Animal Rights? www.bbc.co.uk/bitesize/guides/zc3c7ty/revision/5.

102 The Lankavatara Sutra, A Mahayana Text. Translated for the first time from the original Sanskrit by Daisetz Teitaro Suzuki, 1932. Published online 2005. http://lirs.ru/do/lanka_eng/lanka-nondiacritical.htm.

103 M. Ricard, 2016. *A Plea for the Animals.* Boulder: Shambala Publications.

104 Website of His Holiness the 14th Dalai Lama of Tibet, u.d. Routine Day. www.dalailama.com/the-dalai-lama/biography-and-daily-life/a-routine-day.

105 C.C. Lewis, 07/10/20. Dalai Lama Promotes the Compassion of Vegetarianism for World Animal Day. www.buddhistdoor.net/news/dalai-lama-promotes-the-compassion-of-vegetarianism-for-world-animal-day/.

106 C.C. Lewis, 13/08/18. Dalai Lama Advocates Global Need for a More Compassion-based Diet. www.buddhistdoor.net/news/dalai-lama-advocates-global-need-for-a-more-compassion-based-diet/.

107 Plum Village, u.d. What Can I Do When I See Animals Suffer? Thich Nhat Hanh Answers Questions. www.youtube.com/watch?v=78qgek8GJ9k.

108 Thich Nhat Hanh: Why Everyone Should be Vegan. www.youtube.com/watch?v=GDMwYC9qZ-w.

109 Dharma Voices for Animals, u.d. Thailand Project. www.dharmavoicesforanimals.org/thailand/.

110 *Pacific Roots* magazine, 26/11/19. Engaged Buddhism & Animal Rights: Interview with Andrew Bear, DVA [Dharma Voices for Animals] Chapter Leader.

111 Dharma Voices for Animals, 2018. The Venerable Dhammananda and the Importance of Not Eating Animals. www.youtube.com/watch?v=CYJxWMSqodo.

112 K. Wortley. 26/04/17. Japan's Meat Appetite Breaks Records. www.foodnavigator-asia.com/Article/2017/04/26/Japan-s-meat-appetite-breaks-records.

113 K. Allen, 26/03/19. Why Eating Meat Was Banned in Japan for Centuries. www.atlasobscura.com/articles/japan-meat-ban.

114 https://unu.edu/publications/articles/tokyo-drifts-from-seafood-to-meat-eating.html#info.

115 National Bureau of Agricultural Commodity and Food Standards. Good Manufacturing Practices for Pig Abattoir. /www.acfs.go.th/standard/download/eng/pig_abattoir.pdf.

116 K. Hodal, 11/06/19. Death by Clubbing: The Brutality of Thailand's Pig Slaughterhouses. www.theguardian.com/environment/2019/jun/11/death-by-clubbing-brutality-thailand-pig-slaughterhouses.

117 Wikipedia, u.d. Prevention of Animal Cruelty and Provision of Animal Welfare Act [Thailand]. https://en.wikipedia.org/wiki/Prevention_of_Animal_Cruelty_and_Provision_of_Animal_Welfare_Act.

118 BBC, u.d. What Does Buddhism Teach about Animal Rights? www.bbc.co.uk/bitesize/guides/zc3c7ty/revision/6.

119 Animal Protection Index, 2020. Thailand. https://api.worldanimalprotection.org/country/thailand.

120 Cruelty Free Soul, u.d. 9 Animal Testing Facts to Know about Japan. https://cruelty-freesoul.com/animal-testing-facts-japan/.

121 Animal Protection Index, 2020. Japan. https://api.worldanimalprotection.org/country/japan.

# 6 Beyond the Major World Religions

## Teaching and Practice regarding Humanity's Relationship with Animals

The Abrahamic faiths may recognise animals as creatures of God, they may call on humanity to care for animals and avoid causing them suffering, but they still place humans at the centre of creation. We can be careful stewards of animals, but it is WE who are in charge.

Hinduism and Buddhism take different and differing approaches. In the cycle of birth and rebirth, both faiths believe that an animal incarnation is lesser than a human incarnation. Many in both faiths believe that it is only possible to gain liberation, moksha, nirvana, by being born into at least one human incarnation, probably many, many human incarnations. Once again humanity is placed at the epicentre of the story.

In this chapter, I would like to give attention to some apparently different ways of viewing the human-animal relationship, as well as including some important faiths which are not usually considered under the title "The Five Major Faiths".

## Indigenous Beliefs and Practices

The United Nations tells us that Indigenous peoples represent only 5% of the world's population, but their lands cover 22% of its surface and 80% of the world's biodiversity is found within Indigenous lands.[1] These facts alone imply that the future of life on earth may rely on these peoples and their beliefs and practices.

There are thousands of Indigenous peoples, many of whom self-identify with their land and the environment in which they live and this stems from having specific cultural and ancestral ties to place. Their beliefs seem to share a very different approach to animals and to the natural world.

Whereas in the modern, scientific world of global economics we tend to see the natural world and its creatures as there for us to use, Indigenous beliefs seem to see a togetherness, a joined-up community of beings. How many worthy papers on sustainability have I read which speak of "ecosystem services", which of course the authors want us to protect. Are ecosystems only to be viewed as providing "services" for us?

DOI: 10.4324/9781003292555-7

To my surprise therefore, in July 2022, I read from a Report by the Intergovernmental Science-Policy Platform on Biodiversity and Ecosystem Services (IPBES), that:

> the authors present four general perspectives. These are: living from, with, in and as nature. Living from nature emphasizes nature's capacity to provide resources for sustaining livelihoods, needs and wants of people, such as food and material goods. Living with nature has a focus on life 'other than human' such as the intrinsic right of fish in a river to thrive independently of human needs. Living in nature refers to the importance of nature as the setting for people's sense of place and identity. Living as nature sees the natural world as a physical, mental and spiritual part of oneself.[2]

While most Indigenous peoples would of course understand that one needs to take from nature to feed oneself and survive, they would see themselves as living with nature, living in nature but perhaps most of all as living AS nature, seeing "the natural world as a physical, mental and spiritual part of oneself" (as above).

## First Nations Living in North America

In her lovely book "Braiding Sweetgrass", Robin Wall Kimmerer, member of the Citizen Potawatomi Nation, quotes from the Thanksgiving Address which is declared in schools in the Onondaga sovereign territory (situated within New York State) before the school week begins.

The Address gives greeting and thanks to all aspects of nature including animals. The children give thanks to

> all the beautiful animal life of the world, who walk about with us. They have many things to teach us as people. We are grateful that they continue to share their lives with us and hope that it always will be so. Let us put our minds together as one and send our thanks to the Animals. Now our minds are one.[3]

This is surely a lovely example of seeing oneself living "as nature".

How different life can be for these children from the fate of so many of their ancestors. Kimmerer's own grandfather was one of many children who were taken from their families and sent to schools where speaking their own language was an offence and she says that the general rule was "Kill the Indian to Save the Man".

In recent years, political controversy has plagued the Onondaga people, who form part of the Haudenosaunee Confederacy established several centuries ago. Although George Washington destroyed most of the lands and Onondaga people, their descendants live on and their claims to their land were agreed by the US Supreme Court in 2005. However, in 2010 the Federal court dismissed their claims for restitution of their lake which has been polluted by chemical companies. At that time Clan mother Audrey Shenandoah, said, "In this action we seek justice.

Justice for the waters. Justice for the four-leggeds and the wingeds, whose habitats have been taken. We seek justice, not just for ourselves, but justice for the whole of Creation".[4] This is another example of how the original inhabitants of North America view animals as of equal importance to humans.

Generally, although each group will have their own beliefs, many of the native tribes living in northern America recognised a Sky Father deity, who controlled the planets, stars and the wind and rain and an Earth Mother, who nourished her children by helping crops to grow.

Different peoples have their own stories of creation, but in the Indigenous belief systems of North America humans are not necessarily the centre of the story or they may even be regarded as the younger brothers of creation. They may learn from the animals, who preceded them and with whom they co-exist. Some peoples may see themselves as descended from a particular animal, such as a raven or a coyote, or from the soil.

Another important Indigenous woman, Jenny Leading Cloud of the White River Sioux, is recorded as saying in 1967: "Man is just another animal. The buffalo and the coyote are our brothers; the birds our cousins. Even the tiniest ant, even a louse, even the smallest flower you can find – they are all relatives".[5]

Chickasaw writer Linda Hogan, explains, "the animals are understood to be our equals. They are still our teachers. They are our helpers and healers. They have been our guardians and we have been theirs".[6]

It would seem odd to the Indigenous peoples of North America to have to lobby governments to have animals recognised as "sentient beings". They already see animals as kin, as "someones" not "somethings", as "who" and not "which" or "it".

## Hunting and Trapping

The peoples of the Plains survived primarily by hunting the buffalo (more accurately, the "bison"). Some say that the relationship with bison goes much deeper and that in Amerindian cosmologies, this meant that the bison existed for more than just providing resources. One author comments:

> They were also there to teach humans how to live. A great number of common cultural motifs amongst Great Plains societies can be traced back to watching bison interact and modelling social behaviour upon them. For example, many Amerindian nations of the Great Plains have very strict rules about treating the elderly with respect, raising young children as a community, using resources responsibly, maintaining healthy diets, staying physically active, and promoting gender equality. These ideas were all modelled on the interactions of bison within their herds.[7]

One Oglala tribal Elder, John (Fire) Lame Deer, put it thus:

> The Buffalo was part of us, his flesh and blood being absorbed by us until it became our own flesh and blood. Our clothing, our tipis, everything we

needed for life came from the buffalo's body. It was hard to say where the animals ended, and the human began.[8]

University of Montana anthropology professor S. Neyooxet Greymorning stated:

> The creation stories of where buffalo came from put them in a very spiritual place among many tribes. The buffalo crossed many different areas and functions, and it was utilized in many ways. It was used in ceremonies, as well as to make tipi covers that provide homes for people, utensils, shields, weapons, and parts were used for sewing with the sinew.[9]

Because the buffalo is one of the most sacred animals, they are regarded with respect. Many Indigenous peoples generally believed that successful hunts required certain rituals. The Omaha Tribe had to approach a herd in four stages. At each stop the chiefs and the leader of the hunt would sit down, smoke the pipe and offer prayers for success. The Pawnee performed the purifying Big Washing Ceremony before each tribal summer hunt to avoid scaring the bison.[10]

Before the introduction of horses, bison were herded into large chutes made of rocks and willow branches and trapped in a corral called a buffalo pound and then slaughtered with bows and arrows. Alternatively, the bison were stampeded over cliffs, called buffalo jumps. Both pound and jump archaeological sites are found in several places in the US and Canada. In the case of a jump, large groups of people would herd the bison for several miles, forcing them into a stampede that drove the herd over a cliff.[11]

In animal welfare terms, the fear of the chase would be frightening for the bison, but the actual death might well have been instantaneous. Bows and arrows were probably an inadequate method of achieving a quick death. So, when the westerners arrived with guns and horses, the Plains peoples adopted them too.

"The Indian was frugal in the midst of plenty," says Luther Standing Bear, a member of the Lakota tribe. "When the buffalo roamed the plains in multitudes, he slaughtered only what he could eat and these he used to the hair and bones". Indeed, for thousands of years the huge bison herds were able to accommodate the loss of the relatively few animals taken by native Americans.[12]

Kimmerer describes the ethics behind the buffalo hunting:

> The taking of another life to support your own is far more significant when you recognize the beings who are being harvested as persons, nonhuman persons vested with awareness, intelligence, spirit – and who have families waiting for them at home. Killing a who demands something different from killing an it. When you regard those nonhuman persons as kinfolk, another set of harvesting regulations extends beyond bag limits and legal seasons.[13]

She calls it the honourable harvest.

It may seem an anomaly to western minds that those who recognised the animals as beings, as persons with spirit, should then kill them on a regular basis.

But there seems to have been a realisation that for the humans to survive, some of the animals must be killed. The hunt could not be done gently – no hunt ever has been – but the victim creatures were still respected by their killers.

Black Elk, an ageing Oglala Sioux holy man, told his story to John G. Neihardt in the early 1930s and describes how he and his father went to look for deer to hunt and his father killed two of them. As they were butchering the animals Black Elk says, "I felt sorry that we had killed these animals" so he asked his father "should we not offer one of these to the wild things?"

His father takes one of the deer and cries out "Grandfather, the Great Spirit, behold me! To all the wild things that may eat this flesh, this I have offered that my people may live and the children grow up with plenty".[14]

Millions of bison once roamed the US, but they were hunted nearly to extinction in the 19th century, when Indigenous Americans were forced on to reservations, damaging their sacred bond with the land and its creatures. A wholesale slaughter of bison by the newcomers began. Some were hunted for their skins and tongues with the rest of the animals left behind to decay on the ground. After the animals rotted, their bones were collected and shipped back east in large quantities.[15]

Among the earliest waves of settlers were trappers and traders, people who made their living selling meat and hides. By the 1870s, they were shipping hundreds of thousands of buffalo hides eastward each year. More than 1.5 million were packed aboard trains and wagons in the winter of 1872–1873 alone. Some US government officials even promoted the destruction of the bison herds as a way to defeat their Native American enemies, who were resisting the takeover of their lands by white settlers. One Congressman, James Throckmorton of Texas, believed that "it would be a great step forward in the civilization of the Indians and the preservation of peace on the border if there was not a buffalo in existence".[13]

Though buffalo were being slaughtered in masses, many tribes perceived the buffalo as part of the natural world—something guaranteed to them by the Creator. In fact, for some Plains Indigenous peoples, buffalo are known as the first people.[16]

Although the bison had been hunted, they had never been hunted in numbers that would lead to their extinction. Many tribes did not grasp the concept of species extinction. Thus, when the buffalo began to disappear in great numbers, it was particularly harrowing to the tribes. As Crow Chief Plenty Coups described it: "When the buffalo went away, the hearts of my people fell to the ground, and they could not lift them up again. After this nothing happened. There was little singing anywhere".[17]

The cattle that largely replaced the buffalo often killed off native vegetation. Agricultural and residential development of the prairie is estimated to have reduced the prairie to 0.1% of its former area. The plains region has lost nearly one-third of its prime topsoil since the onset of the buffalo slaughter. Cattle are also causing water to be pillaged at rates that are depleting many aquifers of their resources. Research also suggests that the absence of native grasses leads to topsoil erosion – a main contributor of the dust bowl and black blizzards of the 1930s.[18]

Today, Native people and Nations on the Northern Plains are working to restore bison populations and protect them from threats such as commercial hunting and disease. The InterTribal Buffalo Council (ITBC) believes that reintroduction of the buffalo to tribal lands can help to heal the spirit of the peoples and protect the traditional relationships between the people and the buffalo. The ITBC includes 58 tribes from 19 states and a collective herd of over 15,000 buffalo.[19]

The Rosebud Sioux Nation in South Dakota have begun collecting bison on the Wolakota Buffalo Range. They hope to reach 1,200 buffalo by 2023 – they want it to be the largest Indigenous-owned bison herd in the country. Clay Co-lombe, CEO of the Rosebud Tribe's economic development agency, said: "Buffalo are central to who we are as Lakota. When we bring them back on to our land and into our lives, it heals and strengthens us". The meat from the first animal slaughtered by Wolakota was given to homeless members of the Rosebud Sioux reservation community.[20]

US Indigenous leaders hope Congress will help tribes return bison to their lands: the Indian Buffalo Management Act was passed by the House of Representatives in December 2021 and is, at the time of writing, awaiting Senate approval.[21]

It is unlikely that these buffalo will be hunted. Will they in fact have to endure frightening animal transport to slaughterhouses, like the cattle who for so many years replaced them on the land?

One spokesperson said:

> We're trying to strike a balance of letting the buffalo express their natural behaviors, making sure they have plenty of room to roam, and being able to manage where they're grazing so we can make sure we're still improving the range health and habitat quality for other wildlife.[22]

As with the buffalo hunting, so with the fishing for salmon. Kimmerer describes how the coastal peoples would await the annual return of the salmon to their birth rivers. Once the salmon were seen to be swimming in great numbers upstream, the people would wait for four days before they began to fish. The First Salmon was fished by the most revered person and once the salmon had been feasted on, the head and bones were replaced in the water, facing upstream, so that the spirit could follow the other salmon.[4] The honourable harvest principle still applied. That principle has now been violated by modern fishing methods, damming of the rivers and industrial fish farms, where these migratory beings are kept caged until slaughter.

## Dietary Principles

Many Indigenous peoples of North America did not live close to the bison plains. They may never have seen a bison in their lives. For the Potawatomi peoples and others in the more eastern parts of the land their staple foods were what Kim-merer calls the Three Sisters of beans, corn and squash.[23] These crops have a mythical origin, having been presented to the ancestors by three strange women (the sisters) at a time of hunger.

The three crops worked well in a kind of symbiosis. Corn draws nitrogen from the soil, while beans replenish it. Corn stalks provide climbing poles for the bean tendrils, and the broad leaves of squashes grow low to the ground, shading the soil, keeping it moist, and deterring the growth of weeds.[24]

Rita (Hina Hanta or "Bright Path of Peace") Laws, who is of Choctaw and Cherokee descent, says the Choctaw people believed that corn was a gift from Hashtali, the Great Spirit. (Hashtali is literally "Noon Day Sun". Choctaws believe the Great Spirit resides within the sun, for it is the sun that allows the corn to grow.) Their traditional homes were constructed not of skins, but of wood, mud, bark and cane. The principal food, eaten daily from earthen pots, was a vegetarian stew containing corn, pumpkin and beans. The bread was made from corn and acorns.[25]

Laws recounts that a Cherokee legend describes humans, plants, and animals as having lived in the beginning in "equality and mutual helpfulness". The needs of all were met without killing one another. When man became aggressive and ate some of the animals, the animals invented diseases to keep the human population in check. The plants remained friendly, however, and offered themselves not only as food to man, but also as medicine, to combat the new diseases.[26]

In the mid-19th century, under the Indian Removal Act, the Choctaws and other tribes were forcibly moved from the Mississippi and other fertile regions to what became the state of Oklahoma, on the disastrous "Trail of Tears". Thousands died on the long journey. The survivors settled and continued to farm and eat from the land, with the government supplying rations of new (often unhealthy) foods. However, even these allocated lands were absorbed into the new state of Oklahoma in 1907.[27] Laws says that many of the Choctaw foods cooked at celebrations even today are vegetarian.[28]

However, many descendants of these survivors have been drawn into eating processed foods and their health has deteriorated as a result. Amanda Fretts, Ph.D., M.P.H., an epidemiologist at the University of Washington and a member of Mi'kmaq tribe, points to rates of heart disease doubling in these communities, saying: "Several studies have shown that unhealthy, non-traditional foods like canned meats and fast-food, are a large part of the problem. Many of these processed foods contribute to diabetes, which is a risk factor for heart disease".[29]

In both cases, the loss of the buffalo by the plains people and the loss of their traditional growing fields by the Choctaws, Cherokees and others, have broken the bonds between the people, their environment and their fellow creatures and fellow plants. It seems that there was a deliberate attempt to "break their spirit". In this volume, there is not space to delve deeper into this history, but it is good to see the descendants of these peoples making strong efforts to restore the equilibrium and relationship they used to enjoy with the land and with the other beings who shared it with them, perhaps truly "living as nature".

# The First Nations Peoples living in Australia

## Introduction

Like many other people, I have heard the terms "Indigenous peoples" and "Aboriginal people" used to describe the First Nations Peoples who have lived in the land we now call Australia for many thousands of years, probably for over 60,000 years. I shall use the term First Nations People(s) in this chapter, using the word "Aboriginal" only as an adjective, for ease of reading. With around 250 distinct groupings, beliefs between each First Nations group may vary.

Even though no official figures exist, estimates of the Aboriginal population in 1788, when white people first claimed part of Australia, range between 250,000 and 750,000. By 1911, the number was 31,000.[30]

Numbers have since been recovering to about half that original number, but only in 1967 did Australians vote that federal laws also would apply to First Nations Peoples and most did not have full voting and citizenship rights until 1967.[31]

The appalling treatment of the First Nations Peoples is well documented and makes shocking reading. Thousands were massacred, others had the land they lived on taken away and, as with some First Nations Peoples in America, children were sometimes taken away from families and sent to (often abusive) schools for cultural "re-education", where girls were groomed to become domestic servants and boys often trained to work as stockmen for white farmers. In all cases, they worked for very low or no wages at all. Their lives were in effect, "stolen".

First Nations Peoples have only been included in the National Census since 1971. In 1996 the National Census recorded that 352,970 or 1.97% of the population were of Aboriginal and Torres Strait Islander (Melanesian) descent.[32]

It was not until 2008 that the then Australian Prime Minister, Kevin Rudd, issued a national apology for the country's actions toward Aboriginal Australians of the Stolen Generations.[33]

## Beliefs about Animals

The Dreaming (formerly often called the Dreamtime) is not a historical concept for First Nations Peoples. It encompasses the past, present, and future; it is non-linear.

The Dreaming includes many stories of the Ancestral Beings, who created everything – animals, plants, rocks, and land formations – as they moved through the land, often in human form. They also created a system of relationships between the individual, the land, animals, and other people.[34]

The Ancestral Beings were not models of sanctity like gods or saints. Many behaved badly and faced the consequences. So, their stories are in many ways morality tales too. Many First Nations Peoples believe in and live by the stories and teachings of the Dreaming today, maintaining a deep interconnectedness with all aspects of their particular Country and its Dreaming. Law is also integral to the Dreaming and the rules by which the various nations lived.

The Dreaming stories often include animals. Koalas feature in many of these stories. One common theme is the association of koalas with drought, perhaps because they can survive on very little water. Some believe that koalas have power over the rain, and it is when people behave badly that the koalas send drought. One Dreaming story tells of the origin of koalas when a boy, Koobor, who was neglected by his family, learned to live on the leaves of the gum tree.[35]

First Nations People usually have totems, which are often totem animals. They feel close to this animal and responsible for its wellbeing. So, if someone has a koala totem, they would try to protect koalas; if they have a kangaroo totem, they would try to protect kangaroos for future generations. Although other people might hunt and eat koalas, they might not join in. Having a particular totem may prescribe a responsibility to learn particular songs, dances and stories.

Another important belief is about Country. This does not mean just the countryside. Country includes the physical land, its hills and valleys and rock formations, but it is much more than that. Country includes one's relationships with other beings, human and animal, and with the Ancestors and with the earth too.

If any aspect of Country is under attack, a First Nations person will feel under attack themselves. This is a relationship with one's environment which is incredibly close and one that may be hard to understand for a westernised urban dweller.

One respected First Nations website, Common Ground, explains: "Each First Nations individual has a unique and spiritual relationship with animals on their Country and holds storylines that ensure they live sustainably with the environment". The site quotes Worimi Elder, Uncle Steve Brereton, "Healing Country is healing us. We are Country and Country is us. We are all one".[36]

Sissy Pettit, Deputy Chairperson of the Victorian Aboriginal Heritage Council, explains the huge sadness that is felt when one's totem animal dies:

> When our totem dies, our connection with the spirit is compromised. The spirit and totem are as one and once our totem dies, a bit of our spirit dies as well. We feel the whole of Country in ourselves and its loss is felt in our whole spirit, not just the body that carries the spirit.[37]

Palyku woman, Ambelin Kwaymullina, explains the relationship to Country:

> For Aboriginal peoples, Country is much more than a place. Rock, tree, river, hill, animal, human – all were formed of the same substance by the Ancestors who continue to live in land, water, sky. Country is filled with relations speaking language and following Law, no matter whether the shape of that relation is human, rock, crow, wattle. Country is loved, needed, and cared for, and Country loves, needs, and cares for her peoples in turn. Country is family, culture, identity. Country is self.[38]

This kind of understanding and relationship with the natural world, with Country, is both "Living in Nature" and "Living as Nature" as mentioned previously.[39]

These First Nations Peoples believe that to keep the land alive and well, they must sing to it. They can navigate the landscape from place to place by singing songs about the sacred landmarks that traverse it. The tradition of singing songs as a map or guide is known as Songlines.[40]

The Songlines represent the journey that the Ancestors (some of whom were animals) took through the land. This again is a different way of "seeing" one's environment, as all the significance in that landscape comes from what the Ancestors did and then handed down to the people through the Songline ceremonies.[41] Songlines connect people to the earth. Songlines may include information about animal behaviour or about a particular place or the best plant medicine for an ailment.

In an interesting article in the Guardian, Paul Daley, who spent much time in Australia, interpreted Songlines thus:

> At the most basic conceptual level, perhaps think of the Songlines as the oral archives of Indigenous history that chart the very creation of the land and sea by the Dreaming totems (animals), and the various marks – trees, waterholes, rocky outcrops and creatures – along them. The Songlines also hold the stories of the people and the eternal spirits who inhabit them. Because melodic variance is used to describe the land, the Songlines – which also manifest in artworks, dance, the yirdaki (special didgeridoos – Ed) and clapsticks – transcend language. The Songlines or tracks transcend the language groups. If you know the song, you can navigate.[42]

## Hunting and Food

The First Nations Peoples believe in taking from the earth only what they need. In this way the earth, its creatures and plants can continue to flourish. As the Common Ground writers explain: "Each First Nations individual has a unique and spiritual relationship with animals on their Country and holds storylines that ensure they live sustainably with the environment".[43]

One Aboriginal elder, Tom Dystra, explained: "We cultivated our land, but in a way different from the white man. We endeavour to live with the land; they seemed to live off it".[44]

Traditionally, First Nations Peoples managed the land, often using fire, and cultivated a wide range of plant foods like yams and spinach and many seasonal fruits like bush bananas and tomatoes. They also ate the large moth larvae, known as witchetty grubs, and hunted animals such as kangaroos, wild turkeys, possums, emus, lizards and snakes. The animals were hunted using tools like small daggers and spears made from sharpened stone.[45] Fish traps were built on rivers and coastal communities ate fish and shellfish and some seabirds.[46]

This kind of hunting comes into the subsistence category and cannot be compared to so-called "sport" hunting of foxes, hares and deer in western countries, nor to the so-called "trophy hunting" of westerners who pose happily beside the lions, elephants or giraffes they have killed. Subsistence fishing bears no relation to today's huge commercial fishing operations and large-scale fish farms.

While the actual death of these animals may have been, on occasion, prolonged and painful, the creatures themselves enjoyed their natural lives until that point, unlike the billions of animals kept confined and cramped for most of their lives in industrial farms across the globe today.

Today there are several state and national laws in Australia, which allow continued hunting of traditional species by First Nations Peoples, such as the Native Title Act of 1993. However, in 2012 the state of Queensland withdrew its exemption for Indigenous hunting from its animal welfare legislation.[47]

The First Nations Peoples of Australia have this extraordinary feeling of oneness with their environment and all its beings, human and animal. This feeling of living on Country, being an intrinsic part of Country, feeling connected to the land through a multitude of cultural practices such as Songlines, is an experiential state which is missing in modern societies. Perhaps we are the poorer for it.

# Jainism

## Introduction

Jainism arose in northern India at around the same time as Buddhism. Both rejected the animal sacrifice of the earlier Vedas and both influenced Hinduism. Jains believe that their faith began many thousands of years ago, and that it has had 24 Tirthankaras or enlightened teachers, the last of whom was Vardhamana, known as Mahavira, (the "Great Hero"), who lived around 500 BCE. A Tirthankara is literally a "ford-maker" – in this case one who creates a fordable passage through the cycle of endless rebirths (samsara) to kevala or liberation.

A story is told of how, in a previous life, Mahavira had been born as a lion. Two monks taught him about non-violence and not killing others, whereupon the lion stopped eating meat and starved to death only to be reborn in heaven and eventually becoming Mahavira.[48]

This story reflects the outstanding principle of Jain teaching: ahimsa, non-violence towards all beings. Of all the faiths considered in this book, the Jain code of behaviour towards all kinds of animals is the strictest, the most uncompromising.

That respected Jain, Satish Kumar, recounts a well-known story of the life of the 23rd Tirthankara, Parshwanath, who was born a prince. On the way to his wedding to a princess, Parshwanath saw many animals cooped up outside her palace and to his horror found that they were being kept to be slaughtered for his wedding feast.

He told his future father-in-law:

> Animals have souls, they have consciousness, they are our kith and kin, they are our ancestors. They wish to live as much as we do; they have feelings and emotions…Their right to live is as fundamental as our own. I cannot marry, I cannot love and I cannot enjoy life if animals are enslaved and killed.

Whereupon he left, became a monk and devoted his life to informing everyone that they must be compassionate to animals. He made such an impression that his bride-to-be also renounced her comfortable life, became a nun and devoted herself to animal welfare and her father ordered that there would be no hunting, no shooting, no caging and no pets in his lands.[49]

Those few individuals who have achieved kevala or enlightenment are called Jina (literally, "Conqueror"), and the monastic and lay adherents are called Jains ("Follower of the Conquerors"), or Jaina.[50]

Today, most followers of Jainism live in India, with estimates of upwards of 4 million adherents.[51] Jains have travelled throughout the world and there are substantial communities of Jains in North America, the UK and other countries, some settling in these "western" nations as a result of forcible expulsion from Uganda or political unrest in other east African countries in the late 20th century.

## Teaching and Holy Books

There are no Gods in Jainism. Jains revere all 24 of the Tirthankaras. Mahavira's predecessors are all venerated and are the source of authority within Jainism. Their existence lays emphasis on the idea of lineage and continuity.[52]

Jains believe that all living things, even the tiniest insects, plants and aspects of nature such as water, have a jiva or soul. Jains believe in reincarnation, with the soul having a better or worse rebirth as a result of karma. The destiny of the soul is kevala, full enlightenment. Then one can achieve moksha, liberation from samsara, which can only be achieved through getting rid of one's karma. Harming living beings creates bad karma, sometimes described as like dust settling on one's karma. The best birth is to be born a human, as only a human birth allows the possibility of achieving liberation.

Souls are believed to be a unique substance in the universe, taking different living forms in the cycle of birth, death, and rebirth. This cycle has been going on forever as the universe has no beginning or end; it has always been and always will be.[53]

In a similar way to the Buddha, Mahavira, who was born into the kshatriya or warrior caste, left his home and lived for many years as an ascetic until he became enlightened. He came to the conclusion that there are three essential elements which bring true liberation of the soul. He called them ahimsa (non-violence), sanyama (simplicity) and tapas (the practice of austerity).[54]

Ahimsa is the most fundamental principle of Jainism. No living being has the right to injure or kill any other living being. There are four forms of existence in Jainism – gods humans, hell beings, and animals and plants. This last group is further divided into beings having a different number of senses. The general laity should avoid harming organisms with two or more senses while monks/renunciants are supposed to refrain from harming any living beings at all, which would include plants.[55]

Sanyama is the second principle and calls for simple living, self-restraint and frugality. This is in direct contrast to today's consumerist culture of having more and more "stuff" and more and more "experiences", forever acquiring.

Tapas, the spiritual practice of purification, austerity, self-sacrifice and fasting is the third important Jain principle. It refers not only to purifying the physical body but also purifying the soul by practices like fasting, meditation, restraint, pilgrimage and service to others.

There are four practices to which every Jain aspires, in order to attain inner liberation. The first is satya (truth), which means understanding and realising the true nature of existence. The others include non-stealing, which means refraining from acquiring goods or services beyond one's essential needs and non-possessiveness, such as not accumulating stuff or displaying wealth. Jains should also follow bramacharya. For monks, bramacharya means total abstinence from sexual activity and for lay people it means fidelity in marriage.[56]

The greatest good a Jain can do is give someone protection from fear of death. It is called Abhaydaan. This is translated into avoiding harm to the smallest form of life to the biggest.[57]

There are two main divisions within Jainism and these emerged quite early on in its history: the Swetambar (white-clad) sect and the Digambar (sky-clad) sect. The Digambar monks favour not wearing clothes – as even these are possessions. In their temples, the holy figures are depicted as nude. Both sects have further subdivisions. Whereas the Swetambars believe that Mali, the 19th Tirthanka, was a woman and that other women are capable of achieving kevala, the Digambars disagree and do not believe that one can attain enlightenment until one has a male human incarnation.

The Sacred Books of Jainism are collectively known as Agam literature. It consists of Lord Mahavir's teachings that were compiled by his disciples.

The Agam Sutras show great reverence for all forms of life and contain strict codes of vegetarianism, asceticism, non-violence, and opposition to war. The existing Agam Sutras are accepted as the authentic preaching of Lord Mahavira by the Swetambar sects, but the Digambar sect does not accept them as authentic. Digambars follow two other main texts written by great Acharyas (scholars) from 100 to 800 CE.[58]

The Acaranga sutra says: "All breathing, existing, living, sentient creatures should not be slain, nor treated with violence, nor abused, nor tormented, nor driven away. This is the pure, unchangeable, eternal law, which the enlightened ones who know have proclaimed…".[59]

Not only do Jains respect the contents of sacred texts. They also venerate them as holy objects in themselves. Both Śvetāmbaras and Digambaras have a festival in honour of scriptural knowledge which is the occasion to clean and restore manuscripts or books and to worship them as embodiments of knowledge.[60]

## Jains and Diet

Jains follow a restricted vegetarian diet. They avoid all meat, fish and eggs, but they also avoid eating vegetables that grow under the soil because insects and worms would be harmed or even destroyed as these vegetables were harvested. Each of these little, possibly microscopic beings has its own jiva (soul) and must not be harmed. Each carrot or potato would also be killed by being uprooted. So, potatoes, carrots, garlic, onions and other root vegetables and tubers are avoided. Onions and garlic also come under the 'tamasic' category which means they have the quality of darkness.[61]

Jains are lacto-vegetarians as they do consume dairy products. They do not usually consume yoghurt or any food which has been kept overnight, as in both cases, microorganisms may have developed.

In 2021, the Pew Research Center published its research on diet in the Jain community. Roughly nine in ten Indian Jains (92%) identify as vegetarian, and two-thirds of Jains (67%) abstain from root vegetables. More than eight-in-ten Jain vegetarians also say they would not eat food in the home of a friend or neighbour who was non-vegetarian (84%) or in a restaurant that served non-vegetarian food (91%).[62]

Jains do not worship the cow as sacred, as many Hindus do. The cow is regarded as a being with all five senses and must be treated with gentle care. In the past, in India, it was easy for Jains to get milk from cows living locally and who were allowed to rear their calves. Modern, urban life and the intensification of the dairy industry have made this harder to achieve. There are movements among Jains to support a move towards a vegan diet, using plant-based milk instead of milk from cows. For example, there is an international Jain Vegans e-group, in the UK, there is the Jain Vegans Working Group (JVWG), and in the US, there is a vegan Jain awareness-raising group called "The JAINA Eco-Vegan Committee of Jaina", as well as an informative blog site called "veganjains.com".[63]

## Looking after Animals

The Jain concept of jiv-daya – jiv meaning life and daya meaning compassion – runs parallel to ahimsa. It is the desire to alleviate the suffering of others, and it is also an established form of charity. In every Jain temple and at many pilgrimage sites, there are a variety of donation boxes, each designated for a specific purpose. One of these is always marked "jiv-daya".

This compassion may extend to many "human" causes such as care of orphans or widows, but some often goes to taking care of animals. There are an estimated 3,000 animal sanctuaries, called pinjrapoles, in India, the majority associated with the Jains. Most are in Gujarat, the state in northwestern India with the highest population of Jains, who provide the necessary funds and impetus to establish and maintain them.[64]

There are also homes for unwanted cows, called gaushalas (gau means cow and shala is a place of protection). Both Jains and Hindus may set up these cow sanctuaries and sometimes co-operate in their management.

Animal welfare-minded veterinary surgeons and some western campaigners criticise these cow sanctuaries, as sick and dying animals are not euthanised.[65] Hindus will not allow the sacred cow to be killed.

Jains will not allow the taking of life, and although a sick animal will be cared for, he or she will not be killed, humanely or otherwise. Outsiders see an animal suffering unnecessarily; a Jain believes that it is the karma of that animal to die in their own time. Meanwhile the animal will be looked after and kept as comfortable as possible, as that is showing compassion.

Jain monks and some committed lay Jains used not to brush their teeth because they would harm the microorganisms living in the mouth. Unfortunately, this has had a bad effect on their dental health.[66] Nowadays modern Jains do brush their teeth. [67]

For the same reasons, Jain monks and nuns can be seen walking down the streets in towns in India, wearing their white robes, covering their noses and mouths with white face masks, to avoid breathing in airborne insects, and sweeping the ground in front of them as they go to avoid stepping on any little creatures on the road ahead. If possible, Jain monks do not use any form of transport. They only walk from town to town as part of their belief in ecology and not using animals as a form of transport. The Jain laity or householders have a duty to provide food and look after the needs of the monks and nuns.

It may come as a surprise then to find that the Jain community is well represented in India's pharmaceutical industry, with many companies under Jain ownership. How the company owners can reconcile the inevitable animal experimentation involved in the pharmaceutical industry with their Jain beliefs, is a question for them to reflect on.

Some Jains living in the UK are also involved in this industry. In a debate in the Westminster Parliament on 1 May 2019, Gareth Thomas MP, Chair of the All-Party Parliamentary Group for Jains, drew attention to one such:

> An important example is Sigma Pharmaceuticals... It is the largest independent pharmaceutical wholesaler in the UK and was a national champion in the European Business Awards back in 2017. It is a family-run company with Jain principles at its heart, and for almost 40 years it has served independent pharmacies, dispensing to doctors and hospitals across the UK.[68]

In general, Jains seem to have prospered and they value education highly. In India, roughly a third (34%) of Jain adults have at least a college degree, compared with 9% of the general public, according to India's 2011 census.[69]

## Conclusion

The Jain belief and practice of ahimsa, non-violence, and its commitment to compassionate action, jiv-daya, is exemplary. Historically, these Jain beliefs have been an influence on many Hindus and may have helped the Hindus move towards abandoning animal sacrifice and adopting vegetarianism.[70]

The great leader Mahatma Gandhi, a Hindu himself, admitted his admiration for Jainism and he always attempted to put ahimsa into action in his personal and political life.[71]

Nitin Mehta, a committed Jain, explains another important concept in Jainism:

> To put this concept of Ahimsa or non-violence into practice, Jainism advocates an idea called Anekantwad. It means that truth can be arrived at from different angles. In practice this means that you respect another way of looking at things. Different religions and ideologies are different ways of looking at things and there is no need to fight over that. If we look at history, we see that tens of millions of people have been killed by people claiming their religion is the only right one and that the others should not exist. Tens of millions of people have died in the name of Communism, Capitalism and

in the name of a superior race looking down on those who are perceived to be inferior. All this would have been avoided if the Jain idea of accommodating differences had been practiced.[72]

One Jain scholar, Hampa Nagarajaiah, is quoted in "The Hindu" newspaper: "The contribution of Jainism to the overall glory of Indian culture, art and architecture, sculpture and literature is enormous. The Jain community has always been in the mainstream strengthening the Indian culture".[73]

In the state of Gujarat in a place called Palitana there are 700 Jain temples on the hills of Shatrunjaya. Pilgrims have to climb 3,700 steps, preferably without taking any food or water. The intricate workmanship on the temple walls is fascinating.[74]

Apart from such wonders, at the everyday level, the Jain diet displays extraordinary concern for living beings.

From the outside, looking in, it does seem to be an anomaly that most Jains continue to drink cow's milk. Today's dairy industry is ruthless in its exploitation of the cow for maximum yield and profit, and insensitive to the needs of cow and calf after the calf is born. It is good to know that increasing numbers of Jains are moving towards a vegan, non-dairy diet.

While Jainism requires a Jain to have a non-violent lifestyle, it is a further anomaly to see so many Jain-owned and managed pharmaceutical companies. Safety-testing of most pharmaceuticals still requires animal-testing, although more and more alternatives are being developed. It would be good to see Jains in the pharmaceutical industry leading the way towards adopting non-animal alternatives.

# Sikhism

## Introduction

Guru Nanak (1469–1539), the founder of the Sikh faith, grew up in a Hindu family in India at a time when relations between Hindus and Muslims were antagonistic. He underwent a deep spiritual experience, as so many religious founders have done, and came to the conclusion that there is no Hindu, no Muslim. He declared that we are all children of the one God, often named "Waheguru" or the "wondrous enlightener". So, Sikhism is a monotheistic faith. Guru Nanak rejected the caste system of Hinduism and declared all humans equal. He also recognised women as equal to men.

Nine Gurus followed Nanak and developed the Sikh faith and community over the next centuries. Two of these gurus were executed by the Mughal rulers of India. The last Guru was Guru Gobind Singh (1666–1708), who continued to militarise the Sikh community in order that it could defend itself from attacks which came sometimes from invaders who came from what is now Afghanistan. Horses became a vital part of the fighting force.

Before he died, Guru Gobind Singh said there would be no more human gurus, but that the Sikh holy book, the Guru Granth Sahib (GGS), would be the Eternal Guru. Every Sikh gurdwara (temple) has a copy which is kept on a raised platform under a canopy, out of respect. The Guru Granth Sahib consists of 5,894 verses in which the works of the gurus are preserved, as well as works from some Muslim Sufis and Hindu saints.

There are an estimated 25–30 million Sikhs in the world. The vast majority live in India, centred on the Punjab area, but there are significant Sikh communities in other countries from the UK to Canada, the USA and Australia. The city of Amritsar in Punjab is home to the prestigious Golden Temple (Sri Harmandir Sahib), of the Sikhs, where the Guru Granth Sahib is recited every day.

Guru Nanak said religion should be based on selfless service and meditation. This can be achieved by following the three principles of Naam Japna (focus on God), Kirat Karni (honest living) and Vand Chakna (sharing with others). Sikhs should adhere to the following virtues – Sat (Truth), Santokh (Contentment), Daya (Compassion and kindness), Nimrata (Humility) and Pyare (Love). He said Sikhs should shun various negative human vices, one of which is cruelty to others.[75]

Guru Gobind Singh modified this, teaching that the five qualities/virtues which the Sikhs should emulate are: Daya (Compassion), Dharam (Righteousness), Himmat (Courage), Mohkam (detachment) and Sahib (Majesty/Dignity).[76]

## Sikh Beliefs about Animals

Charanjit Ajit Singh, a Sikh author and animal welfarist, reminds us that every prayer said by Sikhs individually or in a congregational setting, ends with "O God, may your will prevail and may the whole creation benefit".[77]

Sikhs believe in reincarnation and that the soul may be reborn as a human, an animal or a plant. As with Hinduism and Buddhism, humans are the highest level to be born into.

Brandon Foreman writes: "Thus, not only do Sikhs place the highest value on humans whereby they are the closest beings to holiness, but they give a clear separation between humans and other animals".[78]

The concept of "Mukti" or Liberation in Sikhism includes both freedom from the cycle of birth and death but also absorption or surrender into a state of merger with the divine. In the world at large this is often referred to by other words; such as nirvana.[79] Sikhs may aim to attain Liberation in this life (Jivanmukti) by their devotional activities and selfless service to the community.

Sikhs pray three times a day for the wellbeing of all of humanity, prosperity for everyone in the worldwide community and global peace for the entire planet.[80]

There are some texts in the Guru Granth Sahib which show real concern for the wellbeing of animals. Guru Nanak wrote: "There are beings and creatures in the water and on the land, in the worlds and universes, form upon form. Whatever they say, You know; You care for them all".[81]

There are many animal analogies within the Guru Granth Sahib, such as this from Guru Tegh Bahadur:

> Those who make pilgrimages to sacred shrines, observe ritualistic fasts and make donations to charity while still taking pride in their minds - O Nanak, their actions are useless, like the elephant, who takes a bath, and then rolls in the dust.[82]

Animals, along with nature, are viewed as meditating on the Divine: "Mortals, forests, blades of grass, animals and birds all meditate on the Divine".[83] Therefore, animals are in relationship with God.

Another beautiful verse from the Guru Granth Sahib demonstrates concern for animals and those humans who are suffering:

> Always cognize the near presence of God, through the practice of the Name,
> Avoid hurt or injury to any sentient being so that peace may come to your mind,
> Be humble by helping and serving those afflicted with misery and want, so as to achieve God-consciousness.
> Nanak testifies that God is the exalter of the fallen and lowly.[84]

The verse in the Guru Granth Sahib which puts concern for animals in the strongest light is:

The merit of pilgrimages to the sixty-eight holy places, and that of other virtues besides, do not equal having compassion for other living beings.[85]

So, compassion for other living beings is clearly seen as the highest quality which humans can demonstrate.

In modern times Sikhs have issued statements concerning the Sikh relationship with animals. At the major meeting of the faiths in Assisi in 1986, the Sikhs issued a statement on our relations with animals. It reads:

Humans should conduct themselves through life with love, compassion, and justice. Becoming one and being in harmony with God implies that humans endeavour to live in harmony with all of God's creation.[86]

A further statement was made in 2003:

The world, like all creation, is a manifestation of God. Every creature in this world, every plant, every form is a manifestation of the Creator. Each is part of God and God is within each element of creation. God is the cause of all and the primary connection between all existences.[87]

## Hunting

What was the example of the gurus of Sikhism? Guru Har Rai (1630–1661) was known as an animal lover and kept many animals himself. Two of the gurus were known as hunters. Guru Hargobind (1595–1644) was an avid hunter who enjoyed falconry, although he also said that Sikhs should not eat meat or fish.[88] Guru Gobind Singh (1666–1708) was also a keen hunter who said: "Through various sports I hunted in the forest and killed bear, nylgao and stags. Witnessing many a wonderous feat there we camped on the bank of the Yamuna river. Selectively we killed many lions, bears and nylgao". This Guru was often portrayed with one of his hunting dogs or with his pet hunting falcon perched on his arm.[89]

The scale of this hunting seems to go far beyond subsistence hunting for food and seems more akin to the western so-called "sport" hunting of foxes, deer and hares.

Of course, we recognise that hunting was taken for granted in many parts of society at that time and long before we knew that many wild animals are becoming threatened with extinction. However, hunting does not seem to sit easily with the teaching that all creatures are created by God and should be cared for. Nowadays few Sikhs are associated with hunting.

## Farm Animals

Sikhism is the majority faith in Punjab, practised by 16 million people representing 57.69% of the population of Punjab, making it the only Sikh-majority state in India.[90] So, it seems fair to see what kind of animal farming is practised in Punjab.

There are many small-scale farmers in Punjab, who may keep a cow or two and some chickens. They may be devoted to their animals and keep them as best as they can.

Dairy farming is widespread within Punjab and dairy consumption is an intrinsic part of the local diet. (See Hinduism chapter for a description of dairy farming in India.)

So-called "modern" intensive farming practices have also been adopted. These pay scant regard to the wellbeing of the animals whom they farm.

It seems that poultry farming follows the usual pattern in the state. Punjab has 500 laying hen farms with a capacity of nearly 30 million birds producing around 25 million eggs daily.[91]

This equates to about 60,000 birds per farm. It is likely that such huge numbers of birds are not kept in free-range conditions but in cages or intensive indoor units.

There are around 400 broiler (meat) chicken farms in Punjab. It appears that the government of India is encouraging the growth of the chicken industry as stated in the National Action Plan for Egg and Poultry, 2022.[92]

While there are small-scale backyard farms rearing chickens, and these provide for household consumption and some local sales, the vast majority of poultry farms in Punjab and elsewhere in India appear to be intensive. Some of the big poultry farms are even named after the Sikh gurus, such as "Guru Nanak Poultry Farm".

The intensive farming of poultry by Sikhs does raise the question asked in the Guru Granth Sahib: "You say that the One Lord is in all, so why do you kill chickens?"[93]

## Food and Diet

Sikhs are divided on the subject of meat-eating. Sikhs living in India will not eat beef, possibly out of respect for their Hindu neighbours.

Guru Gobind Singh prohibited Sikhs from the consumption of Kutha, which is meat slaughtered by Muslims or Jews, because of the Sikh belief that sacrificing an animal in the name of God is not correct. Some Sikhs who have committed to their faith through Amrit or baptism, will become vegetarian.[94] Baptised Sikhs become Khalsas (Pure ones) and are devoted to their guru, even being prepared to die for the faith.

However, several sects within Sikhism advocate a vegetarian diet, possibly because in the early days of Sikhism, they attracted many followers who were Vaishnavite Hindus and were opposed to meat-eating. Some Sikhs are strongly vegetarian and quote many edicts about this.[95]

Nearly all Sikh gurdwaras (temples) run langars, community kitchens, which cook only vegetarian food and distribute it free to everyone, regardless of caste, religion, social status etc. The food is often rice, chappati and dahl (lentils) with vegetables. Everyone sits on the floor, be they royalty or homeless (of course facilities exist for those who physically cannot manage such sitting). The langars are run by Sikh volunteers.

The langar attached to the Golden Temple in Amritsar, Sri Harmandir Sahib, is said to feed 65,000 people a day. In 2011, Amritsar became one of the founding cities of the Green Pilgrimage Network and committed to providing organic and pesticide-free food. Plastic water bottles and bags have been banned and solar panels are being installed in order to cook the langar food.[96]

The first three gurus established the langars and they really were – perhaps still are – revolutionary. Hitherto, people of different faiths, such as Muslims and Hindus, would not eat together and high-caste Hindus would not eat with lower castes or "outcastes". Now the langars have demonstrated that "...the Light of God is in all hearts".[97]

It is recorded that the great Emperor Akbar came to visit the Golden Temple and was told that he too must sit on the floor with everyone else in the langar. [98]

Some modern Sikh spiritual guides are sympathetic to vegetarianism. For example, Sant Rajinder Singh writes:

> Many also find such plant-based diets are beneficial for spiritual growth. Those who meditate and connect with the Light within them see that same Light also shining in all other human beings and all living things. Thus, they choose to treat other forms of creation as younger brothers and sisters in one family of God. Such people often choose a plant-based diet as consistent with their spiritual values.[99]

He goes on to explain the spiritual reasons for caring for all creatures:

> This Light (of God) exists as much in the humble ant as in the powerful lion. It shines in the snake as well as the cow. It shimmers in the fish, as well as the birds. When we look at life through the eyes of the soul, we witness God in even the humblest and most grotesque of creatures. With that angle of vision, we develop love for all that exists.[100]

## Slaughter

The preferred method of slaughter for those Sikhs who eat meat is called Jhatka and consists of beheading the animal with one stroke. Sikhs believe this to be the most painless method for killing an animal.

Jhatka carries no religious meaning or symbolism. Sikhs have always opposed the attachment of religious rituals to the slaughter of animals.

In Jhatka, the head of the animal is attached to a stable column and the posterior legs are stretched out in the opposite direction. The animal is beheaded from the backbone side with a single stroke of a sword or axe.[101]

Some slaughter experts say that this will cause the sudden death of the animal because the spinal cord is cut, and the circulation of blood to the brain has been immediately stopped, resulting in brain failure within seconds.[102] Other experts estimate that decapitation may not induce total unconsciousness for about half a minute.[103]

In the European Union, decapitation without prior stunning is not permitted.[104] In countries where Jhatka meat is not widely available, Sikhs may often eat meat slaughtered in the modern, western way, where the animal is stunned and then cut. They will not eat halal or Kosher meat, because religious beliefs and practices are involved in the slaughter.

## Conclusion

Sikhs regard animals as creatures of God and respect them. The Guru Granth Sahib contains some beautiful verses about compassion for all beings.

Many Sikhs follow a vegetarian diet, while others eat meat.

There does seem to be some inconsistency regarding intensive farming and compassion for all creatures.

The Sikh langars are a wonderful demonstration of community action, concern for all humanity and respect for animal life.

## References

The Sikh holy book is the Guru Granth Sahib (GGS). The abbreviation GGS with the relevant verse number is used in these references. The GGS can be accessed online at www.srigranth.org/servlet/gurbani.gurbani.

# Rastafarianism

## Introduction

Most of the faiths considered in this book began hundreds or thousands of years ago. Rastafarianism is a 20th-century faith, which started in Jamaica, has spread globally and has around 1 million adherents. However, Rastafarians, or Rastafari, believe in the Biblical God Jehovah, referred to as Jah, and many of their beliefs and practices are rooted in Biblical references.

The black inhabitants of Jamaica were the descendants of slaves, brought to Jamaica during the notorious slave trade and subjugated by the white ruling and land-owning elite and by many of the white Christian missionaries.

Marcus Garvey was a political activist and promoted black self-empowerment in the early 20th century. Many Rastafari think that he was a prophet, akin to John the Baptist's role in Christianity. Garvey urged those of the African diaspora to not only return to Africa, but to also "look to Africa, when a black king shall be crowned". That prophecy was realised in 1930, when Haile Selassie I was crowned the Emperor of Ethiopia. Rastafarians consider the Emperor their messiah, naming the movement after his birth name, Ras Tafari Makonnen.[105] Many regard him as the Second Coming of Jesus and Jah incarnate, while others see him as a human prophet. Among the titles the emperor took for himself was "King of Kings, Lord of Lords, and Conquering Lion of the Tribe Judah". In doing this, he claimed descent from the Biblical King David and many Rastafari saw a reference to the Book of Revelation 5:2–5, where only the Lion of the tribe of Judah can open the sacred scroll.

On 21st April 1966, Haile Selassie visited Jamaica and although he is said to have denied his personal divinity (he was a member of the Ethiopian Orthodox Church), the Jamaican Rastafarians gave him a massive and vociferous welcome. The date is now considered holy and is celebrated as Grounation Day.

Other Rastafari practices are also biblically referenced. Smoking ganja, marijuana, is regarded as a sacrament and they believe that this "herb" is the tree spoken of in Revelations 22:2: "In the midst of the street there was the tree of life, and the leaves of the tree were for the healing of the nations". Usually, Rastafarians refer to marijuana as the "wisdom weed" or the "holy herb".

When Rastafari men gather together for their "Reasoning" sessions, they may pray, chant, sing and smoke ganja in a serious way, believing that it heightens their meditation and brings them closer to Jah. Before it is used, a prayer is uttered by all: "Glory be to the father and to the maker of creation. As it was in the beginning is now and ever shall be World without end: Jah Rastafari: Eternal God Selassie I".[106]

Many Rastafari do not cut their hair and the men's dreadlocks are said to resemble a lion's mane – a sign of strength and a tribute to the Lion of Judah, Haille Selassie. It is seen as more natural to let one's hair grow. Women often cover their hair too.

Jah is regarded not just as god out there, but as dwelling in each person. Rastafarians therefore say they don't "believe" in God, they "know" him. He is immanent within them.[107]

## Political and Cultural Aspects

While Rastafarianism is undoubtedly a faith, it has strong political aspects too. Many Rastafari believe that they should return to Africa, the homeland of their ancestors. They often call Africa, or specifically Ethiopia, "Zion". Some Rastafari people have returned to Africa, often to Ghana, from where many of the slaves were captured and transported. Others have taken up Haile Selassie's offer, in 1963, of 500 hectares of land near the small southern Ethiopian town of Shasemene. The believers who have settled there are from a particular Rastafari sect, the Twelve Tribes of Israel.[108]

Western consumerist culture is derided as "Babylon". Rastas' economic beliefs are anti-capitalism. Capitalism is part of Babylon, the way the white world rulers enrich themselves and enslave others. Rastas believe that possessions should be shared. This is not Communism as Rastafarianism rejects all rules and everyone finds their own way within the faith.

This strong mixture of faith and community is demonstrated in the way Rastas never use the words "I", "we" or "us". They say, "I and I". Rastas use the word to connect themselves to God, to show that that God is always part of them. A Rasta will never say "I am going there"; instead, it would be "I and I am going there". The Rasta does this to show that God is part of him, and that he is not separate from any other person.[5]

Rastafari believe in being close to the earth and living in harmony with their environment. They do not believe in plundering the earth for profit. They see Babylon destroying the planet and living greedily off the earth's so-called "resources". In this belief, they have been ahead of the Babylon world, which is only beginning to see that its resource-intensive lifestyles cannot go on forever.

Rastafari see Babylon in the neocolonialism of foreign aid and structural adjustments. These programmes, sponsored by institutions like the International Monetary Fund and the World Bank, are supposed to be aimed at reducing debt within developing nations. The reality is that they have often ended communal control of land, seized land for debt, and forced upon developing nations new agricultural programmes aimed at increasing capital. With these programmes cash crops have replaced traditional farming and subsistence agriculture. The drive towards industrialisation and large-scale agriculture has been relentless.[109]

## Health and Diet

Rastafarians believe their body is a temple, so they should only eat pure foods. They follow the "ital" diet (the word being derived from "vital" and vitality), eating organic, preferably home-grown or organic plant foods, preferably in season. They do not eat meat or eggs, and many do not eat fish, especially shellfish, as they are scavengers. They believe such a diet will promote "livity" or life energy. Livity is a contraction of "live" and Leviticus. They believe that eating dead animals turns their bodies into cemeteries. Some will eat small fish, shorter than 12 inches in length, to avoid the Babylonian sin of greed.

Some Rastas avoid salt, which is believed to harm the kidneys and liver, and many adhere to a vegan diet, considering dairy to be harmful or not strictly ital. Others avoid any food that has been preserved or has been prepared using metal instruments. Clay pots and wooden bowls and spoons are often used in the preparation of ital food. Many adherents avoid alcohol and stimulants like tea and coffee, but this is less strictly followed. Herbal tea is the exception due to its low caffeine content and natural herbal properties.[110]

A label is being developed in the United States for official recognition of this increasingly popular ital diet.[111]

The BBC ran an article in 2016 about a young Rasta couple who have established an ital food truck cafe in Liverpool. The young man, Dan, was asked if the reason for this was animal protection. He replied:

> Well, that's probably not the primary idea behind the movement, but it plays a big part. If an animal has been bred for slaughter and kept in a space where it's not allowed to move freely or live a happy life and then you eat that animal, you take all of that history on. It's all about being mindful of what you're putting into your body, as well as where your food comes from.[112]

In an interesting interview, the well-known Rastafari dub poet, musician, actor, educator, and radio host, Mutabaruka, declares, "I think we should respect the lives of all creatures on earth".[113]

In spite of the Rastafarian respect for animals and the earth, at first it was quite a male-dominated faith. Although Rasta women were called "queens" they were meant to do as they were told. Now more Rasta women are declaring their independence and confidence.

Sheeba Levi Stewart, a member of Rastafari Movement UK, told "The Voice" magazine about how she saw Haile Selassie on his visit to Jamaica when she was just eight years old. "I remember looking at His Majesty and just feeling this like an electric charge," she said. Her family moved to Britain and did not share her enthusiasm for Rastafarianism. She said:

> But then once I realised the spirituality of His Majesty and the dynasty back to Solomon and Sheba, and the Bible and Ethiopia as the world history that just gave me that confidence and that push where I couldn't be anything else, but a Rasta.

She added: "I've always been independent, and I've always felt it's important to be independent".[114]

## Outspoken Rastas

Two of the best-known Rastafarians are the late Bob Marley, whose songs touched so many people both in Jamaica and around the world (and whom I have quoted at the top of this chapter) and the famous writer and poet Benjamin Zephaniah.[115]

## Conclusion

The Rastafarian ital diet, with its emphasis on home-grown, organic plants, is undoubtedly a planet-friendly, healthy way to eat. Many health, animal welfare and environmental groups are now proposing diets that are more akin to this way of eating.

Rastafarians respect the earth and all its creatures. Their scorn for the western capitalist system of food production with its industrial farms and lack of concern for the marginalised is understandable. "Babylon" has indeed been destructive of the environment and negligent in caring for the earth and its creatures. Rastafarian farming is naturally agro-ecological and regenerative.

Rastafarianism offers an attractive alternative lifestyle.

## Notes

1 K. Sena, 22/10/20. Recognizing Indigenous Peoples' Land Interests Is Critical for People and Nature. WWF. https://tinyurl.com/2p88yvxd.
2 Intergovernmental Science-Policy Platform on Biodiversity and Ecosystem Services, 2022. Summary for policymakers of the methodological assessment of the diverse values and valuation of nature of the Intergovernmental Science-Policy Platform on Biodiversity and Ecosystem Services (IPBES) (Version 1). IPBES Plenary at its ninth session (IPBES 9), Bonn. Zenodo. https://doi.org/10.5281/zenodo.6832427.
3 R.Wall Kimmerer, 2020. *Braiding Sweetgrass: Indigenous Wisdom, Scientific Knowledge and the Teaching of Plants.* First published Milkweed Editions 2013, London: Penguin Books 2020.
4 Quoted in R.Wall Kimmerer, 2020. *Braiding Sweetgrass: Indigenous Wisdom, Scientific Knowledge and the Teaching of Plants.* First published Milkweed Editions 2013, London: Penguin Books 2020.
5 R. Erdoes and A. Ortiz, 1984. *American Indian Myths and Legends.* New York: Pantheon, quoted in L. Kemmerer, 2012. *Animals and World Religions.* New York: Oxford University Press.
6 L. Hogan, 1998. First People, in L. Hogan, D. Metzger and B. Peterson (Eds). *Intimate Nature: The Bond between Women and Animals.* New York: Fawcett Columbine, quoted in L.J. Eichler, 2020. Ecocide is genocide: Decolonizing the definition of genocide. *Genocide Studies and Prevention: An International Journal,* **14**: 2, pp104–121. https://doi.org/10.5038/1911-9933.14.2.1720.
7 Study.com, 08/06/17. Native Americans & Buffalo: Symbolism, Uses & Importance. study.com/academy/lesson/native-americans-buffalo-symbolism-uses-importance. html.
8 John (Fire) Lame Deer, Oglala-Lame Deer Seeker of Visions, with Richard Erdoes, 1972. https://americanindian.si.edu/nk360/plains-belonging/itbc.
9 T. Hubbard, 2014. *Buffalo Genocide in Nineteenth Century North America: "Kill, Skin, Sell".* Colonial Genocide in Indigenous North America. Duke University Press, p294. https://doi.org/10.1215/9780822376149-014.

10  J.R. Murie, 1981. Ceremonies of the Pawnee. Part I: The Skiri. *Smithsonian Contributions to Anthropology*, **27**, p98.

11  S. Taylor, 2011. Buffalo hunt: International trade and the virtual extinction of the North American Bison. *American Economic Review*, **101**:7, pp3162–3195. https://doi:10.1257/aer.101.7.3162. S2CID 154413490.

12  PBS, 1998. American Buffalo: Spirit of a Nation. Nature, S17 EP3. www.pbs.org/wnet/nature/american-buffalo-spirit-of-a-nation-introduction/2183/.

13  R.Wall Kimmerer, 2020. *Braiding Sweetgrass: Indigenous Wisdom, Scientific Knowledge and the Teaching of Plants.* First published Milkweed Editions 2013, London: Penguin Books 2020.

14  Black Elk and J.G. Neihardt. 2014. *Black Elk Speaks, The Complete Edition.* Lincoln: University of Nebraska Press.

15  T. Hubbard, 2014. *Buffalo Genocide in Nineteenth Century North America: "Kill, Skin, Sell".* Colonial Genocide in Indigenous North America. Duke University Press, p294. https://doi.org/10.1215/9780822376149-014.

16  T. Hubbard, 2014. *Buffalo Genocide in Nineteenth Century North America: "Kill, Skin, Sell".* Colonial Genocide in Indigenous North America. Duke University Press, p294. https://doi.org/10.1215/9780822376149-014.

17  D. Smits, Autumn 1994. The frontier army and the destruction of the Buffalo: 1865–1883. *The Western Historical Quarterly*, **25**: 3, pp312–338. https://doi:10.2307/971110.

18  PBS, 1998. American Buffalo: Spirit of a Nation. Nature, S17 EP3. www.pbs.org/wnet/nature/american-buffalo-spirit-of-a-nation-introduction/2183/.

19  InterTribal Buffalo Council, u.d. https://americanindian.si.edu/nk360/plains-belonging/itbc.

20  Positive News, 16/4/22. In the US, indigenous-led conservation efforts are boosting buffalo numbers, reviving a culture and feeding homeless people.

21  H.R.2074 - Indian Buffalo Management Act, introduced 03/18/2021. www.congress.gov/bill/117th-congress/house-bill/2074.

22  M. Krupnick, 2022. "It's a Powerful Feeling": The Indigenous American Tribe Helping to Bring Back Buffalo. *The Guardian.* www.theguardian.com/environment/2022/feb/20/its-a-powerful-feeling-the-indigenous-american-tribe-helping-to-bring-back-buffalo.

23  R.Wall Kimmerer, 2020. *Braiding Sweetgrass: Indigenous Wisdom, Scientific Knowledge and the Teaching of Plants.* First published Milkweed Editions 2013, London: Penguin Books 2020.

24  L.E. Frank, 11/11/21. History on a Plate: How Native American Diets Shifted After European Colonization. The History Channel. www.history.com/news/native-american-food-shifts.

25  R. Laws Ph.D, September 1994. History of Vegetarianism: Native Americans and Vegetarianism, published by The Vegetarian Resource Group in *The Vegetarian Journal.*

26  R. Laws Ph.D, September 1994. History of Vegetarianism: Native Americans and Vegetarianism, published by The Vegetarian Resource Group in *The Vegetarian Journal.*

27  History.com, 28/07/22. Trail of Tears. www.history.com/topics/native-american-history/trail-of-tears.

28  R. Laws Ph.D, September 1994. History of Vegetarianism: Native Americans and Vegetarianism, published by The Vegetarian Resource Group in *The Vegetarian Journal.*

29  NIH, 21/11/16. Native American Foods, Dietary Habits Take Center Stage. www.nhlbi.nih.gov/news/2016/native-american-foods-dietary-habits-take-center-stage.

30  B. Stone, 07/09/99. Report Details Crimes against Aborigines. www.wsws.org/en/articles/1999/09/geno-s07.html.

31  Education Services Australia, 2005. The 1967 Referendum. www.civicsandcitizenship.edu.au/cce/default.asp?id=9589.

32  E. Blakemore, 31/01/19. Aboriginal Australians. *National Geographic*. www.nationalgeographic.com/culture/article/aboriginal-australians.

33  E. Blakemore, 31/01/19. Aboriginal Australians. *National Geographic*. www.nationalgeographic.com/culture/article/aboriginal-australians.

34  Common Ground, 2022. The Dreaming. www.commonground.org.au/learn/the-dreaming.

35  Common Ground, 2022. The Significance of Koalas for First Nations People. www.commonground.org.au/learn/the-significance-of-koalas-for-first-nations-people.

36  G. Pol, 2022. What Is Country? Common Ground. www.commonground.org.au/learn/what-is-country.

37  Victorian Aboriginal Heritage Council, 2021. Plants and Animals. www.aboriginal-heritagecouncil.vic.gov.au/taking-care-culture-discussion-paper/plants-and-animals.

38  J. Korff, 03/09/21. Meaning of Land to Aboriginal People. Creative Spirits. www.creativespirits.info/aboriginalculture/land/meaning-of-land-to-aboriginal-people.

39  Intergovernmental Science-Policy Platform on Biodiversity and Ecosystem Services, 2022. Summary for policymakers of the methodological assessment of the diverse values and valuation of nature of the Intergovernmental Science-Policy Platform on Biodiversity and Ecosystem Services (IPBES) (Version 1). IPBES Plenary at its ninth session (IPBES 9), Bonn. Zenodo. https://doi.org/10.5281/zenodo.6832427.

40  L and J. Morcan, 2016. *White Spirit*. Tauranga: Sterling Gate Books.

41  D. Wroth, 2021. Why Songlines Are Important in Aboriginal Art. https://tinyurl.com/pakk7p3p.

42  P. Daley, 04/07/16. Indigenous Songlines: A Beautiful Way to Think about the Confluence of Story and Time. www.theguardian.com/commentisfree/2016/jul/04/indigenous-songlines-a-beautiful-way-to-think-about-the-confluence-of-story-and-time.

43  R. Glynn-McDonald and R. Sinclair, 2022. Connection to Animals and Country. www.commonground.org.au/learn/connection-to-animals-and-country.

44  T. Dystra, Aboriginal Elder. *TimeOut Sydney*, 21–27/5/2008, p7.

45  Watarrka Foundation, 2022. Traditional Aboriginal Foods. www.watarrkafoundation.org.au/blog/traditional-aboriginal-foods.

46  Watarrka Foundation, 2022. Traditional Aboriginal Foods. www.watarrkafoundation.org.au/blog/traditional-aboriginal-foods.

47  J. Kotzmann, 24/02/20. Condemning Indigenous Hunting Practices: Are We Throwing Stones from Glass Houses? https://sentientmedia.org/condemning-indigenous-hunting-practices-are-we-throwing-stones-from-glass-houses/.

48  P.S. Jaini, 1979. *The Jaina Path of Purification*. Berkeley: University of California Press, quoted by C. Chapple, 2006. Animals and the Jaina Tradition, in P. Waldau and K. Patton (Eds). *A Community of Subjects*. New York: Columbia University Press, pp241–249.

49  Satish Kumar, 2022. Jain Religion. *Resurgence & Ecologist*. www.resurgence.org/satish-kumar/articles/jain-religion.html.

50  Britannica, u.d. Jainism. https://www.britannica.com/topic/Jainism.

51  National Geographic, 20/05/22. Jainism. https://education.nationalgeographic.org/resource/jainism.

52  Nalini Balbir, 23/09/19. An Introduction to the Jain Faith. The British Library. www.bl.uk/sacred-texts/articles/an-introduction-to-the-jain-faith.

53  Jain Students Group at the University of Michigan, 1997. General Facts about Jainism. http://websites.umich.edu/~umjains/overview.html.

54  Satish Kumar, 2022. Jain Religion. *Resurgence & Ecologist*. www.resurgence.org/satish-kumar/articles/jain-religion.html.

55  Byjus Exam Prep, u.d. Jainism. https://byjus.com/free-ias-prep/jainism/.

56  Satish Kumar, 2022. Jain Religion. *Resurgence & Ecologist*. www.resurgence.org/satish-kumar/articles/jain-religion.html.

57  Nitin Mehta, 29/08/22. Personal communication.
58  P.K. Shah, u.d. Jain Agam Literature. www.cs.colostate.edu/~malaiya/agamas.html.
59  Acaranga sutra 1.4.1. 1–2, pp41–42, quoted in K. Armstrong, 2007. *The Great Transformation*. London: Atlantic Books.
60  Nalini Balbir, 23/09/19. An Introduction to the Jain Faith. The British Library. www.bl.uk/sacred-texts/articles/an-introduction-to-the-jain-faith.
61  Gautam Batra, 25.4.18. This Is Why Jains Don't Eat Onion and Garlic. The Reason Will Make You Respect Them. www.rvcj.com/this-is-why-jains-dont-eat-onion-and-garlic-the-reason-will-make-you-respect-them/.
62  K.J. Starr, 17/08/21. 6 Facts about Jains in India. Pew Research Center. www.pewresearch.org/fact-tank/2021/08/17/6-facts-about-jains-in-india/.
63  Plantshift, 20/05/14. Veganism in the Jain Community: Then and Now. https://plantshift.com/blog/the-vegan-movement-in-the-jain-community.
64  B. Evans, 2013. Ideologies of the Shri Meenakshi Goushala: Hindu and Jain motivations for a Madurai Cow Home. *ASIA Network Exchange*, **20**:2,pp1–10.
65  A. Sharma, C. Schuetze and C.J.C. Phillips, 2020. The management of cow shelters (Gaushalas) in India, including the attitudes of shelter managers to cow welfare. *Animals* (Basel), **10**:2. https://doi.org/10.3390/ani10020211.
66  M. Jain, A. Mathur, S. Kumar, P. Duraiswamy and S. Kulkarni, 2009. Oral hygiene and periodontal status among Terapanthi Svetambar Jain monks in India. *Brazilian Oral Research*, **23**:4, pp370–376. https://doi.org/10.1590/s1806-83242009000400004.
67  Nitin Mehta, 29/08/22. Personal communication.
68  Hansard, 01/05/19. Jain Community: Contribution to the UK. Vol 659. https://hansard.parliament.uk/commons/2019-05-01/debates/93A69D0F-11C9-4428-857E-097031BC4B98/JainCommunityContributionToTheUK.
69  Kelsey Jo Starr, 17/08/21. 6 Facts about Jains in India. Pew Research Center. www.pewresearch.org/fact-tank/2021/08/17/6-facts-about-jains-in-india/.
70  Farzana Ahmad, 15/06/10. In Brief: Jainism. *The Review of Religions*. www.reviewofreligions.org/2312/in-brief-jainism/.
71  M. Mahanta, 2020. Jainism: Philosophy That Inspired Mahatma Gandhi. *Prācyā*, **12**:1. https://doi.org/10.22271/pracya.2020.v12.i1.98.
72  Nitin Mehta, 29/08/22. Personal communication.
73  P. Sujatha Varma, 14/02/12. Jainism Can Never Be Popular Due to Its Asceticism. *The Hindu*. www.thehindu.com/news/cities/Vijayawada/jainism-can-never-be-popular-due-to-its-asceticism/article2891791.ece.
74  Nitin Mehta, 29/08/22. Personal communication.
75  Sikhi Wiki, u.d. Guru Granth Sahib against Cruelty. www.sikhiwiki.org/index.php/Guru_Granth_Sahib_against_cruelty.
76  Charanjit Ajit Singh, 26/08/22. Personal communication.
77  Animal Interfaith Alliance, u.d. Sikh Teachings About Animals – by Charanjit Ajit Singh. https://animal-interfaith-alliance.com/sikh-teachings-about-animals-by-charanjit-ajit-singh/.
78  B. Foreman, 27/01/17. Sikh Reincarnation and the Boundaries of "Animal". https://sites.duke.edu/lit290s-1_02_s2017/2017/01/27/sikh-reincarnation-and-the-boundaries-of-animal/.
79  Sikh Dharma International, u.d. The Path of Sikh Dharma. www.sikhdharma.org/ideology-beliefs/.
80  Sikhi Wiki, u.d. Guru Granth Sahib against Cruelty. www.sikhiwiki.org/index.php/Guru_Granth_Sahib_against_cruelty.
81  GGS, p466.
82  GGS, p1428.
83  GGS, p455.
84  GGS, p322.
85  GGS, p136.

86 M. Palmer and V. Finlay, 2003. Faith in Conservation: New Approaches to Religions and the Environment. Directions in Development. Washington, DC: World Bank. © World Bank. https://openknowledge.worldbank.org/handle/10986/15083 License: CC BY 3.0 IGO, p134.

87 M. Palmer and V. Finlay, 2003. Faith in Conservation: New Approaches to Religions and the Environment. Directions in Development. Washington, DC: World Bank. © World Bank. https://openknowledge.worldbank.org/handle/10986/15083 License: CC BY 3.0 IGO, p134.

88 Charanjit Ajit Singh, 26/08/22. Personal communication.

89 Sandeep Singh Brar, 11/12/05. Sikhism and Pets. https://tinyurl.com/57t8kkcp.

90 Wikipedia, u.d. Demographics of Punjab, India. https://tinyurl.com/ubnuvzv8.

91 *The Times of India*, 26/03/20. Punjab's Poultry Sector in Deep Crisis as Bird Feed Stock Running Out. https://tinyurl.com/495e2xxt.

92 Minister of Agriculture, 2017. Seeking Comments on the National Action Plan for Egg & Poultry, 2022 for Doubling Farmers' Income by 2022. https://tinyurl.com/2tph4kse.

93 GGS, p1350.

94 Weston Area Health NHS Trust, u.d. Sikhism. www.waht.nhs.uk/en-GB/NHS-Mobile/Our-Services/?depth=4&srcid=2008.

95 Sikhi Wiki, u.d. Cruelty and Food. https://www.sikhiwiki.org/index.php/Cruelty_and_food.

96 S. Weldon and S. Campbell, 2014. *Faith in Food*. London: Bene Factum Publishing.

97 GGS, 282.

98 Charanjit Ajit Singh, 26/08/22. Personal communication.

99 Sant Rajinder Singh Ji Maharaj, u.d. World Vegan Day. www.sos.org/sant-rajinder-singh/world-vegan-day/.

100 Sant Rajinder Singh Ji Maharaj, u.d. Vegetarianism and Spirituality. www.sos.org/vegetarianism-and-spirituality/.

101 Z.A. Aghwan and J.M. Regenstein, 2019. Slaughter practices of different faiths in different countries. *Journal of Animal Science and Technology*, **61**:3, pp111–121. https://doi.org/10.5187/jast.2019.61.3.111.

102 Z.A. Aghwan and J.M. Regenstein, 2019. Slaughter practices of different faiths in different countries. *Journal of Animal Science and Technology*, **61**:3, pp111–121. https://doi.org/10.5187/jast.2019.61.3.111.

103 N.G. Gregory and S.B. Wotton, 1986. Effect of slaughter on the spontaneous and evoked activity of the brain. *British Poultry Science*, **27**, pp195–205, reported in E.M.C. Terlouw et al., 2008. Pre-slaughter conditions, animal stress and welfare: Current status and possible future research. *Animal*, **2**:10, pp1501–1517. https://doi.org/10.1017/S1751731108002723.

104 European Commission, 2009. Council Regulation (EC) No 1099/2009 on the Protection of Animals at the Time of Killing. http://data.europa.eu/eli/reg/2009/1099/2019-12-14.

105 IslandOutpost.com, u.d. 10 Things Everyone Should Know About Rastas. www.islandoutpost.com/outpostings/2016/01/18/10-things-everyone-know-rastas/.

106 Re:Online, 2022. Prayer and Meditation. www.reonline.org.uk/knowledge/rastafari/prayer-and-meditation/.

107 Wikipedia, u.d. Rastafari. https://en.wikipedia.org/wiki/Rastafari.

108 Black History Month 2022, 2020. Rastafari Culture. www.blackhistorymonth.org.uk/article/section/real-stories/rastafari-culture/.

109 E. David, April 22,1998. *Nature in the Rastafarian Consciousness*. The Dread Library,theUniversityofVermont,Burlington. https://tinyurl.com/mpfxjxf9.

110 K. Aidoo, 16/05/17. Ghana's Entwined History with Rastafarianism. https://theculturetrip.com/africa/ghana/articles/ghanas-entwined-history-with-rastafarianism/.

111 E. Sauphie, 08/06/21. The Ital Diet, A Rastafarian Recipe for Eating Right. https://worldcrunch.com/culture-society/the-ital-diet-a-rastafarian-recipe-for-eating-right.

112 C. Varley, 13/06/16. Ital - The Vegan Rasta Movement You've Probably Never Heard of Until Now... www.bbc.co.uk/bbcthree/article/a81ed43e-0f31-43c0-9cf8-e2134ec5ad2a.

113 INeverKnewTV.com, 22/12/21. Mutabaruka Speaks on The Hypocrisy of Animal Rights Activist Who Eat Animals. www.youtube.com/watch?v=fjTOXP6aX6Y.

114 The Voice, 2/3/22. Rastafarian Women in Britain: 'I Couldn't Be Anything Else but a Rasta'. www.voice-online.co.uk/news/features-news/2022/03/02/rastafarian-women-in-britain-i-couldnt-be-anything-else-but-a-rasta/.

115 Website: https://benjaminzephaniah.com/.

# Conclusion

There are around 8 billion humans on the earth.[1]

For our food alone we slaughter ten times that many other sentient beings each year. Over 80 billion individual land-based animals[2] – and well over a trillion of wild-caught fishes – are eaten by us on an annual basis.[3] Figures for consumption of farmed fishes range from half a billion to well over a billion a year.[4]

Over 100 million animals are used in animal testing each year.[5]

Many thousands of animals are shot or hunted for "sport", others used for our entertainment in films, circuses and zoos (which is not to deny that many zoos are involved in breeding animals for release back into their original environment).

We humans appear to be a highly predatory species.

Many people look to the teachings of their faith and to its current leaders to guide them in making ethical decisions as to how they should lead their lives. From the Ten Commandments to the Five Pillars of Islam, from the Laws of Manu to the Five Paramis of Buddhism, the faiths have indeed given guidance and sometimes absolute instruction as to how one's life should be led.

So, it is a bit surprising to see so little guidance overall in determining how we should relate to animals. There are calls for compassion but, on the whole, human interests come first. Could it be that we are so afraid of death and the possibility of an eternal afterlife or continual rebirths, that we always put our personal interests first?

I know many sincere and kind people who do much good in the world, but who sit down to factory-farmed meat for supper without a second thought. Some of them are deeply religious people.

Is this not a sign of a fundamental failure of the world's faiths?

If we added up all the sermons and talks given by the priests, bishops, imams, rabbis and gurus of the world, I wonder what proportion would have addressed the issue of our relationship with other creatures on this planet? I fear that the answer would be in very low numbers. At least in this book I have been able to give some encouraging examples.

So, here's the challenge: animals globally are suffering at our hands. We can act to change this. If you are a faith leader, please talk about this. If you are just an ordinary believer, please ask or challenge your faith leaders to investigate the issue and to talk about it publicly. If you are an unbeliever, then please question your

DOI: 10.4324/9781003292555-8

faith friends or faith leaders locally or nationally and ask them to do something about this.

My research into the faiths' teachings has encouraged me. I hope it has encouraged you too! Let's find creative ways to make the teachings and exemplars known in our communities.

We can be sure that trillions of creatures will be spared immense suffering if we take up this challenge.

Surely that can only be A VERY GOOD THING?

## Notes

1 UN DESA, 2022. World Population to Reach 8 billion on 15 November 2022. https://tinyurl.com/3ud6d8rt.
2 Calculated from FAOStat, www.faostat.org.
3 M. Pellman Rowland, 24/07/17. Two-Thirds of The World's Seafood is Over-Fished – Here's How You Can Help. www.forbes.com/sites/michaelpellmanrowland/2017/07/24/seafood-sustainability-facts/?sh=6ef35ae54bbf.
4 Fishcount.org.uk, 2022. Numbers of Farmed Fish Slaughtered Each Year. http://fish-count.org.uk/fish-count-estimates-2/numbers-of-farmed-fish-slaughtered-each-year.
5 RSPCA. Animals in Science. https://tinyurl.com/5x5vbbvy.

# Glossary

## Judaism

| | |
|---|---|
| Chalaf | A knife used for animal slaughter. |
| Halacha | The body of Jewish law supplementing the scriptural law and forming especially the legal part of the Talmud. |
| Korban(ot) | Sacrifice(s). |
| Kosher | Fit or proper. Usually refers to food which is fit to be eaten according to Jewish law. |
| Nefesh | Life force, urge for survival. |
| Neshama | A spiritual soul, which seeks fulfilment in God, said to be only possessed by humans. |
| Rabbi | A teacher of Judaism. |
| Sabbath (shabbat) | Day of rest, ordained in the scriptures. From Friday evening to Saturday evening. |
| Shechita | Slaughter according to Jewish rules. |
| Shochet (-im) | The person/people who carry out Jewish slaughter. |
| Shtreimel | Fur hat worn by some Ashkenazi Jewish men, mainly members of Hasidic Judaism, on Shabbat and other Jewish holidays. |
| The Tenakh | The Hebrew Bible. |
| Torah | The five books of Moses at the beginning of the Hebrew Bible. |
| Tsa'ar ba-alei chayim | The pain or suffering of living things; a fundamental Jewish teaching is that human beings must avoid tsa'ar ba-alei chayim. |

## Christianity

| | |
|---|---|
| Catechism | A manual of religious instruction in the form of questions and answers. |
| Encyclical | A circular letter from the Pope to all Catholics (sometimes to all people). |
| The Evangelists | The four authors of the gospels, Matthew, Mark, Luke and John. |
| The Trinity | Three persons in One God: Father, Son (incarnated as Jesus) and the Holy Spirit. |

# Islam

| | |
|---|---|
| Allah | The one God, probably a contraction of al-ilah, the god in Arabic. Used by Arabic-speaking Christians and Jews as well as by Muslims. |
| Bismillah | Saying meaning "In the name of God". |
| Hadith | Collections of the sayings and actions of the prophet Muhammad and his companions, next most important to the Qur'an. |
| Halal | "Acceptable" "permitted" or "sanctified", applies widely to a multitude of products and actions, not just to food. |
| Insha allah | Saying meaning "God willing". |
| Khalifah | The role of humans in relation to the world, variously translated as "vice-regent", "trustee", "agent" (of God), "having a sacred duty". |
| Qur'an | Islam's most sacred book, believed to be the word of God revealed to Muhammad by the archangel Gabriel and written down in Arabic. |
| Sharia | Divine law, based on teachings in the Qur'an and Hadith. |
| Taqwa | Having reverence towards God and caring for his creatures. |
| Tayyib | Pure, healthy, good or natural food. |

# Hinduism

| | |
|---|---|
| Advaita | Non-dualism. Brahman and Atman are one. Sometimes referred to as Advaita Vedanta. |
| Ahimsa | Non-violence. |
| Atman | The "higher self", identified with Brahman. |
| Bhagavad gita | Dialogue between the warrior Arjuna and his charioteer, the god Krishna. |
| Bhagavata purana | Holy book from 8th to 9th CE, smriti. |
| Bhajan | Devotional song. |
| Brahman | The one divine essence behind and within every being. |
| Brahmins (Brahmans) | The traditional priestly caste. |
| Dharma | One's duty in life, how to live. |
| Gaushala | Sanctuary for cows. |
| Karma | Action and the results of action, can determine one's rebirth. |
| Kshatriyas | The warrior caste. |
| The Laws of Manu or Manusmriti | Books of religious and moral teaching from 100 CE approximately, smriti. |
| Mahabharata | Epic tale, includes the Bhagavad Gita, smriti. |
| Moksha | Release from samsara, eternal bliss. |
| Ramayana | Epic tale of the god Rama and his wife Sita, smriti. |
| Samsara | The cycle of rebirths. |
| Sanatana Dharma | The Eternal Law of Righteousness, the words many Hindus prefer to use, rather than "Hinduism". |
| Scheduled castes | Official term for those outside the main caste system, previously called untouchables, Dalits (scattered ones) or Harijans (children of God). |
| Shudras | The worker caste. |
| Smriti | Holy books accepted as being written by people, literally "that which is remembered". |
| Sruti | Divinely revealed teachings given to the sages, e.g., the Vedas. |
| The Upanishads | Later sacred books, more philosophical, also sruti. |
| Vaishyas | Traders, farmers and business people caste. |
| The Vedas | Ancient holy books: Rig Veda, Sama Veda, Yajur Veda and Atharva Veda, all sruti. |

# Buddhism

| | |
|---|---|
| Anatta or an-atman | The concept of non-self or no-self. It is linked to the concept of anicca, impermanence – everything is constantly changing. |
| Arhat | In Theravadan Buddhism, one who fully realises the teaching and can thus attain nirvana (nibbana) or enlightenment and freedom from the cycle of rebirth (samsara). |
| Bodhi tree (tree of awakening) | Usually refers to the tree under which Gautama meditated until he became the Buddha or enlightened one. |
| Bodhisattva | One who foregoes nirvana in order to be reborn and help others to achieve enlightenment. |
| Buddha | The Enlightened One. |
| Dhammapada | An anthology of 423 verses mostly contained within the Pali canon. Dhamma can mean law, discipline, justice, virtue, truth - that which holds things together. Pada means way, path, step, foot. So, The Dhammapada is the path of virtue, or the way of truth. |
| Karuna | Compassion. |
| Mahayana | One of the two main divisions within Buddhism: the Great Vehicle, found mostly in China, Tibet, Japan and Vietnam. |
| Paramis | Perfections or moral virtues of giving, morality, renunciation, discerning wisdom, energy, patience, truthfulness, determination, loving kindness and equanimity. |
| Samsara | Cycle of birth, death and rebirth. |
| Sangha | The community of monks and nuns, sometimes refers to the wider Buddhist community. |
| Theravada | One of the two main divisions within Buddhism: The Way of the Elders, found in India, Sri Lanka and other south-east Asian countries such as Thailand and Myanmar, sometimes referred to as the Hinayana (Lesser Vehicle). |
| Tripitaka or Pali canon (1st c BCE), also called Tipitaka ("Triple Basket") | The oldest Buddhist written teachings. |

# First Nations Australia

| | |
|---|---|
| Country | The land, its formations, includes one's relationships with other beings, human and animal, and with the earth. |
| The Dreaming | Stories of the Ancestral Beings, who created the land, the creatures and the relationships between them. |
| Songlines | These songs represent the journey of the ancestors. The songs act as a map or guide across the land and include knowledge about animals and plants. |
| Totem | Usually an animal, unique to that person, who feels a strong affiliation with that totem. |

## Jainism

| | |
|---|---|
| Agam literature | Holy book accepted by Swetambra Jains. |
| Ahimsa | Non-violence, key teaching in Jainism. |
| Gaushala | Sanctuary for cows. |
| Jiva | Soul. All beings have a soul. |
| Jiv-daya | A life of compassion (daya), relieving suffering, compassionate action. |
| Karma | Action and the results of action, can determine one's rebirth. |
| Kevala | Full enlightenment, liberation. |
| Moksha | Liberation from samsara. |
| Pinjraproles | Animal sancutaries. |
| Samsara | Cycle of rebirths. |
| Tirthankara | Enlightened teacher, lit. "ford-maker" – in this case one who creates a fordable passage through the cycle of endless rebirths (samsara) to kevala or liberation. |

## Sikhism

| | |
|---|---|
| Gurdwara | Sikh temple. |
| Guru Granth Sahib (GGS) | The ultimate teacher or "Eternal Guru", book containing teachings from the Sikh gurus and others. Regarded as the highest authority in Sikhism. A copy is kept in each gurdwara. |
| Jivanmukti | Realisation of mukti whilst still living. |
| Jhatka | Preferred Sikh method of slaughter. The animal is beheaded in one stroke. |
| Langar | Community kitchen/feeding place in a gurdwara, distributes free vegetarian food daily to all-comers. |
| Mukti | Liberation from samsara, the cycle of rebirths, and merging with the divine. Similar to Moksha. |

## Rastafarianism

| | |
|---|---|
| Babylon | Western consumerist culture, neo-colonialism. |
| Ital (diet) | Diet based on plant foods. |
| Jah | God (from Jehovah). |
| Livity | Life energy, increases through eating an ital diet. |

# Index

harmony in 167; foreign aid as
neocolonialism for 167; ganja, smoking
of 166; glossary entries 180; health, diet
and 167–9; "I and I," connectiveness in
use of 167; "ital." diet in 167, 169; Jah
Rastafari: Eternal God Selassie I 166–7;
Liverpool, Dan's food truck cafe in 168;
origins of 166; political aspects 167;
practices, biblical references for 166–7;
reasoning sessions, meditation and
166–7; rules, rejection of 167; women
and 168–9
*Rebirth: A Guide to Mind, Karma, and
Cosmos in the Buddhist World* (Jackson,
R.) 115–16
Ricard, Matthieu 121, 130, 132
Rinpoche, Yongey Mingyur 118
Roberts, Peter 14; court action against
intensive veal farming by Norbertine
friars 41
Rohr, Fr. Richard (Franciscan theologian)
29, 35, 36
Rose, Kenneth 47
Rosebud Sioux Nation in South Dakota
148
Rosen, Rabbi David 8; on factory farming
13, 14; on principle of not causing pain
18–19; on slaughter of animals 17;
on vivisection 21; on wearing animal
products 23
Royal Society for the Protection of
Animals (RSPCA) 39, 122
Rudd, Kevin 150

*Sacred Animals of India* (Krishna, N.) 100
sacred scriptures, inspiration from 1–2
sacrifice: Ashvamedha (horse sacrifice)
84–5; Buddhism and 129–30; Cardozo,
Rabbi Nathan Lopes on animal sacrifice
20; Christianity and 50; Eid ul Adha,
Islamic sacrifice at festival of 76; God
and rejection of animal sacrifice 19–20;
Hinduism and 84–5; Islam and 76; Jesus,
sacrifice of 47, 50; Judaism and 19–20;
Qur'an, animal sacrifice in 76; Union of
Reformed Judaism on animal sacrifice
20
Saeed, Professor Abdullah 75
Saheb, Sant Dariya 91
Sahib, Sri Harmandir 164
Saint Augustine 47
Saint Bonaventure 38
Saint Cuthbert 37
Saint Francis of Assisi 38, 52

Saint Gerasimus 37
Saint Isaac the Syrian 1, 37
Saint Kevin 37
Saint Martin de Porres 38
Saint Paul 29; Letter to the Romans 35
Saint Peter 46–7
Saint Thomas Aquinas 31
sanctuaries 108, 136; cow sanctuaries
102–3, 157, 178, 179; elephant
sanctuaries 126; gaushalas (sanctuaries
for cows) 102–3
SARX - For All God's Creatures 40
Saudi Ministry of Environment, Water
and Agriculture (MEWA) 67, 73
Saudi National Commission for Wildlife
Conservation and Development
(NCWCD) 74
Schwartz, Dr Richard H.: on factory
farming 14; on Judaism and compassion
for animals 10; proposal on Rosh
Hashanah LaBeheimot (New Year for
Animals) 23–4
Schweitzer, Dr Albert 39–40, 42
SEKEM farms in Egypt 67
sentient beings 2, 3, 35, 47–8, 59, 60, 129,
161; Acaranga Sutra and protection for
all 156; animals as, Indigenous North
American lobby for recognition of
145; bodhicitta (mind which aspires
to enlightenment for the benefit of all
sentient beings), aim for development of
117–18, 119; Buddhism, loving kindness
for all within 114, 116, 120–2, 130, 131,
136; ecosystem and sentient beings,
calls for care of 8; India, Prevention of
Cruelty to Animals Act (1960), partial
recognition in 107; Laws of Manu and
104
Seventh Day Adventist Church 47
Shah-Kazemi, Reza 69
Shankara, Adi 91
Shantideva 119
Shasemene, Ethiopian town of 167
Shenandoah, Audrey 144–5
Sigma Pharmaceuticals 158
Sikhism 160–5; animals, beliefs
about 161–2; Daya (Compassion
and kindness), virtue of 160; farm
animals 162–3; food, diet and 163–4;
glossary entries 180; God, animals in
relationship with 161; Guru Gobind
Singh 160, 162, 163; Guru Gobind
Singh, qualities for Sikhs to emulate
160; Guru Granth Sahib (GGS),

# Redcoat's Rifle

## Book 2 in the Soldier of the Queen Series

## By

## Griff Hosker

# Redcoat's Rifle

*Published by Sword Books Ltd 2023*

SWORD
BOOKS

*Copyright ©Griff Hosker First Edition 2023*

## Dedication

To Betty, the newest member of the family and a most welcome one too.

# Contents

# Prologue

## Brecon 1880

I had joined the British Army as a soldier of the Queen because an old soldier, Trooper, had told me he had enjoyed the life. He was right and my life was good after the Battle of Rorke's Drift. I had returned from South Africa with just a service medal but I had been promoted to corporal and I had extra pay. I had spent a precious week of leave with my family and I was able to give them some of my back pay. My needs were less than theirs. They were comfortable but that was because they did without luxuries. I was able to give them a few more treats. I felt guilty that I was not supporting my family.

My nan had been close to death just before I returned and the whole family thought I had died at Isandlwana. My unexpected return brought joy to them all. Although my grandmother recovered after I walked through the door, it was a warning that her time amongst us was limited. I spent as much time as I could with her and my mother. I knew I only had a short leave and that I would be back at Brecon for we needed to train men to replace those who had fallen, not at Rorke's Drift, but at Isandlwana. Many of the men I had served with like Fred Hitch had been invalided out of the battalion while others, like Hooky, had fulfilled their enlistment and left.

I said goodbye and took the familiar trains back to Brecon. Now that I was an NCO, I enjoyed more privileges. I was under a new sergeant, Sergeant Bob Williams. He had not been in South Africa and he treated me well. Colour Sergeant Windridge was also a familiar face to help me learn how to be an NCO.

I could not help smiling at the new men who had to learn the drills, recognise the bugle calls and work out how to keep the vast array of equipment in good order. I think I was more sympathetic to the men having had to endure the mysteries of service life relatively recently. Life was good until the day that Lieutenant Harding-Smythe arrived. He had not purchased his commission, the Cardwell reforms had eliminated that route, and every officer had to climb the slippery ladder through their own endeavours. Having said that Lieutenant Harding-Smythe must

2

have used the connections of his father, a retired general from the Crimean War to ease his way through officer training for he was an incompetent and arrogant officer. Captain Bromhead, who had commanded us at the Mission Station, had appeared to be a little aloof but that was largely due to his deafness. Lieutenant Harding-Smythe was just a nasty piece of work and a bully to boot. It did not help that when he arrived Bob Williams suffered a hernia and was in the battalion hospital and I had to deal with him, unaided. I think it might have been easier if I did not have two or three new men who needed to be treated gently. I was more than capable of that. Hooky had taught me how to use discipline but to be fair as well. The new lieutenant wanted to make his platoon the best in the battalion.

He began on day one and ordered me to take my section on a ten-mile forced quick march with full equipment. It was high summer and whilst I did not find it a problem the new lads did. Most of them came from poor homes and they were not as fit as they might have been. The officer did not march with us but used his horse to ride and chivvy those at the rear. Albert Hepplewhite was a thin lad from Lancashire and whilst he was keen he was patently unfit. I don't think he had eaten well and was all skin and bone. The losses at Isandlwana meant we took men we would not have in previous drafts. I used the men who had been in South Africa to lead the march and I stayed at the rear to encourage Albert and another of the weaker men, Leonard Jones. Neither was fast and a gap opened up before us. I felt that the forced march was unfair as the new men had only joined us a fortnight earlier. They were still learning.

"Come on, boys. You are doing well. Take it one step at a time and just count your steps until we reach the top of that rise, eh?" Neither answered me as they were both out of breath but they gritted their teeth and tried to catch up with the redcoats ahead of us.

Lieutenant Harding-Smythe had stopped to allow his horse to drink from a farmer's trough and I heard him galloping up behind. "This won't do, Roberts! These two are forty yards behind the others. Make them march faster."

"Sorry, sir, but they are doing the best that they can."

"Nonsense. You just need to encourage them." It happened that Albert was the last man and the lieutenant rode behind him and smacked his back hard with the cane he carried. The lieutenant was a good rider. The blow came as a shock to Albert who fell forward and hit the ground hard. I helped him to his feet. "Now you are even further behind. Get a move on man."

Albert was hurt, His hands had scraped along the ground and his nose was bleeding. "Sir, the man needs medical attention."

"Then he will have to run hard for we still have three miles to go."

What I did next exacerbated the problem. I can see it now but at the time I felt sorry for the lad from Lancashire, "Here, Albert, give me your gun." It was little enough but the gun he carried was heavy, it weighed nine pounds and with his grazed hands was a weight he could do without.

"What are you doing, corporal?"

"Sir, I am helping the private and trying to minimise the effect of the fall, sir." I added, quietly, "Come on son. Not far to go."

"Right Corp."

It was a supreme effort but we gradually caught up with Jones who had almost caught up with the others. I wondered how and then realised that the rest of the section was helping us. They were looking after one of their own and had slowed down.

When we reached the camp I said, "Private Hepplewhite, go and see the MO. The rest of you fall in."

I stood and watched as they shuffled into their lines. The lieutenant did not dismount but rode along the length of them. "I can see that I have inherited the worst and most slovenly soldiers in the army. Let me tell you that I will make you the best or I will break you. Do you understand?"

They remained silent and he glared at me, "Are they being insolent, corporal? Why do they not answer?"

"Against Queen's regulations, sir."

He rode over to me and put his cane under my chin, "I do not like you, Corporal Roberts. I shall see the colonel about having you removed from my section."

I said, "That is your right, sir."

He glared at me, "Tomorrow we shall see if they can drill. I want them all to spend the next three hours drilling. Do you understand, Corporal?"

"Yes sir!" he had made the mistake of keeping his face close to mine and when I barked my response, he recoiled. The men were not stupid enough to laugh out loud but smiles crept across their faces and he saw it.

When he had gone, I did as he had ordered. By the time we had finished, they were perfect, even Leonard Jones. As I dismissed them, he said, "Thanks for that, corporal. I'll do better the next time."

I smiled, "Don't worry about it. If I had been asked to do a forced march in my first month, I would have still been puking my guts up."

I sought the advice that night of Colour Sergeant Windridge. He shook his head, "Sorry about this, Jack, but there is nowt we can do about him. Hopefully, the colonel will see what he is like and have a quiet word. I will see Lieutenant Bourne and ask him to see the colonel." The lieutenant had been Colour Sergeant Windridge's predecessor and had been the best soldier in the regiment. I went to bed feeling better. What I did not know was the Colour Sergeant would not see the lieutenant until the next day.

The MO put salve on Hepplewhite's hands and bandaged them. What he did not do was give him a chitty to excuse duty. I had the section up and ready before the lieutenant arrived for his inspection. It gave me the chance to talk to Albert, "Just make sure you obey every order promptly, eh lad? Don't give the officer the excuse to find fault."

"I do try, Corp, honest I do but sometimes I get left and right mixed up."

"Which hand do you hold your pint in?"

I saw him frown and then beam. He nodded to his right hand, "This one Corp."

"Then that is your right. When I say right then think pint hand. Can you do that?"

"Yes, Corp."

The anger on the lieutenant's face was still there as he strode belligerently up to the line of red-coated soldiers. I knew that their equipment was perfect, I had checked it myself. They were all ramrod straight and at attention. Their faces were set and as he approached, I said, "Section, attention!" I would not risk abbreviating the command as I normally did in case he took offence to that.

He marched along the line peering at every face and every uniform. Despite seeking he found no fault.

"Very well, Corporal Roberts, let us see them go through the drills."

The drills went perfectly. Even Hepplewhite who had missed the extra training session I had put in, thanks to '*pint hand*', managed.

"Now let us see them use their bayonets."

"Prepare to fix bayonets."

Every right hand went directly to the bayonet and was ready to draw as one.

"Fix bayonets."

The bayonets all came out together and rose as one so that the socket was ready to be placed on the end of the rifle. The clang on the cobbles as Hepplewhite dropped his echoed across the parade ground. Even as Albert bent to retrieve the weapon, I saw the look of joy on the officer's face. It had been the bandage on Hepplewhite's hand that had caused the accident. That was clear to all but I don't think that the lieutenant was bothered.

He strode over to me and handed me his cane. "Corporal Roberts, I want this man to bare his buttocks and for you to cane him. Twenty strokes should teach him a lesson."

I stared ahead and did not take the proffered wooden cane.

"Did you not hear me, Roberts, I gave you an order?"

"Sir, it is against regulations to use physical punishment on any soldier. Flogging was banned some time ago."

"This is just caning. I was caned at my school and it did me no harm."

"No, sir. Hepplewhite has injured hands and he could not help what he did."

The lowered voice was a warning, "So you are refusing to obey my order?"

"With respect, sir, yes."

As it happened Colour Sergeant Windridge was close by and he was spied by Lieutenant Harding-Smythe. "Colour Sergeant."
"Sir?"
"This man has refused to obey an order. I want him confined to barracks while I see the colonel." He gave no explanation but turned and marched off. The colour sergeant had no idea what was going on. He said, "Refused an order, Jack?"
I nodded, "I was ordered to tell Hepplewhite to bare his buttocks so that I could cane him."
The whole section nodded and it was some comfort to know that I had their support.
"Right, come with me. You lot, at ease and await my return." As we headed for the barracks he said, "Soon have this little lot cleared up, Jack. I know there are officers who still like to birch or cane but the colonel doesn't approve." Once in the barracks, I sat on my bed. He grinned, "A morning off work is not a bad thing, eh Jack?"
I sat and I brooded. I was in the right and he was in the wrong. I did not want a morning off. I had a good section and I wanted to work with them. I hoped that the colonel would realise that the lieutenant was a bad apple. There were ways and means for the colonel to put the martinet out of harm's way. He could make him adjutant and let him deal with paperwork. We did not really need an officer. Although Captain Bromhead had been a rock at Rorke's Drift it had been the steel of the non-commissioned officers and chosen men that had won the day.
The noonday meal came and I was still confined to barracks. I had expected to be back with my section within the hour. When Colour Sergeant Windridge returned, Captain Bromhead accompanied him. "Come with us, lad. The colonel wants a word." The colour sergeant's tone was not encouraging. It sounded like the tolling of a death knell.
As we left Captain Bromhead said, loudly as he always did, "Sorry about this, Roberts, but the lieutenant has connections at the war office and the colonel has the regiment to think about."
"Sir, it was not a lawful order."
Colour Sergeant Windridge said, "We all know that, lad, but there is still a great deal of blame attached to the regiment

because of Isandlwana. Our regiment managed to avoid amalgamation in the Cardwell reforms, the colonel..."

We had reached the office and Colour Sergeant Windridge flicked some imaginary fluff from my uniform. "Keep your face straight and your mouth shut."

"Yes, Colour Sergeant."

I was marched into the office and ordered to take off my cap. Lieutenant Harding-Smyth smirked at me. I kept my eyes fixed on the map of Wales above the colonel's head.

"Corporal Roberts, Lieutenant Harding-Smythe has made a very serious accusation. He attests that you have tried to undermine him at every turn." My mouth almost dropped open. "He says that on the march yesterday, you carried a soldier's gun and allowed men to lag behind others and that today you refused to obey an order." It was clear that I was not going to be allowed to speak for he went on quickly. "We cannot have dissension in the regiment." He looked up and smiled, "Captain Bromhead has spoken on your behalf. Perhaps you might be better off in another regiment. The Shropshire Foot has a need for experienced men, especially non-commissioned officers for they are about to go on foreign service. You are to be transferred to that battalion with immediate effect. You will still be a soldier of the queen but you can use your experience to help the Shropshires become better."

That was not good enough for the bully, "Sir, I protest. I want Roberts to lose his stripes."

There was steel in the voice of the colonel, "Lieutenant, your father may have sway in Whitehall but here I run this regiment, now take Colour Sergeant Windridge who will assist you today."

"Sir."

"And have Hepplewhite sent to the MO again, Colour Sergeant."

"Sir."

The silence in the room felt oppressive. I had been told to remain silent but I could not, "Sir, this is unfair. The officer should be punished and not me."

The colonel leaned back and put his fingers together, almost as though he was at prayer. "Roberts, you are highly thought of in this regiment but we cannot afford a scandal and if you remain here then there would be ripples that would show us in a poor light. You have the chance for a new start with a new regiment. I hear they are being sent to India in the next year or so. You are a good soldier and could make a sergeant within the next ten years."

India! I was being sent abroad so that the lieutenant and I would never cross paths again.

Captain Bromhead said, "It is unfair, Roberts, and I have done my best but we have the regiment to think of. We need to build on the success at Rorke's Drift and put Isandlwana behind us."

It was done. That I had the sympathy of the whole battalion just made my punishment worse. Poor Albert was particularly upset. I did not know if that was because he would be left at the mercy of the martinet or was genuinely upset. My world had been turned upside down and I could not think straight. The next day I was given my railway warrant and took a train to Shrewsbury. I had thought to be a soldier in the 24th for my whole career. I was wrong and as I sat in the carriage I wondered if I had chosen the wrong career. Was it too late to do something about it?

# Chapter 1

**Shrewsbury 1881**

The bulky manilla packet, sealed with wax, the colonel had given me was my pass into the barracks at Shrewsbury Castle. The colonel was away and the adjutant, an aged officer, Captain Philips, was the one to free me. He had the office door closed by his orderly and invited me to take a seat. He had the look of an old soldier who was coming to the end of his time in the army. His office felt like a comfortable study. He lit his pipe and studied me and then broke the seal and began to read the contents. It was my service file but I could not help but notice letters there. He glanced up from time to time as he read each document and then placed it neatly in a pile.

When he had finished reading, he smiled as he leaned back in his chair. "Roberts, I have served in this regiment my whole career and I have never heard a shot fired in anger. When the regiment was in India, I was here training the replacements. I have read, with interest, this letter from your colonel and Captain Bromhead." He tapped the letters, "You fought at the battle where so many VCs were won. I envy you. I shall never know how brave or cowardly I am. I shall grow roses and wonder." He leaned forward, "There are two pieces of news which should interest you. First, this regiment is to be amalgamated with another. Second, I have heard that we are to be sent abroad." He shook his head, "Perhaps my chance to discover what is within me, eh? I know that you regard this move to a new regiment as a punishment. I can see it in your face and looking at the letters I can understand those feelings. Let me say that it is not. We really do need men like you. When this regiment fights you may well be one of the few who has endured battle. You were at Rorke's Drift." He said it as though my mere presence there elevated me. I nodded, "And while the newspapers tell us how glorious the battle was, I know it must have been bloody."

I spoke for the first time, "It was, sir."

"Then you should know that your colonel thinks that you should have had more reward in terms of honours and that you could and should be a lance sergeant. I will put the case forward to the colonel when he returns. It would mean more pay."

I nodded, "Yes sir, unless an officer took a dislike to me and had the stripes removed."

"Don't be bitter, Roberts. You have a good service record. I do not know this officer but he is in the past."

"Sir, if we are amalgamated then you cannot know the calibre of the officers from the regiment that is joining us and, with respect, you are leaving the regiment."

He nodded, "But not until it is posted abroad. You have to trust me, Roberts. I will do all that I can to ensure that your time with us is a happy one."

"Do you mind me asking why, sir?"

He nodded, "I know Gonville Bromhead and Lieutenant Melville was my cousin." He tapped the letter. "I know what you did, all of it." I knew then that letter from Captain Bromhead had to have been written before the incident with Hartington-Smythe. The officers in the army were a network of old families and the product of the public schools. It was like a secret society. I wondered how Lieutenant Bourne would cope in the new world.

"Yes, sir, I just want to be a good soldier."

The captain tapped the letters in his hand, "And this tells me that you are. Let us use those skills to make this new regiment even better."

I thought back to Trooper. He had told me of officers like Harding-Smythe. Trooper had also said that the non-commissioned officers made the real army. I was now one.

In the event, my arrival went almost unnoticed as old soldiers were given their pensions and new ones arrived. The colonel did not arrive back for a week and I saw that Captain Philips was the driving force behind this regiment. I was put in command of a section. We were part of a platoon and that was part of a company. A sergeant commanded the platoon. The sergeant who commanded the company was a senior one and above them all were the colour sergeant and sergeant major. My new rank was yet to be confirmed and so I had just the two stripes. However, word had gotten around about my adventures in the Zulu wars and both rank and file were keen to know all the details. The captain had been right, this regiment had enjoyed a peaceful time since they had returned from India in 1860. That was twenty years earlier and none remained from the time when the regiment had earned five VCs. I was a novelty. I passed for a veteran and that gave me status.

I threw myself into the training. The captain was a man of his word and the officer who commanded me and the platoon was not a young man. He was still a lieutenant but Lieutenant Hodges had served the regiment for ten years and knew how to be an officer. He had nothing to prove and, indeed, was keen to learn from me. The story of our defence of the mission had appeared in many newspapers. Everyone wanted to know the reality. The section themselves were also, in the main, good lads and despite the fact that I was younger than many of them, they took both my orders and my advice. Captain Philips had been right. It was a new start and one I should embrace. My bitterness began to seep away. I had closed one door but thanks to Captain Bromhead and Captain Philips another had opened.

After the first month, I felt brave enough to go into the town and enjoy a pipe and a pint. The other NCOs all recommended a pub called the *'Eagle and Child'*. There were unspoken rules and that particular pub was used by NCOs. I began going there because I felt sorry for myself. The other soldiers had all made me welcome but it was not my regiment and, at first, I was still resentful about the injustice of it all. It did not help that I still wore my old uniform. I would be getting a new one but as it was still serviceable and there was the prospect of foreign duty when all the regiment would be issued new gear it was deemed that I did not need one. The other corporals and sergeants soon realised that I wished to be left alone and I had my own little corner where I sat. I enjoyed the solitude. I never had more than two pints and I smoked my pipe and wrapped myself in the comfortable blanket of memories of Natal.

The pub had girls who, for a handful of coins would provide comforts other than beer. That was not to say that all the girls were as free and easy with their favours. One such girl was Annie. She was only eighteen or so and, as I discovered, an orphan. She lodged with some of the other girls. They were the ones who were happy to sell their favours. In return for the room, Annie cooked and cleaned for them. It was a worthwhile arrangement. All the soldiers respected her attitude but some of the men who also used the pub did not see the demarcation line. It was not a whorehouse. The girls decided if they wanted to lie with the men who sought comfort and company. In the main, it was a system that worked and was not abused. The landlord, Geraint, took no commission. His trade was increased by the arrangement and he seemed to be quite paternal towards the girls.

A month or so after I had begun to drink there I went for a drink; I only ever drank two at the most. I enjoyed drinking good beer and smoking my pipe, and, if I am honest, feeling sorry for myself for there had been no word about foreign service. Annie was serving and I liked her. She had a lovely smile and a good sense of humour. I had been chatting with her while she hand-pulled the beer and enjoying the conversation when a bunch of young men entered. They were labourers, navvies, working on the railway. They would be gone in a month. They were relatively well paid for their work. They were only given a few opportunities to make the most of such freedom. Bill, who had been on the iron gang at Pritchard's had been one and he had told me the tales. I knew that they thought of themselves as tough young men. As soon as they entered, I went to my corner. They were loud and they were young. They also thought that they were good fighters. Bill had told me of bare-knuckle contests in the navvy camps. The largest of them made the mistake of brushing against Sergeant Thomas and spilling his beer. The sergeant made Colour Sergeant Windridge look slim.

Flicking the beer from his red tunic the Welshman said, "Son, if you can't handle your beer, stick to pop!"

The young man squared up to the sergeant. As Sergeant Thomas was not alone the loudmouth quickly realised his mistake and backed off. I saw him glowering at their backs all night. When they left, he turned his attention to Annie and Mary, the two barmaids. Mary did take money for favours. However, when he heard the price she asked, he turned his attention to Annie. I smiled. The girls raised their prices when they did not wish to go with a man. Annie, however, was clearly uncomfortable. I had planned on just one pint but seeing her discomfort I finished my beer and went to the bar for a second.

"Come on, love, you don't charge as much as this stuck-up cow do you?"

Geraint, the landlord said, "Eh, son, watch your language."

The young man had clearly had too much to drink for he waved a contemptuous hand at the diminutive landlord. "I asked you a question, how much do you charge?"

She looked at me, "A pint again?"

"Yes please."

As I counted out the money, she pulled my pint and said, with a smile on her face, "I am sorry, but I am not like that. There are others who are but not me."

He laughed and put half a crown on the bar, "Here, half a crown for ten minutes around the back."

"That will be four pence, Jack."

As I handed over the money the young man seemed to see my uniform for the first time. "Jack, eh? I see, so a uniform gets you what you want. Typical." He pushed me, clearly intent on beginning a fight. "I bet you are a typical soldier, all mouth and trousers!"

I turned and grabbed his hand which he had bunched into a fist ready to hit me. I began to squeeze, "Listen you loudmouth, you are not welcome here," I looked at Geraint, "Isn't that true, landlord?"

"Aye, finish your drinks, sling your hook, you are all barred."

There were still a couple of soldiers in the bar as well as some locals and they all stood and edged towards the labourers. The rest saw the writing on the wall and one said, "Come on, Joe, there are plenty of pubs."

Joe's hand was hurting but he was bigger than I was and I saw what was coming. He pulled back his head to butt me. I simply tucked in my chin and his nose smashed into the top of my skull. The rest of the pub burst into laughter as blood erupted from his nose. The butt made his eyes water and I pushed his hand away, "You lads get him out of here before he really gets hurt."

They led him out and the pub cheered and applauded. The landlord said, "Thanks for that, Jack. I am getting too old for fisticuffs."

Annie looked worried, "Will you be alright, Jack? It was very gallant of you but I wouldn't want you to get hurt on my account."

I shook my head, "I will be fine."

I sat down and drank the beer which tasted better. The pipe I lit smoked sweeter and the smiles from my fellow non-coms and the other clientele made me feel better about myself. I knew why. For the first time, I wasn't thinking about myself. When I had finished the beer, I took the tankard back to the bar. "Thanks Annie."

"No, Thank you. I know this is a bit forward but I get Sundays off. Is there any chance of meeting up and having a walk in the park?" She shook her head, "If you are a young lady and walk by yourself then people get the wrong idea. I can see that you are a gentleman and I have been trying to pluck up the courage since you first started drinking here."

I did not think she had even noticed me. I smiled, "Of course, I can meet you outside the castle after church parade if you like."

Her smile and nod made me feel even better.

As I stepped outside into the cool air my sixth sense kicked in. The outside of the pub was empty. The street was unlit and I had six hundred yards to the barracks. I was not a fool and guessed that Joe would want some revenge. I looked to the left and right and saw no one but I did smell unwashed bodies. That was not unusual. Most people took a weekly bath and this was in the middle of the week. However, this was the stink of a labouring man. Joe was somewhere close. I stepped into the middle of the street. The only traffic might be a horse-drawn hackney cab but they were rare and I walked in silence and in the dark. The wooden stave that swung from my right came suddenly but my time hunting for the colours of the 24th had given me good reactions. I ducked beneath it and swung my left hand at the stomach of the man who had wielded the wood. It was one of those who had been in the pub but it was not Joe. Joe had allowed his friend to initiate the attack and he brought his stave down to smash at my head. I moved towards him and my movement meant his stave hit my back and not my head. I hit him hard in the gut with my right hand. The hands on the stave brushed my head but there was no force behind the blow. I hit

15

him hard in the ribs with my left fist and then on the other side with my right. I heard bones crack. The first man had recovered and I sensed the stave coming for me. They had both had too much to drink and I stepped out of the way. The stave smashed into Joe's head and he fell in a heap.

Just then I heard a whistle and two constables arrived. I was also aware that others had come from the pub when they had heard the altercation. Joe's mate was standing with his hands on the stave while blood dripped down the face of the unconscious Joe.

Geraint pointed at the two men, "Those two caused bother in my pub, Constable Rees, and they attacked the corporal."

The constable nodded, "Aye, we heard there had been some bother. We will take them down to the station where they will be charged with breach of the peace. We don't need their kind here. You alright corporal?"

One of the sergeants who had been in the pub said, "That is Lance Sergeant Roberts and he will be alright. He is a soldier. Don't worry, constable, we will see him home. Come on Jack."

From that moment I was not only accepted but welcomed into the regiment and I began to feel less sorry for myself. The story spread and it became clear that everyone approved of my actions. The fact that I had taken on two hulking great labourers and soundly thrashed them was a badge of honour for me. I had no injuries, except for grazed knuckles and my tunic was undamaged.

Sunday was our day off. We had one duty every four weeks and, as it happened, I was able to take advantage of Annie's offer. I now had two medal ribbons on my uniform. It made me feel less like a novice. I had the Zulu War Campaign medal and the South African General Service medal. I felt proud to be wearing them. With my boots polished until you could see my face in them and my forage cap at a jaunty angle, I tucked my swagger stick under my arm and awaited Annie. I was ribbed, of course, by other NCOs but that was to be expected. It was all good-natured. When Annie arrived, I saw that she too had made a real effort. She wore what was patently her best dress and bonnet and shoes that had a slight heel on them. There was the tiniest amount of rouge on her cheeks and a little more on her lips. As she neared me, I caught the faintest whiff of toilet water.

I gave a slight bow, "You are beautiful, my dear, and I am honoured to walk with you in the park." Standing I put my right hand on my hip and said, "My arm?"

She slipped her arm into mine and nestled a little closer to me. I was becoming intoxicated. It was a lovely afternoon. I had coins in my pocket and there was an Italian ice cream seller in the park. I bought her an ice cream and it was as though I had given her a diamond. She was a lovely bubbly girl. Apart from my sisters and Hooky's wife, Ada, I had little experience of women and it showed. She chattered on about the girls in the pub and the house in which she lived. She told me that one of them had loaned her the shoes and it was they who had applied the rouge. I told her of my family in Liverpool and St Helens and she was genuinely interested in them. her family had lived on a small hill farm close to Builth Wells and it had been illness which had wiped them out.

"I know not why I was saved, Jack, but I determined to make a good life. I work in the pub as it is the only job I could get but I save each week and one day I will make something of myself. I know not what that shall be but I have dreams."

I found myself captivated by her and when it was time to return to her lodgings, I found myself reluctant to leave. "Shall I see you again, Annie?"

She laughed, "As you come into the pub two or three times a week, I think that you shall."

I shook my head, "I mean, like today."

"Walking out with me, Lance Sergeant Roberts, what will people say?"

"I care not. Next week?"

"Next week."

We enjoyed more walks and I found myself looking forward to Sunday and the chance to talk to the sweet Welsh girl with the lilting voice and sparkling eyes. Three weeks later she invited me into the house where she lodged. She was keen to show me her culinary skills and had made a cake and scones. It was all very prim and proper. I think the other women in the house were amused by it. Some of them had clients and I heard the bump of a headboard from upstairs but everyone tactfully avoided mentioning it. I loved every moment and the girls seemed to enjoy my company. I told them the same tale of Rorke's Drift I had told my family, the acceptable version and they squealed when I told it.

Doris was the oldest of the women and she smiled and shook her head, "You are a natural storyteller, Jack. People pay good money to hear such tales at the music hall. You could earn a good living."

"Not for me, Doris. I am a soldier pure and simple." I stood, "Anyway, I must be going. It wouldn't do to be on a charge."

"And next week come here, Jack. You are good company and it is nice to talk to a real hero. You won't mind will you Annie?"

I had come to know Annie, not well but well enough to know that while she said, "Of course, not." She did not mean it. She would rather have me all to herself.

The next week saw a return to the house. The ladies had made a real effort and put on their version of a high tea. There were no crusts cut off the sandwiches and they were rough ham and mustard while the scones just had butter and no cream but it was a nice gesture. I could see, however, that Annie just wanted us to be alone. We laughed, sometimes until our sides ached but I saw that Annie was not as happy as I had thought she would be. She saw me to the door when I left and then to the end of the street. She linked my arm and when we were out of sight she turned and held my hands in hers.

"Next week, Jack, just you and me, eh? I don't like sharing. I will meet you outside the barracks and we will go to the park again."

"Of course, I could see that you were uncomfortable."

"They are all good girls but they all have boys or men in their lives. I only have you and I am selfish. I want to keep you all to myself."

"And so you shall."

The following Sunday saw us in more familiar territory and she squeezed my arm as we walked through the park. The clouds that suddenly appeared and sent a deluge to drown us spoiled an otherwise perfect afternoon. We ran to her home and raced up the stairs to her tiny room. Our clothes were soaked. She opened the door and I said, "I will let you get changed then, Annie. I shall see you next week."

She took my hand and shook her head, "No, Jack. Wait here while I get changed then you can come in and we can talk."

I looked around, nervously, "Is that proper?"

She smiled, "It is."

The door closed and I took off my tunic in the hallway. The good thing about the tunic was that it kept our moisture for longer than ordinary clothes. My shirt, beneath, was barely damp and my trousers were already drying.

Doris appeared and laughed, "Got a soaking, did you, Jack?"

I nodded, "Annie is just changing."

She gave me a knowing look, "You two are right together, you know. We all see that." With those enigmatic words hanging in the air she returned to her room.

The door opened and I saw that Annie had donned a dressing gown. "Come in and we can dry your things. I shall get a fire going."

I saw the smallest fireplace I had ever seen in my life in the corner. It obviously fed off the main one downstairs. I shook my head, "I will do that. It is not a job for a lady."

She had all the makings but my flint, the one I always kept with me, was better than hers. The kindling soon caught and I had a fine fire going quickly. I put the fireguard before it, the room was so small that sparks could have started a fire, and hung my tunic from it. It soon steamed as the moisture evaporated.

"Take off your boots, Jack. They will need to dry too."

"Are you sure?"

She laughed, "The only place to sit is on the bed and the last thing I want are your muddy boots on it."

I took off the boots and placed them close to the fireguard. She sat on the bed and patted the space beside her. It was a single bed.

"I feel so safe when you are here."

"I will always be here to protect you, my lady."

She laughed, "My lady! I do like the way to speak to me, Jack. It is so much nicer than the way the regulars talk to me. Oh, don't get me wrong, they are not rude but just, well, over-familiar, you know? They call me love or honey. One chap who comes from Nottingham calls me ducks. They mean nothing but…"

"I know." Auntie Sarah and my mother had brought me up to speak to all women as though they were ladies.

She nestled her head on my shoulder, "This is nice."

We sat in companionable silence and the smell of her hair and the remains of the toilet water drifted up to my nose. Her fingers played with mine. She stroked them and, I know not why, I found that it aroused me. The winter's days were short and as the room darkened, we were only lit by the light from the fire. Annie shifted a little so that her back was to the wall. She looked up at me, "Jack, I have never been kissed."

"If you are inviting me to kiss you then you have chosen the wrong man for the ways of women are foreign to me."

"All the girls have told me about kissing and… well, you know. I should like my first kiss to be from you, Jack. Is that brazen of me?"

I shook my head, "Not a harmless kiss but don't expect much, Annie."

I cupped her chin in my hand and lifted her head. When our lips met, I was not expecting it to have the effect it had. It made my whole body change. The one kiss lasted longer than I had expected and when it ended her eyes were wide.

That was the moment I should have risen and left but I was caught up in that first kiss and I obeyed. It was a mistake. That first kiss became many kisses and our hands explored each other. I know I never intended for what happened to happen but it did and afterwards, spent, I found myself wishing that I could go back in time and say goodbye at the door. I lay there and wished I was not there. When the church bell tolled, I had the chance to leave.

"I had better go, Annie."

"I love, you, Jack."

I held her hands and said, meaning every word, "And I love you, Annie, but this is too sudden. It is like the rain that came before."

"Will I see you next week?"

"I hope so."

I did not put my boots on in the room but carried them downstairs. At the door, she stood on tiptoe to give me a kiss. I knew then that I loved Annie but, as I hurried through the rain to the barracks, I still regretted what we had done. It was not right and I had been brought up better.

# Chapter 2

Sometimes events conspire to change your life. I know not how the events occurred but on Monday morning all the officers and non-commissioned officers were summoned to a meeting. The regiment was to travel to London to take part in the Trooping of the Colour, a celebration of Queen Victoria's official birthday. It was an honour for the regiment to take part although we would be on the periphery. The new colours of the amalgamated regiments were the reason for our inclusion. It meant three weeks in London as there would have to be many rehearsals to get everything just right. There would be no opportunity for me to visit the house and inform Annie as we were due to leave Shrewsbury by train, that day. I confess that the three weeks were so busy and full of new things to learn that Annie was not in my mind. It was good for the regiment as all of us were having to learn new drills. It made us better soldiers and I never thought that drill would do that.

When we returned there was a rumour that we would be going to India. When we were issued with tropical uniforms the rumour gained meat. I did not get the chance to go to the pub as the whole regiment was confined to barracks for a month while we trained and drilled. We were all checked over by the regimental doctors as the colonel did not wish to risk us taking a disease to a country where tropical diseases were rife. After a month we were allowed to leave the barracks, but, and I regret this still, I did not bother to go to the pub. All the work with the Trooping of the Colours, not to mention the possibility of tropical service made me focus on my job. I did not forget about Annie. I still dreamt of her at night but I began to think that this was for the best. I felt like a cad. I had taken advantage of a young woman and I knew that if my mother ever found out she would be ashamed of me and I did not want that.

When Doris turned up at the barracks asking to speak to me, three months after the rainstorm and the wet uniform, I was mocked by the sergeant on duty who knew Doris in the Biblical sense.

"Eh, up, Roberts, you must be something special that you are sought after here at the barracks."

Doris stood with her hands on her hips, "You are so sharp you might cut yourself, Sergeant. I don't think any woman will bother seeking your favours." The derogatory glance she gave to his midriff made the two sentries smile and him to redden. "I need a word, Jack."

"Of course." I turned to the sergeant, "I shall just be there, Sergeant Harris. I am not leaving the barracks."

He nodded his agreement.

I had no idea why Doris was here. Her face was serious and that was unusual for a woman who grinned all the time. "It is Annie."

"She is alright, isn't she? I mean I would have called around again but we were in London and then…"

She nodded, "We know you have been busy and as for being all right, well, Jack there is no easy way around this. She is pregnant. You are going to be a dad."

If she had slapped my face, I could not have been more shocked, "What?"

"I know you have both only done it the once, Annie told me, and that you have been unlucky but there is no getting around it. She is going to have a baby and that means she will lose her job at the pub."

"I…, I er…"

She smiled, "Look, come around to the house on Sunday. She needs looking after and I know that you are a gentleman. You will see her alright."

"Of course. Of course. She is well?"

Doris beamed, "Blooming. Don't worry, some of the girls have been pregnant. I have two bairns myself. We know how to look after girls in her condition."

I returned to the barracks in a state of shock. A picture of my mother came to my mind. I was telling her what had happened and she was telling me to wed the girl. That was not as easy as it sounded. I was a serving soldier and had to have permission. I knew from Hooky and Ada that being married did not guarantee married quarters. I went to the adjutant. Since I had joined the regiment, he had often sought me out to talk to me. Our joint connection to Lieutenant Melville helped.

He was an astute man and knew that something was amiss as soon as I entered his office, "Sit down, Roberts." He took out his pipe, "Smoke your own if you wish, Roberts. I can see from your face that this is something difficult and I find smoking a pipe helps to comfort me."

I did as he suggested. The silence was an easy one as we both filled and lit our pipes. I told him the whole story, including the part with Joe the labourer. When I had finished my pipe had gone out although the larger bowled pipe of the adjutant still burned. As I scraped out the remains into the ashtray the adjutant spoke. His voice was like that of a kindly uncle and was without prejudice, "I think you have been unlucky. A little foolish too but from your words, this was your own misjudgement and I think luck had more than a little part to play. You must marry the girl." He looked me in the eyes and I nodded. We both knew that such a lofty ideal as love was not even to be considered. "I would say the sooner the better. I can arrange for the padre to officiate. I am not sure that the local vicar would approve. From what I understand the house where your young lady resides is considered a house of ill repute."

"Annie is not like that!"

He held up his hand, "I know and I am trying to help here. You can be married in three weeks."

"If Annie agrees."

He smiled, "I am confident that, from what you have told me your young lady will be agreeable. Now I am afraid that there are no married quarters at the moment and, if I am to be honest, little likelihood in the near future. Added to that we may be sent abroad…"

"She can live where she does until the baby is born and then, Captain, if I could have compassionate leave, I can take her and my child, home to my family. They will look after them both."

"Are you certain of that?"

I shook my head, "I confess, Captain Philips, that I am in completely unknown territory. I will write to my mother and tell her. I have been frugal with my pay and I will see that she does not go short."

"I admire your resolve, Roberts. I am a bachelor although I have known women. I would like to think that if I was in the same boat as you, I would behave in the same way."

We finished the details and as I rose, I said, "I would like this kept quiet until the last moment, sir."

"Of course," he waved his arm around the office, "Consider this the confessional."

I sat and spent an hour writing the most difficult letter of my life to my mother.

When I arrived at the house on Sunday, I found my feet dragging. I would be judged, quite rightly, by the other women in the house. I wondered how Annie would view me. Even as the thought came to me, I knew that my mother's reaction would be even harder to bear. I was a defiler of women. Surprisingly there were smiles when I entered and Annie was sitting in the room they called the parlour. All the others left but Doris remained, "I will stay... well to put it bluntly to see if either of you need me. Whatever you say shall not leave this room."

I nodded. Annie reached out for my hand and I took it, "I have missed you."

My voice broke as I said, "And I, you." That was the signal for the dam to burst and she stood and threw her arms around me. "I am sorry, Annie. I should have had more control."

She pushed me away and the tears stopped as she wiped her arm across her eyes, "There were two of us in my room that day and we both did what we did... out of love so do not diminish it."

"But I am the man and it was my..."

"You are a man and did what a man does. It is done now and we need to decide what we do. You need not marry me."

I nodded, "Yes, I do and it is arranged. Three weeks from today we will be married in the regimental chapel. It will be done and done well. I will support you until the baby is born and then I thought to take you to my home. I am to be sent abroad and I want my family to look after you."

"Will they do that?"

I sat, deflated, "In all truth, I know not. I hope so for I have a caring family but this is unprecedented. I have written to my mother and I will let you know. Whatever happens, you will be looked after."

The letter with the Liverpool postmark arrived at the end of the week. I left it on the stand next to my bed for most of the day as I was afraid to open it. After mess, I stood in front of the mirror and counselled myself, "You have faced four thousand Zulus trying to kill you, Jack Roberts. This is a letter from your mother and she loves you. Open it!"

I slit it open with my pipe knife and sat on the bed to read it.

*My Dearest Son,*

*It was good to read a letter from you but I confess that its contents made me cry. The tears were not tears of judgement but rather the realisation that another woman has your heart. You have to marry her, that is only right and proper. My sadness is that I will not be able to be there for the ceremony. That is not because I do not wish to be there, I do, but Nan is ill. She is close to death and we dare not stir for fear of missing the moment. Do not fear, this is not because of you. We have not told her the news but as she drifts in and out of this world into a world of her childhood, I think it matters not. It is our duty to be here for her until she passes. When that is done, I intend to come to Shrewsbury for I would like to see you and to reassure you both that your family here, in Liverpool, will always be here for you. Aunt Sarah, Billy, Alice and Sarah, all know your news.*

*Your letter made me fear for your spirits. This is not a bad thing, Jack. Bringing a child into the world is a wonderful thing. I have experienced it four times and I am proud as Punch of all my children. You will be proud of yours. This is not the way I would have wanted things to turn out but God often presents us with trials to see how we deal with them. I know you, Jack, and you will handle this. It will make you a better man.*

*Hoping to see you soon,*

*Your loving Mother*

I read the letter three or four times and that night slept better than I had in a long time. I know not what I was expecting, the worst probably.

The wedding itself was a simple affair. The captain and the padre along with Doris and Geraint were the only witnesses. I wished my family could have been there as the chapel was festooned with flags and standards and the chapel itself was ancient. Despite her bump, Annie looked radiant. I did love her but there would always be the nagging doubt in my mind that our hasty liaison had distorted things. Geraint and the ladies had laid on food at the pub and my comrades who were off duty came to toast us. There would, however, be no wedding night. After the food, Annie put away her dress for she would still be working and the captain escorted me back to the barracks.

"You are a lucky man, Sergeant Roberts, she is a lovely girl and I envy you."

I stopped, surprised by the grey-haired captain's words, "Envy me, sir? I have got a girl into trouble and as I am about to be sent abroad, I have no idea if I will even see my child."

He nodded, "You are right, there are negatives but more positives in my view. She looks to me like a lovely girl and, more importantly, is clearly besotted with you. That is a good start. You are both young and you will make this work." He tapped out his pipe, "And you have made a mark on this world. When I die all that will be left is a pile of earth with, perhaps, a stone. It will be untended. You have now a child who would, at least, put flowers there now and then." I had thought the captain had all that he wanted. I was wrong,

The conversation made me think that he was right. I was given permission to spend the weekends away from the barracks and we were able to snuggle up on Friday and Saturday nights in the single bed. It was a relief to me as during the week we were training harder than ever. It was clear that we would be sent to Egypt and, it was rumoured, the Sudan. There was trouble there and with the Suez Canal so important to the Empire, then Egypt had to be kept safe. Every moment was spent in exercises, often with cavalry regiments. It was clear that this war would be fought differently from the Zulu war. Lessons had been learned and there would be more cooperation. Captain Philips, who had taken a shine to me, managed to get my temporary rank of sergeant confirmed and that meant more money. I had always been a saver and in the months left before the birth, I smoked less and barely drank at all.

When my mother arrived at the barracks, I knew that it meant my nan had died. Mother was philosophical about the whole thing. I walked her to the pub where Geraint insisted on giving her a room for her three-day stay. She had arranged it so that she arrived on Saturday and would leave on Monday. I would not be able to see her off but Annie would. As we walked, she said, "Your nan almost died after Isandlwana. When you returned it was as though she had been gifted extra life. The first six months were wonderful, Jack. She was so proud of you and what you achieved. It was only the last few months when she deteriorated." She suddenly stopped, "Eeeh, I have just thought. She couldn't have known it but it was around the time your young lady became pregnant. It is a sign."

"A sign?"

"Yes, Jack, one leaves this world and another one joins."

Geraint had arranged for Annie's shifts to be at lunchtime and so the first time my mother saw my wife she was pulling pints with an apron on. I waited until she came around the bar before I introduced them. Mother just held her arms wide and Annie rushed into them. It was perfect. I saw the other girls as they wiped away tears. Any fears they had harboured were dispelled. The two were as one. I breathed a sigh of relief. The two days saw my mother spending more time with Annie than with me. She even cajoled Geraint into letting her finish early and the three of us enjoyed a walk in the park.

I was not there for the parting as it was on Monday but Doris and Annie, helped by Geraint, took my mother to the railway station and there were more tears all around. Often tears are not a bad thing and, in this case, were a clear sign that all was well.

Our orders to prepare to embark came when Annie was just two weeks shy of her due date. I never understood how these things worked but the others in the house were prepared for the birth and, indeed, seemed to be looking forward to it. I rarely saw Annie in the last weeks of her pregnancy. Everything that would be needed in the Sudan and Egypt had to be checked and double-checked. The tropical gear had to be tried and, inevitably, there were issues.

I was with my section when one of the sentries came for me, "Sarge, Captain Philips said you are to go and see your wife."

"What's up?"

He was a new man and young, he shrugged, "No idea. Just telling you what I was told."

I ran out as fast as I could. There were neighbours gathered outside the house and they parted when I entered. Doris looked tearful as she greeted me, "It's a boy and he is healthy. The doctor is with Annie."

I went from euphoria to despair in a heartbeat. Women delivered babies and doctors were only called when there was trouble. I took the narrow stairs two at a time. The doctor heard me and he greeted me at the door, "I am sorry, Sergeant Roberts, but while your son is healthy, your wife has suffered internal bleeding. Go to her."

"You can save her, can't you?"

He put his arm around me and said, "Give her what comfort you can. It is out of my hands and is now in God's."

Annie was nursing our son and he was feeding. She looked as white as a sheet. "We have a boy, Jack."

I knew I had to be strong and I smiled, "And he is a beautiful babe. What shall we call him?"

We had avoided naming him in case we jinxed the birth. She kissed the top of his head, "I would like to name him after my father, Griffith." She turned and looked fearful, "You do not mind, do you?"

"Of course not, it is a lovely name."

Doris appeared behind me, "Well it looks to me like young Griff is asleep so I will take him from you, Annie, so that we can clean him up and Jack here can give you a cuddle."

The baby gone, I sat next to her and cradled her head in my arm. "It was harder than I thought, Jack, and I feel so weak. Still, that is to be expected, eh? I hope it did not harm our son."

"He looked healthy, let us make you well now. I have not told you enough, Annie, but I love you. I think I loved you from the first moment I saw you in the pub."

"And I love you. When you strode in looking so handsome and spoke kindly my heart melted and now that I have met your mother, I cannot wait to meet your aunt, brother and sisters. I will have a family again. The only thing is,"

"Yes,"

"I have never lived in a big place. I hear that Liverpool is a busy port. Shrewsbury is the biggest place I have made my home. Will I fit in?"

I was fighting back tears as I said, "You will fit in. You could fit in anywhere and my family will look after you." She suddenly winced and I shouted, Doctor!"

He must have been waiting outside the door for he rushed in and took her pulse, "Do you want something for the pain?"

She nodded and could barely get the words out, "That last spasm was as bad as the birth, doctor, and I feel so sleepy but I want to see my baby and husband."

He gave her a spoonful from a jar. I recognised the smell. It reminded me of the hospital at Rorke's Drift, it was morphine. "Ah, that is better. That is good medicine, doctor." She looked up at me, "Is it wrong that I wish you to kiss me?"

"Of course not."

I inclined my head and our lips met. It was like the first kiss and my heart lifted. She went slack in my arms and her head lolled away. The doctor was still there. He took her pulse and shook his head, "She is gone, but that was well done, sergeant. She died happy and the good lord will care for her now."

I buried my head in her chest and sobbed uncontrollably. This was not fair and she deserved a better life than the short one she had. I cursed myself for ever having come into her life. Had I not done so then she would be alive.

It was Doris who lifted me from the corpse, "Come, Jack. You have a son to care for now. Annie would have wanted that. Love him the way you loved her and she will be happy in heaven. She loved you, you know and counted herself the luckiest woman in the world."

"But if I had not met her, she would be alive."

She shook her head, "You cannot think that way. These last ten months were the happiest in Annie's life. There are many people who live far longer and do not have a tiny piece of the happiness she enjoyed. Never forget her but you honour her by caring for your son. Now go to him and hold him while we see to Annie."

Alice, one of the other girls, handed Griffith to me and I looked at his sleeping face, "I am sorry, son, but I shall have to be a mother and a father to you. I am a soldier and will often be away but know this, not a day will go by when I do not think of you and each night I shall say a prayer for you, no matter where I am. You will be loved but I think that for me, my heart will have a hole the size of your mother."

That first talk to my sleeping son was one of many. I know he could not understand a word but I somehow felt that Annie's spirit was close. Things happened quickly and I seemed to be riding an unbroken stallion. The captain gave me compassionate leave for a week but told me that the regiment was leaving the barracks in eight days and I had to be back by then. Doris and Geraint did more for me than I could have hoped. A funeral was arranged quickly and the regulars in the pub all chipped in to pay for the coffin. Doris managed to get some of the new-fangled babies' drinking bottles and teats and Griff was dry-fed with goat's and cow's milk. As one of the other women, Alice said, "Mother's milk is best but try to get a mixture of milk for him." I barely remember the funeral except that it rained and I sheltered Griff beneath my greatcoat as rain dripped from my head onto the muddy ground as the priest's voice intoned the rite of passage to the next world. I had almost no time to mourn as immediately after the funeral I had to take the train home. I needed as much time as I could manage with my family and Griff. Before I left for Egypt I needed to be certain that he was comfortable. Doris and the girls waved me off at the station. It was like going to war. I had my haversack filled with the paraphernalia of infancy. All that I had of my gear were my changes of socks and underwear. Griff's bed was a wicker basket and he nestled neatly in the bottom covered with swathes of blankets to help him to sleep.

"Come back to the pub before you leave, Jack, we would like to say goodbye to you." I nodded, Doris' last words made tears spring to my eyes, "She loved you, Jack, and the evidence is in that basket. You take care of that boy."

There were others in the compartment and the men looked at me strangely. Men did not look after babies. I was watchful for the whole journey. Feeding him was easier than I had expected. The girls had made the baby accustomed to the rubber teat and bottle. The changing of the nappy was hard but I was lucky. There was a woman in the compartment and she aided me. Some of the men snorted when it became clear what I was doing.

The woman said, angrily, "It is a baby and once upon a time you were all babies so stop acting like babies and let this soldier see to his bairn. Here, sergeant, let me help you."

Alice had advised me to use a piece of oilskin to place beneath Griff when I changed him. It made life a little cleaner. After we had changed him, I cringed when I had to use the nappy pin to fasten the nappy. I wrapped the nappy in the oilskin. The next time I changed him I would have to pray for a wet nappy. The woman chatted to me after we had changed him. Her husband tried to pretend he was not with her. I smiled for I knew that he would suffer for that later. Griff was a good baby. He needed one more feed before we arrived in Liverpool and although I thought he might need his nappy changed I decided to get to Aunt Sarah's as soon as I could.

The captain had sent a telegram for me and so I knew that they would be ready at the house. When I emerged from the station, I hailed a hackney carriage. Normally, I would have taken a bus or walked. I used some of my precious horde of coins and was at Aunt Sarah's fifteen minutes after the train arrived.

My sisters were still in St Helens but my mother and my auntie made up for their absence by fussing over us both. I saw Aunt Sarah cry for the first time. Obligingly Griff began to cry as the wet nappy was beginning to irritate him and he became the focus of our attention. By the time he was settled and in the cot my mother had found for him, Billy had arrived home from work and we were able to sit and talk. Our meal was ham sandwiches and as I had not eaten all day I was starving. I then took them through the procedures they would need to care for my son. Mother had only breastfed and Aunt Sarah had never had a child. The bottles were something new.

"I think those new cans of evaporated milk might be something you could try with him. Alice, one of Annie's friends, said that if you could get hold of them then they were the safest milk to give him."

"Cold?"

I smiled, "He prefers warm, like breast milk. The milk I gave him on the train was kept warm in my socks."

Billy wrinkled his nose and I realised I had forgotten to empty the oilskin, "What is that stink?"

I went to my haversack and took out the offending item, "Come with me, Bill, you will have to do this." I went to the outside toilet. Aunt Sarah had ensured that we had a flush toilet rather than a hole with night soil. The night light gave a dim glow. I shook the nappy to empty it down the toilet and then flushed. It was the only one in the street to have a flushing toilet. It would make life easier. "Get me a bucket, Bill, and fill it with water."

He returned and I dropped the nappy into it.

"This is a daily job, Bill. The girls said that he will get through between six and eight a day."

As we entered the house Bill said, "I am sorry about Annie, Jack. Mother was much taken with her." It was still too raw for me to talk about and I just nodded, not daring to risk speech. "I will do my best while you are away. Where are you off to this time?"

"Africa again, but Egypt."

He stopped as we neared the kitchen, "The Dervishes?"

"I think so."

"I have read of those in the papers. They are terribly fierce warriors with great long swords. You take care, our Jack."

I smiled, "If they are like the Zulus then they will find that a redcoat's rifle is more than a match for them and we know how to use our lungers."

"Lungers?"

"Bayonets. Listen, Bill, I am not afeard of any enemy but having to look after Griff makes me shake with terror."

"Aunt Sarah and Mother will see to his wellbeing. I doubt that I will be any good but once he can walk and talk, I will do my best. You always looked after me and I will do the same for my nephew." He stopped and grinned, "I am an uncle, Uncle Bill! I like the sound of that."

The leave went all too quickly. I slept in the same room as Griff for the first two days and then Mother sensibly pointed out that it would be their job and he was moved into the room used by my mother. Every time he woke in the night I was up and I helped but the arms that comforted him were those of his nan. He took to her so quickly that I wondered at her words about one life leaving and another arriving. Was the spirit of my nan in my son? I do not have the words to describe my feelings when I left. Mary and Alice had managed to get a day off work and they adored him the moment that they saw him but that made the parting even harder. I envied them all the time that they would spend with my son. Their questions about Annie also made it hard for me. I knew we had not enjoyed the time together we deserved. My sisters and Annie would have got on really well and that saddened me. The biggest revelation was Auntie Sarah. She had seen us grow from a distance but suddenly she was with a living growing piece of clay that could be moulded. She would never have children but from the moment Griff entered her life he became the focus of it.

My one consolation, as I slung my almost empty haversack over my shoulder and tramped down the road was that Griff would have more love than most babies and he would be safe. His father might not be but his mother was in heaven and he was in the bosom of five people who would guard him as well as the crown jewels. It allowed me to sit on the train, smoke my pipe and think of Annie and the life we might have had.

**Egypt 1882**

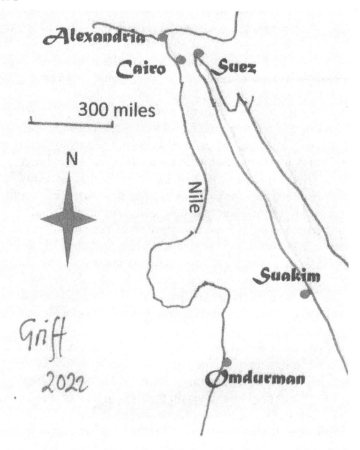

# Chapter 3

### The Mediterranean 1882

Back with the regiment, my self-indulgent fantasies had to end. I prepared to return to Africa and I made sure that I had all that I might need. I bought the things that we could not buy in Africa. Mint Imperials were good for you could suck them for a long time and they seemed to relieve the need to drink as much. I bought two spare pairs of socks. The army never had enough. I know that I shouldn't have had to use my own money for what was, essentially, army equipment but I was sensible enough to know that I would reap the benefit. I bought some bar tobacco and put it in a new pouch. When we reached warmer climes, I would buy an orange and put the peel in the pouch to keep it moist. I bought a spare flint as well as a spare couple of boxes of matches that I put in an oilskin pouch. I stained my new helmet with tea to darken it. My preparations made, I bade farewell to Captain Philips who would now retire to the small house he had bought and grow roses. He gave me a couple of ounces of tobacco. With the tobacco I had would have enough for a few months. "I know you have cut down as you needed the money for little Griffith but a pipe soothes a man. When you smoke this tobacco, reflect on the good parts of your life, Jack. You were lucky and have already enjoyed more than most. I think you are a good fellow and I am proud to have known you. Enjoy your life and I will grow roses and reflect on what my life might have been like had I met my Annie."

I was sad for the officer. The regiment had been his life and, a little like Trooper, the ending of it would be as though part of his life had ended or he had lost a limb. I saluted him and left the office. That chapter of my life was over. I was now a father and a sergeant. Both had changed me.

He had been right. The troop train to Southampton reminded me of when we had gone to South Africa and the waiting steamships made me wonder if my life had been a dream. Was I reliving the same events over and over? My experiences from the first time aboard the Danube, enabled me to get the best berths for my section and they were grateful. This time we would not sail down the Atlantic coast of Africa but head across the Mediterranean and land at Alexandria. It would be a shorter and I hoped a more peaceful voyage. As usual, the ship was rife with rumours.

Corporal Bob Walters was my corporal and as we stood watching Sicily to the north of us and Malta to the south, we smoked our pipes. He too had heard the rumours and he brought up some of them. For some reason, they thought my experience in Natal made me prescient. "They say we will be fighting Turks, Sarge, what do you reckon?"

"The Turks lost Egypt years ago and I think they were glad to be rid of it. This chap, Arabi Pasha, the one who has rebelled against the Khedive, won't want another imperial power taking over. I reckon that if we did not have the Suez Canal to worry about, we wouldn't be here." I pointed to the fleet of warships that had begun to pass us some hours ago. There were French and Royal Navy vessels. "They guarantee that whatever we want to do, there will be no interference."

"You have done this before, sarge, what is it like?"

"That is a good question if you know what the '*it*' is you are talking about." He looked puzzled, "Do you mean the fighting?" He nodded, "It lasts a shorter time than you think. The lads who died at Isandlwana fought for just over an hour. At the Mission Station, we had a day and night of fighting and that was rare. Marching into Natal we had short, sharp and savage fights. You needed quick reactions. When you are fighting you have no time to think and worry. At the end of it, you will either have survived and be as happy as a sandboy or dead and have no worries at all. The rest of it, the day-to-day life as a soldier, is harder. There are flies and mosquitoes that bite all the time. There are creatures that will bite, sting and kill you. Some are spiders and scorpions and others are snakes. The dust gets everywhere. There are few hard roads and you have to watch where you are marching and you march all the time. Your boots will wear out and your red tunic fade to a fashionable shade of pink. When it is hot you will melt and when it rains then look for the chap Noah and his boat. You can't drink the water and you will soon get sick of bully beef. Your uniform will be like rags after a month or two and your skin burnt so bad that it looks like someone has flayed you alive."

He shook his head, "But why us, Sarge?"

"Simple, lad, we are soldiers of the Queen or, in this case, the Empress and we have to protect the canal as that connects Britain to her Empire, India, New Zealand, Australia and so many little islands that most don't even have a name."

He tapped out his pipe over the side, "What do we get for it? The pay is not that good."

"What did you do before you joined up?"

"Farm labourer down Ludlow way."

"Well paid?" His look told me it was not. "Life is easier for us and, the pay is guaranteed. A failed crop does not mean poverty. As I said, the fighting and the dying are a tiny part of what we do. In battle, there is a lot of luck. One chap at Rorke's Drift spent twelve hours lying behind the Zulu lines playing dead. He survived. Another four were found and tortured, it is down to luck, but the rest of it is down to what we do, you and me. Our job is to keep the sections alive." I now had two sections to lead. Corporal Cole led the lads I had yet to meet properly.

"What about Lieutenant Hodges?"

"He seems a decent bloke but he has served for ten years and never heard a gun fired in anger. Officers are different to rank and file, Bob, as they should be. They have been brought up differently. They went to schools where they were beaten and learned Greek and Latin."

"I was clipped around the ear when I was at school."

"And I bet you left before you were ten."

He nodded. "I only went to the Dame School and I started work at 8 helping my dad on the farm." It wasn't until 1871 that children were obliged to go to school between the ages of five and ten.

"When the fighting starts listen to the NCOs, the officers will."

By the time we woke we were nearing Egypt but the faster-moving fleet was no longer in sight. We were mustered on deck and addressed by Colonel de Winter. He had managed to buy his first rank but earned the colonelcy. As I had not heard any evidence that he had seen action I reserved my view of him. The honorary colonel, still in England, General Sir Henry de Bathe, 4th Baronet KCB, had been in the Crimea but like most of those who had fought with Trooper, they had retired from active service.

"Men of the King's Shropshire Light Infantry, tomorrow we will disembark in Egypt. We are here to restore Tewfik Pasha, the Khedive of Egypt and Sudan, to his rightful position as leader of this country. This will be the first time that the amalgamated regiments will have fought side by side but the training you have undertaken leaves me in no doubt that there will be more battle honours coming our way. When you are dismissed, I wish to speak to all the officers and ranks of sergeant and above. We will meet in the fore mess."

I groaned. It meant we would have to keep the top buttons fastened and stay below decks which would make it unbearable. At least when he had paraded, we had enjoyed the natural breeze from the sea. We were still wearing the red coats we had worn in Zululand. The cork hats were a light improvement but as they would not stop a bladed weapon from splitting our skulls I wondered if they were a wise choice. We had been told that the cloth puggaree we had been issued might slow a blade down. I knew that it would help to keep the sun from my neck.

"Ten 'shun!"

We all stood as the colonel and other senior officers entered the large mess used by other ranks at mealtimes. It was Major Pulleine who addressed us. He had seen some active service having been seconded to the general staff in the campaign leading to Ulundi.

"Despite the high expectations of the General Staff, the colonel and I have a more realistic view of our expectations. This is an untried regiment and we cannot get around that. The dozen or so men who have seen active service will have to pass on all that they know as quickly as possible. General Wolsey intends to make a diversionary attack on Alexandria. Our intelligence tells us that it is unlikely to find a safe route to Cairo through Alexandria. Ismailia is a better prospect. The attack will be commanded by Sir Archibald Alison South Staffordshire Regiment and a battalion of the King's Royal Rifle Corps. They will be combined with a battalion of Royal Marine Light Infantry as well as two sections from this regiment." He smiled, "I know Sir Archibald and the colonel and I were keen that this regiment, new though it is, should begin to earn honours for our new standards. We have chosen 1st Platoon numbers two and three sections, Lieutenant Hodges commanding, to join the South Staffs. In training, they have demonstrated great skills and they have the most experienced leaders in the regiment. They will disembark first and will be brigaded with their counterparts in the South Staffs. We are telling the whole regiment of these plans as we do not want anyone to think that we have come here to watch others fight and die for queen and country. We will be at the fore of the coming battles. Lieutenant Hodges merely has the honour of drawing first blood. I will brief the lieutenant and his sergeant on the foredeck."

I dutifully followed the lieutenant. He turned as we left the mess, "A great honour, sergeant but, equally, a great responsibility. You know the chaps better than I, are they ready?"

I nodded, "I know number three section better than number two sir but they seem as ready as any, sir, but until you load your rifle and face a charging enemy you never know. I would prefer going into action with the rest of our own regiment and not the South Staffs."

"They have been chosen by the general and that means he must view them highly." I did not say it but it could be the opposite and they were sacrificial goats. This was the land for such metaphors.

The major and Sergeant Major Lowery were waiting with a map. Major Pulleine tapped the map, "The delta. It is a swampy, pestilential piece of earth but we have to cross it if we are to get to Cairo. You may well be advancing in the dark, gentlemen and I want no men becoming lost. Keep them together, Lieutenant Hodges."

"Sir."

"Roberts, you have a fine record in the 24th and I am relying on you to use all the skills you learned in Natal. Keep them safe and give the whole section the wisdom you acquired in the glorious action three years since."

"Sir." The lieutenant had not asked any questions but I would, "Sir, how much ammo is being issued?" The Sergeant Major gave me a frown. No one had asked for questions. "I only ask because the 24th lost at Isandlwana because they ran out of ammunition."

The major had seen the sergeant major's look and nodded, "The sergeant is quite right to bring the matter up and he has shown that he is the right man for the job. Fifty rounds seem about right, sergeant?"

I smiled, "A hundred would be heavier but would be a safer choice, sir."

"A hundred it is. See to it Sarn't Major."

"Sir."

I had given the confidence to Lieutenant Hodges, "Sir, might I ask to be issued with a rifle? From what I read of the reports of Rorke's Drift the officers there all used rifles to great effect." He tapped his revolver, "This little pea shooter does not have the range."

"Of course. Times are changing and we must adapt or men will die. Any further questions?" We shook our heads, "Then dismiss."

As we left Lieutenant Hodges said, "Quick thinking there, Roberts. Any more pearls you would like to cast before me?"

"I will get the lads to find as much food as we can and as much water as we can take in our canteens. If you could get a few extras from the QM it would help." I smiled, "He has spares but as soon as he knows people want them, they will become as rare as rocking horse droppings, sir. Play the innocent, sir."

"I shall do my best, Roberts." He paused, "Is the Martini-Henry an easy rifle to use?"

"Watch the kick sir, but, yes. The only problem we had at Rorke's Drift was that we fired so many bullets that some rounds jammed in the breech. Luckily, we had spare rifles from the wounded and I doubt that this little action will see a sustained fire like that."

Heading back to the section to tell them the news I felt more confident about the lieutenant. He was more like Lieutenant Melville and nothing like Harding-Smythe. The section was proud at having been chosen but as it was likely they would have to fire their weapons then there was understandable nervousness too. I liked that. Overconfidence was not what was needed.

"Now if there is any food you can grab between now and when we disembark then do so. We share whatever we have. Fill your canteens tonight and drink as much tea as you can before we leave the ship. Dehydration can be a killer here."

Private Potter laughed, "You can't die from a lack of water, Sarge."

"You can, Potter, but it is not just the lack of water than can kill you. If you have an empty canteen then any water seems an attractive prospect and looking for water can get you killed just as easily. Get plenty of sleep tonight and remember when we leave the ship, we take everything we need with us and that includes greatcoats. It might be as hot as Hades during the day but it can get cold at night and a greatcoat makes a good blanket."

As with the lieutenant, I was impressed by the questions. It showed they were taking this foray seriously. The one thing I was short of was pipe tobacco. I planned on finding some as soon as time allowed.

Just before they departed Private Davis asked, "Sarge, why is your helmet brown and ours are white?"

I smiled, "I stained mine with tea. A white helmet makes for an easy target."

I watched as they all began to seek methods of staining their headgear. If the sergeant approved then it was alright for them to.

One difference in this campaign was that the helmets now had a puggaree around the tope. A piece of cloth, it served two purposes. It could slow down the slice of a blade and protect the helmet and it could be attached to the bottom of the helmet to shade the neck from the sun. Lessons had been learned in South Africa.

That night I carefully packed my bag. I had placed most of the ammunition in the bottom but I had twenty rounds in my valise and another ten in my tunic. That done I lay down and closed my eyes. I had developed a ritual and with hands folded together, I spoke to Annie and to Griff. The conversation was directed at God. I was keenly aware that we were now close to the place where his son had been born. Trooper's Sunday School lessons were still vivid memories. As I said, '*Amen*', I felt much better. When as a child I had intoned, '*if I should die before I wake, I pray my soul, the lord to take,*' I had felt fearful. My new prayers made me feel close to not only Annie but also God.

We disembarked and joined the other three and a half thousand men who would be making this diversionary attack. We were directed to the South Staffs and were ordered to tuck in at the rear. I did not mind that we were relegated to that position. I was obeying the major's orders and would keep as many men safe as we could.

Marching through the burning city of Alexandria was chastening. The Egyptians had been driven from the city by a mixture of naval bombardment and an attack by Royal Marines. Now those same marines were summarily hanging looters. I did not think that any of my section were light-fingered but the swinging corpses we passed ensured that they would not even consider stealing. We stopped regularly and I made sure that the men only took sips of water.

The officer commanding the South Staffs before us and Lieutenant Hodges chatted each time we stopped. It was how I learned that the enemy had dug trenches at Kafr El Dawwar. It was still some way ahead but I had every man put a bullet in the chamber. "Keep the safety on but be ready to fire when you hear the command." Technically it would be the officer who gave the command but I was quite willing to override the lieutenant if it was necessary. We were on the left flank and marching on the west side of the Mahmoudiyah Canal. The canal and the railway line formed our boundaries. We heard the pop of rifles and that told me we were about to go into action. The South Staffs were ordered to drop their packs. I was already forming the words when the lieutenant said, "Give the order, sergeant, to drop packs. Make sure the chaps have enough ammo."

"Yes sir. You heard the officer. Keep your canteens with you."

I slipped another ten rounds into my tunic before refastening my pack and piling it with the others.

The order was passed down the line, "Form skirmish order." We spread out. Corporal Walters took the left flank and Corporal Cole the right. As I did not know him well I was to the right as well. The lieutenant was in the centre. This was not the way we had fought in Rorke's Drift. We would be the attackers now. The muskets and rifles began to pop from ahead of us. Some were ancient weapons and spouted more smoke than the newer rifles. I saw one or two men raise their rifles.

"Do not fire until ordered. Take off your safeties." Taking off the safety catch was a risk but I wanted them secure in the knowledge that they could fire if they needed to.

We were on the extreme left of the South Staffs. Some of their platoons were eager and ran forward. I saw one hit and fall and heard the order given, "Open fire."

I growled, "That is the order for the South Staffs. Lieutenant Hodges will give the command."

I was prompting him and he responded, "Take cover and return fire."

As most of the bullets and balls were flying over our heads, we did not really need to take cover but it was a wise command. I knelt and rested my forearm on my knee. Through the smoke, I saw the faces peering from the ditch. It explained why their bullets were missing. They were resting their barrels on the edge of the trench and most were flying way up in the air. I took a breath and squeezed the trigger. I kept my eye on the man as I reloaded. His head was thrown back. I moved my rifle slightly to the right and a face loomed into view. I saw a barrel aimed at me. I hit another man. All along our line, my section was firing far faster than I was but it was having an effect. The sheer weight of shot was wounding and killing the defenders. They outnumbered us but had no Colour Sergeant Bourne to stiffen their resolve.

I knew what would happen next and I shouted, "King's Light Infantry, fix bayonets."

A heartbeat later I heard the same order being given to the South Staffs. I stood and the lieutenant saw me. He rose and waving his rifle shouted, "King's Light Infantry, forward."

"The South Staffs will advance!"

I don't know if any of the men thought that we would run and charge them but my stentorian tones left them in no doubt that it was not an option. "Walk, boys. This is not a race!"

I had chambered another round and as an Egyptian rose my bullet caught him in the back. He flew forward and his arms were spread like a crucifix. Some of the South Staffs were getting excited and running. The ones that did soon realised their folly as they tripped over discarded equipment left by the fleeing soldiers. We reached the trench and saw that we had killed at least ten men. After navigating the obstacle we formed our skirmish line again and advanced. I fired at one man but he was two hundred yards ahead of me. I clipped his pack. I did not think I had hurt him but he ran far faster after the bullet struck. Ahead of us was a white house and as we neared it the word came down the line that we had reached our objective.

Lieutenant Hodges was in an ebullient mood. "Not a man hurt and I counted twelve bodies. We have acquitted ourselves well, sergeant."

I nodded, "Yes sir."

"Take charge while I have a chin wag with my opposite number."

"Sir." I waved Bob and Cole over. "One man in three on watch. The rest can get a fire going and make a brew." I nodded to the canal. "I wouldn't like to drink that but if we boil it then we can make a pot of tea."

"A pot, sarge?"

"Improvise, Bob." I let my subordinates allocate the sentries but I went along the line to ensure that they knew their duties. Some couldn't stop talking while others were morosely silent. It was in the nature of a first combat. My questions made them forget the memory of the recent action, at least temporarily. "How many rounds did you use? Are your feet holding up? Do you need to use your neckerchief to keep your neck out of the sun? Keep your eyes to your front and listen for sounds that shouldn't be here." Every question and command was meant to give the men something to do. When I was satisfied that the sentries were all more alert I headed back.

I joined Bob and took out the can of bully beef I had carried in my valise. "When we have made a brew cut this up and share it amongst the lads."

He nodded, "I should have thought of that."

"Don't worry, Bob, next time you will."

He stood and then said, "Where did you get it?"

I winked and tapped the side of my nose. The truth was I had stolen it from the ship's larder. I had another two in my haversack. I did not bother drinking any water as I saw that Bob had found an old cauldron and there was a fire going beneath it. It would be tea without milk but it would refresh more than water and having a hot drink seemed, somehow, to make you feel like you had enjoyed some sustenance.

It was as I peered south that I saw a second white house, a mile away. When the lieutenant returned, I said, "Sir, is this the right target only there is another while building a mile from here?"

He wore binoculars and he looked at the building. Shaking his head he said, "Probably is, Roberts. I mean the colonel of this regiment seems to know what he is doing."

It was just before dusk that the general appeared and scanned the Egyptian defences through his glasses. Seemingly satisfied with what he saw he went to the colonel of the South Staffs. A few moments later a runner came to tell us that once darkness fell, we were to withdraw back towards Alexandria. I went around the men to ensure that they had everything and knew that we had to march away from the skirmish as alert as when we had advanced. Bob went to remove his bayonet and I shook my head, "Keep your bayonets attached, lads. It will be too dark to see too far and a bayonet is a better weapon in the dark. Another thing, tie something white to your back. It will make it easier for us to stay together." I used my puggaree to attach to the bottom of my helmet. I tied it to the top strap. It would stand out against the dark of my uniform.

The lieutenant loomed up, "Are we all set?"

"Sir. If you and Corporal Cole act as rearguards then Corporal Walters can lead the men. I will be the scout."

"Shouldn't I lead, Sergeant?"

I nodded, "Perhaps but as the only one in the section who has experience of fighting at night, it makes sense for it to be me, doesn't it, sir?"

"I suppose you are right."

Darkness suddenly dropped. It was not gradual like it was in England. One moment there was light and the next it was as though someone had turned off the gaslight. I waved my arm and began to walk. I had chambered a round but I had the safety on. I was not arrogant enough to think that I might not trip. We were not all walking along the road and we had obstacles before us. I warned Potter, whom I had placed behind me, of every danger. My eyes were moving all the time as I looked for obstacles and danger. There were damaged buildings and bodies covered in carrion that fled at our approach. My ears were listening for the sounds of danger. My time in Zululand had taught me how to identify such sounds. My most useful weapon was my nose. The stink of the bodies was a different smell from that of one who was living. When I caught the smell of sweat mixed with what seemed to me to be a perfume of some sort then I was alert. It was not a dead body but there was someone waiting in the darkness. The Egyptian officer who came at me from the side must have been cut off by our advance. I am still unsure if he intended simply to attack us or if I surprised him as he made his way back to his own lines. All I know is that he swung a sword at my head as he stepped from the shadows.

The night attacks at Rorke's Drift had honed my reactions and as the curved blade sliced towards my face, I brought up the rifle. My lunger caught the blade and sparks flew. Even as I blocked him, I was aware that I had novices behind me. "Hold your fire!" I used the stock of my rifle to punch at his middle. He was not expecting that and I heard the grunt of pain. It was time to go on the offensive and I pulled back the Martini-Henry and rammed it towards his middle. The officer was skilled with a sword and deflected the bayonet. In Natal, I fought recklessly. Now I had a son and flicking off the safety I fired at the officer. At a range of three feet, it was a mortal strike. He was thrown back. The crack of the gun in the night caused a ripple of orders down the line. I went to the officer and began to search him. He had a map with him and I stuffed that in my tunic. He also had coins in his pocket. I took them as well as the sword and his pistol in its holster. He had some cigarettes and while I did not smoke them, I knew others that did. Everything went into my tunic or my valise. I fastened the scabbard to my belt.

The lieutenant hurried up, "Everything alright, Roberts?"

"Yes sir. It was an Egyptian officer. Sorry about having to shoot sir but he knew how to use that sword. I have his maps and the like."

The lieutenant looked down at the body with the blood puddling around him. We had not dwelt close to the men we had killed during the advance and the sight of the corpse in the shadows of the night was a little macabre.

By eight pm we had reached our haversacks. Once again, a runner came to tell the lieutenant that we were heading for the camp the rest of the army had made. We had another mile to march. I transferred everything I could to my haversack and we headed back to our camp.

Major Pulleine showed that he had experience for there were two privates waiting on the road to escort us to the tents that had been erected. He greeted the lieutenant and the relief on his face was clear.

"Everything went well?"

"Yes sir. The men have been successfully blooded. I would like to mention Sergeant Roberts. His advice was sage and he prevented what might have resulted in a death on the way back."

The major nodded, "I heard you were a good chap. Well done, Roberts."

I took out the map I had taken, "I found this, sir, on the officer I killed."

"Excellent, Roberts. I shall study this. We have a pot of something for you. I daresay you are hungry."

I led the men to the fires. Our first action in Egypt had been a success. I prayed that the ones that followed would have as good an outcome.

# Chapter 4

We spent a week in our camp before General Wolsey finally landed and ordered us to push towards the Suez Canal and Ismailia. Unlike in the Zulu war, we had reliable cavalry. Now that their horses had become acclimatised to Egypt, they were able to scout ahead. The Household Cavalry looked particularly splendid and it was no surprise to us that Ismailia was abandoned by the handful of Egyptian troops who held it as the heavy cavalrymen approached. Our attack at Kafr El Dawwar had fooled the enemy and they had shifted their forces to prevent us from moving south to Cairo. We were amongst the first into Ismailia and I took advantage of that. I led my sections to ensure that all the enemy had gone and we were the ones who found their deserted camp. They had left in a hurry and as in all such departures had left behind what they could not carry. The men looked mystified when I ordered them to collect the pots, bags of grain and discarded uniforms.

"But sarge, why do we need the bits of uniform?"

"They are handy as we can use them for disguise and you never know when you are going to need a spare piece of cloth. Learn to scavenge, Potter, and this will be an easier war for you. When you see something then take it and decide later if it will be useful." The gold that I found was a pouch of pipe tobacco. I sniffed it suspiciously as I knew the Egyptians also smoke other things than pipe tobacco but I recognised the smell and tucked that treasure away in my haversack.

The march to Ismailia had been a testing one. It showed everyone the problems of marching in the desert and in heat. The roads were not the best and it took its toll. No men were wounded but there were men in the temporary hospital with heatstroke and other desert-related complaints. This was before the engineers managed to take control of the railways. Until we had transport, we used the roads. Many of the officers, of course, rode. The rest of us tramped down dusty roads with a permanent shimmer of heat ahead of us obscuring what was in the distance. We had marched as far when in England and on exercise but that was England and not in a temperature that seemed to make your blood boil. Sweat and heat made feet swell. Soon there were blisters and bloody feet. Every time we stopped, I had the men take off their boots and allow them to cool a little. We soon ran out of the salve we carried but one of the treasures I had taken from the Egyptian camp was a jar of olive oil. I had taken it to use for cooking but it proved to be useful on the men's feet. The cloth we had taken also proved useful. We used it to hang from our helmets and keep the sun from our necks. I know that Sergeant Major Lowery and some of the officers did not approve as they thought it made us look less than smart. It did but we were no longer trooping the colour. The one thing we could do nothing about was the woollen tunic. It was every bit as bad as I remembered from Natal. It was hot and the collar chafed our necks. Those were the days when the War Office, in its infinite wisdom, deemed that the army should march to war much as it had done for the last two centuries.

When we camped, we sought shade. Once again, my experience had given me an eye for such things and I always managed to find a wall that could be used, allied to a judicious use of the pieces of Egyptian tents we had salvaged, to make shelters to protect us from the sun. The spices I had found enlivened our stews. On the march, each section cooked for itself. The officers had their own mess and servants to cook for them but my section was catered to by me. Even when we had shelter and our stomachs had been fooled into thinking that we had eaten well we had the nightmare of insects at night. Some men smoked cigarettes and one or two did not smoke at all. Those of us who smoked pipes became the mosquito-free parts of the camp. The one time we had to endure the bites was when we had a sentry duty. Then the silence of the night was punctuated by the slaps of hands against biting bugs.

The Egyptians in Ismailia fled the city when the red snake approached and so some of our men had roofs over their heads. We also had camp kitchens set up so that we no longer had to cook our own food. Of course, my sections still scavenged. Unlike the rest of the regiment, my sections had learned from me. The pieces of tent we took from the Egyptian camps had proved to be of great benefit and my enterprising sections became adept at finding things that we could use to make life easier. I saw my sections for once we reached Ismailia we saw less of Lieutenant Hodges. That was the usual way in the British Army. The unique nature of the battle of Rorke's Drift had forced us to spend longer in the company of officers than was normal. We all liked the lieutenant but he was an officer and it was clear that he was more comfortable with other officers and men from his own class.

A week after we had arrived, we were ordered to escort a company of Royal Engineers, the 8th Railway Company, to repair the railway line to Suez. Before they had fled the Egyptians had tried to sabotage the crucial railway line to Suez and the canal. Once the railway was open then we could be supplied and reinforced far more easily than the road down which we had just marched. The railway troop were good lads and the week we spent with them saw friendships that lasted a long time. Our sections were seen as being experienced. The two corporals got on well. Our battle experience was still the only evidence that the regiment had fought and they listened to us. It meant that I commanded thirty men, the largest body thus far for some of those who had been ill before our first action had recovered. Lieutenant Hodges and Captain Jennings, the commanding officer of the Engineers, got on well as did I with the non-commissioned officers of this unique unit. They were armed with rifles and at that time still wore the red tunics like us. However, they were not the same as we were. They were builders.

We marched along the shores of Lake Timsah. Any thoughts we might have had of bathing our hot feet in its waters were soon dispelled. Its local name was crocodile lake and its shallow waters teemed with the reptiles. We learned to camp as far away from the water as we could and spent as much time on sentry duty watching for the terrifying creatures as we did looking for Egyptian soldiers.

The Egyptians had tried to damage as much of the track as they could. The Engineers were contemptuous of their efforts. With their guns stacked and tunics discarded they happily worked to make good the damage. I remembered that Mr Chard had been a Royal Engineer. I wondered where he was now. While they laboured, we watched for the red fezzes that would mark an Egyptian fellah, their version of us. We were learning all the time and it became clear to me that the Egyptian fellah did not like to fight at night, or noon. First light was their preferred time of attack. Although they had fled Ismailia, they still had mounted patrols. We watched for their camels and their horses. We had been working for a couple of days when one of their patrols found us. Their first attack was signalled by the smell of camels. The British Camel Regiment had yet to be fully established and camels meant the enemy.

It had been Bob Walters who had been on duty that night but I always rose early. I remembered Rorke's Drift. Colour Sergeant Bourne never seemed to sleep. No matter what time I woke in Natal he was always ready for duty and I used him as my model. I was awake and had washed and dressed well before dawn. I quite enjoyed that time of day. The insects had yet to awaken and it was cool. As soon as the sun rose it would become unbearable. I had the latrines to myself and I was able to make a brew of tea. Once I had drunk a cup, I took my rifle and joined Bob.

"Quiet night, Bob?"

He nodded, "Like the grave." He shook his head, "It is funny, sarge, but that lake stinks worse at night than it does during the day."

"What?"

"Sniff the air, Sarge," he pointed to the southeast and the canal, "It is coming from over there."

I sniffed and he was right, there was a stench, but it was not the crocodile-infested lake, "Corporal, the lake is the south of us. That is not the smell of the lake, it is camels. Have your lads stand to and I will wake the others."

I went to the lieutenant to wake him first, "Sir, I think that there might be Egyptians about. I will wake the lads."

He rubbed the sleep from his eyes, "What time is it?"

I had no watch but I had learned, on the march from Alexandria, how to judge time over here, "Not long off dawn, sir."

"Right, I will wake Captain Jennings. It would not do to have our charges slaughtered while they slept."

I shook awake the men. I did not want a hidden enemy to hear us preparing. "Stand to, there may be enemies about. Look sharp. Fix your bayonets and put one up the spout."

The men had learned that if I gave an order, there was a reason. Even Potter had stopped questioning every command. I suspect one of the other lads had given him a slap for his constant carping was more than annoying.

I had just returned to Corporal Walters when the sun began to rise in the east. Here in Egypt, it did not rise slowly as it did at home. It seemed to rush into the sky. At the same time, I heard the snort in the distance of a camel. It could have been innocent. Arab traders still used camel trains, called caravans, to transport their goods but better to look foolish than be caught out by a camel charge. We had learned to use whatever we had to hand to make a defence and we had borrowed the railway troops' gloves to rip up and make a barricade of the thorn bushes. They were the flimsy defence before us. We had managed to embed a couple of stakes fashioned by the railway troop from sleepers too badly damaged to be reused but if we were attacked then it would be down to the rifles of the thirty men I commanded.

We stood in a loose semi-circle. All of us held our rifles the same way. Held before our bodies we could either kneel and fire or hold our bayonet-tipped rifles before us. I saw that one or two of number two section had not yet fixed bayonets. The heavy bayonet was not perfect and some men did not like to use them.

"Corporal Cole, have your lads fix bayonets. If these are camels then we need to keep the nasty beasties as far from us as we can."

"Yes, Sarge. Come on you dozy pair, fix bayonets."

Lieutenant Walters and Captain Jennings arrived, and the captain had a pistol in his hand, "Trouble, Sergeant?"

I nodded, "Yes, Captain Jennings. I think there are Egyptians out there on camels. The smell is coming from the southeast and…" I got no further for the Egyptians Camel Troopers rose, like the sun from a depression where they had been hidden. They were just three hundred paces from us and I guessed that they had camped closer to the lake than we had. Perhaps they had their own methods of deterring crocodiles. There were more than a hundred of them. This was the first time I had experienced a camel charge. The camel is bigger than a horse and also noisier. It is not like a horse in that it is not elegant when it moves. It has a strange undulating motion and I know not how the riders managed to stay on the backs of their beasts and how they avoided vomiting from the motion.

I looked at the lieutenant and he nodded. I shouted, "At two hundred yards, volley fire." I dropped to my knee. I was unsure if the camel riders would fire weapons as they charged but I intended to be as small a target as I could and the kneeling position was one which gave me the greatest chance of an accurate shot. I heard, behind me, the sound of the engineers forming a line behind our thin red line. They would be moral support for it would be our thirty rifles that did the damage. I had noticed that Lieutenant Hodges had brought his rifle although he had not bothered with the bayonet. He had his sword.

The camels were far faster than I had expected, "Fire!" Even as I aimed and fired at the officer with the sword in his hand, I was choosing my next target before smoke swirled before us. I loaded my second bullet, "Fire!" The camels were closing fast. When I had loaded my third bullet I shouted, "Independent fire." I had noticed that the second volley was more ragged. I knew it was not my section. I had drilled them so that we all fired as one. My fifth bullet smacked into the head of a camel. Its front legs folded and the surprised trooper sailed over the dying animal's head. He landed just thirty yards from me. I stood and levelled my rifle. I was seeking a leader. I saw the trooper with the stripes on the white arm of his tunic turn and urge his men on. He was forty yards from me and I did not need to kneel. I squeezed the trigger and he flew from the back of the camel. I suspect that the troopers might have had enough but some of the camels had been maddened by nicks and grazes from bullets and they came at us.

"Aim for the camels!" All the rifles of my men and the engineers barked and bucked as the railway troop were able to add to the fusillade. When I saw the camel's snapping teeth coming for me, I had no time to reload my gun and I slashed with my bayonet. It tore into the camel's throat and blood spurted as the animal began to fall. I stepped to the side as did the two soldiers next to me and the camel landed in a heap.

Private Potter lunged at the rider who was trapped beneath the animal and bayoneted the fellah. It was the last action of the skirmish and the survivors raced off to the southeast.

I chambered another round and ordered, "Section two stand fast. Number three section come with me." We headed through the charnel house before us. None of the Egyptians was alive. I saw that we had killed more than twenty. Six camels had been hit and one was still thrashing. I ended its misery.

"Corporal, collect the Egyptian dead and burn them. If we leave them here then it will just attract crocodiles."

"Yes, sarge, and the camels?"

"I have never eaten camel meat, what say we take what meat we can and then burn the rest."

"Right Sarge. Hargreaves, you were a butcher, weren't you?"

"Yes, Corp."

"Let's see how much meat we can get from these dead animals then."

I rejoined the officers and reported, "The enemy soldiers have gone, sir. There are twenty odd of them dead. The men are going to burn their bodies and we will try some camel meat."

"Thank you, sergeant." The captain turned to his men, "We are all up so let's start work earlier. This has been a chastening lesson for us all. We will eat later. Our guardians have done their work. Let us do ours."

The troop of engineers set to with a will. The smell of burning bodies acted as a spur to them. I kept a skirmish line of sentries one hundred yards to the southeast in case the Egyptians returned. They did not but when four huge crocodiles began to move menacingly towards the pyre, I ordered my men to shoot the leading animal. Its thick hide could not stop the .303 bullets. The three survivors began to drag the crocodile's carcass back to the lake.

"Sarge, the sooner we are away from this lake the better. Those beasts are scarier than any enemy soldier."

"I agree, Walker. Let us hope that the engineers can work a little quicker today."

By the time the meat was ready the engineers had repaired the section of track. Captain Jennings called the lieutenant and me over, "When we have eaten we will march to the next damaged section. I think it is the last one before Suez. I am loath to remain here overnight. Lake Timsah is a very unhealthy place.

I don't know what I expected from the camel meat but it was tough. I suspect it needed slower cooking. It was meat and a different taste. While we ate the rest of the meat was boiled. We would take it with us. The cooking would stop it from stinking and slow down the process that would lead to its becoming rotten. The engineers had a wagon and we could carry it in that. One advantage of the captain's order was that we marched in the late afternoon. It was slightly cooler and as we neared the canal itself, we enjoyed the breeze from the water. Lake Timsah was too shallow to give any benefit to a breeze. We put the partially cooked meat on to cook overnight and I made sure that we had a defensible camp.

It took just another two days to repair the line and then we marched to Suez. Suez was in our hands and we were able to sleep in the barracks there. The captain found an engine that had been abandoned and his railway engineers soon had it ready to be used. They found a couple of wagons too and they were hitched to the locomotive. We filled three of them with supplies intended for the army and then we enjoyed a pleasant return to Ismailia in a relatively comfortable wagon. The breeze generated by the train kept us relatively cool and we endured the soot from the engine. As one of the engineers told us, the Egyptians had not maintained their engines well. There was work to be done in Ismailia.

In the time we had been away the camp at Ismailia had grown. All the troops needed to bring the enemy to battle were there. Now that we had successfully repaired the railway line then there was nothing to stop us from moving west along the Sweet Water canal. Lieutenant General Sir Garnet Wolseley was keen to defeat the Egyptians.

After the lieutenant had reported to the colonel he came back to our camp with disturbing news. While we appeared to be winning in Egypt a leader, the Sudanese called him the Mahdi, had arisen and had slaughtered Egyptian armies. Muhammad Ahmad bin Abd Allah was too far away from us to be of much concern but I did not like the lieutenant's tone. It seemed that, despite the opposition of Prime Minister William Gladstone to any more imperial expansion, our general was keen to bring the whole of the Sudan under British control. I just wanted to go home and see my son.

# Chapter 5

**The Battle of Kassassin Lock**

The regiment was part of the small force that left the camp at
Ismailia first. We were to march down the Sweet Water Canal
and make a fortified camp at Kassassin Lock. The rest of the
army would follow. Our friends from the railway troop would,
once we had secured both the lock on the canal and the station,
be able to bring troops to build up our forces. We only had
twenty miles to march but I envied those who would enjoy the
journey on the train in our wake. We were with the South
Staffordshire regiment again but this time we had four artillery
pieces with us. We were also supported by cavalry. They
followed us and for that I was grateful. It was no fun to ride in
the dust thrown up by horses. As the regiment had more
experience than ours, the South Staffs led. It was only twenty
miles but the heat made it seem much further. We reached the
lock in the late afternoon and I was looking forward to some
shade, water and food. We dropped our haversacks and prepared
to make a camp. It was as we began to fortify the lock and the
station that the attack began. Once again it was precipitated by
camels aided this time by horses. They were backed up by the
whole rebel army. With just two battalions we were heavily
outnumbered and Major Pulleine did not wait for any counsel of
war. He sent a rider for help. The guns were quickly unlimbered
and fortified. We formed two ranks between the canal and the
railway. Some of the Staffordshire regiment were echeloned to
the north to prevent us from being outflanked.

As I had learned in Natal, the bigger picture was never seen
by the rank and file. Our company, commanded by Captain
Wilberforce, was close to the canal again. Number two section
all looked to me in the absence of their own sergeant. Repulsing
the camel attack at Lake Timsah had given them courage.

"Right, lads, make sure your ammo is close to hand. Mark
your targets and listen for the command. Remember a camel
rider or a cavalryman is going nowhere without his animal.
Shoot for the camels and the horses first." I grinned, "I have tried
camel meat and I would like a taste of horse, just for comparison

you understand." It was a poor attempt at humour but it worked and there were nervous laughs.

This time it would not be me who repeated the orders but Sergeant Major Lowery. We had the colours with us and the colour party would act as a magnet for the enemy. I did not envy them. This time we had four pieces of artillery and with a longer range, they commenced firing first. The booms sounded almost simultaneously and then smoke covered the ground before them. It made it harder for us to see the enemy and we had to hope that they had caused casualties. As we waited, I intoned, "Mark your target and wait for the command. Steady now, lads." I spoke in a monotone and I was deliberately emulating Colour Sergeant Bourne. It had been his steady voice that had kept me calm when I thought a Zulu assegai was going to end my life. We could hear the thundering of the camels and the horses as they galloped towards us. Four cannons were not enough. When they closed with them then the gunners would switch to canister but by then the rifles would be adding to the harvest.

"At two hundred yards volley fire." Captain Wilberforce shouted the command, the nervousness in his voice reflecting the fear he undoubtedly felt.

That was a longer range than we normally gave our first volley and showed that the brigadier was worried by the wall of cavalry that raced at us. We were tightly packed and would make a tempting target for the enemy horsemen but it was reassuring to feel the touch of the rest of the battalion that close.

I aimed at the mount of one of the leaders, a man on a camel waving a sword. The weird motion of the camel meant I had more chance of hitting the camel than the officer who bounced atop the beast.

"Fire!"

The order was repeated by every officer and NCO even though we all heard the stentorian tones of the Sergeant Major. The rifle bucked and I chambered another cartridge.

"Fire!"

The Martini-Henry is capable of twelve rounds a minute but as we had discovered at Rorke's Drift such a rate of fire could not be maintained. Hands became sweaty. Cartridges would not cooperate and nerves made a man look up at the danger and not concentrate on reloading. What we achieved on the training ground could not be repeated on the battlefield. However, in the time it took the enemy cavalrymen to cover two hundred yards we managed to fire eight rounds. I was not optimistic enough to believe that every round struck something. Some men still closed their eyes as they fired. Others would not aim properly. In addition, some bullets would merely score a line along the flank of an animal. It would not make them fall but merely madden them. It was when the cannons began to fire canister that great swathes of riders fell. The guns were spread out along the line and where there were no artillery pieces then the cavalry closed quickly with us. We had not been ordered to fix bayonets but we were in a solid line. The canal to our left meant that we could not be outflanked but that also meant we had nowhere to flee. We had to stand and fight where we were.

"Independent fire!"

As soon as the order was given then the volleys became more ragged but as the enemy warriors were much closer so we began to hit men rather than animals. Some of the riders had lances. One keen camel rider had managed to get close to me. I had just chambered a round when his lance was thrust at me. I knocked the head to the side with the barrel of my gun and then quickly brought back the rifle to fire at almost point-blank range. The bullet threw the rider from his camel. He kept hold of the reins and the animal fell. Had it fallen the other way then Private Thomas and Private Wilson would have been crushed but, as it was it fell before us, making a barrier. I dropped my rifle and, quickly picking up the lance, rammed it into the camel to prevent it from thrashing its feet and hurting my men. As I picked up my rifle, I saw Lieutenant Hodges walk up to the beast and fire a bullet from his pistol into the head of the camel. It fell still.

The cavalry charge was over and the horses and camels began to move away from our lines. In the west, I saw the sun setting and the serried ranks of the fez-topped Egyptians began to march towards us. They were coming in skirmish order and that gave them an advantage. Our formation was solid and when they fired then they had an even greater chance of hitting flesh than we did. The hiatus gave me the chance to check on my men.

"Anyone hit?"

Joe Wilson said, "No Sarge, but that camel came mighty close to giving Dai and me a trip to the hospital."

I turned to the lieutenant, "Permission to order fix bayonets, sir?"

"Yes Sergeant Roberts."

"Fix bayonets."

I heard the sound of the locking of bayonets in their sockets. Some of the other sections had heard and they copied us. The attack at Lake Timsah had shown the efficacy of a bayonet. This would be a night battle. Just as dawn had come quickly at Lake Timsah so night fell as though someone had switched off the light. The darkness suited the Egyptians although our darker uniforms made us a shadow. The white helmets, however, gave the enemy riflemen a target. The sudden darkness was lit up by the flashes from the muzzles of the enemy rifles.

Then we heard the boom of enemy artillery and they had more than four pieces. The muzzle flashes from the rifles and muskets were like fireflies compared with the flashes from at least twenty artillery pieces. Some were old-fashioned cannons but a bouncing cannonball could still carve its way through files of tightly packed men. This would take old-fashioned courage.

Sergeant Major Lowery's voice shouted, "Fire when you see a target. Do not waste bullets."

The Egyptians were doing the opposite. They were firing constantly and the odd bullets that reached us tended to fly over our heads. They were not good shots. I had heard that their leader, Arabi Pasha, had conscripted men in their droves. They had numbers but they were untrained men and while the noise of their muskets and rifles was terrifying the results were not. The problem would come when they closed with us. We might have the chance to get off half a dozen rounds and then it would be bayonet work. That did not worry me. I had trained the men well but unlike Rorke's Drift, there were no mealie bags to offer protection.

It was the nearing of the muzzle flashes that told us where the enemy soldiers were. I heard the crack of a Martini-Henry further down the line and the response from Sergeant Williams, "That man! Wait for the order!"

I said to my section, all close to me, "If we all fire together then it will have a great effect. Just listen for the order."

Private Potter said, "It is the waiting that gets to me, sarge, and I need a pee."

For some reason his words made us relax and men laughed.

"Next time make sure you empty your bladder before we stand to."

A voice from further down said, "Either that or piss your pants."

Bob Walters said, gently, "Quiet lads." He was a sound soldier.

The order to fire would have to come from either the lieutenant or me as the Egyptian line was advancing at different rates. The flash from the artillery pieces was causing fewer casualties as, in the darkness, the enemy could see the flash and take cover. It made for an undulating line that advanced towards us in the dark.

"Number three section, kneel!" I realised that by kneeling we allowed number two section to fire over our heads and also to make us a smaller target. The closer the Egyptians came to us the more chance they would have of hitting us. In my view, it also gave a more stable platform. I looked down the barrel at the sights, waiting for the first enemy soldiers to come within range. The dead camel before us stank but its bulk and the bodies of the dead Egyptians would be a barrier before us. It was something.

The lieutenant gave the order to fire. I thought that it was about thirty seconds too early but at least he had given the order and that showed his increasing confidence.

"Open fire." He commanded Number One Platoon and every gun barked as one. We heard cries but had no idea if we had hit anything as we were still firing in the dark. "Independent fire." The lieutenant realised that we had hurt their advance with the first volley and now we needed to send as many bullets as we could in their direction. It would no longer matter if we fired in volleys as it was a ragged line that was advancing. We could see their lighter uniforms in the dark. There is something almost hypnotic when you keep chambering rounds and then firing them. It is as though your body has taken over and your mind is no longer needed. The advancing Egyptians were no longer coming in large numbers and we had time to aim.

I reminded the men of that, "Mark your targets, lads and don't waste bullets."

Our bullets had an effect. There was a lessening of muzzle flashes and then we heard the most wonderful sound in the world. It was a cavalry bugle sounding the charge and it was our bugle. The messenger had got through and the general had sent cavalry to our aid. This time the thundering of hooves was cheered as the cavalry flooded the plain to the north of us. The Egyptians would be trapped between the canal and the sabres of the cavalry. The Egyptians knew what was coming and while the flashes of their muzzles diminished, the sound of the cannons and rifles did not. They turned to fire at the Household Cavalry, Dragoons, and Dragoon Guards galloped towards them.

Sergeant Major Lowery's voice rose above the battle, "The King's Shropshire Light Infantry will advance in skirmish order." There was a pause and my section rose. "March."

We were not completely in step; the bodies and the terrain made that impossible but it was a steady advance and with loaded weapons pointing forward then any brave Egyptian fellah who tried to stand in our way found either a bullet or a bayonet. When we reached the enemy lines, we were halted. There were no living Egyptians there to fight us. The cavalry had ridden a long way to come to our aid and, unusually for our cavalry had not chased after the survivors. They had reined in close to the eleven guns that they had captured.

"Sergeant Roberts, set sentries. Sergeant Williams, secure any prisoners we might have. We will relieve you as soon as we have established a camp." The lieutenant was paying our sections a compliment. We were the ones that could be trusted to do the task properly.

We both acknowledged the order. "Come on lads, follow me." We moved through the dead and dying Egyptians until we reached the open ground. "Bob, put a couple of good men close to the canal. Ten yards between each sentry. Keep your eyes and ears open." I know the order sounded absurd but the men would know, after Lake Timsah, what I meant. I slipped my rifle over my shoulder once I had established that there were no enemies and then walked down my line of sentries. No one had been hurt and they were all in a good mood. Had the cavalry not arrived when they did then who knows?

The sound of hooves from the west made me shout the command, "Stand to. Riders approaching." We all aimed our loaded and primed weapons at the approaching riders. "Halt, who goes there?"

The English voice reassured me, "Number 1 Troop 7th Dragoon Guards returning from patrol."

The eight riders reined in next to me. The sergeant grinned, "Glad to see you lads are alert."

"Have they all gone, sergeant?"

He nodded, "Aye, they are digging in up the road at Tel-el Kebir. You lads were lucky, I reckon there were twenty thousand men attacking you."

"Good job you came then."

He laughed, "I must confess a night charge is not the best thing but it was good to let our horses open their legs and for some of these lads this was the first time they had unsheathed their swords in anger."

"Aye, well, we are grateful and if we ever get to civilisation again, I will buy you a pint."

"You are on, right lads, let's get back before Lieutenant Dalrymple becomes too worried."

We stood in silence and then I heard the sound of hooves. This time it was a lone horse and an Egyptian one at that. It galloped directly up to us and I heard Hargreaves curse and back away. He raised his rifle. "Don't shoot, the poor animal is terrified." I laid down my rifle and took off my helmet. Trooper had taught me about horses and when I had followed Lieutenant Bromhead to recover the colours I had ridden then. I suppose that there was a cavalryman hidden within me. I walked up to the horse which stamped and snorted. I began to sing. When I had brought Griff on the train to Liverpool, I had sung to him to get him to sleep. It was a simple song with many repeated phrases. It had calmed my infant son and I hoped it would calm the horse.

"Watch out, Sarge, he has teeth."

"Aye and bloody big legs."

Bob Walters growled, "Just shut your gobs. He knows what he is doing."

The horse was already calming and I slowly reached out to take the reins. I had, in my tunic, a couple of mints left and I took one out and held it to the horse. The beast sniffed suspiciously, "Come on, it is just a sweetie." It took the mint and crunched it. I stroked the mane and walked the animal in a circle. When I sensed that it was calm enough, I led it back to the other men. Their teeth shining in the dark showed that my men had enjoyed my little show. "Corporal, take charge and I will take this animal back to the lieutenant."

I donned my helmet and slung my rifle and then led the now obedient animal back to the camp. There were fires now glowing and some men were preparing to sleep. They would be roused early to relieve some of the sentries. The lieutenant was speaking with Major Pulleine and they looked surprised when I walked in.

"Found a horse then, Sergeant Roberts?"

"Yes, Major Pulleine. I couldn't leave it out there." I tailed off lamely.

The major leaned over and examined the rump of the animal. In the light from the fire, I could see that it had been wounded. A blade, probably a bayonet had scored a long line. "The animal is hurt. You did well, Roberts. I know horses and a wounded horse can be a harrying sight. Where did you learn to do this? Were you brought up on a farm?"

I laughed, "No sir, in a town but a trooper from the cavalry taught me about horses. I like them."

"Well get back to your men and I will have this animal tended to by Dragoon Guard's vet."

I walked back to the camp. The smell of cooking food reminded me just how hungry I was. All was quiet on our picket line and we stood watching the dark. We were relieved in the middle of the night as the Highland regiments arrived. We simply rolled into our greatcoats and blankets and slept the sleep of the dead before being rudely awakened a couple of hours later.

Although we were woken early, we had little to do other than to make our camp more secure and to make shelters from the sun. This was August and the sun was at its hottest. The scraps of tent we had taken, augmented by broken lances made shelters beneath which we sheltered as the general and his senior officers rode to inspect the Egyptian force that barred our way to Cairo. We were close to the canal and while I would not dream of drinking the rank green water it did help us to keep cooler. As August drifted towards September increasing numbers of men suffering from heatstroke were ferried on trains back to Ismailia and the hospitals there. When we were not on duty, I had the men take shelter beneath the pieces of tent and when we did go on duty our necks were protected by cloth hanging from our helmets. Our faces and hands turned first pink, then red and finally, after using the oil we had captured to ease the blistering, a nutty brown. I rationed my smoking to just the nighttime and evening when the mosquitoes from the canal threatened to make life unbearable. Other soldiers suffered bites and one or two had to be sent back to Ismailia. It was in the evening when we were not on duty that we got to speak of the battles and what lay ahead.

"What do you reckon, Sarge, can we beat this Arabi Pasha bloke then?"

I do not know what they expected of me. My battle in Natal had been a fierce one but was nothing like this. I tried to answer. "I have seen nothing so far that worries me, Corporal. Our platoon is a good one. We stand our ground and do not flinch. We have good rifles and if it was not for this damned heat then I would be even more confident. Oh, we will beat them but then what? I hope we are sent back to England."

"You have a kiddie, don't you?"

I nodded, "And the last time I saw him he was less than a month old. He will be almost toddling now and I would like to see him." We had not been sent any letters yet. That did not surprise me but I hated the lack of word from my family. I wondered if I was cut out to be a soldier. Before Annie, I had not considered any other life other than being a redcoat but now I had a son and that changed everything.

## The Battle of Tel-el-Kebir

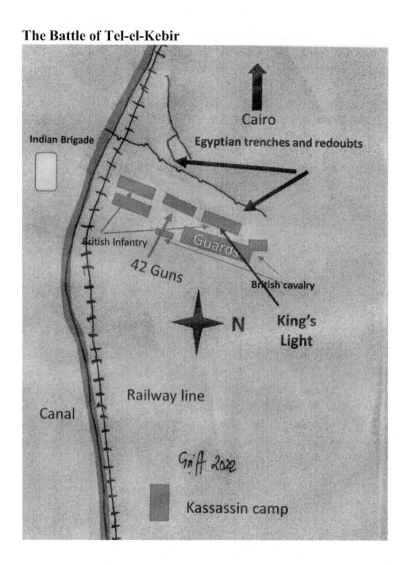

# Chapter 6

## The Battle of Tel-el-Kebir September 1882

When the word came to us that it would be a night attack then the lieutenant and I were summoned to a meeting with the other officers and NCOs from the regiment. Our experience of the first night march was considered invaluable. I did not mind that the lieutenant took credit for my idea of having a piece of white material hanging down from our helmets. The colonel thought it was a good idea and the lieutenant's star rose a little higher. I liked the lieutenant and he and I had become closer as a result of the actions in which we had fought. The colonel was worried that marching over unfamiliar terrain, in the dark, was a recipe for disaster and he ordered the whole regiment to adopt the white cloth.

The day after the briefing we met a patrol of the 7th Dragoon Guards and it was the same sergeant we had met before. He reined in and I could see, from his face, that he had good news to impart. "What is new Sergeant?"

"We had a bit of luck, yesterday, one of our patrols caught a civilian and brought him back to the general. It turns out he is the best leader the Egyptians possess, General Mahmoud Fehmy. The general was pleased and gave our troop an extra rum ration! Happy days, eh?" I knew what he meant. I did not know this general but I knew from the lieutenant that the rebel generals were not the best and if we had captured the one with talent then that boded well for our attack. This time we would be attacking as we had the first time. The difference would be it would not be a couple of battalions it would be against an enemy who was dug in, prepared and who had artillery.

Having been in action our platoon was well-placed to prepare for the fight. Weapons were cleaned and bayonets sharpened on a whetstone. I ensured that we had plenty of bullets and the men had learned to do as I did and use the pockets of our tunics to keep them. An overloaded valise made marching, firing and charging, more difficult.

The attack was set for the morning of the 12th of September at dawn. I was happy about that as it meant we were marching in the cool of the night. Even the cool of the night, however, was still warmer than summer in England. We marched in battalion order and we preceded the Guards Division commanded by the son of Queen Victoria, Arthur, Duke of Connaught. We were on the northern flank of our advance and I think that the presence of royalty behind us made everyone nervous. We stopped many times to dress ranks. It proved to be a good thing as we reached the Egyptian lines just as dawn was breaking.

The unlimbering of the forty-two artillery pieces we had brought with us was both time-consuming and noisy. The handful of Egyptian sentries heard us and began to pop off their rifles at us. We heard their bugles call men to arms and we dressed ranks to prepare for the charge. The Egyptian artillery began a ragged bombardment as our own guns fired in response. They fired first but it was an ineffectual barrage. Some shells fell short and some were long. I know not about the other regiments but ours had not a wound between us. The bugle from the Highland Division precipitated the attack and as the Highlanders charged towards the Egyptians, we were ordered to fix bayonets. Our charge was but a short time later. The word charge suggests running but we just marched resolutely forward. Running invited disaster for as we were in battalion order one man tripping could bring down eight or nine men. Walking smartly was the safer option. This was where all the drills paid off. We kept in step and the line was as straight as it was possible to be. The uneven ground, rocks and small craters created by the artillery inevitably meant it sometimes became uneven. We had, however, to endure the fire from the enemy infantry as well as their shells and I dreaded the thought of canister which would scythe through us like wheat. I was scared for this was unlike anything I had experienced. The first night action had been against a handful of men with no artillery. Natal had been fought against natives with assegais. As the shells screamed over our heads and the air was filled with the buzz of bullets, I knew that while I had every likelihood of surviving, an unlucky bullet or shell could make my son an orphan. I concentrated on keeping dressed lines.

"Keep steady lads. Hargreaves, it is not a race. We get there together and then we go in with the lunger."

Further along the line, I heard one of the younger lieutenants, Cartwright-Jones, exhorting his men, "Think of England, lads. The eyes of the son of the Empress are upon us. Let us do our duty."

It was stirring stuff but I knew that the men I led just wanted to survive with all their limbs intact. The redoubts had been hastily thrown up by the Egyptians but they were an obstacle. They rose from the ground and the earth and stakes protected not only the gunners but also the riflemen. The trenches were now filled with the Egyptian fellahs, the red fez they each wore making a good target. We marched and kept a straight line. Had the Egyptians filled their trenches then more of our men would have died but the Egyptians had been woken from their slumbers and were unprepared for battle. Some of them fired a volley and then fled. When we were just forty yards from the trenches and redoubts, the order was given to charge home and we ran. I saw an Egyptian soldier raise his rifle and aim at me. I ran harder but I knew that he would fire before I reached him. I was twenty feet away when I saw him squeeze the trigger and I braced myself for the impact. It was a misfire and I saw the horror on the man's face as he ejected the cartridge to load another. He never made it and I rammed my bayonet into his chest. Around me, my men were doing as they had been trained. They lunged with their bayonets and cleared the Egyptians before us. They chambered bullets and fired at every hint of danger. That some bullets missed was immaterial as it kept the enemy heads down. The bayonet on the end made the rifle harder to fire but we had trained well enough and all of them knew how to compensate. This was not Rorke's Drift where we fired so many bullets that chambers jammed. Here we were firing steadily. At Rorke's Drift, we had fired six or seven bullets a minute, sometimes for twenty odd minutes at a time. Here we were choosing targets and the rate was nearer three bullets a minute. Our guns would not jam. We moved along the trenches and redoubts seeking enemies. It was clear that many had fled but there were others who had remained. I had heard of soldiers at Isandlwana who had found perches in the rocks and held off Zulus for a couple of hours after the battle had ended. A man fights and clings to life beyond all hope. There would be Egyptians who were of the same mind.

As I had learned before, night fighting was a confused and dangerous affair and although the sun was rising behind us, the smoke and the slight mist from the canal made visibility difficult. Faces, bayonets and swords came out of the smoky murk. The flash of muzzles made a man temporarily blind and there was always the unknown factor of the numbers you were facing. We had been told that there were twenty thousand in the enemy army. We had less than nine thousand men and that meant we were outnumbered by more than two to one. The complete rising of the sun revealed that we had killed many in the trenches already.

I had come to trust both my senses and my rifle. As I scanned the trenches, I looked for movement and when I saw a fez move I raised my rifle I sent a bullet into it. It was now an automatic reaction for me to chamber another bullet and then look for another target. There were fanatics amongst the enemy and a couple of dozen of them, hidden behind a redoubt, suddenly ran at us.

"Number three section, ware enemy to the right." I dropped to one knee and, as my section joined me, began to fire. This was like Rorke's Drift all over again. Wild men who were determined to kill at all costs. I remembered the routine. Stay steady and make sure you drop the nearest man. My bullet caught the closest man in the chest and my rifle switched to the next target, the man to his left. I had not even been aware of loading the round but as I squeezed the trigger my bullet spun him around. I fired a third one before I knew that I would have to use my bayonet for two men were closing with me. I had chambered the rifle but they were on me. The rest of the section was all engaged and I was, to all intents and purposes, on my own. I blocked the bayonet of one Egyptian with the stock of my rifle while I parried the sword that came down for my head. I twisted my body so that the fellah who had struck at my stock tumbled. I turned my rifle and fired at the officer. The man who had stumbled rose and I barely had time to swing my bayonet. I was lucky and he was not. My lunger tore across his throat and he tumbled into the trench.

The attack beaten off, I loaded another bullet. There were six men with me. "They came from behind that redoubt. Let's make sure there aren't more there. Skirmish order and shoot first. Do not hesitate."

They chorused, "Yes, sergeant."

The redoubts had been hastily constructed. The barrels of the artillery pieces poked from between gaps. They had built up soil embankments before the guns and used timber to hold them in place with sandbags at the side. It explained why they had remained undamaged in the artillery duel. I waved Hargreaves and Thomas to the left with Lowe while I led the others to the right. The gunners had been killed by shrapnel from one of our howitzers. It had exploded behind the gun where there was no protection and the gun crew had been shredded by the metal from the exploding shell. There was no one left alive but it made sense to check.

"Make sure that they are not playing dead, eh?"

It was a gruesome task but it needed to be done. They were all dead.

Sergeant Major Lowery's voice echoed across the battlefield. "King's Light Infantry, hold at the trenches! Secure the guns."

It was a sensible order for we had cavalry to chase after the fleeing enemy cavalry and camel riders. "Right lads, let's do as we have been ordered." I ran to the nearest breech-loading artillery piece. After checking that there were no enemy soldiers close by, I laid down my rifle. "You four, swing this one around. Corporal Walters, do the same with the next gun. Corporal Cole, have your men swing around the next gun."

I was no gunner but the breech-loading cannons were relatively simple to operate and I loaded a shell. I doubted that we would need it but, should disaster strike and the enemy counter-attacked, they would have a shock as we fired on them with their own guns.

By the time noon arrived, we had every one of the fifty-eight guns we had captured facing west. Our dead had been collected and the wounded were being tended to. Although our regiment had not suffered any deaths the Highlanders had. They had suffered more from the artillery and they had been wild in their charge. Altogether fifty odd men had died. To me, that was too many but Lieutenant Hodges was in good humour. The regiment had suffered fifteen men wounded and although none was of a serious nature, he had been sent by the colonel to report on their condition. It was he who brought us the numbers.

"And the Egyptians, sir?" We had already cleared the bodies from our section of the trenches. We had not burned them as we were waiting for orders but something would have to be done soon as the heat of the African sun began to make them swell and stink.

"From what I can gather, Sergeant Roberts, more than eight hundred bodies have been counted. A victory."

That brightened me, "Then we can go home soon, sir?"

He shook his head, "Sorry, Roberts, we have to take Cairo first and then ensure that the Khedive is securely placed in command again. We don't want to risk the Suez Canal falling into the hands of the enemy of the Queen."

I had, perhaps, been unrealistic in my expectations but I wanted to see my son.

We did not have long to wait at Tel-el-Kebir. We were ordered to bury the bodies and then our friends from the engineers cleared the tracks of discarded engines and we were taken by train to Cairo. The cavalry had pursued Arabi Pasha and his army to an undefended city and had taken him prisoner. We spent a couple of months tented in Cairo while order was established. The enemy had been beaten three times and many of their keenest warriors had fallen. The heart had gone from them. Lord Cromer was appointed as adviser to the khedive. Lieutenant Hodges had it on good authority that his task was to ensure that the huge tracts of land that ran the length of the Nile were properly managed. To that effect, a couple of regiments would stay with him to ensure that order was maintained. I think that some of the officers hoped that we would be one of the regiments but, thankfully, we were not. It became clear that we would be going home and I was delighted. The time we spent in those tents in Cairo was not pleasant. The heat, the stink from Cairo and the flies were worse than the battle had been.

Thanks to our victory we had all taken from the dead. It was in the nature of war. The winners always took the spoils. The officers might not approve and the generals certainly wouldn't.

73

They did not need any extra money and viewed it as banditry. We were realists and knew that if we didn't take it then the locals would. As the coins we had taken were Egyptian there was little point in taking them back to England and we spent all of them in the souks, the markets of Cairo. I bought gifts for my family. Griff was too young to need anything that we found in Cairo but there were many pretty items of clothing for my mother, aunt and sisters. I knew that Billy had begun to smoke a pipe and I bought two matching tobacco pouches for us. They were beautifully decorated and so cheap that I thought they had been given away. I had a present in mind for Griff and it was one I hoped he would like. I just had to find it.

With the railways under British control, the journey back to Alexandria was a more comfortable one than the march west had been. We rigged shelters over the tops of the wagons in which we travelled but the engineers had done a good job and we made excellent time. We had to wait in Alexandria for a fortnight for the ships to arrive to take us home and it was an unpleasant time. When we first arrived the bombardment and the subsequent fires meant that much of the city was destroyed. There was rebuilding and clearance of demolished buildings all around us. It was like living on a building site and we were all glad when the transports arrived and we were allowed to board and leave Egypt.

I was relieved that we had not been one of the regiments ordered to stay in Cairo. I had found the city hot, dirty and smelly. We had seen the pyramids and whilst they had been impressive the squalor in which the people lived was not. Lord Cromer, the new governor, would have his work cut out to ensure that he improved the lot of the common man. If he did not then there would be another revolt.

We saw less of the lieutenant on the voyage home for he messed with the officers and we only saw him at the daily parade. When we did see him, he was a different man from the slightly diffident officer who had seemed to lack confidence on the way south. He would occasionally join Bob and me as we smoked our pipes at the stern. When he did so he gave us news. He was to be promoted. The colonel and the major were pleased with his performance. Bob too was to be made a lance sergeant. I was pleased for them both. I had my promotion and I was happy with that. The soon-to-be captain also told us of trouble further south, in the Sudan. "Egypt, it seems, has lost control of half of the country. Sudan now has more rebels than we fought in Egypt."

"Does that mean we will have to go back, sir?" The last thing I wanted was another war that would deprive me of the chance to see my son and my family.

He shook his head, "The Prime Minister, it seems, is loath to have British lives wasted. The colonel has heard that it will be the Egyptians who will fight against the rebels. They will be given British officers and NCOs. As we saw the soldiers are brave enough but badly led." He looked at Bob, "If you wished to transfer, Walters, I could put a word in. You get more pay and an increase in rank."

Bob shook his head, "Thank you for the offer, sir, but that little jaunt in Africa was enough for Mrs Walters' boy and besides I like this regiment."

"So do I, Walters, but some of the lieutenants in other regiments stayed in Cairo. They are guaranteed the rank of major. For some chaps that is the be-all and end-all. Not for me. I want to stay with this regiment and earn my promotions." He smiled, "I want to thank you two chaps for all that you did. I know I was a little green when we landed but I appreciate that you looked after me."

Bob shook his head, "That was Sergeant Roberts, sir. He is an old hand at this sort of thing."

I was not and I knew it but my experience in Natal had stood me in good stead. The question remained, would I want to stay in the army when my son and family lived so far away?

The voyage back was less pleasant than the one out had been. After we passed through the Straits of Gibraltar we were hit by an Atlantic storm. I learned then that I had sea legs. Many of the others did not. It might have been the result of heat stroke in Egypt and other illnesses contracted in camp but more than half of the regiment became very ill as a result of the tossing and turning. When the storm burnt itself out there were more men in their beds than reporting for the morning parade on the foredeck. Once again fewer of the men in our platoon were incapacitated. We had eaten better and protected ourselves from the sun more.

There were men who were seasick; Potter and Hargreaves were particularly ill but they soon recovered.

"A lesson for you, Bob. When you take over number two section then you need to think as much about the welfare of the section as their battle efficiency."

"Where did you learn all this, Jack?"

I smiled, "From the lads in the 24th. Hooky, Sergeant Windridge and Colour Sergeant Bourne. They made me the soldier I am today. I reckon that is how the British Army works. We don't go to officer training; we learn from those who have risen up through the ranks. Don't get me wrong, there are some bad 'uns out there but not as many as the solid backbone of the British Army."

The storm also delayed us and we did not dock in Southampton until three weeks after the storm had struck. We had to wait for three days for our trains and had a tortuous journey back to Shrewsbury and our barracks. Once there it was back into the routine. With Captain Philips gone we needed a new adjutant and Captain Hodges was given the post on a temporary basis. He was pleased with the job although I would not have been. It seemed to me to be all about paperwork. He was quite philosophical about it all. "I will learn how the battalion works and that is no bad thing. I learned about active service in Egypt but one day I might be in command of a battalion and I need to know how it works." He grinned, "Besides, I am not a fan of marching and parading."

"Nor am I sir, but we saw in Egypt that drilling makes for better soldiers. That and some good training on the firing range. I intend to make my section the best in the platoon."

"The thing is, Roberts, you won't have the section anymore. You have been put in command of the whole platoon. Sergeant Hughes took a lance in the leg and he can't walk properly. He is being invalided out and the major himself put your name forward. Until we get a replacement for me you will be in command. I am confident you will do a good job."

I groaned, "Sir, I hoped for a leave to go and see my family."

"As do the rest of the regiment." He flourished a packet of papers, "One of my first tasks is to arrange a rota. You will get your leave but it won't be for a week or two. Perhaps a month."

"Sir." I was a victim of my own success. Had I performed less well then, I would not have been given the platoon and until a new lieutenant arrived, I would not be able to leave. I hoped it was not another Lieutenant Harding-Smythe.

On my first day off I went and picked wildflowers from the hedgerow and then went to the graveyard. There was a stone there. Doris, the girls and Geraint must have arranged that.

### 'ANNIE ROBERTS, WIFE TO JACK AND MOTHER TO GRIFFITH, BORN 1863 DIED 1881'

It was a simple stone and inscription but it made tears spring to my eyes.

"Well, Annie, I am home. I haven't seen our bairn yet but I know my family will have looked after him. I promise that I will tell him all about you. As you watch, from heaven, you will see him become a fine young man."

I spent an hour there and then headed to the '*Eagle and Child*'. Alice and Betty were serving behind the bar and they squealed with delight when I entered. Geraint had been in the cellar and his head appeared, "What is all this commotion?" His smile appeared when he spied me, "Jack, you are back. Have a beer on the house." As he pulled the pint he said, "We heard you lads were back and did well out there."

I nodded, "Thank you for the gravestone, how much do I owe you?"

Betty shook her head, "It wasn't us, Jack. The vicar said a Captain Philips paid for it."

"He was a good man. Where is Doris?"

Their faces clouded and Betty's voice was filled with anger, "She ran off with a chap last year. They went to London. He was a bad 'un, Jack. Little pencil moustache and he was a smooth talker. She fell for him, hook line and sinker. We tried to tell her but…"

Geraint handed me the pint, "I reckon that Annie dying like that made her look at her life and she grabbed at the first lifebelt she saw."

Alice snorted, "More like a dead weight. Doris had a little bit of money and I reckon he ran off with her to get the money."

Life was like that. You could not predict what was going to happen. I had thought Doris was the most stable of the girls and the one least likely to do something stupid but in matters of the heart, there are no rules. When I returned to the barracks, I wrote a letter thanking Captain Philips and offering to repay him for the stone. I went to Major Pulleine to ask for an address and he said, "He left for America, Jack. He told us that before we left. He wanted a new start. I am afraid I have no idea where he is."

"The thing is, sir, he paid for a gravestone for my wife and I would like to repay him."

He smiled, "Captain Philips thought well of you, Jack. He had no family of his own and he would not be happy if you repaid him."

I held the letter, "I wrote a letter, sir."

"Give it to me and I will send it to the Army and Navy club in London. He is a member there and they will see that he gets it." I handed the letter over. My life, it seemed, was to be filled with friends departing and the one constant was that I was always left alone. I now understood Trooper a lot better. He had seemed to me friendless and yet everyone liked him. Many of his comrades had died but life in the service, for all the camaraderie could also be a lonely place.

I was lucky that I had Bob Walters in the platoon as well as number three section. Three of them had been promoted to corporal and that meant I had a good spine of men. The sections I had led in Egypt had proved the most efficient and I spent the first two weeks dragging the rest up to the same standard. It was hard work as some of the other sections had not been led as well as ours but we persevered. I made it a competition so that on the firing range we had prizes for accuracy and speed of firing. I also endeavoured to make the men fitter. Africa had taken its toll on many of the men. We ate well in the barracks and I ensured that we had a two-mile run every day in full kit. I was mindful of Albert Hepplewhite and when we went on the run, I stayed at the back to jolly along any who lagged behind. I was helped by the fact that there was no officer yet.

We were told that we would have a two-week leave in a fortnight when Lieutenant Callow arrived. I could not believe how young he looked. I wondered if he was even shaving. I met him in the battalion office with Captain Hodges. The captain made it easy for me and stressed to the young officer how experienced I was. It turned out he was nothing like Harding-Smythe and was eager to learn. It made for a more harmonious time. I tried to treat him the way Hooky had treated me when I joined the 24th. He might be an officer but he was also a young man and I knew how hard he would be finding the transition from civilian life to the life of a soldier of the queen. A fortnight was not enough and it would be hard for the young man to adjust to life in the battalion with the whole platoon on leave. Captain Hodges showed that his promotion had been a good one as he took the young officer under his wing and taught him how to be a good officer.

# Chapter 7

As I headed north, I reflected that it had been two years since I had left my family. I had no idea what to expect. The letters sent to Egypt were now on their way back, unread as I had not received them, and there had been no news. If there had been bad news then I would have been sent a telegram and so I took comfort from that. I virtually ran from the ferry to the house. They knew I was coming as I had invested in a telegram home. I arrived on Saturday afternoon and the whole family was waiting for me. The calls from the neighbours as I strode down the street alerted them to my arrival and Billy, now sporting a moustache and brilliantined hair, greeted me. He had grown but I was still bigger. I dropped my kitbag and shook his hand.

He looked me up and down, "By heck our Jack, you have changed colour."

I laughed and, picking up my bag, entered, "The African sun burns hot, our Bill. I shall never complain about a cloudy day again, that is for sure." I dropped my bag in the hall and put my forage cap on the coat hook. I smoothed down my hair, "How do I look, our Bill?"

"They just want to see you."

"This will be the first time my son will see me. I want him to be impressed."

"Don't worry, he will be. Mother and Aunt Sarah talk about you all the time to him. Come on they will be waiting."

He opened the door to the parlour and stood back. My sisters were now women and they beamed at me. Aunt Sarah and Mother both looked older. All four gave their widest smiles and I felt the love from them all. The hint of a tear was in my mother's eyes but my eyes were drawn to my son. He had my hair and his mother's eyes. He stood, nervously hiding behind his grandmother's leg.

My mother said, "Now then, Griff, this is your dad. Say hello."

"He can talk?"

"A few words," said Auntie Sarah, "His first word was Nanna."

I dropped to one knee and held my arms out, "Son, I am your father and you can't know how much I have dreamed of this moment."

My mother said softly as he continued to hide, "It will take time, Jack."

I reached into my tunic. One of the lads in the section was good with his hands. I had given him a couple of bob and he had carved me a wood soldier, a redcoat with a rifle, and I had painted it on the voyage home. One of the sailors in the crew had given me some varnish and it gleamed. I took it out and said, "Here, Griff, a present, a toy soldier to remind you of me. See he has three stripes just like me." The temptation was too much and he stepped out and grabbed hold of it with two hands. I picked him up and stood. "We have two weeks, son, and I want to make the most of them."

He was so fascinated with the toy soldier that he said nothing and almost ignored me. I did not care. I held my son and I never wanted to let him go.

The fireside chair which had been normally occupied by my nan was vacated for me and I sat on it, with Griff on my knee. He was happy to be playing with the soldier and I stroked his hair and wondered how the tiny bundle I had left became a toddler. I had missed so much.

"You are a good colour, Jack."

I nodded, "I know, Aunt Sarah, I said to Billy that there is no shade in Egypt and it is as hot as a Pilkington's glass furnace. I am glad to be home."

I could see that my sisters were keen to tell me something and when I looked at Alice she blurted out, "And Sarah and I are walking out. We have young men. You shall see them tomorrow."

I winked at my mother, "Well we shall have to see if they pass muster. I am the man of the house."

Billy laughed and Sarah turned and snapped, "And our Billy has a young lady and he is engaged."

Alice pleaded, "You won't be horrible to them, will you, Jack?"

Aunt Sarah rose and came over to kiss me on the top of the head, "Our Jack is just teasing, Alice and well you know it. He hasn't changed and I can see he is still a credit to his family and his country. I'll put the kettle on. How do you take it these days, Jack?"

"Any way that it comes. When we have milk, it could be goat milk, camel milk or dried powder and as for sugar…"

Mother came over to stroke my hair too, "We take so much for granted. Was it hard, love?"

"Not as hard as you might think. The lads in my platoon are good lads."

"But we hear there were battles!"

"There were, Alice, but we won them all easily." I leaned forward, "You know the worst part of Africa? It was the crocodiles. We were at one place and the crocodiles were longer than this room and there were hundreds of them. Trust me, the battles were less dangerous than those reptiles."

Both girls put their hands to their mouths in shock. My mother said, "Let's talk of more pleasant things. If it is a nice day tomorrow, we will all take a walk in Sefton Park. You can meet the young men and Billy's young lady. Griff likes feeding the ducks. I bought a nice joint for dinner. You will be glad of that, I dare say."

I beamed, "And your roast potatoes and Yorkshire puddings." I had arranged for half of my pay to be sent to my mum but I said, "And I will pay my way while I am here. I have money for you. You do enough for me already."

"Your pay is more than enough to give Griff what he needs."

"I want to give you and Aunt Sarah things too. I have presents in my kitbag for you." I hugged Griff, "Right now, I am just enjoying the moment."

Griff had been patient but he soon tired of the lack of mobility and when he was allowed, he raced off to play with the soldier. Even though I spoke to the others I never took my eyes off him.

"So, Billy, do you have wedding plans?"

He nodded, "We might have married earlier this year but I wanted my big brother there. We shall make plans now. You will be there, won't you? Katherine has been patient."

I nodded, "I will move heaven and earth to be here." I knew that with Captain Hodges as adjutant I had every chance of being given compassionate leave.

The simple stew we ate tasted like a feast served up to the Queen. Billy went to the pub and brought us back a few bottles of beer. I confess that tasty as the food was, I only had eyes for Griff and I watched as my mother tempted him with morsels. He was not a picky eater but he had been spoiled by his grandmother and great-aunt. I could not criticise for I had not been here but I wanted him to eat by himself. He had a good appetite. It was at bedtime that I saw the first signs of a problem. He kissed his aunties and uncle goodnight but shied away from me. I made do with a hug and, even worse, he did not want me to take him to bed. He gripped onto his nan as though his life depended on it.

Aunt Sarah saw my face and said, as she put her arm around me, "It will take time, Jack. Don't force it. He sees us every day and looks on your mother as his. It is understandable."

I nodded, not risking speech which might show the catch in my voice. I sat in the chair and lit my pipe. Billy lit his and I could see that he was still a novice. I did not embarrass him by offering advice. When his pipe was going, he said, "It will be cosy tonight with all of us staying here."

I had not thought of that. "Where do we all sleep?"

Alice said, "We will be in with Auntie Sarah. She has a nice big bed. Griff sleeps with mother and you will have Billy's bed."

I shook my head, "No I will not. I shall have the settee."

Billy looked upset, "No, Jack. I insist. You have the bed."

I took the pipe from my mouth, "Look, I am an outsider in this family now. I know that it is my choice but I won't have you put out because of me. I am a soldier and this settee will be far more comfortable than most of the beds I have endured. There will be no argument." I realised that my tone was harsher than it should have been. It was my sergeant's voice. I modified it, "Besides, I shall have the fire. I am used to the heat of Africa."

The silence was awkward. Aunt Sarah said, "I shall put the kettle on. You boys alright with the beer?"

I nodded and she left. Billy said, "I have my eye on a little place of my own for when Elizabeth and I wed."

I was surprised, "You have enough money to buy somewhere?"

"We were all left a little bit by nan when she died. She had an insurance policy. Mother kept yours to give you now."

I shook my head, "She can use it for the family and Griff."

He continued, "And I have been promoted. I am now a manager. I make more than Aunt Sarah." He saw my look and said, "I know it is not right, Jack, as she does the same work as I do but that is life. It is not fair. I have saved up with a building society, the Liverpool and Formby. I am the next one on the list for a house."

"Building Society?"

He nodded, "People like me," he nodded to his sisters, "and the girls, all agree to save a certain amount each week and then you can take out what you need to buy a house. When everyone has a house then the society folds."

Aunt Sarah had come back in, "Except it doesn't work that way as there are always new people coming in who join. Billy started saving when he joined the firm. My mother's money has helped but he will still be paying into the society for ten years."

"But at least I will have a house and not have to rent as our father did."

Betty said, "And when we get married, we will start an account."

I had never even thought of a home. I was a soldier and the barracks was my home. Now I was a father I needed to think of the future. I realised that I needed money. That was the moment when the idea of fighting in Egypt came to mind. If I joined the Anglo-Egyptian Army I would be paid more. I could save more and buy somewhere of my own. It was an idea that lurked at the back of my mind but the thought of being like Trooper and renting a room in a stranger's house did not appeal. I had a son now and I needed to look after him.

When mother came downstairs, I answered all their questions about Egypt. All that they knew was what came from the newspapers and I knew how unreliable they were. Hooky had said the best use for newspapers was wrapping up your fish and chips and I agreed with him. They glorified events that were not glorious and told downright lies about others. I knew for I had been in battles and then read about them. Mother and I were the last ones downstairs for the rest had all retired.

"Are you still happy about looking after Griff?"

She laughed, "Happy? His coming into our life was sad because poor Annie died but that apart it has been the best thing that has happened to me. He is a joy, our Jack. When you were growing up, I had to worry about your father and if he thought what I was doing was right. Our Sarah and I just get on with it. There are no rows and he has two mothers who fuss over him." She saw my face, "Don't get me wrong, I would prefer it if his father was here but we know that can't be, at least not for a while. Billy adores him and even when he is wed, he will be there for Griff. I know, son, that you were upset about tonight but be realistic. Coming home for two weeks at a time can't make you as close as Sarah and me who have him every waking and sleeping moment. We are not taking him from you but we are there, well, for Annie. Would you be as upset if Griff had wanted to go to bed with his mum and not you?"

I shook my head, "You are right, but for the last couple of years I have dreamed about coming home and about my son throwing his arms around me and calling me dad." I sighed, "I have been fooling myself."

"Listen, Jack, we speak of you constantly but he is a baby yet. He can't speak in sentences and I am not sure how much he understands but the older he gets the more he will understand. Your father was not happy about the way you preferred Trooper to him. It hurt him. Being a father is not easy and your circumstances, well they would test anyone. Let us enjoy this leave, eh, Jack? You are right, you are the head of the family now and, trust me, it is not an easy job." She kissed me on the cheek, "It is good to have you home, son."

I smoked a last pipe and watched the fire fade before lying on the settee and trying to get some sleep. It was hard. When I was at the barracks or on campaign then life was easy, I knew what I had to do. Orders were given and I obeyed. I told men what to do and they did it. Family, that was harder.

After a fry-up breakfast, which I thoroughly enjoyed as there was black pudding, sausages and fried bread, the family dressed up for it was Sunday. We all walked down to church and Griff took my hand and his nan's. It was a start. When the church service had finished then Billy went for his young lady and my sisters headed to the bus station to meet their beaus. While mother and Aunt Sarah prepared the vegetables for the Sunday dinner I played with Griff. He liked to play hide and seek. He was not very good at it and went to the same place but he giggled and squealed when I caught him.

"Come on, I have put the meat in on a low light and the potatoes will be ready to roast when we get back." Aunt Sarah would have made a good Sergeant Major. She was very organised.

We closed the front door and I asked, "Where are we meeting them?"

"At the bandstand."

Mother and I swung Griff between us as we walked and he laughed and screamed as we did so. It made the journey even shorter than it was. The park was packed for this was Sunday and the only day when people could, in the main, guarantee to be off work. Everyone was dressed in their best. Men wore suits and smart hats. Some still wore the flat working man's cap but there were many fine hats on show. The ladies all wore a hat and had not only their best dresses and shoes but also a parasol. There was little sun but it was a fashion accessory. In mother's capacious bag she also had a bottle of juice and pieces of fruit for Griff. He was a grazer. Aunt Sarah had the bag of stale bread for the ducks. I was one of the few soldiers and I had made sure that my boots and buttons gleamed while my hat was at a jaunty angle. Annie had loved it when I made an effort on our Sundays. Thinking back there were precious few of them.

Griff could not say much and he tended to point when he wanted something but he had learned the word '*ducks*' and when we came to the path that led to the ducks he squealed, "Ducks!"

His nan said, calmly, "When we have met up with your aunts and uncle. The ducks will wait."

He seemed satisfied with the answer. Had I said anything then he might have pouted. I had to be careful in all that I said and did with my young son. I was desperate for him to like me.

I spied the three couples in the distance. Billy saw me and waved back. My red uniform was easy to pick out. The three of them headed towards us. Billy was clearly the eldest of the three young men but the other two were smartly dressed in polished shoes, brilliantined hair and the inevitable moustache. I was the only one who was clean-shaven. The moustaches were like the parasol, a fashion accessory.

They stopped before us and Billy did the introductions, "This is my brother Jack, Sergeant Jack. This is my fiancée, Elizabeth."

I stood to attention and saluted, "My pleasure, I am sure."

She squealed with delight making Aunt Sarah's eyes roll.

"This is Geoffrey, Alice's young man."

I held out my hand for the flaxen-haired young man to shake, "My pleasure, Sergeant."

I firmly shook the hand and said, "It will be good to become acquainted."

"And this is Archibald, Archie, Sarah's young man."

Archie was the youngest and with fiery red hair, he put out his hand and said, "I am so pleased to meet a hero of Rorke's Drift, sergeant. I have been looking forward to this more than you can know."

He gripped my hand tightly and I smiled, "A fine handshake, Archie, and I, too, look forward to getting to know you too. Now shall we get to the ducks for my son is desperate to feed them?" Aunt Sarah turned to scrutinise the three couples as they walked behind us to the ducks. She was happy to allow Billy to hold hands for he was engaged but the other two had to make do with mere proximity rather than actual contact. I suddenly felt guilty for Annie had linked me from the first moment we had walked out.

I heard Elizabeth behind us. She was trying to be quiet but I heard every word. "Your brother is so handsome and dashing in his uniform, Bill. You did not tell me he was so good-looking."

Billy was a confident young man, "As people say we look alike, Bet, I take that as a compliment."

The problem with feeding the ducks was preventing Griff from going headfirst into the water. Aunt Sarah grumbled, "I knew we should have brought the reins."

I laughed, "If he goes in it is shallow enough for me to fetch him out."

"How does this compare with that crocodile lake you were talking about, Jack?"

"That was more like a small sea and the water was so murky that even though it was barely four feet deep you couldn't see anything."

Archie said, "Crocodiles? Little ones?"

I shook my head, "The little ones were fifteen feet long but I saw one beasty, more than twenty feet from snout to tail, take a horse that was drinking."

Mother said, "Our Jack! The bairn is listening."

"Sorry."

It was a very pleasant hour that we spent. We headed back to the house only when Griff began to yawn. He even allowed me to pick him up and he was asleep before we had even left the park. I happily carried him, his head nestling into my neck. I wondered how we would all fit around Aunt Sarah's tiny table but my unspoken question was answered when Archie said, "It is a shame that we cannot all stay this afternoon for I should love to hear more of your stories, sergeant."

"It is Jack and I thought you would be dining with us."

Aunt Sarah snorted, "How big a piece of meat did you think I bought, Jack? Archie and Geoff will escort the young ladies and their bags back to their lodgings. They have work in the morning."

Archie nodded, "I live in the next street and Geoff is not too far away."

While my mother and Aunt Sarah prepared the Sunday lunch, I said goodbye to my sisters and their boyfriends. I shook their hands and as Alice kissed me on the cheek she whispered in my ear, "Well, what do think?"

I whispered back, "I think they are two charming young men and I look forward to seeing them again next weekend."

Her smile made my heart melt, "Oh, Jack, you are the best of brothers."

Back in the house, I sat with Griff on my knee but it was Elizabeth who amused him. I could see that Billy had found a good one. She liked Griff and was a natural with him. Where I was awkward and uncomfortable, she was at her ease. She was also funny and had a natural wit. Many young women in her position would have put on a face for her prospective in-laws but not Elizabeth. She had no guard up and laughed and giggled as though she had not a care in the world.

"Do you work, Elizabeth?"

She nodded, "I am a typist. I work in Billy's office. It is where I met him."

"Do you like the work?"

She shrugged, "It is noisy but at least it is clean in the office. I know I was lucky. My parents paid for me to go to college so that I could learn a useful skill. They have a small shop and they work long hours. My mum said that a typist gets regular hours and will never be out of work. I find it easy if a little dull. I am paid well and even after paying for board and lodging at home, I have enough to put into the Building Society. We will both be paying for the house we buy."

I looked over at Billy and I envied him. He was going to marry a sensible girl and the two of them were embarking on a journey that they would take together. If I had not made Annie pregnant, would we have had a life together? I would never know. You cannot go back and change the past as much as you might want to. But, as I jiggled Griff on my knee, I knew that Griff would not have been born but for that accident. Even though he had yet to warm to me I knew I loved him more than life itself.

Griff ate in a highchair. I smiled when he began to throw food around but the scowl from Auntie Sarah and the admonishment from mother made me adopt a more serious face. My son took the criticism well and it was a sign, to me at least, of the man he would become. He could take punishment when he had done wrong. As soon as we had finished the food, there had been an apple crumble to finish then Griff, after having his nappy changed, was put down for a nap. I insisted on doing the dishes and Billy aided me. The three ladies, with Griff asleep in his cot, sat and enjoyed a cup of tea. It gave Bill and me the chance to talk.

"She is a lovely girl, Billy, you have been lucky."

He nodded, "Mother said that Annie was lovely too. When she told us I was sorry. I never got to meet her."

"Griff has her looks. She was a lovely young woman." I shook my head, "You can't live in the past. What is done is done. Make sure you give me plenty of notice of the nuptials. I will have to apply for leave."

"You still like the army then?"

I shrugged, "I am not clever like you. I don't have much education. If I came out, what would I do, labour? Work at Pilks?"

"The money would be better."

"It isn't about the money, or at least it wasn't. Your words have made me realise I need to think about the future and when Griff grows up. I want him to have an education."

"Every child now gets schooling from the ages of five until ten."

"I want more than that. I am not sure what but...," I had washed the last dish and I pulled the plug from the sink, "I have met officers and they are no cleverer than you. I know I am not stupid and Griff won't be. I want him to have choices when he grows up." I wiped the dishcloth around the sink, "The trouble is I don't know how to give him those choices."

"Listen, Jack, I know you have chosen the army and that means you are likely to be away more than you are at home. I promise that I will keep an eye on Griff. If I can help it, he will want for nothing. I am well thought of at work and there is no limit to where I can go."

"And I appreciate that Bill, but one day you will have your own family and they will be your priority. That is as it should be. I will wrestle with this problem." As Billy put the last dish in the cupboard I laughed, "Until I came home, I didn't even know that it was a problem. I have a fortnight to get to know my son and then when I am back in Shrewsbury, I can tackle the problem of my future."

The couple left before dark for Billy to walk her home. Griff had woken up and did so in somewhat of a bad mood. He cried when Bet, as he called her, left. It told me much; Billy was the one who called her Bet and if my son was emulating his uncle then Billy had as much influence as my mother.

Over the next week, I spent as much time with Griff as I could. I played with him while Mother did her chores. Aunt

Sarah still worked. I did get closer to him and I learned how to make him laugh. He was tickly and if I put my hand down his back beneath his top he would squeal and laugh. He liked to be bounced on my knee as I sang, '*Half a pound of tuppeny rice.*' When I came to the end and dropped him between my knees he laughed and screamed with delight. He had some wooden building blocks and we played with those too. By the time Friday came and my sisters returned, I was allowed to take him up the stairs to bed and he would happily kiss and hug me. It was still Nan who put him to bed but I settled for that.

The second weekend at home was harder than the first for I had to share Griff with his aunts as well as Elizabeth. I found myself resenting them. They would see my son far more than I would. I would be leaving on the following Saturday and my leave would be over. I put on a brave face. With more faces to amuse him, Griff seemed to forget his father. My mother saw my reaction and came over, ostensibly to give me a cup of tea but in reality, to give me sage advice, "Our Jack, I can see by your face that you are not happy. Now listen to me. Your son has more love than any other child I know. Why, Queen Victoria has so many children that I am not certain she knows all their names. Everyone in this house loves little Griff. Would you rather he only looked for you?"

She had cut me to the quick and she was right. I was being petty and I had to get over it. "You are right, mother and I am sorry."

She shook her head, "No, I am sorry. I thought we had done the best for you but that wasn't true. Your father wanted you to be like him and that meant a factory and when Trooper came and filled your head with stories of glory then there was bound to be a problem." She sighed, "Billy and the girls have the best of it. Your father put all his effort into making you like him. I know you want to go back in time and change the way things were, well so do I but we can't and we make the best of what we have. You are a good father. I have seen that this week and in a perfect world you would be up here and Griff would see you every day but if you were then you would be at work for ten hours and when you came home you would be too exhausted to play. This

91

is a compromise, Jack, and that is what life is all about. You make compromises."

For the first time, I wondered why she had married my father. Had that been a compromise? He had been a good earner. What had been the other choices she might have made? Captain Philips had made a choice. He had chosen the regiment over a life of his own. I now had a life and a son. How our lives turned out would depend largely on me. I would not let life happen to me. I would make decisions to change my life. Colour Sergeant Bourne had become an officer, why could I not emulate him? The following week, as I bade a tearful goodbye to the whole family and Griff hugged me so tightly that I thought I might choke, I determined to make a new start and begin a life that would see us all better off.

# Chapter 8

When I returned to Shrewsbury there were more men who filled the ranks of those invalided out after illness and wounds. I was thrown into the training. A month after our return there was a parade and those of us who had served in Egypt were given two medals: the Khedive Star, a medal awarded by the Khedive of Egypt and the Egypt Medal. Neither was for gallantry or heroism but merely marked our presence there. Still, they looked smart on my tunic. Billy and Elizabeth were keen to be wed and when the date for the wedding arrived the colonel granted my request for four days' compassionate leave. I took every advantage of that and took a five a.m. milk train to speed up the journey. With my new medal ribbons sewn onto my best tunic, I hurried north to be with my family.

I went with Bill to the pub the night before the wedding. Neither of us was what you might call a big drinker and Mother warned me not to get him drunk. We had just two pints and I treated Billy and myself to a double whisky which we slowly sipped.

Billy was in a good mood as one might expect, "We have the house. It is tiny, just like the one we lived in on Central Street but it is ours. I have good prospects and we are both savers. Bet doesn't need fancy clothes and doesn't want them. She wants bairns. She adores Griff and can't wait to have her own."

"That means you won't have as much coming in." When a woman had a baby, she lost her job.

He nodded, "Aye, but the thing is that there are people who need documents to be typed. Writers and the like. Not everyone has masses of typists. We have a plan. We are going to invest in a typewriter, not yet but when she falls pregnant. That way she can work from home and still earn a few bob."

I laughed, "I can see that you got all the brains, Bill. That is a cracking idea."

"No, Jack, what I got was common sense. You are far cleverer than me but I am the lucky one. I got to make my own choices."

I was not sure he was right. "I am not sure that I will be able to get home when Alice and Sarah decide that they are to wed. It will be you who walks them down the aisle, Bill."

I saw that he had not considered that, "But you can get another leave, surely."

"I may not be in the country. Regiments get sent to the West Indies, India, not to mention Africa and Canada. The odds are in favour that we will be abroad, Queen Victoria has a vast Empire and we are her soldiers, we get to defend it for her."

He shook his head, "And we reap the benefit. Trade is good and so is business. Work might be hard in factories but it brings in money. Folks are lucky that there are soldiers like you, Bill. Cheers."

The wedding was lovely. Mother and the rest of the family had been denied my wedding and they made the most of Billy's. They had fine dresses and new hats. They had sewn an outfit for Griff to wear as page boy and my sisters were bridesmaids. I was proud and guilty at the same time. My marriage had been a hurried affair. Annie would have loved the day that Elizabeth enjoyed.

I had less time to spend with Griff but in the time that had elapsed since my first visit, he had grown. He was out of nappies and no longer had a nap in the afternoon. Even better was that he could now speak and I was Dad. I had wondered if he would call me father as we had done to ours but I was happy with Dad. It made me feel special. The parting was a hard one but I left Griff with some lead soldiers I had bought in Shrewsbury. They were redcoats marching with rifles and I had picked the set with a sergeant. I hoped he would see the sergeant and think of me.

As I left, reluctantly, for the train, I said, "This time I will write and as soon as we get a leave I will be home again."

When I returned to Shrewsbury, I threw myself into my work. The new lieutenant was keen and we made the platoon the best in the regiment. The colonel himself praised us. Captain Hodges seemed inordinately pleased too. It did not bring any more pay but I knew that if I kept my nose clean, I might gain a promotion, but as the normal time to reach the rank of sergeant was twelve years, I knew that I had been lucky to have been in action. War was the best place to win promotion.

Six months after the wedding Captain Hodges called me into the office, "Sergeant Roberts, I thought you should be the first to know, I am to be promoted to company commander. Lieutenant Erskine will be the new adjutant."

I smiled for I was genuinely pleased, "Congratulations, sir." I wondered why he was telling me. I had wondered if he would be like Captain Philips and spend his whole career in an office.

"You can smoke your pipe if you like, this is quite informal."

"That is alright sir."

"That is not the main reason I have sent for you." He nodded at a newspaper, "Have you read of the disaster at El Obeid?" I shook my head. I did not read newspapers. "Three thousand soldiers, Egyptians, were ambushed and slaughtered by a Dervish Army." I could not comment as when I had fought in Egypt it had been with a British army and we had been fighting the Egyptians. "The thing is, Roberts, General Hicks, who commands the army out there, has realised that the officers in these Egyptian regiments are simply not good enough. He has sent a request to regiments over here. He needs officers and good sergeants to be seconded for a year to train and command his army for him. The colonel and I thought you would be the right man. I know you have the ability. Our section was the most successful in the campaign."

"I am not sure, sir. I don't speak the language and a year is a long time to be away from my family."

"Don't worry about the language. All that you need is to learn the orders and I am sure you could manage it but it would be more than a year, Roberts, your service would begin from the moment you landed in Alexandria and end when you left. Think of it as nearer to eighteen months."

I did not answer straight away. I fingered my pipe. Eighteen months was a long time but there was no guarantee that I would be based in England if I did not take up the offer. Eighteen months was a fixed contract. "I think I will take you up on the offer of being able to smoke, sir. It helps me think."

"Take all the time you like and ask any questions."

I got my pipe going and asked, "What about my position here, sir?"

"You will retain your rank and the year of service will go towards your total service in the British Army."

"And I get foreign service allowance like the last time?"

He smiled, "Even better, Roberts, is that from the moment you leave here until you return you will have the rank of Sergeant Major and the pay that goes with that." My eyes widened. To reach that rank in a British battalion I would need to serve for twelve years at least. He smiled, "Who knows, when you return, there may be an opening here? The experience can do you no harm."

I was not thinking of that I was thinking that I would just be away for eighteen months but with the extra pay, I would have double the income. It meant I would have no domestic leave for eighteen months and Griff would grow up without seeing me but it was a chance to take a leap forward.

"If I accept, sir, when do I go?"

"You will need a new set of fatigues. You will be issued a new uniform in Southampton. As soon as you decide then you will be given a warrant. The troopship leaves Southampton in a week's time."

An idea sprang into my head, "Sir, the travel warrant is it route specific?"

"No, just time limited. It will expire on the day that you reach Southampton." Realisation dawned, "Of course, you want to go home. In actual fact, that might prove beneficial. The trains from Liverpool to Southampton involve fewer changes, just one I believe in London. So, I shall tell the colonel then?"

"Yes, sir, and thank you."

"No, Roberts, thank you. Many of the men who are volunteering are doing so for the most dubious of motives. You are a stout fellow and will do the regiment proud."

I was pleased that he could not read my mind for I was also doing this for dubious reasons. "One more thing, sir, could I have my pay paid to my mother?"

"Won't you need money in Egypt and Sudan?"

"I can take what I need, sir. I have a little saved up and, if anything happened to me, it would be good to know that my family wouldn't suffer."

"You are a man with a good heart, Roberts, but you will return. Of that, I have no doubt."

By the time I had been issued my new kit and received my railway warrant it was too late to leave and I would have to get the milk train. I sent a telegram and then went to the *'Eagle and Child'*. I told Geraint and the girls that they would not see me for some time and I was touched by their reaction.

Betty said, "You come back, you hear?"

"I will try."

I had not been told not to and so I took not only my rifle, which I disassembled to make it easier to take but the sword and pistol I had captured from the Egyptian officer. I was at the station an hour before the train so keen was I to get home. I reached Aunt Sarah's house by eleven thirty. Mother had received the telegram at eight-thirty. The rest of the family had already left for work They would have a surprise when they came home. It meant that there was just my mother and Griff in the house. While I played with Griff, I told my mother my plans. "It means I have five days here at home. I will put my affairs in order. I need a will."

She put her hand to her mouth, "Why? You aren't going to die?"

I laughed as I bounced a giggling Griff up and down, "We all die, mother, and I have no plans to die anytime soon but I will be fighting and if I haven't planned for such an eventuality then I will curse myself in the next world. I have arranged for my pay to come to you. It means you will be more comfortable. If you can save some then that means I can leave the army sooner rather than later."

"We don't need much. I will save most of it."

"And I want a couple of photographs of the three of us and one of Griff and me. I will have copies made for you but I want a picture to hold. I should have had one done of Annie but..."

She nodded, "You didn't know what was going to happen."

We went directly to the photographer's studio and had the photographs taken. When he heard that I was shipping out he promised me them by the next day and I know that he did not charge me as much as regular customers. The uniform and the medal ribbons ensured that. We then bought some good paper from a stationer as well as some meat. We would celebrate my return.

It was after Griff had been put to bed that I sat with the other three and we wrote the will. Aunt Sarah was more practically minded and she thought it sensible. I had Bill as my executor and we would have the neighbours witness it the next day. I slept better that night knowing that no matter what happened Griff would be looked after.

The days flew by. The visit was too short and did not coincide with a Sunday and so I never got to see my sisters but Elizabeth came around one night to see me. She cried and I was touched. I had ordered three copies of each of the photographs. Mother had an old pair of frames and her set was placed above the fire. I left the other set for Mother to use as she saw fit. Mine went in my kit bag.

I rose early the day I was to leave and although I moved around the house quietly, inevitably I woke them all up and by six the house was awake. I had bought a pocket watch from a pawnbroker. It was not expensive but it was a good make. If I was to be a sergeant major then I would need to tell the time. I looked at the face as I wound it up. It was a sign of my rising status. After breakfast, I sat with Griff. I had all morning with him and my mother but she let me have him to myself and we played with his lead soldiers. We ate a little lunch and then we went for a walk to the park where we fed the ducks. Mother made me sandwiches for the journey as we played. It was not conversations we had but I could talk and he would understand almost everything I said, "Now, Griff, I am going away and by the time I return you will be at school. I will bring you presents when I return. I know you are a good boy for your Nan, but I want you to be even better behaved while I am away. Do your best at school. If you need any advice then Uncle Bill is the best man I know. He will keep you straight."

"Are you going to die?"

I felt my throat constrict and I had to cough to clear it, "I hope not but if it is my time then so be it." I nodded to the photograph over the fire, "I have one of those and I will look at it every day. You look at this one and imagine what I am doing. There is less chance of me dying than you think. The men I knew who died in the battles were just unlucky. More were luckier. I shall write when I can but if you don't get letters then do not think the worst. Egypt is a long way away."

He nodded and then whispered, "Stay away from the crocodiles."

I hugged him and said, hoarsely in his ear, "That I will promise to do." I did not speak again until I reached the train. Had I done so then I would have unmanned myself.

The train journey to Southampton was long and tedious. While I was able to board the train at Lime Street, I had to travel to London first and then change stations to find my train to Southampton. This was an even bigger adventure than when I had joined up. I had a whole new language to learn and the men I commanded would not be British. Those thoughts and the memory of my conversations with Griff filled my head as I endured the eight-hour journey. I arrived in the early hours of the morning and headed for Waterloo where I took the first train to Southampton.

The organisation was remarkably impressive. I had taken the night train so that I arrived on the morning we were due to leave. There were many people on the train taking ship but I was the only soldier. I had the directions from Captain Hodges and I headed for the quay and the building with the union flag flying from it. A sentry checked my identification, also given to me by Captain Hodges and I entered what was, essentially, a Quarter Master's store.

An ancient sergeant was smoking his pipe as I entered. He saw my rank and said, "You are keen, sergeant, or should I say, Sergeant Major." He nodded to a cubicle, "You can go in there to try on the uniform. It is up to you which uniform you travel in but when you dock you will be wearing the uniform of the Egyptian army. He cast an experienced eye over at me and then made a pile. He put two of everything. There were boots, gaiters and the white uniform they called a tarbrush. I still do not know why. There was a red fez, greatcoat, blanket and pack. There were the usual belts and bayonet frog. I noticed that the leather belts and straps were all black. Perhaps that explained why they called the uniform the tarbrush. "While you are getting changed, I will get you the bayonet and rifle you will need."

He had a good eye and the uniform fitted well, or as well as any army uniform that was not tailored made, like an officer's. "Good fit. Are you wearing it?"

I shook my head, "It will get dirty enough anyway. I will wear my regimental uniform."

"Fair enough." When I emerged, he helped me to pack the uniform into my kit bag. His eyes widened when he saw the array of weapons already in there. He said nothing about them. He handed me the rifle. Its weight was about the same as the Martini-Henry but it was longer. "This is the Remington Rolling Box rifle. The rate of fire is about the same as yon rifle," he nodded at my kitbag, "but you can fire for longer before it jams. It doesn't use the same ammunition, it fires a .43 French. Similar but not the same. You might be able to use a .303 but…"

I nodded, "I will stick with what I know."

He gave me the sword bayonet, "This sword bayonet is almost the same as the one you are used to. It will need sharpening."

"Of course. I have a whole sea voyage for that."

"Last of all, mess tin, mug, dixie and canteen." He pushed them over. Grinning he said, "One last thing, your new stripes, Sergeant Major." I know that it was only the Egyptian army but I felt as though I had reached the top of the tree. I was a sergeant major. "Good luck. When you get back, if you get back, then the rifle and bayonet will be left here. The rest will be pretty much ruined by then." He pointed to the door, "Head down the quay until you come to the *'Jervis Bay'* she is your transport. Some of the lads and the officers arrived last night and they are aboard. Someone will sort you out."

"Thanks, Quarter Master."

"Warrant Officer White. I hope you survive out there."

With that cheery goodbye, I hefted the kit bag and rifle over my shoulder. They were incredibly heavy. I marched down the quay looking for the steamship that would take me to a new life.

I saw two redcoats smoking at the top of the gangplank of the steamship. There was a young cadet officer with a clipboard at the bottom, "Name?"

I used my title for the first time, "Sergeant Major Roberts."

He looked down his list. He could not have been more than fourteen years of age, "The Kings' Shropshire Light Infantry."

"That is right."

"Cabin 238 on the port side, next deck down."

I could not help a smile. A cabin was a luxury. When I had travelled the previous two times it had been a hold that had provided our accommodation. "Thanks, cadet." I hefted the kit bag which weighed a ton as well as the haversack and rifle and struggled up the gangplank.

When I reached the top the two redcoats grinned, "You did well. It took us two trips."

I dropped my bag, haversack and rifle. Holding out my hand I said, "Sergeant Major Jack Roberts formerly of the Kings' Shropshire Light Infantry."

The older of the two flicked his cigarette butt over the side, "Sergeant Joe Adams, 33rd Regiment of Foot."

"Sergeant?"

"I was a corporal and there was little chance of promotion in the Duke of Wellington's so I jumped ship, so to speak. They gave me the rank of sergeant."

The one who looked to be slightly younger and had the tan of one who had served in the tropics, held out his hand, "Sergeant Major Harry Dean." He chuckled, "I still can't get used to the title. I was in the Hampshires. We used to be the 67th."

"I can see you have served abroad."

"As have you. I was in India, where were you?"

"Where we are going, Egypt."

Joe lit another cigarette, "I served in Abyssinia but that was more than ten years since. Come on, where is your cabin?" He lifted up my rifle and haversack.

"238."

Harry grinned, "Very neighbourly. We are 236 and 240. Here, grab one end of this bag and I will get the other." As he picked it up he said, "What have you got in here? The kitchen sink?"

I shook my head, "I stripped down my Martini-Henry and I have a sword and pistol I took from a dead officer."

"Very enterprising."

The cabin was surprisingly spacious. "We will see you back at the gangplank. We are officer watching."

"Officer watching?"

"All the officers are majors. We are trying to see which ones are wet behind the ears lieutenants and who are the greybeards who are looking for a better pension."

As I unpacked my gear, I was happy that I had met the two of them. I would not make snap judgements but they seemed like decent chaps and I had wanted friends. I had endured enough of being alone. Everything was stored and in the right place, I donned my forage cap and taking my pipe returned to the gangplank.

"Are there many other NCOs then?"

"I think there are ten of us so far." Harry pointed the pipe of his stem to the north. "Five are Jocks. There are us three, one lad who was in the 16th, the Bedfordhires and another who was in the Prince of Wales' volunteers. They used to be the 40th Foot."

I lit my pipe as a horse and carriage pulled up and a young officer stepped out. Joe grinned, "Another officer. I am putting my money on a wet behind the ears lieutenant."

Harry said, "No bet. You can see from here that he has barely begun shaving."

The man was clearly an officer for he had a servant carry his bag up the gangplank. He came up to us and we snapped to attention. We all intoned, "Sir."

I could barely keep a straight face as he looked to be about fourteen years of age. He squeaked, "Carry on, chaps." Turning to his aged servant he said, "Come on Brown, do keep up."

"Yes, Lieutenant Carruthers."

"I keep telling you, it is Major Carruthers." The man rolled his eyes.

When they had gone Harry and I laughed. Joe shook his head, "He might be in charge of one of us." That wiped the smile off our faces.

We watched another half dozen officers come aboard. Harry had been right, you could see the older ones, some older than Captain Hodges, who saw no promotion at home and then there were the young officers, barely old enough to command. They would be looking for glory while the older ones wanted money for their old age. When we heard the bell sound for lunch we headed to the mess. There was a steward who took our names as we entered and I asked, "How many are we expecting for this little voyage, steward?"

"There will be twenty of you who are bound for the Egyptian army but later on this afternoon we are embarking the cavalry who will be going with you to become the camel regiment."

This would be our last quiet meal. When we were a full mess, we would have to queue up and use our mess tins but as there were so few they were using stewards to serve us. The food was good and plentiful. One of the older stewards confided to us that until the cavalry regiment was aboard, we were to enjoy the same food as the officers and the ship's officers. He was a mine of information. "They will be an interesting collection. There are Guards, Household Cavalry and Marine detachments." He shook his head, "Good luck to them. Camels are horrible beasts."

After he had gone, I said, "They are that but they are not bad to eat."

The three of us got on well. We shared stories of our service. By the time we returned to the deck I had told them of Rorke's Drift. That had really impressed them. "I didn't know your lot were in Natal."

I shook my head, "They weren't, Harry, I was in the 24th first." I hesitated and then decided to be truthful with them. I told them of Harding-Smythe and they both nodded.

Joe said, "Every regiment has one. We had one in Abyssinia. He got half a platoon wiped out in an ambush."

"What happened to him?"

"What do you think? Gave him a medal and covered it up."

The men who would be going to begin the Camel Regiment arrived. I had already worked out why they would choose a duty that was not only hazardous but would be strange to them, promotion. The best way to get promoted was through war. You could show courage under fire and get promoted and men could be killed or wounded. Either way a private could become a corporal and a corporal a sergeant. A lowly lieutenant could become a captain. Promotion meant more pay. I was under no illusions about myself and my motives. I was a mercenary too. I would still be serving the Queen but I would be fighting in a unit that was not British.

"Eighteen months."

I thought I had said the words in my head but Harry asked, "What?"

"Huh?"

"You said eighteen months."

I nodded and tapped the pipe out on the rail, "Ah, I was just thinking out loud. In eighteen months I can come back home. I have a son. He is a toddler and even eighteen months will see a huge change in him."

Harry nodded, "Ah, I see why you are here then. I want a family too but that will have to wait. I am older than you and I have less time to serve. This little lot will see me with enough money to get the lease on a little pub. I will do an extra year after the first one and come back. Do a year in England and then find a wife."

I laughed, "You make it sound easy."

He looked surprised, "It is. You have been in barracks towns. There are plenty of women and bonny ones too. They will jump at the chance of marrying a soldier with money." He turned to Joe, "What about you? Any family?"

He nodded, sadly, "There was a young girl. We were set to wed and then her father refused. He said a soldier was not good enough for his daughter. She married a doctor." He shrugged, "He might have been right, I mean a doctor is a much better profession than a soldier. Now if I had been an officer then it would have made a difference."

I gave him a shrewd look and asked him the question I already knew the answer to, "When was this, Joe?"

"They were married three months ago. I only met her a year ago and I fell for her." He lit a cigarette, "Egypt will be a new start."

He was leaving to forget a woman. "So you will stay longer than the initial contract then?"

"Too bloody right. I want the money and the promotion."

I suspected that the motives of many of the other men would be the same.

The troopers marched up the gangplank. They were led by their NCOs and headed below decks. They would have slung hammocks and be together. Their officers would have cabins like us. At least my voyage out would be a better one than the previous two.

It did not take long to board the men for they had no horses to worry about. We left on the early evening tide. We were eating and missed the sight of the setting sun and the Isle of Wight silhouetted against it. We were soldiers and food came first.

# Chapter 9

## Egypt September 1884

The voyage out felt cosy. The officers who were travelling to command and the NCOs had not been told which regiments they would command and so we led separate lives on board the ship. We saluted the officers when we passed them but there was no communication. The three of us chatted with the other NCOs but that was generally about our past experiences. The cavalrymen and naval ratings who ate with us had a slightly superior attitude. They would not be fighting alongside what they called, 'natives'. There was a certain snobbery about that. The result was that we tended to eat at the same table and socialise together. I think it helped us as it bonded us. When we joined our new battalions, we would be isolated and only mix with those who were like us and had volunteered.

The exception to all of this was Major Dickenson. We met him on the first day at sea. He held a class every day for the officers and NCOs who would train the Egyptians. He had a darkly tanned face and when he spoke it became clear that he had been in Egypt for some time.

"I served with General Hicks, they call him Pasha Hicks, in Egypt. I can speak the language well and the general has sent me back to teach you the basics of the language." There were groans and he held up his hand. "Generally, you will still use the British commands for left, right, march, fire and the like, but there are other words that will make your life much easier. I am here to teach you. I will be here for an hour after breakfast, an hour after lunch and an hour before dinner. That will give you three hours a day. I am not saying that you will be fluent by the time we arrive but you won't be like fish out of water."

I liked the young officer and he was a good teacher. He reminded me of Trooper for he was very patient. The numbers in the class dwindled alarmingly. By the third lesson of the first day, the officers had voted with their feet and it was just the twenty NCOs who turned up for the last session of the day. The major looked disappointed but he forced a smile, "Well done, chaps. I will see you in the morning."

106

When we turned up for the morning session there were just twelve of us left. The Scottish NCOs had decided that if the officers were not going to turn up then they wouldn't either. Joe and Harry had both learned some words when they had served in Abyssinia and India respectively. I felt guilty that I had not bothered and I knew that learning a language could only help me. The Egyptians would be terrified when they met the Dervishes and as a leader, it was my job to speak to them. The smaller numbers helped and the major proved to be a good teacher. By the time Alexandria hove into view, we could hold conversations with each other. He had encouraged us to try to use our newfound skills when we did not have a lesson. Harry, Joe, and I enjoyed the challenge. We played dominoes and cards when off duty and it became fun to use the Egyptian word for knock.

His last lesson, the night before we would disembark, was to tell us to use Arabic whenever possible. "You chaps will not be commanding the Sudanese elements. They will have officers from the Egyptian Army. They will be the equivalent of you, men who have been given an extra promotion to command. The Egyptians you will command will be used to their own officers. They will have been moved on so that you can train them. Using their language will make them less resentful. They speak Egyptian Arabic. It means that if you meet anyone who is not from Egypt then you should be able to speak to them too." Just then there was the hawking, high-pitched laughter of some officers in the next mess. He shook his head, "As your officers may not speak the language it will be up to you chaps to rally your men and believe me, they will need it." He leaned forward, "At the first battle of El Teb, earlier this year the Egyptian battalions panicked and fled. General Hicks does not want that to happen again." We nodded, "One more thing. This is the last night that you will wear your old uniforms. Tomorrow, you don the fez and the rest of the uniform." He stood, "I will go and inform my fellow officers of that fact. I don't think that they will be best pleased but any that land in redcoats will be sent back to their regiments."

That was a sobering thought. That night we indulged ourselves. I was not sure that we would be drinking in a Muslim country. On board the transport we had enjoyed our rum ration and that night we did so to the full. We were not drunk but, let us say, that we slept well. I did not forget to soak some of the bar tobacco in rum. It made it last longer and smoke sweeter. The next morning I dressed in the unfamiliar uniform. The most alarming piece of equipment was the fez. I was used to a helmet which, whilst not metal, afforded some protection from both bullets and bladed weapons not to mention the sun. I felt foolish in my new uniform but when at breakfast I saw the others, including the officers, wearing it I found myself smiling. The officers looked even more uncomfortable. Although we dined separately from the officers the two entrances were next to each other. Harry, Joe and I took our usual seats and I put my fez, like the others, on the table. It was not done to eat wearing headgear.

"Well, this is us, lads, for the foreseeable future, eh?"

I nodded, "The thing is, Harry, the fez apart, it is not as bad as the red tunic, is it? It is thinner and it is white. It feels cooler."

"Aye, I suppose you are right."

Major Dickenson entered and we all stood to attention, including the Camel Regiment NCOs. He waved us to our seats, "I just wanted a word with my chaps. At ease." We were all seated in our usual place. "I know that you will find this uniform hard to get used to." He nodded towards my fez, "I know that you can't attach anything to the fez but you can use a keffiyeh or shemagh." We all looked puzzled. "It is a square of material that Arabs wear on their head. It is secured by an agal, a sort of band. Now your officers may not approve of it worn as the Arabs do but I would suggest you get yourself one and use it around your neck. Eventually, even the most hidebound Englishman will realise that it makes life easier and you will not be marching along Horse Guards parade. This is Egypt and as some of you know, it is hot!"

I knew the item he was talking about and it made sense. Harry asked, "Will any of us be serving with you, Major?"

He shook his head, "I am destined for other work. I can't talk about it but I will still be a soldier of the queen. Good luck chaps and keep up with the language. You have all done well and I am confident that it will stand you in good stead. Major Hall will be waiting for you landside with more instructions. He is a good chap and has served with the general for as long as I have. We are both old hands."

Alexandria was in sight an hour before we docked. Keen to be off the three of us waited with our kitbags and we smoked as we watched the rebuilt port grow closer. There were four gangplanks waiting to be used. The officers would use the one at the bow, the camel regiment the centre two and we would use the one at the stern. I saw the union flag flying from a hut-like structure and guessed that within would be Major Hall. We left the ship having bidden farewell to the stewards whom we had come to know well. We were all good soldiers and we marched in order to the hut. In contrast, the officers, the majority of whom were young, just ambled along. I saw a line of Egyptian soldiers lined up behind the hut taking advantage of its shade. They were unarmed.

As we had marched, we reached the hut first and Harry knocked on the door and said, tentatively, "Major Hall?"

A tanned but young looking young officer smiled and said, "Come in out of the sun." I saw that a native was operating a crude fan above the head of the officer and the soldier next to him. "Leave your bags outside. Now then, give me your name and I will tell you your regiment. Then if you go behind the hut where there is some shade you will find your servant. He will carry your bag to the railway station for you."

"We aren't going to be based here then, sir?"

He looked up at me, "No, you will muster at Suez." I idly wondered why we had not gone there by ship but I assumed there would be a reason. It might not be a good reason but someone with red tape on his neck would have thought it a good idea. "And you are?"

"Roberts, Sir."

He smiled, "Third battalion second regiment. Your chap is called," he scanned his meticulously written list, "Malik al Tammar. He is a good chap." He looked up at me, "You will have plenty of time for a smoke. I have all of you chaps to process and when they get here the officers."

I went outside and picked up my kit bag. I had retained the rifle which was slung over my shoulder. When I went outside the forty-odd men all snapped to attention. It was time to test my

Egyptian, "At ease." It is hard to describe the pleasure I felt when they not only obeyed but something else, I saw respect in their eyes. "Malik al Tammar?"

An older soldier came forward and stood to attention. He saluted and said, in English, "I be your man."

I replied in Egyptian Arabic, "I should like to learn your language." It was one of the first phrases we had been taught. "Please correct me if I make a mistake."

Not only his face but the rest of the servants broke into a grin. "Of course, Sergeant Major." He took my bag and moved his fellows out of the way. He led me to a shady spot at the end of the building. As we stood there, I lit my pipe and then asked him, in my halting Arabic, his story. When he looked confused, I asked him which word I had said wrong and, in this way, my Arabic continued to improve without Major Dickenson. I learned that he had fought against the British at the Battle of Tel-el-Kebir and that he had great respect for the men in redcoats as he put it. He corrected me when I called him a fellah and explained that I was calling him a peasant. He was a private. When I apologised, he told me that it was understandable as their officers all referred to them in that way. It made sense as no one ever spoke to a common soldier. When we had prisoners then they were officers. He said that officers and the British were called effendi. That first hour as I smoked my pipe and chatted to my servant the many gaps in my knowledge were filled in. I learned that there was a huge armed British and Egyptian camp close to Suez. It explained why we had landed at Alexandria. Most of the British regiments that would be fighting had returned from India and it cut the time that we would be reinforced. Only the new officers for the Egyptian Army came through Alexandria although I knew, from what Malik told me, that if we went south to take on the Mahdi and his Dervishes then we would have to return to Alexandria. Suez was where we would train the men.

Before speaking to Malik I had no idea of the way the Egyptian army operated. I learned that it was through conscription. All the servants were not conscripts. They were the equivalent of British corporals and Malik was a full-time soldier. He had a wife and family in a village in the Nile valley where they farmed. They had a good living for, by Egyptian standards, Malik was well paid.

When Joe and Harry joined me, we learned that each of us had been assigned to a different battalion. General Hicks, Pasha Hicks as Malik called him, was spreading his redcoats thinly.

Harry shook his head and grinned, "I like Major Hall. The officers barged in and demanded to be attended to first. The Major said, '*First come, first served.*' We are to march to the railway station when all the sergeants have been processed."

Joe nodded, "That means we will be first on the train."

Harry warned, "Don't expect the best seats. The first class will be officers and we will be in cattle class, as usual."

He was proved right. We marched to the railway station where an officer directed us to what were the third-class carriages. It was as we headed past the engine that I was accosted, "Sergeant Roberts, is that you?"

I turned, "Captain Jennings, yes sir. I am temporarily assigned to the Egyptian Army to help to train them. I am Sergeant Major Roberts now."

"Good fellow."

"So you are still running the railways then, sir?"

He patted the locomotive, "Lovely engines these. They just needed a little bit of love and attention. That is what we have been doing since we last saw you. The torn-up lines were easy to repair but the engines had not been maintained. My lads enjoy repairing and then running them."

I was hailed by Ned and Matthew, two of the sergeants. They were in the cab of the locomotive. "Until you spoke, sergeant, I would not have recognised you. You can't hide your flat vowels. Are we taking you to Suez then?"

"Yes, you are and we are in third class so mind how you drive."

"It will be smoother than a baby's bottom."

"Come on Jack, we want good seats."

"See you lads, later."

"Sarge, I would use a toilet before you go." He pointed at a fly-covered hut. It was the toilet.

"Thanks for the advice."

We needn't have worried about having good seats. Malik appeared to be some sort of senior servant and he had put my bag in the luggage rack and the three of us had a whole carriage to ourselves. There was no corridor on the train and Malik said, "Sergeant Major, it is a long journey and you may need refreshment."

I nodded and took out some coins, "Here, get what you can for this and make sure there is some for you."

He shook his head, "There is no need, Sergeant Major."

I put my hands on my hips, "If you don't eat then I don't. They are my rules. Like it or lump it."

I said the last part in English as I didn't know the Arabic. He frowned and then nodded, "I will do as you command, effendi."

Joe and Harry gave similar orders and we settled on the wooden seats. I stood and opened my kit bag. I took out my greatcoat and blanket. "These will make it a little softer." The alternative for the long train ride was an uncomfortable-looking wooden bench.

That done we went to test the facilities. The toilet was a bucket and it stank. We just made water whilst holding our breath. Anything else would have to wait until we reached our new camp. As we walked back to our compartment Joe pointed to the head of the train. "I am not sure the officers will be happy. There is only one first-class carriage. They will be cosy!" We laughed.

By the time the officers had passed by, heading for first class, Malik and the others had arrived back. They had a dixie of tea and a selection of cheeses, bread, figs and dates. He looked worried as he said, "It was all they had, Sergeant Major."

"You did well, now settle yourselves down and make yourself comfy."

We heard a furore and we looked down the platform. Three of the officers were complaining to Captain Jennings that they did not have enough room. I saw him shake his head and shrug. They would have to endure cramped conditions. Had I been an officer I would have sought second class as there were empty compartments. None of them did and that told me much about the calibre of the men who would be leading us.

The train soon pulled out and it took us from the stink of the latrine. We opened the windows to allow cooler air to blow through the compartment. The servants did not seem bothered by the heat but we were. I understood, from past experience, that I would get used to it and the new uniform helped but I knew that the journey would have to be endured rather than enjoyed. The three of us had chatted on the ship and knew all that there was about each other. We talked, instead, in halting Arabic, to Malik and the other servants about the battalions and the officers. It was illuminating and helped us to improve our Arabic. Two hours into the journey we had a water stop for the engine. If this had been England then we might have been tempted to walk outside. The sun was almost at its zenith and we stayed inside. We drank some of the cold tea and ate. We insisted that the servants ate and drank too. They were uncomfortable with the order but I knew I would not have enjoyed the tea and food if they had not eaten and drunk too. It was a relief when we pulled out again and the air moved through the windows. The journey was more than two hundred miles and by the time we arrived in Suez I was hot and I was sweaty. One thing we had learned was that the army had good Quarter Masters' Stores and the three of us determined to get spare uniforms as soon as possible. I intended to wash my uniform each day. We had only travelled in a railway carriage but the white uniform already looked grubby and was flecked with soot from the engine.

I could not help smiling when I saw the officers descend. Being cramped and cooped they were even sweatier and dirtier than we were. Malik and the other servants hefted our kitbags on their shoulders and lined up behind us. Harry shouted, "Attention!" and we all stood to attention. Each of us had our rifles slung over our right shoulders. He had seen what we had not, the general striding down the platform. The officers had not seen him and the clutch of officers with him. They were busy complaining to Matthew and Ned our engine driver and fireman. I saw them shrug although I did not hear the words.

The general looked up at them as he stopped before us, "I am guessing that you are the sergeants and sergeant majors?"

We all chorused, as one, "Sir, yes sir."

He turned to an aide, "Find out where they should be and send them to their camps."

"Sir."

"Your work begins tomorrow gentlemen." He turned to the officers, "The rest of you come with me and we will see what the officers are complaining about."

I liked General Hicks. He had been an Indian Army officer who had retired and had been brought out of retirement to give the Egyptian Army some sort of shake-up. He had forgotten more about soldiering than any of the officers who were still moaning would ever learn.

The camp was not far from the railway station and that made sense. The aide pointed out the sergeant's mess first. He had obviously done this before and knew the routine. Then the latrines were identified and, that done he took us, one by one to the camp of each of our battalions. I was the fourth one to be dropped off. We did not bother with farewells. We would be seeing each other at mealtimes and my work began now. As the senior non-commissioned officer I had a tent to myself and not just any tent but one that had a footlocker, a camp bed as well as a small folding table and camp chair. There was even an outer tent. In England, it would have been to keep the tent drier but here it was to keep it cooler.

Malik gave me my first lesson in having a servant. He began to unpack my kitbag even while I was still examining the interior. When I tried to stop him, he said, "It is my job, Sergeant Major and I am proud to do it. Do not take that away from me, I beg you."

I respected his wishes and sat to smoke a pipe. When he came to the disassembled Martini-Henry he stopped and I smiled, "I think, Malik, that this is where I take over. Lay it out on the bed and I can show you how to assemble the gun." I nodded to the Remington, "It is far superior to that weapon."

He watched as I quickly put the gun together. Back in Wales when I had first joined, I had been taught to do it so many times that I had once managed it while blindfolded. When it was ready, I handed it to my servant.

He nodded, "It is shorter and easier to hold."

He handed it back. When he found the sword and the holstered pistol, I decided to be honest with him, "I took these from an Egyptian officer I killed in battle."

He placed the sword in the footlocker and hung the holster from the camp chair, "What you will learn, Sergeant Major, is that most of the original officers are not even Egyptian. They are of Turkish descent and despised the men that they led. You have not offended me."

Malik and I got on well. When that was done, I had him take me on a tour of the camp. Most of the men were being drilled but I wanted to look in their tents and see how tidy they were. Some were immaculate and would have met with the approval of Colour Sergeant Windridge but many were a mess. It was nothing major, in the scheme of things, but an untidy and disorganised tent often meant a disorganised soldier and that was dangerous.

Malik said, quietly, "Some of the men have no pride, Sergeant Major."

"Then we shall have to give them some, eh?"

I went to the Quarter Master Stores and was relieved to find that there was not only an English Warrant Officer but also an armourer. Albert Prosser was an old soldier. The cropped white hair and veined hands told me that before he spoke. I snapped to attention and said, "Sergeant Major Roberts, Warrant Officer, just arrived from Alexandria."

He nodded, "Aye, but you have served here before."

"Natal, Warrant Officer, and I was in the campaign that led to the fall of Arabi Pasha."

"Albert Prosser. I am glad that they have picked some men with experience rather than the ones who just come for the extra pay. What can I do you for?"

"The uniform, Warrant Officer, it…"

He shook his head, "What is your first name?"

"Jack."

"Well, Jack, I have been in the army for forty years. By rights, I should either be pushing up daisies or growing roses but here I am in Africa. We are both roughly the same rank and I can't be doing with this Sergeant Major here and Warrant Officer there. You are a soldier, I can see that. I am Albert." He held out a hand and I shook it. His attitude was unusual but refreshing and I took a liking to the old man immediately. "Now I am guessing that you want a spare uniform so that you always look smart, am I right?"

"Yes…Albert."

"It makes sense." He turned to an Egyptian soldier. "Get a full set of kit for the Sergeant Major." He spoke in English and I raised my eyebrows. "I am too old to learn the language, Jack. Ahmed is a bright lad and he has picked up the English." He nodded to the armourer who was working on a Gatling gun. "This is Will, he is the armourer."

The man looked up and nodded, "Pleased to meet you." He then went back to his gun.

Albert chuckled, "His parents named him Warrington Wilberforce Wilson. Some folks are cruel, eh? He answers to Will."

"What is your story, Albert, I mean you said yourself you could be retired?"

He shrugged, "I stayed in too long. I enjoyed life and finished up as top sergeant. All my mates were either dead or had left the army. What was I to do when it came time to hand up my swagger stick? I should have got out sooner. I might have had a family. It might be nice to have grandkids listening to me telling tall tales about the Northwest frontier. No, when the chance of this job came I jumped at it. England is too cold for me. I have served all over the world. When I was a younger man, in the Crimea, it didn't bother me that much but now my bones are full of arthritis and I like the heat."

I nodded, "You get plenty of that here."

"Aye, you are right."

"What do I need to know about the battalion?"

"Best you find out for yourself. You are the one who will have to mould them into soldiers. What I will say is that there are some good lads in this camp and some who I wouldn't trust further than I could throw them. Make no mistake, Jack, it is not the officers who are in charge here it is the sergeants that Hicks Pasha has put in place. The old general knows his stuff. I served with him in India. The officers, well," he leaned over to speak conspiratorially, "they want the pips on their shoulders and the chance to shine so that they can get further promotions and return to England. You keep yourself and your lads safe."

Ahmed returned and Malik took the pile. "Is there any chance of some .303 ammo?" The armourer looked up and Albert took the pipe from his mouth. "I brought the rifle I am familiar with. I like the Martini-Henry. It served me well at Rorke's Drift." For the first time, I saw surprise on Albert's face. He looked at my chest with the medal ribbons. I shook my head, "I wasn't one of those that were given the Victoria Cross. I was like the rest, just happy to be alive."

The armourer stood and lifted a small box from the floor. "Here, Jack, it will save me having to load these into a magazine for the Gatling. Just keep them out of sight, eh?" He put them on the table and then saluted, "You lads did well in Natal."

Real soldiers knew what we had done. The stories that had come back to England and been spread in the messes and on the parade grounds were the reality and not the glory paraded on the front of newspapers. I picked up the box, "Thanks, to both of you."

I left feeling that I had two more friends. I was not as alone as I had been. I also thought about Albert, Trooper and Captain Philips. All three had dedicated their lives to the army. Only Captain Philips appeared to have taken the opportunities that retirement offered. It was a lesson that stayed in my head.

Malik had not understood much of the conversation as it had been in English. He asked, "Why did they give you bullets, Sergeant Major?"

"Because I asked for them and... well Malik, in our army there is a sort of unspoken bond between soldiers."

He beamed, "And in our army too. Those of us who fought against you and survived share memories."

"Don't you hate us?"

"I should but we now serve the new Khedive and he trusts your general and your Queen. Life is better now for me but I am sad for my friends who died." It took all the way from the QM to understand all that Malik said. He used many words that Major Dickenson had not taught me. I was patient and asked for explanations. Malik was also patient. My Arabic would improve and I knew that would help me to make my battalion into a fighting force.

When the bugle sounded for mess then I was ready. I dismissed Malik, telling him that I would not need him anymore. He looked hurt and asked me if I did not need help undressing. I realised that it would take some adjustments to be used to having a servant. I did not change into my new uniform, I would do that the next day. I looked as grubby and grimy as the rest as I entered the sergeants' mess. I made for Harry and Joe. We were served our food and, again, it was hard to get used to being waited on.

"Have you met your officers yet?"

"No, Joe, you?" He shook his head as did Harry. "I didn't see any when I was touring the camp."

Harry leaned forward and said, "I heard a commotion in the officer's mess. I am guessing they were being welcomed."

The soup we had been served was good although the meat base was hard to identify. I sipped the soup and said, "We have our work cut out here, lads. From what I have learned we are the ones who will have to train these lads; looking in their tents they are a mixed bunch."

Harry grinned as he noisily slurped the soup, "Well you know what they say, don't volunteer if you can't take a joke."

We shared what we had learned. There were eight battalions in the camp. There were another two camps. The Scottish NCOs had been sent to the one made up of Sudanese conscripts. Malik had been scathing about their quality or lack of it.

Joe sat back as the mess orderlies took our bowls, "I reckon a good three months and we will have them whipped into shape."

The rest of the meal was a good one and we wandered around the camp in the dark, our pipes keeping away most of the wildlife. We did not stay out late. Some of the new arrivals had found some beer and were drinking in the sergeants' mess. We three knew we would need to be up early.

When I reached my tent, I saw that Malik had laid out my new uniform and polished the boots and leather belts until they gleamed. I fastened the two tent flaps and undressed. Malik could wash my original uniform in the morning. I said my usual prayers. Each time I said them they grew longer but they were a comfort as I felt closer to, not only my family but Annie. Her face came to me each night in my dreams. I enjoyed my sleep.

# Chapter 10

I had trained my body so that I was up an hour before reveille. When I undid the flap, after dressing, Malik awaited me. "Good morning, Sergeant Major, and what are your orders for the day?"

"Do the dhobying and then take the Remington. Go to the practice range."

"Me, Sergeant Major?"

"You are a soldier, aren't you? When we go to war you will carry the Remington. If we fight then I want you to be able to defend yourself. Oh, and put an edge on the sword, too."

When I was satisfied with my appearance, I took my swagger stick and headed for the mess. I had almost reached it when reveille sounded. Joe and Harry were not far behind me. We were the first ones in. What I realised was that as this was an Egyptian camp there would be neither bacon nor sausages. There was a fry-up of sorts, fried eggs and the flatbreads from the previous day fried in oil. It was not the same as a breakfast cooked in lard and bacon fat. I opted for the porridge instead.

The previous night, when we had eaten, we newcomers had been aware of the scrutiny of the rest of the NCOs. They were all Egyptian or Turkish. That morning the three of us returned the scrutiny and I wondered what my NCOs would be like. There were eight companies, or so Albert had said. He had shaken his head and said, "Of course, that might be just a number so that someone can claim their rations but, in theory, you will have eight companies with a hundred and twenty or so men. There will be a sergeant and two corporals in each company. They are like the curate's egg, Jack, good in parts."

I hoped that Joe was right and that we would be given plenty of time to whip them into shape.

We finished first and headed for the parade ground. It was huge. Unlike an English parade ground, it was dusty and unpaved. The tramping of boots on its surface would make it a dustbowl. There was a recently erected dais on one side and we headed to it. The freshly sawn ends told us that it was new. I surmised that we would be introduced to the men together. The other five sergeant majors arrived. We knew each other, of course, but it was natural for men to form friendships. We nodded to each other and made the usual comments about the food and the camp.

Sergeant Major Dixon, a huge ex-guardsman, said, "Watch out. Here comes the brass."

I recognised General Hicks and with him were the rest of the officers. The colonels all had the tanned faces of men who had been in the sun for some time. Albert had told me that they were all ex-Indian army. Half of the rest were the ones who had come over with us while the other half had the tanned faces of men who had been here for more than six months. Then there were the ones below the rank of major. They were all either Turkish or Egyptian. It was as they approached that my heart sank. I recognised one of them. It was the former Lieutenant Harding-Smythe. He was now a major. If I had to serve under him…I put that unpleasant thought from my mind. The odds were seven to one that I would not. I was not a gambling man but as I waited, I prayed that the odds were in my favour.

I kept my head down but reasoned that it was some years since he had seen me and might not recognise me, especially now that I was tanned and wearing a different uniform.

The officers neared the dais and I heard the bugle sound the call for parade. Had this been England, all of us would have known what to expect but this was Egypt. General Hicks, however, was an eminently practical man and he climbed onto the dais. "Gentlemen, those who are new to the Egyptian Army, form two ranks before me, officers to my right and NCOs to my left."

As there were only eight of us, we were well outnumbered by the officers who made three ranks.

"Normally we would hold this meeting in the mess hall but I am afraid we do not have time for that. We need to move quickly. I know this is all new to you but you will have to think on your feet. The regiment will be leaving this camp in two weeks. We will join General Graham when he advances towards Khartoum to secure the road for the relief force now being assembled in India and England. It has been decided to rescue General Gordon and those in the beleaguered city of Khartoum."

Two weeks was a ridiculously short time and I feared that this advance might end in disaster.

"Now, you know which battalion you are assigned to and rather than me reading out a list of names I would like you to arrange yourselves in battalion order and look lively for the men are arriving."

I smiled for the others, like me, had already stood in battalion order as had the colonels and the officers who had been here for some time. The pale officers shuffled somewhat awkwardly into line.

The general smiled, "Colonels, lead your officers and sergeants off and stand before your battalions."

Unlike Harry and Joe, I had one officer I did not want to go with me. The colonel of my battalion nodded to me, "You must be Sergeant Major Roberts. I have heard good things about you. Come with me."

As he led us off, I saw that my nemesis was in another battalion, number five battalion. That meant that neither Harry nor Joe would have to endure him. It was Sergeant Major Dixon who would have to deal with him.

As we walked the colonel said, "I introduced myself to the officers in the mess last night. I know I should have sought you out but..." his voice tailed off lamely. He could not think of a reasonable explanation. "I am Colonel Bellamy. My adjutant is Major Hodgkin. The other new officer is Major Carruthers." I recognised the officer who had arrived with a servant and looked to be about fourteen. He had grown a moustache on the ship in an attempt to look older. It did not work. "The rest of the officers are all either Turkish or Egyptian. They are all good fellows." It was only then that I realised that he had been speaking English the whole time. "Roberts, you will stand next to me, eh? Senior NCO and senior officer, what?"

I surveyed the men and the NCOs as we faced them. The officers I ignored. The ones I would command were before me.

Sergeant Major Dixon shouted, "Parade, attention!" I guessed the general, who was just behind the ex-guardsman had given him the order. He looked to be the sort of NCO who could be heard a mile away.

The majority of the battalion snapped to attention as one. There were half a dozen or so who were a heartbeat tardy. I did not look for them but, instead, looked at the corporals and sergeants whose eyes identified that the men were in their sections.

General Hicks spoke in Arabic. I realised that he would have been used to speaking languages other than English during his time in India. "Men of the Egyptian Army, the Mahdist rebels are causing great damage to our country and we will soon be leaving to defeat them. That means hard work. You have new officers here with you today and they will drill you and train you until you are ready to fight the rebel rabble." I did not understand the word for rabble but I was learning to work out the meaning of unknown words. He changed to English. "Colonels, take command. There will be an officer's meeting immediately after the parade."

That meant I would be alone with my battalion. I had already worked out that there were just six hundred men in the battalion. It was under strength.

The colonel said, "I had hoped we would spend the morning with you and the battalion but obviously the general has other ideas. What do you intend, Sergeant Major?"

I looked to the east. There was desert there but the canal was close enough for some breeze. "We need to drill the men sir until they react without thinking. I would have liked to give them some tests of endurance but we do not have enough time. This morning I will drill them and then, this afternoon, take them to the firing range. We need to see how well they use their weapons." All my words had invited comment from the officer who should have known the answers. There were none and it told me that the officers did not know the men.

"Very well, we shall join you in the firing range this afternoon if the meeting is finished."

"Sir." He strode off and I said, "Bugler."

The battalion bugler hurried over to me, "Effendi?"

"Sergeant Major, if you please. The officers have gone. Sound officers' call." The bugle sounded and the sergeants and corporals hurried smartly over. It was a good sign. I left the men at attention. I was grateful for Major Dickenson's and Malik's lessons for I was comfortable as I spoke to them all in Arabic. In my head, I had already practised the words. "We have a tough job. We have two weeks to make this battalion a fighting unit. I don't know your names yet but I will get to know them. I am Sergeant Major Roberts and you should know that I fought against the rebel army of Arabi Pasha." I saw some of the eyes widen. "That is in the past and we are one now. This morning we drill. We all know that there are some sloppy soldiers in this battalion but there are already too few for us to be able to get rid of them. We make them good soldiers. At the moment we are just a number. I do not like that. I like an identity. For now, I will use numbers but I will be watching. Now, we will march further east where there is space and we will drill until it is time for food. Then we will march back to camp. I want the other battalions to see that this one is the best. Now rejoin your men. Bugler, you stay by me." When they left, I asked, "What is your name?"

"Bugler Bey, Sergeant Major."

"Right, Bugler Bey, today you will be my shadow. You are going to teach me the names of all the corporals and sergeants in the battalion." I waited until the companies were formed up and then shouted, "Battalion, right face." This time I did identify the ones who were slow. "Forward march!"

I took longer strides so that I began to overtake the companies. Already the heat from the sun was becoming unbearable. By the time we had finished, I would need a clean uniform. The place I had chosen was half a mile away. Behind me, I heard the others shouting at their battalions. I smiled for it would be confusing. My decision to have a longer march would give us a little privacy. As we march and passed companies, I asked the bugler for the names of the sergeants and corporals. By the time we reached the open piece of desert, I had most of them.

I knew that I had to be patient and that morning tested my patience to the limit. The drilling with the weapons and marching in companies became more rather than less ragged. I worked out which men needed to be barked at and gave them a tongue-lashing. Malik had taught me some choice words and I used them. The Arab way of insults was to compare men with animals. I worked out that I needed competition and so I had one company drill while the others stood at ease. Having the eyes of their peers on them worked and the drills became better and smarter. The standing at ease also gave the other companies rest. I took out my pocket watch when my stomach told me that it was time to be refilled. We had half an hour to get back to the mess tents.

As we marched back, I noticed that the ones who had been sloppy as we marched east were less so on the way west. It was a little thing but a sign of hope. I had also worked out who the best sergeant was. Malik had told me that the senior sergeant was Sergeant Mahmoud ibn Mohammed. I marched next to him and spoke on the way back.

"We have much work to do, Sergeant."

"I know, Sergeant Major, but the men are good at heart. They just need to be led." I glanced at him. I knew he meant the officers and he was right but it did not do to criticise officers. "I was at Kassassin, Sergeant Major. I know that your British regiments have more discipline. I hope that you can give it to us."

I nodded, "This afternoon we will have them at the firing range. How many bullets can they fire in a minute?"

"On a good day without men firing at them then perhaps five or six."

"That is not good enough. I can see we have our work cut out. When we eat this evening, I would be honoured if you and the other sergeants would sit with me."

"But Sergeant Major, the British usually sit together."

"As the general said, we are all in this together. I can talk to my friends after we have eaten."

Having the furthest distance to march meant we were the last to arrive. There was, however, plenty of food. I sat and ate with my sergeants. I spoke little and listened more. I was happy with their attitude. There was neither moaning nor complaining. They seemed to get on and that was a good thing. I learned that all of them had fought at Tel-el-Kebir. Many had enjoyed promotion after that battle and when they were reformed under the new Khedive. Most of the men were conscripts and had not seen action.

Sergeant ibn Mohammed asked, "Sergeant Major, what brings you here to Egypt?" I did not answer straight away and he said, "I am sorry if my question offends you."

"It does not. I suppose that I saw it as a chance to command. I have had some good teachers since I joined the army and I saw this as a chance to compare myself." I stood, "Right, I will go and get my rifle and join you at the firing range. I leave you in command, Mahmoud."

I deliberately used his given name as opposed to his rank and I saw that the gesture worked.

At my tent, I saw my uniform drying. Malik ran over, "How did it go, Sergeant Major?"

"Well. I need you this afternoon. Did you manage to fire the Remington?"

"Yes, Sergeant Major."

"Good." I strapped on my holster and pistol and picked up the Martini-Henry. I made sure I had plenty of ammo in my valise and then said, "You bring the Remington."

I found the firing range on my tour. If another battalion was there then there might be a problem but it was empty except for the men who maintained the range and hoisted the flags to warn that there was live firing.

I saw that it was the armourer who was on duty, "My battalion will be using the firing range this afternoon."

He nodded, "There is a booking system but no one else has booked it. It is yours, Sergeant Major."

I took out the pistol, "Have you any ammo for this weapon?"

He picked it up, "A Webley, aye, we have. I will get you a box. What is a sergeant doing with an officer's pistol?"

"Spoils of war, my friend, spoils of war."

While I awaited the regiment, I took the opportunity of firing the pistol. It took a few shots to get used to the kick but, at close range, it proved to be accurate. Its six bullets might be the difference between life and death in a closely fought battle.

The battalion arrived and I selected Mahmoud's company, A Company, first. I left it to the sergeant to organise his men. he looked at me. "I want five smart volleys." Warrant Officer Warrington Wilberforce Wilson had placed a marker one hundred yards from the firing line. The sergeant gave the command and the guns were raised, fired and lowered five times. I saw his frown as the volleys became more and more ragged. When they had finished, I stepped before the battalion. As I did so I saw the colonel and the officers striding over.

Sergeant ibn Mohammed shook his head, "That was not good enough, Sergeant Major."

I nodded, "Let us say that is the start of our journey. Malik." My servant handed me the Remington and I gave him the Martini-Henry. "Sergeant, when I begin to fire, I want you to count out loud."

The Remington was an unfamiliar weapon to me but I had to use it rather than the Martini-Henry. I had the bullets to hand for my valise was open. I chambered a round and raised the rifle. It was longer than the one I was used to and I adjusted my grip. Unlike the company who had just fired I had a target. The piece of wood was one hundred yards from me. There was silence all around me and I was aware that the officers were also watching. I was challenging myself. Was I good enough to be a Sergeant Major?

I squeezed the trigger and heard the sergeant intone, "One, two, three."

I was soon in the rhythm and I chambered and fired. In my mind, I was seeing a sea of Zulus coming towards me and knowing that if I slowed then I might die.

"Fifty-nine, sixty."

I stopped firing. The armourer shook his head and pointed at the shredded target, "Impressive, Sergeant Major, with a rifle you don't know, but you have made a mess of my target. Corporal, stick another one up, eh?"

I looked at the ground and saw fourteen shell casings. I handed the Remington to Malik. "So, that is what you can do in one minute. "B Company, your turn."

I stepped to the side and B Company lined up. As they did so the officers joined me. The young officer, Major Carruthers said, "Sergeant Major, how did you do that?"

"A great deal of practice, sir."

Major Hodgkin said, "Major Carruthers, Sergeant Major Roberts is one of the heroes from Rorke's Drift."

I saw his mouth drop open. Colonel Bellamy nodded to the rear of the firing range, "A word, Sergeant Major." I followed him and we stood in the shade of the armourer's hut. "From now on, Sergeant Major, my officers will be with their companies. All these meetings with the general, whilst informative, do nothing for the battalion. We need the battalion to be as one. To have an esprit de corps."

I nodded, "I agree, sir. May I offer a suggestion, sir?"

"Of course. You and I have to be of one mind."

"Might I suggest a name for the battalion?"

He frowned, "A name?"

"Yes sir, something to shout and help them to rally. Number 3 Battalion sounds like all the other battalions. In the heat of battle, how will that make them rally?"

He nodded and lit his pipe, "You may have something there. Go on."

"The biggest insult you can give to these chaps is to call them an animal, dog, snake, crocodile and the like but the one animal they all admire is the lion. We shall be fighting further south anyway why not call them the Lions of the Desert?"

"You know I like that." He smiled at me, "If you don't mind, Sergeant Major, I will suggest that as my idea."

"Of course, sir."

We returned to the firing range. My demonstration and the natural competitiveness of the sergeants meant that every company improved dramatically. Of course, the Warrant Officer was not happy about the expenditure of ammunition but the colonel and I thought it was a small price to pay.

The colonel gathered the companies around him and spoke to them much as a father would. I realised at that moment that Colonel Bellamy had skills. He reminded me of Captain Philips. "You have all done well today but it is just the start. I have decided that we will no longer be Number Three battalion. That makes us sound like the rest of this army and we are going to be something special. From this moment forward we will be the Lions of the Desert."

Strictly speaking, the reaction of the battalion might have been deemed a breach of discipline for they all cheered and whooped but the smile on the colonel's face told me that he was pleased. We had a name and from that moment on the battalion marched with a spring in its step. They were the Lions of the Desert and even if other battalions emulated us, they would never have such a good name. We had stolen a march on them all.

That evening after we had eaten, the English sergeants gathered together. Just as I had done, they had sat with their own battalions. We were all experienced non-coms and it made sense to us all. As we walked around the camp, smoking, we shared our experiences. It was Sergeant Major Dixon who had the biggest complaint. The ex-guardsman had met Major Harding-Smythe and in the short time they had been in each other's company John Dixon had discovered that he did not like the man. "He is everything I despise in an officer. He is still wet behind the ears and has yet to hear a shot fired in anger yet he lords it over everyone. He has connections at Horse Guards and it shows."

Harry said, "That is what Jack said. Tell them how you met him, Jack."

I would not have brought it up but now I had to. I told them of the story and how I had been forced to leave my regiment. Dixon nodded, "Aye, that is about right."

Joe asked, "But what about the soldiers? Are they up to muster?"

Harry shook his head, "Even if they are not then we have less than two weeks to make them so. We will be marching with British soldiers but you can bet that the Dervishes will see us as an easy target. Jack, you were the only one to use the firing range today, what do you think?"

"They fire too slowly. By the end of the afternoon, they were better but I have fought against them and know that a British regiment would be able to fire three volleys to every one of theirs."

Sergeant Major Dixon said, "Right, let us decide on a rota. We take it in turns so that every three or four days we have a session on the firing range."

"And don't forget bayonet practice and forming a square."
They all looked at me, "It stands to reason that we will be using the square more often than not. The Dervishes have camels and

horses. A rank of bayonets can hold them off but the other ranks need to keep up a rapid rate of fire."

"That is it then, firing, using the bayonets and forming a square." He nodded, "I will go and report to General Hicks." He allowed a rare smile, "Because I was a guard, he seems to think I should be the top sergeant." His eyes dared us to object but none did. None of us wanted an extra responsibility. We had enough as it was.

As we had enjoyed the firing range, we had two days of using bayonets and then forming a square. It soon became clear that the Egyptians had problems not only forming a square but marching in a square. If we moved across the desert then we would have to do so in a square. By the time it was our turn on the firing range we had improved dramatically. John Dixon had spoken to the general and three days before we were to leave, we had the monumental task of forming a square made up of eight battalions. Although it took a whole day, we managed it. We really needed to perform that same manoeuvre a dozen times but we had just the one attempt and it would have to do. We prepared to take the train to Alexandria where we would be loaded on boats and head down the Nile.

We had suffered desertions already but the night before we were to march to the railway station some battalions lost up to twenty men. The Lions lost just two and they were the worst soldiers in the battalion. The result was that we boarded trains more than two hundred men shy of the number we had trained. General Hicks was not a happy man. It was not the best way to go to war.

**Sudan 1884**

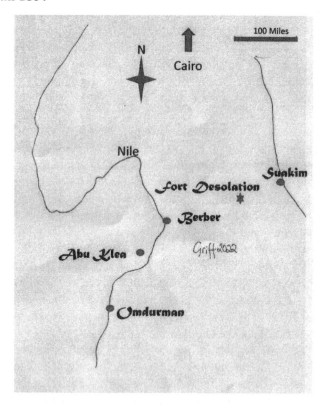

# Chapter 11

We left Cairo and boarded a mixture of vessels, mainly whale boats, to take us down the Nile. The cataracts meant that we would still have some marching to do but the bulk of the journey would be by water. The boats and ships took, generally, one company. The colonel and his staff, along with me, travelled with the smallest company, Company G. They had fewer men to start with and it was their company who had suffered the desertions. Sergeant Ahmed Sayyid was not the best sergeant. Mahmoud had tried his best with him but he had been over-promoted and was not a natural leader.

The colonel had allowed me to wear the holster and as we headed down the Nile I said, "Colonel, the one thing we have not had the chance to practise is firing at enemies."

He nodded, "I know but that is almost impossible to actually practise anyway Sarn't Major."

I patted my holster, "What I mean, sir, is will the officers be able to use their weapons judiciously? When it is close quarters, then a pistol can do serious damage."

He nodded, "An omission on my part, Roberts, I will speak to them when we land. Keep coming up with these ideas, Roberts. You are an asset that I will try to use." He also confided, "We shall not be going the whole way by boat. We and a column of British soldiers will land close to Korti and we will cut the large loop out of the river. It will be one hundred miles and will test the battalion."

As I digested that information I took in the full implications. We would be isolated and the mounted Dervish could pick us off at will. We would have to march through the inhospitable desert. It would not be an easy task.

The one advantage of the river was the breeze afforded by the river but the insects were in even greater numbers. It was the British officers who suffered more than the Egyptians. It was not that they were immune but they seemed to be able to endure it better. I learned that we were in a race to get to Khartoum before it fell. The politicians had prevaricated, as usual, and left it almost too late. The one advantage of their dallying was that we were moving in December when it was the coolest that it would be. When we landed on the west bank of the Nile, at Korti, it was hard to see how any sense could be made of the confusion. There were heavy guns to be moved as well as Gatling and Gardner guns. The camel regiment we had travelled with was now an operative unit and had to disembark camels with whom they were unfamiliar. The 19th Hussars were our cavalry but they were riding horses and we also had naval detachments with their guns. The Egyptian element consisted of our eight battalions. Whilst we were the largest single unit, I knew that we were, probably the weakest, if only because we had not yet been under fire and that was the true test of any warriors.

General Graham would push on down the river. It led directly to Khartoum but the cataracts meant that the journey would take much longer as the boats would have to be unloaded, carried overland, refloated and reloaded. The desert column was General Gordon's hope. If we could get close to Khartoum then the defenders might be able to hold on a little longer.

It soon became clear that General Stewart was also lacking confidence in General Hicks' army. We were relegated to guarding the left flank of the main British column. We outnumbered them but they would travel faster having the luxury of camels and horses to use as a screen. Further humiliation was heaped upon us as we had to help unload the whaleboats and leave two battalions to guard the boats and ships. It meant our six battalions marched towards Khartoum two days after the main column.

General Hicks decided that as the Dervish element of the Mahdist army was the most dangerous, we would move across the desert in a square. The one practice we had enjoyed was not enough. It was Sergeant Major Dixon's company which was given the honour of spearheading the square while the Lions of the Desert had what I considered the hardest duty, we were the rear of the square and if attacked we would have to turn through one hundred and eighty degrees to face the enemy. We had with us non-combatants whose task it was to lead the draught animals carrying the tents and the food and they, along with our servants were in the centre of the huge square. We had more than a hundred miles to march. Malik had managed to acquire another four canteens for I knew that water would be crucial. I had hoped for water skins but they were like gold dust. General Hicks was also in the centre of the giant square, his staff officers were with him. Our officers were also mounted. With a keffiyeh around my neck and my face and hands oiled I was as protected as much as I could be from the sun. I missed my helmet and I could not get used to the fez. The first night we camped and I had the men gather as much material as they could to make a barrier around us. Each battalion would be responsible for its own section of the square and I detailed the companies who would have that duty. I had half a company do the first watch and the second half the later watch. I did not know how many days it would take us to reach Khartoum but I reasoned we would all have one duty. As the senior NCO, I did at least two hours on the first night. In that, I was copying Colour Sergeant Bourne who seemed to be awake the whole time during the Battle of Rorke's Drift.

It took ten days of marching to get almost halfway across the desert. The heat and the slowness of marching in a square hampered us. It was getting close to the middle of January when we heard firing from the southwest. It had to be the main column commanded by General Stewart. As soon as we heard the firing then my battalion was ordered to about turn. I was impressed by the speed with which the Lions managed the feat. I ordered them to fix bayonets. Malik brought me my Martini-Henry. He would place himself close to the animals and use the Remington. A square of infantry was the best defence against cavalry but it could be broken and a square that lost cohesion risked being massacred. I had the men in three ranks with the front rank kneeling. It presented a triple wall of bayonets to face the enemy.

The gunfire did not last as long as I had expected and after an hour, we were ordered to continue our march. Despite the extra weight I did not tell my men to remove their bayonets. Whilst it was unlikely that the British manned column would have been defeated, Isandlwana had shown me that it was possible. The thundering of hooves and the dust cloud in the distance told me that we were going to be attacked. The general saw it too but the order took ten minutes to be given. As soon as it did, I had the Lions about face.

I did not wait for an order from Colonel Bellamy who was, in any case, busy speaking with the other colonels and General Hicks and I shouted the command, "Front rank kneel. Chamber a round." We had neither artillery nor machine guns. They were with the British column. When I saw the dust cloud grow closer, I began to worry for it suggested a horde of horse and camel men.

The colonel arrived and he and the other officers drew their pistols. They were on foot. The non-combatants had moved as close to the centre of the square as they could manage. "The battalion has fixed bayonets and their guns are loaded, sir."

Major Hodgkin said, quietly, "For what we are about to receive…"

It was then that we saw the Dervishes. Most were on camels but at least a quarter of them were warriors on horses. It meant they had none of the men on foot armed with a wicked sword and shield. I had been told that they were very fierce and more dangerous than the camel riders. Sunlight glinted from the spearheads and lances carried by the riders.

"Steady lads. We are the Lions of the Desert and these Dervishes do not frighten us, do they?"

They chorused, loudly, "No, Sergeant Major!"

Colonel Bellamy said, "They have spirit, anyway."

"Don't worry, Colonel, they will stand." I was not sure about the other battalions. John, Harry and Joe had battalions that were almost the equal to mine but some of the others had inherited officers who were weak and Egyptian sergeants who were not of the highest standard. A square meant that you needed every part to be as strong as its neighbour.

General Hicks shouted, "Open fire when they are two hundred yards away."

I was relieved. Although not all the bullets would hit it would give us the chance to fire more volleys and the smoke would make the Dervishes seem less frightening.

"Wait for the order. Mark your target." I heard my sergeants repeating my orders so that it became a hum along the battalion. I stood close to the company I had the least faith in. Sergeant Mahmoud did not need me but Sergeant Sayyid did.

The Dervishes knew their business and they had spread out to encircle us and attack all four sides at the same time. They had done this before. The ones near us halted, well out of range of our rifles. Some of the other Dervishes were already attacking the opposite end of the square. The leader of this part of their army obviously intended to inspire his men. He was riding a huge camel and carrying a black flag rode up and down before them. He was four hundred paces away and I lifted my rifle. "Malik, your shoulder." My servant came before me and I rested the barrel on his shoulder. He put his hands against his ears.

Major Hodgkin came over, "What are you doing, Roberts?"

"Just testing the range, sir." I waited until the leader had stopped and raised the standard before I fired. I aimed at the camel. The rifle bucked and I saw a moment later, the flag fall and the Mahdist leader tumble from the back of the camel. It was a lucky shot but my rifle was a good one and the odds were on my side. The battalion cheered and Colonel Bellamy said, "Damned fine shot, Roberts."

"Thank you, Malik. Return to your position."

Grinning he turned and said, "One day I should like to learn to shoot like that."

The effect of the shot was to unleash the Dervishes close to us. They screamed and thundered towards us. It would be like Lake Timsah all over again. The difference this time was that it was more than two thousand who charged at the Lions.

"Open fire!"

"Fire!" The words rippled down the line and I fired too. I found the action reassuring. Fire, eject, chamber, fire. It was almost hypnotic. There were bullets fired at us too as some of the riders had rifles and muskets. They were like buzzing insects. They could only fire once but a lucky bullet could find flesh. I saw that they had slings on their guns and simply dropped them to hang from their waists ready to be reloaded when they had the chance. As with Lake Timsah, we brought down not only riders but also camels and gaps appeared. That meant some bullets missed. The line of Dervishes came closer.

I knew that this would be when nerves failed, "Hold fast, Lions, and let us show these Dervishes our teeth."

The Dervishes were fanatically brave. Even with bullets flying around them they came on, urging their mounts to get close to us.

"Bayonets!" We had practised this move and the front ranks, who had been kneeling, stood and stabbed with their bayonets as animals and riders came within reach. They struck camels and the screams and squeals of the wounded beasts were blood-curdling. The square was broken, not by men running but by camels falling into one corner. The animal crushed five men, two from Company F and three from Joe's battalion. The other Dervishes saw their chance and before we could plug the gap another ten camels had burst into the square. I chambered a round and fired at the leading Dervish. I switched hands and drew my pistol. I emptied it at the others and then dropped my pistol to hang by its lanyard. I drove my bayonet up into the guts of a camel. Just then there was a roar and Malik led the rest of the servants to charge into the few survivors. Major Carruthers showed how much he had grown as he ran up, sword in hand and emptied his pistol at the camel riders who had survived. Before more men could exploit the damage, the gap was filled.

"Well done, sir."

The young officer grinned, "Now I feel like a soldier."

The near disaster had instilled courage into every soldier and bullets scythed through the Dervish ranks. The attack broke down. Men cheered as the Dervishes headed back to the south. There were many Dervishes lying wounded. Major Carruthers sheathed his sword and said, "Some of you fellows come and help me see to their wounded."

Sergeant Mahmoud shook his head, "No, Sergeant Major, they are feigning injury."

I nodded and turned to Major Carruthers, "Let me do this, Major."

"Very well then."

I reloaded my pistol and said, "Sergeant come along with me. Chamber a round." We walked towards the nearest man who was lying half hidden by a dead camel. I still had my Martini-Henry and there was a bullet ready. Mindful of Mahmoud's advice I moved warily and used the body of the camel as a barrier between me and the wounded man. Suddenly not only the wounded man but another three leapt to their feet. Mahmoud fired at the one near the camel and I shot a second. I dropped my rifle and pulled my pistol. I emptied it into the two other Dervishes.

The Major's voice reflected his reaction to the treacherous attempt to kill us, "Thank you, sergeant, I think we will let them rot."

"They are cunning men."

Major Carruthers said, "Sorry about that Sergeant Major. I almost got you killed."

Shaking my head I said, "Not today, Major."

Colonel Bellamy had seen it all unfold and he shouted, "Lions, fire a round into all the bodies that are close to us." As soon as we started to fire then bodies rose like Lazarus and tried to flee. None escaped our wrath.

Just before dark, a rider came in from the main column. He was a hussar. He reported to the general who had the officer's call sounded. When the colonel returned it was with the news that the British column had been ambushed at a wadi called Abu Klea. I remembered seeing a map and knew it was close to the cataract where we would rendezvous with the boats. More than seventy men had been killed and eighty wounded but the Dervishes had lost more than a thousand men. We had also lost men but with just twenty men dead and thirty wounded our losses were lighter. The colonel surmised that the British column had been attacked by more men than we.

We camped in square. Our journey was cutting a loop of the Nile. For this part of the march, we were on the main caravan route and there were oases. The usual well-armed patrol was sent a couple of miles to the nearest oasis to fetch water and I sent a couple of men to hack some steaks from the camels and we added them to the stew we made. My sergeants and I, even Sayyid, were a lot closer now and as we stood around the fire that night, they asked me about the campaign. Malik had brought me a mug of tea and I was enjoying my first pipe of the day.

"Sergeant Major, do we push on? If General Stewart has lost men, then can we carry on?"

I nodded, "A good question, Sergeant." I blew the smoke from my mouth, scattering a small swarm of insects that were approaching. "The general has not lost many men and the Dervishes lost more. We are also in good shape. No, I think we will push on. If we don't relieve Khartoum then we will have lost Sudan." I did not mention the loss of the general there and the garrison. I could not see the Dervishes taking prisoners.

Sergeant Mahmoud persisted, "I have travelled this part of Sudan before, Sergeant Major and we still have more to travel to reach Khartoum than the march we have made."

"Don't forget the boats on the Nile. They won't be attacked."

Even as I said the words, I realised that I was clutching at straws. My sergeants were good chaps and they knew this land. Their doubts came not from a fear of the Dervishes but of the land. We were too few against too many and crossing a land that was as cruel as any enemy. I don't think that any of us enjoyed a good night of sleep.

General Hicks made one decision and that was to close with the main column. We had heard the gunfire when General Stewart had been ambushed but they had been too far away to offer mutual protection. He sent one of the mounted officers to tell General Stewart of his decision and then we turned to march directly for the column. We were now accustomed to our position at the rear. We had learned to avoid stiff necks. Constantly turning was pointless. If we were attacked then the animals would warn us, for they always reacted to camels and we would hear the hooves. Men also had a sixth sense. We could see the dust raised by the British column and our attention was on that when the Dervishes rose from the pits they had dug and were upon the leading battalion before they even knew they had been ambushed. Then camels and their riders rose from the sand. They had hidden themselves and at that precise moment, we heard the thunder of hooves from behind as the trap was closed.

I barely managed the order, "About face," when the wild-haired warriors holding the cross-handled swords and shields raced at us. "Fire at will."

There was little point in ordering volley fire as they were upon us. I fired at point-blank range and the wild face of the Dervish disappeared in a mess of blood and bone. I transferred my rifle to my left hand and emptied my Webley at the Dervishes. All that I succeeded in doing was clearing the enemy from before me. Malik appeared and handed me the Remington. He took the Martini-Henry and loaded it for me. I fired at the nearest warrior and then took off my lanyard. "Here, Malik, load and fire this."

I fired the Remington and dropped it. The Martini-Henry bucked in my hand and another enemy fell into the dust. Although we were killing more than they were we had lost men. I was proud of the Lions for they never faltered even though they were facing fearsome fighters whose weapons were better suited to this type of fighting. I slashed the bayonet across the side of the nearest warrior's head and he fell. I heard the Webley fire and saw men fall. At this sort of range, Malik did not need to be a marksman.

When I fired at the Dervish who ran at me screaming, he was so close that his body almost touched the bayonet and the .303 went through his body, shattering his spine and hitting the warrior behind. In the distance, I heard the bugles as General Stewart and his men fought the same sort of battle as we did. The square was a fine defensive formation but if the Dervish used cunning, as they had, then they could undermine its cohesion. I heard a wail from the front of the square, "We are undone and the heathen are amongst us!" The Dervish had broken into the square.

The pressure on us lessened and I heard Colonel Bellamy's voice, "Sergeant Major Roberts, take a section of men and go to the aid of Sergeant Major Dixon."

"Mahmoud, number one section."

Major Carruthers nodded, "I will take command here. Lions of the Desert, close ranks and remember we are the best battalion this day!" That it was in English did not matter for it was his tone that had the effect. The young man had grown into his officer's pips.

I chambered a round as we ran. The sergeant major was isolated. Around him lay Dervish bodies but it was only a matter of time before the giant of a man was felled. He was trying to rally while he fought on. I saw that his white uniform was bloodied and much of if had to be his own.

"Come on, you fellows. Rally around your sergeant major." My Arabic seemed to halt the flow of men away but when the

140

two-handed sword struck John's left shoulder he stumbled. The triumphant warrior raised his sword to give the coup de grace. Without aiming I fired from the hip and the bullet threw the Dervish away. "Lions, with me!" I stabbed at the nearest Dervish as I placed my body before Sergeant Major Dixon's.

Mahmoud shouted, "Fire!" The small volley from his section cleared the enemy from before us.

"Rally! Rally!" The cry was not for my men but for the ones who had broken. It should have been shouted by an officer but none was close by. My words had an effect and some of the company formed up around me. As much as I wanted to tend to my comrade in arms, I had to plug the gap. I chambered a bullet and said, "Advance in two lines." The ragged volley had created a space and I took advantage of it. We were able to move and form a diagonal line between the unbroken men. Mahmoud and my men formed the front rank. "Front rank kneel. Front rank fire!" We fired and I reloaded. "Rear rank fire." We began to fire and reload in such a fashion that we cleared the Dervishes from the broken square. "Advance."

The wall of enemy dead was a barrier behind which the shattered remains of the company John Dixon had tried to rally, could fight. "Sergeant, take command."

"Yes Sergeant Major." He turned to the broken company, "You men now have the honour to fight alongside the Lions of the Desert. Show us that you have courage."

I chambered a bullet and ran back to Sergeant Major Dixon. He was alive and being tended to but I knew, as I saw his slashed and battered body that his days as a soldier were ended. I knelt next to him and his eyes opened as the medical orderlies staunched the bleeding. "The bastard ran, Jack. The coward fled."

"Who, John?"

"Your mate, Harding-Smythe. He ran and half the company went with him." The effort proved too much and he fainted.

"Take good care of him, boys."

"Yes, Sarn't Major."

Even as I stood to return to the corner of the square I saw Major Harding-Smythe. He was sheltering by the baggage in the centre of the square. He had taken refuge amongst the wounded. I had no time for him and hurried back to Sergeant Mahmoud.

"Fire!" His command sent another one hundred bullets at the Dervishes. They had endured enough and they fled but I saw that they had hurt us. There were more white uniformed bodies than I had seen up to now.

The bugle sounded the cease-fire and medical orderlies ran to tend to those wounded near the front of the square. One of the battalion's Egyptian officers came over to me, "Thank you, Sergeant Major, you may return to your battalion. Your men are well-named."

"Thank you, your men fought well."

He could not help his eyes flicking to the baggage and I saw the contempt in them. "Not all, Sergeant Major."

As I led my men back to the rear of the square, I deliberately took us close to the baggage. I had managed to avoid Major Harding-Smythe up to now and I was not even sure that he would recognise me but I marched the company so close to him that he was forced to look at me and I held his eyes. Suddenly recognition dawned. I said nothing but I would seek retribution for the hurts caused to Sergeant Major Dixon.

We stood to after the battle until the rider came in from the British column. They too had been ambushed and General Stewart and many men had died. It was a disaster and ended our attempt to spearhead the relief of Khartoum. General Hicks took the decision to march closer to the British soldiers for mutual protection. We reached them before dark and I saw the piles of bodies. That there were more Dervishes than British was small comfort. We made a camp, still in the square and ate cold rations. The officers were summoned to a meeting with General Hicks. It was a long meeting and I saw a Hussar leave the square to head for the Nile.

Colonel Bellamy came to see me when the meeting ended. "Bit of a shambles, Roberts. But for you, we might have been broken and that would have been a disaster for this army." He leaned in and said, "We have heard that Khartoum has fallen."

"General Gordon?"

"We don't know but as we have lost a substantial number of men today, not to mention General Stewart we are heading directly back to the river."

"Not going back the same way we came, sir?"

"No, we are taking the shortest route. We will have the protection of the main column at the river as well as water." He shook his head, "We are going back to Egypt. We may not have lost but we failed and that is hard to live with. We have, however, proved that the Egyptian army is more than capable of holding its own. When you and the others have completed your commissions, you can, if you wish, return to your regiments. I hope that you will not but..."

"You will stay, sir?"

He nodded, "The Government failed today, not the army. We owe it to the memory of General Gordon to retake Khartoum. It will not be a swift campaign but we will do so. The general has recommended that you and Sergeant Major Dixon be decorated. In Sergeant Major Dixon's case, it might give him something to reflect on back in England. He is to be invalided back there."

We reached the boats safely. It seemed that we had hurt the Dervishes and that they had been desperate to stop us from relieving Khartoum. We had failed and so they licked their wounds. The Sudan was theirs. We boarded the boats but only after the wounded.

The wounded were transferred to whale boats when we reached the Nile and taken back to Cairo. I saw Sergeant Major Dixon before he was boarded. He was swathed in bandages but was awake, albeit dosed with morphine, and could speak. The general wanted me there so that the whole army could hear that we had each been awarded the DSO. Sergeant Mahmoud had also received the equivalent Egyptian reward, the Khedive Star. John's last words to me were whispered in my ear, "Sort the bastard out Jack. He ended my career and he will hurt good soldiers."

"I promise I will, John." The promise being made, I would have to keep it. Major Harding-Smythe's days in Egypt were numbered, one way or another.

It was not a swift journey back to Egypt and there was, generally, a depressed mood amongst the men. I had time to ponder the problem of removing the danger that was Major Harding-Smythe without being court-martialled and losing all that I had gained. By the time we reached Cairo, I knew what I could not do and had a vague idea of how to succeed. It would take cunning.

# Chapter 12

When we returned to Cairo we were not sent back to Suez. That camp would be occupied by the Indian regiments coming from the sub-continent. Nor were we in one huge camp. Each battalion had its own camp and that, in many ways, made life easier. For me, however, I missed the company of Harry and Joe. On the march south, I had seen them every day and we had been able to share troubles. As a senior non-commissioned officer I could not share with anyone in the battalion but Harry and Joe were different. On the way back we discussed Harding-Smythe.

"But Jack, you can't take the law into your own hands. Let the general or the colonel deal with it."

"Harry, it is common knowledge what he did. If it had been a British regiment then he might have been court-martialled but this is an Egyptian one." The Egyptian officers had seen his conduct and the general was aware that he had sheltered in the centre.

Joe agreed with me, "The word is, Harry, that it will be covered up as an accident and no one was to blame. General Hicks has ensured that John has a full pension. That alone tells you that it is being covered up. Major Harding-Smythe will not rise any higher but it wouldn't do to have a British officer court-martialled for cowardice. It would undermine everything we have achieved here."

I saw that Joe had convinced Harry, "All right then, you are going to do something but what can you do?"

I shrugged, "I don't know yet. I will think about this. If it was another rank and file, we know what we would do, don't we?"

They nodded. We had our own discipline. There were few instances of petty theft being brought before the colonel. Instead, the culprit would be beaten by their comrades. This was different and I did not want to be court-martialled and lose my pension. I would bide my time. I had already decided to see the year out and that meant I would be serving longer than I had said. The truth was I liked the battalion and I wanted to finish their training. I was encouraged by the performance of Major Carruthers but I still had to make Sayyid into a good sergeant. I had already spoken to the colonel about being replaced, when my time was up, by Sergeant Mahmoud. He had shown us all what could be achieved.

We had enjoyed some mail and I had written to my mother to let her know that I might have to extend my contract. I consoled myself with the fact that I would have more money at the end of it. In her letter, she told me that Griff was growing and that he asked about me. I wondered if that was true or was my mother writing what she hoped I would like to hear. She also told me that I was to be an uncle. By the time I returned Billy and Elizabeth would be parents. The dates had also been set for Alice and Sarah's weddings. I would miss them but that could not be helped. Life went on while I served the queen.

I threw myself into the battalion as we trained the new recruits. The action at Abu Klea meant we had suffered losses and some of the older soldiers had completed their duties and returned to their farms. The good news was that having a name like the Lions of the Desert gave us a unique identity and new men were made aware of what we had done. Sergeant Mahmoud had been the only Egyptian to be decorated. We both received our medals from General Hicks. I was touched by the pride shown by the whole regiment in the award to both of us. It was the first medal I received for gallantry. The campaign medals were one thing but when soldiers saw the ribbon of the DSO then they knew what you had done. The red, edged with blue was a prestigious ribbon.

Four months after the battle I was granted a week of leave and I went into Cairo each day. It was only a short walk and I wanted to see the sights. I visited the pyramids and other ancient buildings. I wandered the souks and enjoyed sitting outside the cafes enjoying tea and sometimes a beer. It was as I was on my way back to the camp a day or so after my first trip that I spied Major Harding-Smythe, He was alone and entering a house of ill repute. Such places were congregated together. The officers had women of the night who charged more but it meant they were unlikely to run into their own men. I decided to wait. As in all such places, there were bars and cafes close by. I sat at one and soon dissuaded the streetwalkers from accosting me. They found easier targets. It was as I sat there that I worked out what I would

146

do. My trip up the Nile had told me what I could not do but the officer being alone and in such a place was the perfect place to put my plan into practice. He was in the house for more than an hour and in that time, I refined the plan in my head. I made sure that I was not seated in direct light and that my face was hidden.

When he emerged, a little unsteadily, then I waved the waiter over and paid. His unsteadiness was probably a mixture of alcohol and over-exertion. He was not walking quickly as he headed down the unlit road. His camp was a mile to the east of ours and I knew that I had to put my plan into operation before we left the suburbs and before we reached the crossroads. There were military police at such places to discourage desertion and robbery.

Major Harding-Smythe obliged me by responding to a call of nature. I saw him duck down an alley and I followed him like a shadow of the night. He undid his buttons and I was on him in a flash, ramming his head into the wall. I had my knife at his throat before he even knew.

He could not see my face and had no idea who I was. I suspect he thought I was a local thief, "I am a British officer and I shall have you whipped for this."

I put my mouth close to his ear, "And I am a British soldier and I know who you are, Lieutenant Harding-Smythe."

There was anger and fear in equal measure when he spoke, "Roberts! You will be court-martialled for this. I can no longer have you broken on the wheel but I can make sure that you are punished."

My low laugh should have warned him but just to confirm that I did not care I punched him in the side with my knife-hand. It would have been simplicity itself to ram my knife in his ribs but I did not want him dead. "And where are the witnesses to this? It is your word against mine."

"But I am an officer and you are just a sergeant,"

"No, you are a coward who ran and I am the Sergeant Major awarded the DSO for bravery. Everyone knows what you did. Do you think anyone would believe you over me? Besides I am willing to take that chance. Now, this is what you will do. You will resign from your regiment. Your contract is up in any case and you can also resign from the army. You have hurt enough men as it is."

I heard the sneer in his voice, "And if I do not, what then?"

"We have both been in battle. We will do so again and I am a patient man. The next time you fight you had better watch out for the bullet in your back or the bayonet in the melee. Your choice is simple. Resign or die." Just then I smelled urine. He had not been able to hold his water.

I sheathed my dagger and slipped away while he was still ensuring that he did not soil his uniform. Whilst pee is hard to see when wearing breeches, the white trousers would be stained yellow. I was on the main street before he even knew I had gone. I made my way back to my camp.

I spent the next morning in camp but no one came to question me. I returned to Cairo that afternoon but did not see him. When my leave was over, I returned to training and wondered what the coward would do.

I discovered what he had decided a month later when we were sent by train with another two battalions to the border. Mahdist raiders had attacked a border town and we were sent to garrison an old Egyptian fort. The three battalions were a little cramped in the town but our presence reassured the locals.

I recognised the colonel of Major Harding-Smythe's regiment when he came over to speak to me, "I never got the opportunity, Roberts, to thank you properly for what you did. I know that Sergeant Major Dixon was grateful."

"We are all in this together, sir. Has he been replaced yet?"

"There is a replacement coming out from England and another officer to replace Major Harding-Smythe."

I affected a look of innocence on my face, "Was he wounded too, sir?"

He gave me a knowing look, "Strange you should say that, Sergeant Major, he resigned but not until he had slandered your name. He said you had threatened his life."

"Me sir?" I put as much outrage in my voice as I could muster.

He nodded, "I told him that was impossible for you were the recipient of a DSO and such heroes do not threaten officers, do they, Sergeant Major?"

"Of course not, sir."

"Probably for the best. Some men are meant to be soldiers and others…Anyway, good to see you again, Roberts."

I had gotten away with it but I had been lucky.

Although our mere presence made the townsfolk feel safe, we still had to show a presence and we took out daily patrols. I went with Sergeant Sayyid and his company when he patrolled. He was better than he had been but still needed guidance and he had the largest intake of recruits. I wanted to see what they were like away from the parade ground. We had with us, Lieutenant Karim. He was also a new officer and although he seemed keen, I thought it would be useful to give him the benefit of my wisdom. I strapped on my sword and took not only my pistol but also my Martini-Henry when we headed to the village six miles from the fort.

Four or five of the company had lived in the area and I advised the lieutenant to use that experience. They were happy enough to be a hundred yards ahead of the column of men. We had left just after dawn so that we could rest in the village during the heat of the day.

"What we hope to do, lieutenant, is to reassure the locals that there are soldiers close by." My Arabic had become fluent and that was in no small part thanks to Malik."

"Will we meet Dervishes, the Sufi?"

Sergeant Sayyid answered, "Perhaps, effendi, but our one hundred guns should be enough to deter them."

I liked the answer for it showed a healthier attitude in the sergeant. The road had dropped into a depression and as we rose to the crest the scouts came racing back. Their eyes were on me as they reported to the officer, "There are Dervishes, sir."

"How many?"

Their answer told me that they still had room for improvement. "They are riding camels. Perhaps a hundred or more."

Both Sayyid and the lieutenant looked at me and I nodded to the crest of the ridge and road, "Until we know the precise number let us exercise caution. I would suggest, sir, that we deploy into three lines along the ridge." I looked at the scouts,

"Were you seen?" The white uniforms would have stood out against the desert sand.

Their downcast looks confirmed what I already suspected, "They did, Sergeant Major."

We hurried to the ridge and the top of the road. I saw the Dervishes. They were a raiding party and the appearance of the scouts had attracted their attention. They were galloping towards us. We had time to form a defence for they were more than a mile from us. There were nearer one hundred and forty of them as opposed to one hundred. I went to the right-hand side of the front rank. I nodded to Sayyid and he went to the left of the second line. "Lieutenant, if you would take the rear line and I suggest we open fire at two hundred paces." There were too many new men to risk closer range. I wanted none of them to panic. Flight would invite disaster. He nodded, "Fix bayonets."

I chambered a bullet and opened the flap on my holster. The Dervish line spread out, as I knew it would. The two ends would be exposed. Sayyid and the lieutenant were on the left. I would be the rock on the right.

The lieutenant's voice showed his nerves, "At two hundred yards, volley fire."

I boomed, "Present!" I decided that I would not rely on his judgment of the range. Some of the camel riders had guns which they popped off. It was typical of them and merely unloaded a weapon. They all had spears and swords. If they had been better led then they could have used their weapons to snipe at us. I took aim at the leader of the Dervishes. He had a sword and a helmet with a green plume. I knew that most of the men would not aim. Some might even close their eyes. My finger was on the trigger as I shouted, "Fire!" My bullet was a heartbeat before the volley and I saw the leader clutch his chest. As the bullets struck the line he tumbled from his horse.

"Fire!"

The camels were fast and the second volley was at a range of one hundred and ten yards. More saddles were emptied but the riders on the side were untouched and they were the danger. I switched my rifle to the right and fired one bullet then chambered a second so quickly that I fired it not long after the volley.

"Independent fire at will."

I drew my Webley, holding the rifle like a spear in my left. I aimed at the nearest camel and fired at its head. The bullet threw the rider from its saddle. I switched to the next keenly aware that there were still ten men closing with the right flank. I emptied the pistol and then held the rifle in two hands. The spear that was thrown struck my left arm, tearing through the material to the flesh. Blood stained the cloth. I had been wounded. I rammed my bayonet under the head of the snapping camel and the head came out through the top of the camel's skull. It was dead but a dead weight. I twisted the bayonet and the dying animal fell to my right, releasing the bayonet. I had no time to load another bullet as the last of the Dervishes who had attacked the right had his spear held like a lance ready to skewer me. I jinked my body to the right and then stabbed at his camel as he passed me and the spear hit fresh air. I put all my strength into the strike as well as the weight of my body. The animal began to fall and the rider lost his balance.

I loaded another bullet and saw that we had broken them. There were bloodied, white uniforms showing me that men had died but we had emptied more than forty saddles and the company was still intact. Sayyid shouted, "Fire!" It was a ragged volley but when another five Dervishes fell, the rest fled.

I shouted, "Well done. Reload for this may not be over."

I knew that it was but the words were intended for the officer. The Egyptians had learned from Abu Klea and they bayonetted every single body even if it was clearly dead. They were taking no chances. Many of the Dervishes carried treasure into battle and the men scavenged. One of the men bandaged my arm and Sayyid came over. He held in his hands the helmet, sword and purse of the dead leader.

I said, "Keep them or give them to the lieutenant."

He nodded his head, "I will take the helmet as a souvenir and as the lieutenant's sword broke, he can have this one, but take the purse, effendi. Soon you will leave us and you can have a drink on this company before you do. Today, we came of age and I knew that was down to you."

The lieutenant had also suffered a wound and I saw that he was grateful to be alive. "Thank you, sergeant."

I nodded, "I would suggest you capture any camels that are still alive and make a gift of them to the villagers. Lieutenant, perhaps we should visit the village as we were ordered."

"Of course." We had lost four men and we buried them in the village. The villagers were indeed grateful for our arrival had prevented the raid. We left in the late afternoon. The men had carved hunks of meat from the dead camels and burned the Dervish bodies. The stink of burning flesh hastened our departure. We marched into camp bloody but unbowed and the lieutenant proudly left to present his report to the colonel.

The MO needed to stitch my wound and he was most concerned that it might become infected. He rubbed alcohol all over it. "Three days off duty, Sergeant Major." He saw that I was about to object and added, "Or you could be placed in the hospital."

I saluted, "Three days it is then, sir."

Major Carruthers took out the patrol the next day and I went the following evening to see Harry whose battalion was bivouacked just a mile from us.

"Been in the thick of it again, Jack?"

As we smoked our pipes, I told him of the fight. "The lads are coming on."

"And have you had enough yet?"

"What do you mean?"

"Our contract was up months ago. Joe and I are going home. I reckon I have made enough and, to be honest, I can't stand the heat."

"I had not really thought about it. The battalion still needs work."

"And they always will. Wasn't Sergeant Sayyid your weakest link?" I nodded, "And he did alright, didn't he?" I tapped my pipe out. He was right. Why was I staying here? I had a family at home. "Come on, Jack, give Colonel Bellamy the news and we can all travel back together. None of us wants to go home like John Dixon, do we?"

It was the last part that confirmed it for me. I went back to the camp knowing what I had to do. I went the next morning and saw Major Hodgkin, "Sir, my contract is up and I would like to leave for England."

He nodded at the sling, "It isn't the wound, is it?"

Shaking my head I said, "No sir, but I have done all that was asked of me. Sergeant Mahmoud can take over as top sergeant and the action the other day showed me that the rest of the battalion is ready."

"I know that everyone will be sorry to see you go but this was to be expected. I will get the paperwork done as soon as I can but it will take a couple of days."

"That is alright sir. I have goodbyes to say."

The hardest was Malik. He was genuinely upset. I gave him the sword, pistol and holster. "I will miss you, Sergeant Major, as will the Lions. You gave them all heart and now they fight as soldiers should fight."

"And I will get to see my son. You should think about going home too, Malik."

He nodded, "I would have stayed longer but if you are going," he shook his head, "I cannot serve another and it is better to leave now than serve one who might disappoint me. I can see why you British have made such an empire."

There were gifts too. All were sentimental rather than valuable but all the more welcome for that. Sergeant Mahmoud had made a tobacco pouch from camel skin for me and it was beautifully decorated. The officers bought me a pipe. It was one of the sweetest smokes I ever had and it gave me fond memories of my time with the battalion.

The colonel also gave me not only a railway chit but one for the Palace Hotel in Alexandria. "General Hicks insisted that your last night in Egypt be a memorable one."

Joe and Harry were at the station for the journey to Alexandria. I had thought we would all be staying at the Palace Hotel but when I showed them it Harry laughed, "Ah, the DSO, you move in higher circles than we do, Jack, my lad. Still, we can enjoy a drink with you there, eh?"

I thought of the purse Sayyid had given to me. "Of course, and the drinks will be on me."

The journey back was comfortable. There was a second-class carriage and we enjoyed just watching the land fly by and chatting. They also had chits for hotels but they were not the Palace. We arranged to meet in the bar of the hotel at six o'clock.

We parted just five hundred yards from the prestigious hotel. I felt a little overwhelmed as I approached the liveried doorman. I felt under dressed and as though I had no right to be there. I was not helped by the look of disdain on the man's face. He stood to bar my entry, "Can I help you, Sergeant?"

"It is Sergeant Major and you can help by moving out of the way and having someone carry my bag for me."

He looked surprised, "You are a guest here?"

"I will be just as soon as you get out of my way."

He tried again, "But the hotel is very expensive."

"I know. Now for the last time."

Just then I heard, "Mohammed, let Sergeant Major Roberts in. He has every right to be here."

"Of course, effendi. Saoud, fetch the bag. Apologies Sergeant Major."

I looked up and saw Major Dickenson. He smiled, "Sorry, Sergeant Major, I was delayed in the bar. Welcome. Let us get you checked in and then we can have a little chat."

"You knew I was coming here?"

"I had a word with General Hicks." He saw my confusion, "I was in Cairo and he told me you had resigned. It is perfect timing."

The desk staff were all French. There was a heavy French influence in the city and that was down to Napoleon Bonaparte. "Pierre, this is Sergeant Major Roberts. I spoke to you…"

"Of course. Saoud, take the Sergeant Major's bag to room 42 and run him a bath." He proffered a form, "If you would just sign here, Sergeant Major, I will fill in the rest." As I dipped the nib into the ink he continued, "Major Dickenson, I will bring the key to the bar."

"Thank you, Pierre."

The manager said, "It is an honour to have a hero staying here with us. If you need anything Sergeant Major, then please let me know."

I felt as though I had stepped into a dream world. This was not my world. It was not the Sefton Arms in St Helens, this was a hotel filled with businessmen and senior officers. I was led like a horse to water by an officer who seemed most at ease in the surroundings. He put an arm around my back and propelled me to a quiet table. A waiter followed us, "Drink, Roberts?"

"Er, a beer, please, sir."

"A beer and a gin and tonic." As the waiter disappeared, he said, "I believe that the quinine in the tonic helps keep away malaria. Any excuse eh, Roberts?"

I did not like games and I did not like being manipulated, "Sir, what is going on?"

"Sorry, Jack isn't it?" I nodded, "Jack, all will become clear and all I want you to do is listen to me while we have a drink. If you then so choose, we shall never have to see each other again but hear me out, eh?" I nodded. The drinks came, "Cheers and congratulations on the DSO. It was well earned. Those were the words of General Hicks."

I raised my glass. The beer was icily chilled, "Cheers." It was a lighter lager than I normally drank but the heat and dust of the day made it taste like nectar and it slipped down so easily that I had drunk more than half before I knew. The major smiled, clicked his fingers and pointed at my glass.

"Now, your plans are to go back to England and see your family and then rejoin your regiment, correct?"

"Yes sir, back to my uniform and the rank of sergeant."

The second beer arrived and I finished off the first and handed the glass to the waiter. Major Dickenson drank some of his gin and his smile told me that he liked the taste. He took the lemon from the drink and sucked it before placing it on the napkin. He took out a cigar case, "Cigar?"

"No, thank you, sir, I am a pipe man."

He grinned and looked like a schoolboy, "Then fill it up." I took out the pouch as the major snipped off the end of the cigar and struck a match to warm the end before he put it in his mouth and lit it. He nodded to the pouch as he sucked on the cigar. "Interesting pouch."

I nodded as I packed the tobacco in the new pipe. "The battalion gave it to me before I left."

"You were highly thought of, Jack. I have read Colonel Bellamy's report."

"Report, sir?"

"For your colonel back at the Light Infantry. He thinks that you could be an officer."

I had the pipe going and the sweet tobacco went well with the lager, "Yes, sir but we know that is not going to happen, don't we?"

"You are a realist, Jack, and I like that but one day it might be that a sergeant could be promoted." He tapped the crown on his shoulder, "This isn't a temporary rank. I have been promoted to a full major in the British army and I have been charged, by Colonel Kitchener with raising a unit to serve in East Sudan."

"A new unit, sir?"

"Yes, the colonel is now the governor of East Sudan. Mr Gladstone will soon no longer be the Prime Minister. It will take time but the new Government will want to take back Khartoum. You and I, Jack, are not politicians. We are both soldiers of the Queen but you and I know that had action been taken earlier, then Gordon and Khartoum could have been saved. General Stewart need not have been sacrificed in a meaningless gesture that was doomed to fail from the outset."

"But why me, sir?"

He waved over the waiter and said, "Same again." He drained his glass and the waiter took it away. "You have a unique set of skills, Jack. You speak Arabic well and you understand soldiers. I did some checking up on you and discovered that you are a more than competent rider. You can live and survive in a hot climate and you are a natural leader. If you join my new unit then you would have the permanent rank of Sergeant Major."

"But it means I would be here in Egypt and my family is in England."

"I am travelling to England to recruit the rest of the men I will lead. I am looking for men such as yourself, Jack. I have read the reports of the battles and the units that fought them. I go to poach twenty men. They will not need the linguistic skills you and I possess but they will need to be tough men who can ride. I return in four months' time. That would give you three months with your family." I cocked an eye. "I have the power to give you an extended leave. As our unit would be operating in extreme conditions then you would be given one month's leave each year in England. Colonel Kitchener knows the desert and understands its needs." He saw my face and smiled, as the waiter brought our drinks. "I can see that the idea appeals but you need time to think. We will be sailing home on the same ship and your two fellow sergeants will be on board. By the time we pass the Channel Islands, I shall need an answer." He leaned forward, "And I need someone who is not afraid to do the right thing, even if it means a court martial." My eyes widened. He smiled, "Your secret is safe, Jack. The General is not a stupid man and Harding-Smythe's injuries and his accusations told him what had happened. There are bad apples in the officer's barrel but you should know that I am not one of them."

"I know that, sir."

The major's cigar had gone out and he laid it on the ashtray, "If you cannot do it then Sergeant Adams will be approached. He served in Abyssinia and if he is not interested then Sergeant Dean. You three are the best that I have found and I am hoping that the permanent promotion and the chance to serve in a small unit might be the inducement that is needed."

I drank off the half-finished beer and started on the second. A desk clerk came over with my key. "Your key, effendi."

"Thank you."

The major grinned, "Your accent is perfect. Just think about it, eh Jack."

"I will sir and I have to say that I am interested. It is just that this is so new. What would the unit be called sir?"

"The colonel and I thought something like the East Sudan Camel Regiment."

"Camels, sir?"

"Better for the desert and they are as easy to ride as a horse. They just take some getting used to."

I downed my beer, "Well sir, you have given me much to think about and I am flattered by the offer."

"The ship sails the day after tomorrow. I will see you aboard. Tomorrow, I have business here. There are a couple of men I need to see who might be suitable troopers."

He shook my hand and I headed for my room. The three beers, drunk so quickly, had made me a little lightheaded. The room was, compared with what I was used to, palatial. I suppose that was true of all the rooms. One of the hotel staff was putting my gear away. He gave a bow and said, in English, "When you have taken off your uniform, I will have it cleaned, effendi. Your bath is ready."

I answered in Arabic, "Thank you," I gave him a couple of coins. He handed me a bathrobe. The bathroom was behind a door and I went in to undress. I slipped on the robe and gave him the white uniform. Would I need it again?" When I took off the robe and viewed my naked body in the mirror I smiled. Most of my body was white but the extremities were burnt a burnished brown. My mother, aunt and son would barely recognise me. I rubbed my finger over the white of the scar. She would not see that as it was on my upper arm. I would not tell her of it as I did not want to worry her.

The bath was still hot and the smell told me that they had used bath crystals. I luxuriated in it. When I had finished, I enjoyed the best shave in a long time. A cold water shave is less than perfect. I wondered what the policy of the new unit would be on beards. In the desert a beard was functional. I suddenly stopped mid-stroke. In my head, I had already decided to accept. How had that happened? I dressed in my redcoat and wondered if this would be the last time that I was a redcoat.

# Chapter 13

When Harry and Joe arrived, they were as impressed as I was with the hotel. I paid for the drinks and then we decided to eat somewhere a little less daunting. We wandered the streets to look for an inviting place to dine. We found a small café that had some non-coms eating and they nodded as we entered. While we waited for the food, I told them everything, including the potential offer that might come their way. Both shook their heads.

Harry said, "I have enjoyed my time out here and made a few bob but I want a family now. My days of fighting are done."

Joe lit a cigarette, "And anyway, Jack, you are the one with the skills. I can't ride a horse and as for a camel."

Harry nodded, "If you want this then grab it with both hands, Jack. The thing is, do you want it?"

"That is the point, isn't it? I want to see my son but if I am at Shrewsbury then I will only see him when I am on leave. I could leave the army and live at home with him but what would I do? Go back to the Iron Gang? I suppose I have already decided, for this way I am guaranteed a quality leave once a year and the rank means more money too."

"Then you have decided. Let's drink to that."

It was a pleasant evening and we spoke of other matters. The foolishness of politicians, the perfidy of men like Harding-Smythe and the changes we had affected in the Egyptian Army. We all knew that the army that had fought at Abu Klea was a better one than the one beaten at El-el-Kebir.

The next day we went shopping in the souk. I had more to buy for. It was not just my sisters but also my sister-in-law as well as my niece or nephew. Although I was hotter in my red uniform I felt, somehow, more like a soldier. I saw other soldiers too and saw that many of them were wearing the new khaki-style uniform. I confess it looked cooler and much smarter than the white one I had worn for some time. We ate at the same café on our last night in Egypt. For Harry and Joe, they would never return, at least not as volunteers. We all knew that Whitehall could send soldiers anywhere it chose. As we ate the two of them

laid out their plans for the future. Neither involved the army.
They had saved all their extra pay and now had a tiny sum put
by. Both had the same objective in mind. A pub where they
could serve beer and bar those people that they did not like. They
had a similar idealised view of their clientele. They envisaged
old soldiers and serving soldiers using it. I knew from Geraint
and the girls that running a pub was nothing like that. The fight
with the navvies had shown me the reality. I knew from Annie
that there were long hours with little time off. My friends would
need to choose partners well. Annie could have coped with
running a pub. I could not.

I left the hotel with a little regret. I enjoyed the brief flirtation
with luxury and high living. When we boarded the troopship
heading home, reality set in and the three of us shared a cabin.
Admittedly, it was intended for four people but after the hotel, it
was something of a comedown. The ship was packed with
soldiers returning to England. Some had travelled up the Suez
Canal having come from England and some were regiments that
needed to return to England. War did not take as many men as
illness, heat and disease. I knew I had been lucky to have
survived so well and with so few injuries. My scar had already
healed and all that would remain would be the thin, wiggly,
white line on my upper arm.

The three of us had a cabin that was below decks. There was
a port hole and so we had light but I knew that the officers'
cabins above us would have a large window and would be more
spacious. The rank and file would be below us and some would
have to endure the hold. I was lucky and I knew it.

I did not see the major until the following day. The three of us
had taken to promenading around the deck. There were no
parades and no duty but we were soldiers and we were used to
being active. We met the major coming the other way. He was
alone and he stopped when he met us. I knew I did not need to
but I was a fair man and I wanted the major to be put out of his
misery. The final deciding factor had been the news that neither
Harry nor Joe would take on the role. If I did not accept then the
major would have to look elsewhere. It was not arrogance but the
knowledge of what I had done that made me realise I was the
best man for the task.

"Major Dickenson, I will accept the position you have offered me."

His face lit up. "You will not regret it. Leave everything to me. I will contact your regiment. I do not want you to miss a moment of time with your family." He took out a notepad and pencil, "Write down your address. I know I could get it through official channels but this way I can contact you quicker."

I was suspicious, "And why should you need to do that, Major?"

He held up his hand and counted off his fingers, "Uniform, weapons, information about the unit and, of course, the date when we leave. I shall send you a telegram a week before we are due to leave. It will be from Southampton. I will send your travel warrant by post. I have to say I am really pleased. And you two, what are your plans?"

Harry spoke, "Family and then leave the army. Joe and I have done our time, sir. It is time for us. Jack here is a young lad by comparison with us."

It was only then I realised how much older the other two were. It says much about their character that they had not made a fuss about it.

"I dare say I shall see you about the ship. I am really pleased, Roberts."

The food was not bad on the ship and we were able to buy beer. We played cards and dominoes and spoke in the mess to the other non-commissioned officers. My ribbons invited comments as did our experiences in Egypt. Many of the others were non-coms returning from India after long service out there. They had endured skirmishes and what were termed police actions but none had fought in a battle like Abu Klea. Most were like Harry and Joe, ready to retire. Speaking with them left me with mixed feelings. I wanted to be with my family but I was not yet ready to hang up my rifle. Many of the sergeants had accrued a decent pension but I had not been one for long enough yet. It strengthened my resolve. The major had not given me a time that I would be serving but I would ask if I could leave after four or five years. He could only say no. I worked out that by then I could have saved enough to forego a pension.

We made a swift journey back. Despite the fact that they were steamships and did not rely on the wind, a benign wind could make for a faster journey and we made the fastest passage to Southampton that I had enjoyed thus far. I did not have time to send a telegram although I had sent one from Alexandria telling them that I was on my way home. I jumped on the first train I could, just eager to be home and not to waste a second. The three of us had exchanged addresses although I was not convinced that I would ever see them again. The army was like a sea full of ships that passed in the night. Men who had fought together and put their lives in each other's hands had a bond but sometimes life got in the way of making anything of those unspoken promises.

I managed, thanks to an early arrival and trouble free train journey, to reach my aunt's house by mid-afternoon. It meant that I would have Griff and my mother to myself. Fate determined that the house was empty, they were out. Disappointed I took off my tunic and put my kitbag in the back place. I put the kettle on and fed the fire. The kettle had boiled and the tea was brewing in the pot when I heard the front door open and my mother shouted, "Hello, is someone there?"

I stepped into the hall and smiled. Mother just burst into tears making Griff, looking like a little boy now, start, "What is up, Nan?"

She rushed to me and I swept her in my arms, "You are home, my big boy is back home." She kissed me on the cheek and then turned to Griff, "It is your dad, now give him a hug!"

I feared that he would shy away but he did not and I picked him up. He wrapped his arms around my neck and hugged me so tightly that I thought I would choke. It was wonderful. I held him close and kissed his ear.

"Hello son, I am back, for a while at least."

He pulled his head back. I could not believe the changes the few years had wrought. "Nan says you have a new medal. Can I see it?"

"Of course."

"I will put the kettle on our Jack."

"All done and the tea is made. If you pour, I will go and sort out my kitbag."

I carried Griff into the back place. He was heavy but I did not care. I put him on the washing boiler and opened my bag. "Have you brought me a present?"

"That depends, have you been good for Nan?"

"Of course."

"Then I have but just wait until I take out what needs to be washed and what are presents, eh? There is a good soldier."

I had placed the presents in the middle so that they would have protection from my other gear. I had to take out the disassembled rifle and I saw Griff's eyes widen. "Now you don't touch that." He nodded. I made a pile of dirty laundry and secured the presents and medal case before returning the rest of my gear to the bag. I handed him half of the pile and I carried the heavier half, "Right then, quick march."

Mother had poured the tea, "His teachers said that he was a really good boy today and they are pleased with him."

I stopped in the doorway, "He is at school now?"

She nodded, "And he is doing really well. He can count to a hundred and can sing the alphabet."

I felt as though someone had punched me in the stomach. The wind went from me. I was pleased that he was doing well but I had missed so much. "Well, I shall take you to school tomorrow."

"Will you wear your uniform? And your medals?"

"Of course." I sat on my chair and took out the medal case. The ribbons were on my uniform but I had the actual medals and ribbons in the box. Before I opened it, I said, "Now when I return to duty, I shall leave them here. Do you think you can guard them?"

He seemed to grow about six inches, "Of course. I will let no one get them. Can I touch them?"

"Of course." He liked the Khedive Star. I had known he would but when he saw the DSO he asked, "Is this a special one? It looks special."

I nodded, "Not many soldiers get given these. You have to do something brave to earn them." As soon as the words were out of my mouth, I knew that it was the wrong thing to say. My mother's hand went to her mouth. She put down the tea and fled the room. I knew why.

Griff shouted to her back, "What's wrong, Nan?"

I smiled, "The tea was probably too hot. Now would you like to see your present now?"

"Yes please, but first I will put these away." He reverently placed the medals back in the case and handed them back to me.

"Where shall we put them?"

He went straight to the fireplace and the photograph of the three of us. "Here." There was just enough space before the photograph for the case. I smiled for it felt right.

I took out the box I had bought, not in Alexandria but in Cairo. I had found a market trader who had made lead figures and hand-painted them. Malik had told me of him and I had sought him out. He was an ex-soldier and he carved the figures to make moulds and then cast lead into them. I knew it was a painstaking task for there would be lead flashing that would need to be removed. There were a dozen Egyptian Camel Troops. It was strange that I had bought them before Major Dickenson had even mentioned the new unit. They were heavy and beautifully painted. I had given the ex-soldier double the money he asked partly because he was a friend of Malik's but mainly because they were worth so much more.

"Are these the soldiers you were fighting?" I nodded. "I will go and get the other soldiers and we can have a battle."

I was satisfied. I had expected the same shy boy who hid from his father behind his Nan but what greeted me was beyond my wildest dreams.

My mother came in and I saw that she had been crying, "I am sorry, Jack, I know I shouldn't have been so soft but I always worry about you and knowing that you did something brave meant you put your life at risk. I know it must happen but I shut out the idea."

"I am sorry I wouldn't want you crying on my account."

She grabbed me and began weeping once more, "You are a hero and I am so proud of you that sometimes I am fit to burst but I want you home and safe."

Griff entered and stood there with his mouth open, "Just your Nan giving me a real welcome home. Now then let's clear some space on the table so that we can play properly."

"Don't forget your tea. I will go and start to cook our supper too. It will be nice and cosy with just the four of us."

I had forgotten that Billy had moved out, "What did Elizabeth have, mother?"

"A boy, John William, but they call him Jack."

The day was getting better and better.

"Is Elizabeth well?"

She gave me a sad smile, "Aye, Jack, she is and I thank God for it."

We played with the figures for a happy hour until Aunt Sarah came in from work. Unusually for my aunt, she was a little emotional too and I realised why. I had been away from home for far longer than usual. I had only managed a couple of letters and I now saw the worry that the lack of news caused. The tears that were shed were of relief that I was not dead.

"Now, Griff, time to put these away so that we can lay the table for tea."

"Oh, do we have to?"

I put my hands on my hips and cocked my head to the side, "Now then soldier, when a Sergeant Major gives an order…" his eyes welled up with tears and I realised I had gone too far, "I was only joking, Griff, we will play again after tea."

Aunt Sarah's voice came from the kitchen, "But only for ten minutes. He has school in the morning."

He smiled, "Okay then." I was pleased with the care with which he placed the soldiers back in their tissue paper in the box. He would look after his toys and that was a good thing.

He helped me to lay the table and we sat waiting for the food and we chatted. He told me about his school, his kindergarten, and his teacher. He recognised the naughty boys and told me that he did as his Great Aunt had told him and kept away from them. He told me about his friends and the games he played with them. His favourite was British Bulldogs. It was a rough game but one that would help to make him a good rugby player when he got older as well as teaching him skills that would help him if he ever chose to be a soldier. He then asked me about my job and I was able to explain what a sergeant and a sergeant major did.

The food, when it was brought in, suited me down to the ground. It was a quick meal but delicious for all that. It was sausages, mash, and onion gravy. With thick wedges of bread to mop up the gravy, it was a perfect tea.

"I am sorry, Jack, I forgot to get any beer. You didn't say when you were getting home."

I shook my head, "I am happy enough just to be home. Beer can wait."

"Tomorrow I will do a real treat for you. Cow heel stew and mash."

My face erupted into a grin. It was my favourite food of all time. A slow-cooked calves' foot and shin beef with root vegetables and a gravy that stuck to your ribs, it would take all day to cook. I found myself salivating at the thought of it.

After we had eaten and enjoyed a cup of tea, we cleared the table. But before Aunt Sarah would allow us to play, she insisted that he say his alphabet, count up to one hundred and then write his full name on a blackboard that stood in the corner. I was impressed. We had exactly fifteen minutes and then Mother brought in the tin bath and he was bathed before the fire. He had a cup of warm milk and then it was time for bed.

"Can the Sergeant Major read me the story tonight?"

Aunt Sarah said, "You mean your father?"

He frowned, "But I thought he was a sergeant major."

I ruffled his still slightly damp head, "I am but my most important job is to be your father, Dad. Come on then, which story do you want?"

"The tin soldier."

I smiled. He was just like me.

He soon nodded off. He had enjoyed a busy day and he was excited. That was always tiring. When I came down, I gave them their presents. "You shouldn't have." I could see that despite their protestations they were delighted. Had I not brought them anything then they would have been disappointed.

"You can go to the pub if you like."

I shook my head, "I will get some beer in tomorrow but I am content just to be here in this cosy house and talk to you two. Tell me all about Sarah, Alice and their husbands."

I learned that my sisters were both close to giving birth and I wondered if I might actually still be here when they did. As the clock ticked around, the ever-practical Aunt Sarah asked the inevitable question, "When do you go back?"

I knew this had to be said and I had been dreading it. "I have a longer leave. It will be close to a month." I saw their faces brighten and I shook my head, "I am no longer a redcoat. I have been asked to form a new unit. We will be in the desert and riding camels."

Mother looked the most shocked, "Back to Africa?"

I nodded.

Aunt Sarah was an eminently practical woman, "It was inevitable, Mary, you know that. The Government let poor General Gordon and all those civilians die. It will need soldiers like Jack to win it back."

Mother became angry; a rare event, "Our Jack has done more than enough for our country and our Queen. There are others who can take their turn."

I shook my head, "Mother, I am good at what I do. I can speak Arabic, ride and, well, I am a good soldier. I am now a Sergeant Major. That is the highest rank below an officer. Even Trooper never got that high."

Aunt Sarah was impressed, "You speak Arabic?"

I nodded, "And I can get by with French, too." Egypt had been French and a smattering of French was necessary.

Aunt Sarah nodded, victoriously, "You see, our Mary, he would never have learned those skills if he had stayed at Pritchard's."

With Billy leaving home I had a bed. It was the smallest room in the house but I did not mind. I took my kit bag up and arranged it. There would be no servant for me back in England. As I lay in the bed and stared at the ceiling, I realised that the new position meant no servant and, probably, being isolated from help. I was putting myself in danger. From the odd conversations I had enjoyed with the major on the way back, I gathered that Colonel Kitchener saw our unit as an intelligence-gathering force. We were not there to fight but to find out. I had not said so to the major but it was unlikely that we would avoid fighting. What we had to avoid was capture. When we had come across the bodies of men captured by the Dervishes they had been tortured and mutilated. Malik had told me that there was no malice behind the cruelty. It was just their way. They believed that their holy cause gave them the right to do as they pleased. My last thought, as I turned to sleep, was that I would do all in my power to avoid being taken prisoner. It would be a sin but I would take my own life rather than risk torture.

The next morning I went with Mother and Griff to school. It was not far and as we walked, we saw other children heading to school. Griff was so proud of me. Every child he recognised he introduced me, "This is my father. He is a sergeant major and has won medals. The children seemed impressed as did their mothers. The headteacher stood at the gate. He was an older man than I had expected but there was something about him that suggested a man with a military background.

"This is my son, Mr Myers, Sergeant Major Jack Roberts, he is back for a while and will be bringing his son Griff to school and picking him up."

He held his hand out, "First of all, I can see from your medals that you not only serve your queen and country but do so bravely. Thank you for your service. Secondly, your son is a bright boy. Sometimes he doesn't concentrate but we are working on that, aren't we, Griff?"

"Yes, Mr Myers."

"Now cut along to the playground. I shall be ringing the bell soon."

My mother said, "And I will get to the butcher, Jack, the sooner I get the tea on the better."

When she had gone Mr Myers said, "Your mother is a good woman. Griff needs that in his life. Especially with his father gone so much." Guilt flooded through me as though someone had cut a vein. The headmaster saw my look and put his hand up, "Do not misunderstand me, Sergeant Major. I do not criticise. I served the Queen in the Hussars." He smacked his left leg, "A lance in the leg ended that career but it enabled me to come home and be a father once more. Rest assured that, until your son leaves this school, I will do all in my power to see that he has an education that even the nobility would envy. I am a great believer in this new idea of educating all."

"As am I and I thank you for this."

"When you return to duty, will it be in England?"

I shook my head, "I shall be going back to Africa."

He smiled, "When I returned from India I was as nut brown as you. It fades Sergeant Major, but the memories do not." He looked at his pocket watch, "I must ring the bell. Good to have met you, Sergeant Major, and my wife and I will pray for you when you return to the oven that is Africa."

The bell tolled as I headed, not back to the house but to the river. The cool air felt refreshing after the heat of Africa and I would enjoy walking along a river that was not teeming with mosquitoes.

I reached home at eleven having been out longer than I expected. That was largely due to the number of conversations I had enjoyed with complete strangers. My tan and my uniform told their own story and complete strangers were interested in me. My ribbons were usually the starting point. When I entered the house the wonderful aroma of the stew bubbling on the stove greeted me.

"You had a good jangle then, son?"

I smiled at the local word for conversation, "Aye, people are interested in a uniform."

"What did you make of Mr Myers?"

"Seemed a good chap."

"He is. He encourages the older children to sit for the entrance exams to the grammar school. His church raises money to help children go to school right up to the age of fourteen."

I nodded, "When Griff is old enough, I will find the money to send him to grammar school. If that is what he wants."

"Your Aunt Sarah is of the same mind and she has taken out a policy so that in five years there will be a little lump of money." She stirred the pan and then tasted it. She sprinkled in some salt. "She adores, Griff, you know. I think she sees him as her grandson too. She looked after our mother for so long that she didn't see you and the others growing up. She is making up for it now." She peered into the main room of the house and the clock on the mantle, "The pub is open if you want to get yourself a few bottles of beer." She nodded to a wooden case on the floor. "There are a couple of empties there our Billy drank. You can get the money back on them. They have cluttered up the floor long enough."

I took them and strolled down to the pub. It had been the pub where I had been recruited but they did not know me there. However, my uniform afforded me a fine welcome and I felt duty-bound to enjoy a pint. I made sure it was just a pint and took the four bottles of brown ale back to the house.

"I have made you a sandwich."

"Does our Billy live close?" I took the sandwich and the cup of tea mother poured.

"Just a mile or two away, why?"

"I thought to call in and see Bet and the bairn."

"A good idea but better leave that for tomorrow. You don't want to be late picking Griff up from school."

The leave sped by and the routine I had developed made it fly even faster. After dropping off Griff I would walk to Billy's house. Poor Elizabeth was struggling on her own with little Jack and while I had little experience with babies I could help. I washed nappies and cleaned the house while she fed what seemed like a very voracious baby. I helped her in the kitchen when he slept and I took him for walks in his pram. When I visited with Billy at the weekend he said, "You don't need to help Bet all the time, Jack. She has to learn to cope."

"I need to do this, Billy. I missed out on being a father while I was away. Griff is in school so let me be an uncle, eh?"

"Don't get me wrong, big brother, Elizabeth is very grateful but you are on leave. You shouldn't have to work."

I laughed, "It isn't work, our Bill, it is a pleasure and besides, it is only for three weeks and then..."

His face fell, "And then back to putting yourself in danger. Look, Jack, I can get you a good position. I am a senior manager now."

I shook my head, "It is very kind of you but I am not cut out for office work. I will give up the uniform one day but not yet and when I do come home to look after Mother and Griff, I will find some employment that I will enjoy."

I only saw my sisters and their husbands twice on that leave but that was because they lived in St Helens and the two of them were with child. The house was too small to have everyone there but they came over and I gave them their presents. I told them that they bloomed and I gave my brother in laws my approval.

The telegram, when it finally came, was a real shock, although I had been expecting it. I was due in Southampton in four days' time. It meant I would not see my sisters again before I left. My mother knew as soon as the telegram came and I told Aunt Sarah that night. I saw the upset on her face but she said not a word. She was a strong woman. She would have made a marvellous sergeant major had she been born a man.

That night, after I finished reading the story to Griff, I kissed him on the forehead, "We have just three days left before I must return to the other soldiers."

He nodded, the light from the candle throwing my shadow across his face, "Mr Myers said that when the time comes for you to leave that I should not cry. He said that you are a hero and Britain needs heroes. But I shall miss you, dad. I have enjoyed playing with the soldiers."

"As have I."

He pulled the covers up and then said, in a small voice, "Promise me one thing."

"Anything."

"Don't die. I never saw my mother and I would not lose you too."

I nodded and said, "I promise." I knew that I had made a promise I had no way of guaranteeing that I could keep. Men who shied away from danger were often the ones who were killed first. I had accepted the role in Egypt and I could not go back on my word but now I regretted it. My son and my nephew had changed me. I enjoyed the life I had led and now it would be snatched away from me.

# Chapter 14

The troopship was a large one. We were not the only troops sailing. I arrived in the late afternoon and found that my billet was aboard the ship. We would not be sailing for four days. At first, I was resentful. Major Dickenson could have given me another four valuable days with my family. Once I had spoken with him then all resentment left me. He had found the men he needed and wanted us to begin the training as soon as possible.

"But sir, we will have many days at sea. Surely these four days aren't really necessary."

He looked at me sadly and said, "But they are, Jack. The others arrive tomorrow but you and I need tonight and the morning. There will be an officer but you and I will be the backbone of this unit and I want us to be as one."

I was still upset, "But my family."

He lowered his eyes, "Jack, I understand better than you can know. My father died two weeks ago. I have left a grieving mother whom I may never see again. I did not want to return either but we have a duty. You and I are soldiers and we serve the queen and our country. We chose this life and personal issues have no place in them."

I was mortified, "I am sorry sir, I ..."

He smiled, "You could not have known but I wanted you to know that we both have reasons to live and return to England."

"Right sir, so who else is there in this, what are we, sir? A regiment? Section? What?"

"We are the East Sudanese Exploration Group. We answer only to the governor, Colonel Kitchener, although knowing the man he may well come with us from time to time. There is a lieutenant, Lieutenant Roger Hardy formerly of the Royal Scots Greys. I managed to get nine troopers. I wanted more but the others were not the right sort. I chose the best that I could. Besides we are not going to fight battles, we are going to find ways and means to defeat the Dervishes. Oh, we have one sailor, Midshipman Dunn is an excellent navigator and will be invaluable in the desert."

"A sailor, sir? Why would he give up the chance of being an officer in the navy to become a trooper."

"Midshipman Dunn suffers from mal de mer, he gets seasick. This voyage out will be a hard one for him. Actually, he sought me out. He had heard what we were up to and he wants to serve the Empire in whatever capacity he can. So, let us begin."

"Right sir, and if I might suggest…?"

"That is why I chose you, Roberts. Lieutenant Hardy is a good chap but I see you as my second in command and any suggestions you make will be welcomed."

"Make the midshipman the corporal. You say he has served for some time?"

"Four years."

"Then he is used to command. It will be easier for him."

"A sound suggestion." He paused, "Of course, he won't be able to bunk with the troopers…"

I nodded, "There are two bunks in my cabin and it will help me to get to know him." The memory of the kindness of Henry Hook and the rest of the section came to mind.

"Now tomorrow the uniforms and equipment will be arriving. I am afraid you will have to act as quartermaster too."

"No problem, sir. I take it we wear khaki?"

"We do."

"And we answer to no one?"

"Correct."

"Then keffiyeh and cloaks would help us. The Egyptians wear them and suffer less from the heat." He nodded, "I don't know about you, sir, but I intend to grow a beard. Cold shaves do not suit me and if we are in the desert then the alternative is a dry shave."

He smiled as he stroked his smooth cheeks, "You may be right and with keffiyeh and cloaks over our uniforms, from a distance, we might be taken for Arabs. Good idea."

We spent an hour planning before the bugle sounded for mess. Despite the organisation of the new unit we dined separately. It gave me the opportunity to think about how I would run this group of Explorers. In essence, I was the adjutant. Captain Philips had shown me the skills I would need. If I had to be away from my family then I would do the best that I could. I had now determined that once the East Sudanese Exploration Group was functioning properly, I would ask the major for permission to resign. I would give him at least a year, I owed him that, but then it would be time to put my uniform in a trunk and find a life outside the army. Eating alone helped me to formulate my plans. I looked at the red uniform. This time, when I put it in my trunk it would be for the penultimate time although I suspected that my son might like to see his father in red once more. I would have to wear it until I acquired the new one.

I headed for the communal area to meet with the major. He was eager and there before I was. I think I could understand his excitement. This would be his first command. His superior, Colonel Kitchener, would have the pressing matters of the governorship of East Sudan to concern him. We went through the list of men and he told me what he knew about them.

"They can all ride and have come from cavalry regiments. I chose those who were young and malleable. I spoke to their colonels too. The nine we have may be small in number but they have quality."

"Sir, I do not want to pour water on your idea but camels... none of us have ridden them."

He nodded, "Smoke if you wish. You are right but I was encouraged by how quickly the first three regiments adapted to camels and became effective. I was not there but at Abu Klea, they performed well." I had heard the same. "And we have an Egyptian sergeant attached to the section. Sergeant Saeed is procuring good camels for us. He served with Colonel Kitchener and he will accompany us when we are on patrol."

His answer satisfied me but as my superior officer, it really didn't matter. I took a pencil and made a list of what I thought we would need once in Sudan. "We will need scabbards for the rifles, sir. I assume it will be the Martini-Henry and not the Remington."

"I honestly don't know. I hope it is as it will be easier to procure ammunition."

I made a note of that, "We need extra canteens. The camels might be able to do without but not us."

"Good point. I have asked Saeed to find extra camels as remounts and to act as beasts of burden."

"Sir, I know you have thought this through but I am finding it hard to envisage. From what I can gather our aim is to gain knowledge of the Dervish lands?" He nodded, "And that means to go deep into enemy territory and remain unseen."

"Essentially, yes."

"Then we need to take food that we can eat without cooking. It is too late to get some from here but when we get to Alexandria…"

"Suez."

"Sir?"

We are going to Suez, not Alexandria."

"When we get to Suez, we will need to get pemmican, dried, preserved meat. The lads will be happy enough with bully beef but the empty tins will be evidence to the Dervishes that we are about. We need to stay hidden. We will just use the corned beef at our camp and can bury or reuse the old tins."

"All these are good points, Roberts. You have served longer in Egypt than I have and I defer to your knowledge."

"I think that I have the skills needed to give us a chance of survival, sir, but I am no good at mapmaking."

"That will be down to the lieutenant, the midshipman and me. The troopers I will leave to you,"

It was getting late and my pipe had gone out. I stood, "How long do I have before the troopers arrive?"

"They are from all over the country so let us say noon."

"And where do I find the Quarter Master, sir?"

"The same place he was before, along the quay."

I rose early and was the first in the mess. It was a full fry up and I had extra portions of everything. I would not be enjoying bacon and sausage in the Sudan.

I headed for the wooden building on the quay, "Sergeant Major Roberts come to pick up some gear, Quarter Master."

The Quarter Master recognised me, "Well, well, you survived." He saw my uniform, "And back in a red coat." He saw my ribbons, "And showing courage under fire. Reckless or just lucky?"

"Lucky, I guess, and the redcoat is temporary only, Quarter Master. I am the Sergeant Major of the East Sudanese Exploration Group."

He beamed, "Thank the lord I can get shot of these." He turned and shouted, "You lads, front and centre."

Four men stripped to tunics came from the back. One, a corporal, snapped his heels together, "Yes Quarter Master?"

"Find all the boxes and bags marked with ESEG and put them on the quay. Sergeant Major Roberts here will show you where to take them. Keep an eye on them. There are some thieving bastards around here." He took out a list and as they passed, he ticked the items off. "Uniforms, khaki, two of each for twenty men." I was too old a soldier to correct him. If they gave us too much then so be it. "Twenty helmets with puggaree and sunshade. Twenty sets of webbing. Twenty sets of puttees and boots." He grinned at me, "If you are riding then these might last longer."

"What if they don't fit?"

"So long as your lads bring them to me before they sail I will change them. The same with the uniform but once you are over the sea…"

A sudden thought hit me, "How do you know we are riding Quarter Master?"

He nodded at the next boxes, "Twenty bandoliers. They only issue those to horsemen and the carbines you have been issued." Another box came out, "Twenty greatcoats and blankets. Twenty canteens and lastly, twenty Westley-Richards monkey-tailed carbines."

"Not the Martini-Henry?" I was disappointed,

He smiled, "This is a cavalry carbine. It has an eighteen-inch barrel and will be much easier to use on horseback." He saw I was not convinced, "It fires a bigger bullet, .45." Shrugging he added, "It is what was ordered, Sergeant Major, and it is what you get."

"Saddles and saddle scabbards?"

"I am guessing you will be issued those wherever you land. The fact is I have none for you."

I knew it was not his fault. I would still take my trusty Martini-Henry. "Thanks, Quarter Master." The last box had been taken outside and I leaned over, "I know I am being cheeky but you wouldn't have a pistol and holster going spare, would you?"

He shook his head, "You are right, you are cheeky but as you have the DSO and they don't hand those out like sweeties, I might have something. Hang on a mo."

He headed out to the back and returned with a pistol, lanyard and holster. "A Remington army model 1875. It fires the same bullets as your carbine. The fact is, Sergeant Major, that it was ordered for a senior officer. He died of gangrene and never got to collect it. It is a bigger gun than most officers use. No one wants it. It is the only one I have and…"

"I will take it and thanks, Quarter Master."

He reached under the counter and pulled out a hessian sack, "Stick it in there and then no one can see it."

With my treasure in hand, I led the men up the gangplank to the ship. I only took three men for I needed the fourth to watch for light-fingered dock workers and enterprising soldiers. This would have to keep us alive far from any replacement equipment. The major was up and watching for me. We took the boxes to the two rooms that would be occupied by the men. "Sir, if you keep watch I will have the rest of the gear brought up."

While my three labourers headed back, I secreted my pistol in my cabin.

It took three more trips and the cabin was packed. "If we take our gear out sir there will be a little more room. In the box with the tunics were stripes. The QM had been thoughtful. There was one set of sergeant major stripes, two sergeants and two corporals. The major did not need all of the uniform. His was tailored but he would need a spare. I found mine and took them back to my cabin. The boots fitted well too and when I had them and the helmet, I was almost complete. The blankets were one size and the greatcoats came in large and medium. I took them with the bandolier and that left the carbine. Its monkey tail actuating lever made it look strange but it was lighter and shorter.

"The QM said we would get our saddles and scabbards in the Sudan."

The major nodded, "Saeed is sourcing them. Better to get something local that will fit a camel, eh."

The major was summoned on deck an hour before noon as the first of the men arrived. Lieutenant Hardy and Midshipman

Dunn had travelled together from London and it boded well that they seemed to get on. He brought them down to the crowded cabin and we began to issue the equipment. It was highly likely that the last men who arrived would be the ones tasked with exchanging equipment. It would be a lesson for them. When the major handed the tunic to Midshipman Dunn he said, "And you have an instant, albeit temporary promotion, Dunn. You will be corporal."

"Me sir? Why?"

The major nodded to me, "Sarn't Major Roberts pointed out that he was the only NCO and you have experience of command."

"Thank you, Sergeant Major." Said a happy ex-Midshipman.

"Don't thank me yet, son, you are to bunk with me and I might snore." I took Dunn to our cabin and left him there to organise himself.

When I returned the lieutenant was also fully equipped. "I will show the lieutenant to his cabin," the major said.

"You might as well stay there, sir, and chat about what we are going to do. The corporal and I can deal with the rest of the men."

I saw the relief on his face, "Thank you, Roberts. I can see that you are going to be an invaluable member of this unit."

When Dunn returned, I said, "Right, you can go up on deck and bring the men down here as they arrive."

"Right, Sarn't Major."

"Sergeant Major. I have to let the officers get away with that but not you."

He flushed, "Sorry, Sergeant Major. I am used to the navy."

"What do they call you, I mean, apart from Dunn?"

"My given name is Archibald but I answered to Middy. I quite like that as it reminds me of the navy." He shook his head, "I did try, you know, but I was quite ill."

"You know we have the Bay of Biscay to negotiate before we get to Suez."

He nodded, "And I will be sick but once we are there then my troubles will be over."

I shook my head, "You mean apart from riding a ship of the desert?" I saw that he had not realised that. "Off you go, Middy, we will cross that particular bridge when we have to and not before."

In an ideal world, they would have arrived one by one but they did not. They were servicemen and travelling on trains meant that they gravitated together and soon discovered that they were in the same unit. Four arrived together. I chatted with them as we issued the equipment and I used my questions to begin to get to know them. Paul Poulter was a Dragoon Guard. I later found out he had fallen out with his troop sergeant. I could identify with that. Harry Fielding had been a Hussar but he yearned for action and he had jumped at the chance to be a soldier who would fight rather than simply parade. Tommy Eliot had been in the lancers. His reason for choosing to join us was a sad one. The horse he had ridden since joining the regiment had fallen and had to be destroyed. The thought of riding a camel appealed. Sam Smith was a Light Dragoon who also wanted action. They seemed keen and had the greatest choice of uniform.

I had Middy take the four to the other cabin and then we waited for the next men. Jacob Johnson, known as Jake was unusual. He was of Jewish origins and his family, who had lived in London since arriving from Poland, had changed their name. He did not hide his religion but he had been plagued by bullying and bigotry. He and Paul Poulter had something in common. James Coupe was the youngest of the troopers and he had been a bugler in the Dragoon Guard. His regiment had just returned from India and was destined for home service. He wanted action. James would be using our quarter master's cabin and so he waited with me while Middy returned to the deck.

"So, Sergeant Major, what is it that we will be doing, exactly? The major was a little vague."

I took out my pipe and lit it, "First off, we will be training so that we can stay hidden. From what you told me you seek action. Well, our job will be to avoid fighting but that does not mean there will be no action. What we will be doing will be highly dangerous and you will be in harm's way."

He nodded at my ribbons, "I can see that you are no coward, Sergeant Major. You are young for your rank and you have medals." He suddenly realised what he had said, "Sorry, Sergeant Major, no offence intended."

"And none taken. If there was you would be picking yourself up off the floor." I saw that he had brought his bugle. The major had omitted to tell me that we had a bugler. It might prove handy. Now make yourself useful and take the empty boxes on the deck."

"Yes, Sergeant Major." He raced from the cabin, grateful, no doubt to have avoided censure or punishment. When I had done with him I gave him the bugle. I could not see us using it much but it was part of the equipment and James was a bugler.

The last two to arrive did not reach the ship until after twelve. That was not surprising as they had both had the longest journeys. Kelvin Kemp was a Scot and had travelled from Edinburgh. Syd Richardson was a Geordie from Newcastle, a Scots Grey. They were two men who craved action and both had been former NCOs who had been reduced in the ranks. As I had expected nothing fitted and, while the rest went to eat I went with the corporal and the two men to the Quarter Master. His men had gone to lunch but he went to fetch the necessary equipment. While he was gone, I said, "You both know we are a small unit?" They nodded, "And that means it is more likely that there might be some tension. If I think either of you is a danger to the unit, I will have you shipped out before you can say 'sorry, Sergeant Major'."

Kelvin nodded, "Aye, and quite right too, Sergeant Major, but the thing is it is drink with me. If there is whisky," he chuckled, "well, it gets my blood boiling. Dinna worry, I will be a good boy and I will keep my nose clean. I want to finish my career with a corporal's rank at least, maybe even sergeant."

"And that could happen. You, Richardson."

"Similar reason, Sergeant Major but in my case, it was a woman. She was mine and the troop sergeant took her. He has her but he has trouble chewing these days. I had to get away from both of them. When the major came it seemed a God-given opportunity."

I nodded as the Quarter Master brought out the uniforms and boots. "You are both big lads so try them on now. I would like to eat too."

"Corporal. Close the door."

Their uniforms and boots fitted and carrying their old ones we left to return to the ship. "I am not sure about God-given, Richardson. The desert is hot and the Dervishes are a tough enemy. I saw one take two .303 bullets and keep coming."

They both seemed happy about that, "Bring them on, Sergeant Major, this sounds like my kind of fight."

Middy and I headed to the mess and he said after the two troopers had left us, "I am not sure I can handle being a corporal, Sergeant Major. All the men, James apart, seem more experienced than I am. How will they take orders from me?"

"First of all the orders will either come from one of the officers or me. From what I understand you will be the navigator of the group. Believe me, if they are as experienced as they say they are then they will realise that without you they could die. All of us have a part to play and it is the whole group that will succeed or fail."

The corporal did look young but that was his face. He had a young-looking face. I could see that although the numbers of men I would be commanding were fewer it would not be an easy task. Chatting to Middy, as we ate, I discovered that he came from a naval family. He had joined because the rest had. None had ever risen higher than captain but that was a lofty position in any case.

"We have time until we reach Suez to make you aware of the way the army works but once we reach our base in East Sudan then the hard work will start. Can you shoot?"

"I have been hunting with my grandfather."

I nodded, "That was more than I ever did and is a start. Riding?"

"Yes, Sergeant Major. I enjoyed riding."

I was relieved. "As I said before your skill will be as a navigator. The desert has few roads. The rivers are the nearest we have to roads. You will be an expert. Do not be afraid to tell the officers or me if you disagree with the direction we are travelling. When it comes to fighting you listen to us. When it comes to making our way across a trackless sea of sand then it will be you who has the voice." I was not just telling him to give him confidence. I meant it.

We started work after the midday meal and spent the time training the men on the foredeck. The Major taught them Arabic. The lessons were familiar to me. While he did that, I stripped down the Remington and put it together again. You could never do this enough times. I did the same with the Monkey Tail. Then we taught them about the desert. I had with me my keffiyeh and puggaree. I showed them how to fasten them. We also did drills with the carbines. They were drills to make them, particularly Middy, familiar with the weapons. Then we set sail and I saw the fear on the face of the former midshipman. He did not want to embarrass himself in front of the men.

As we pulled away, I said, to them all, "Now we are heading for sea. It will be a pleasant little voyage until we pass the Isle of Wight and then, well not to put too fine a point on it, some of you will be sick. I never was but then I am a Sergeant Major and we are never sick." They all laughed. "Simple lessons for you: number one, throw up over the side. Two: as the corporal will tell you there is the windward side and leeward side. The windward side blows into your face. Do not hurl into the wind or you will spend the whole voyage dhobying. Three: being sick is not an excuse not to train. Four: if you are ready to vomit then do not waste time raising your hand. Find the leeward side and let rip. Bear up and behave like soldiers. Now, back to the training. Major?" Major Dickenson could not hide the grin.

Every day was like being back in school. We had to teach them things that they might have known once but had forgotten as well as new skills they knew nothing about. Most of them were sick but the Middy was no sicker than the rest and, indeed, his sickness diminished despite the mountainous seas we encountered off Le Havre. I wondered if part of the ailment was nerves and a fear of failure. I did not think he would have much sympathy from other seamen. Their language skills improved. The exceptions were Richardson and Kemp. It may have been their natural broad accents but it did not really matter. Lieutenant Hardy was a natural and the major and I were fluent. It would just make life easier when talking to Saeed and other Egyptians. The major had brought maps and we looked at those in the mess. It was there that I saw Middy grow. He saw things on the map that I had not seen and I knew that he would be a valuable asset.

When we entered the Mediterranean, the seas became calmer and the sun burned hotter. I had acquired some oil and I invited them to use it. Some did and some did not. When the ones who heeded my advice did not burn red, they realised that my advice was sage. Some of them also emulated me and allowed their beards to grow. The major and I had begun earlier than they had and by the time we neared Alexandria all of them had started to grow one.

Lieutenant Hardy had been the last to grow one. He came from a long line of soldiers with neatly trimmed facial hair, "I feel like a damned bandit, sir."

The major grinned, "And that is perfect for where are going the land is filled with bandits. What better place to hide, eh, Lieutenant? We are not going to fight in nice straight lines with cavalry charges. We will sneak around, often at night and some of the things, I can guarantee you, will be less than honourable." He nodded to me, "Sergeant Major Roberts has killed more men than anyone I know. By the time we are done, many of you will be rivalling him."

# Chapter 15

When we reached Suez, it was not Saeed and camels who awaited us but Colonel Kitchener. I did not know who he was for he was wearing Arab dress but when the major stiffened as we descended the gangplank and said, "Step lively men," then I guessed. He did not smile but began to speak to us in Arabic.

"Welcome to Sudan. We have another ship to take us further down the coast and then you will ride to your camp. It is Major Dickenson who will lead you on your exploration but I am the titular head of this unit and, as it is my concept, I would like to see it in action. Right?"

The 'right' at the end was an abrupt question and was there to catch men out. It did. Richardson and Kemp had been struggling to follow the Arabic and while the rest of us heard the word and snapped, "Yes, sir!" in Arabic, the two northern soldiers did not.

He pounced and spoke to them in English, "You two have failed to learn the language sufficiently well and I have a mind to send you directly back to England."

They both stiffened and chorused, "Sorry, sir." It was clear that as he was not wearing any insignia, they had no idea of who he was.

I looked at the major. He said nothing and that was not right. I spoke in Arabic, "Colonel Kitchener, not all men find learning a foreign language easy and Troopers Kemp and Richardson will improve. We have few enough men as it is without discarding perfectly good soldiers. The chances of our survival depending upon their language skills is negligible."

His head whipped around and his eyes bored into me, "You must be Roberts."

"I am Sergeant Major Roberts, yes Colonel Kitchener."

He came close to me and that was a mistake for he was not a big man and I looked down at him. He was perfumed, not strongly but he wore something. "Are you going to be a troublemaker, Sergeant Major Roberts?"

"Me sir, no sir. I shall just do my duty as I have always done. These men are my responsibility and I shall do all in my power to see that they survive the desert, the Dervishes and anything else that is thrown at them, sir." I never raised my voice and I did not challenge him with my eyes for I was walking a tightrope. From the corner of my eye, I saw the apprehension on the face of Major Dickenson.

He lowered his voice, "I have read your record, Sergeant Major, and it is a good one but know this. I command. You and this unit are an experiment. You are few in number so that you can be hidden, from friend and foe. You are also disposable. Is that clear?"

I looked him in the eye, "Crystal, sir, but you don't mind if we survive, do you?"

He laughed for the first time, "That would be admirable. Now come with me and bring your gear." Laden like the camels we would soon be riding, we followed him down the quay to a much smaller vessel.

As we walked, Lieutenant Hardy sidled up to me and said, quietly and in English, "You sail perilously close to the wind, Sergeant Major."

Without turning my head I said, "My first responsibility is not to Colonel Kitchener but to the men we lead. I was not exaggerating sir, survival will be a sign of success, not medals on the chest. Kemp and Richardson will not need to speak Arabic as well as the colonel but this unit will need their fighting skills, sir."

We boarded and then, without further ado, headed down the coast. He took the officers into a small salon while the rest of us watched Egypt slip by.

It proved to be a voyage of more than eight hundred miles. There was food on the ship but no cabins, at least not for rank and file. We made do with sleeping on the cargo. It gave us the chance to chat and get to know each other. The colonel and the officers kept apart. I suspect it was so that the colonel could let the two officers know all his plans. I had anticipated riding the camels this far and so I was pleased with the unexpected voyage. It took just over two days to reach the tiny jetty jutting into the sea. The voyage had become hotter and hotter as we had headed south and as we stepped onto the wooden jetty you could feel the heat through our boots. The colonel waved off the ship which would carry on south to Suakim. The colonel would be coming with us.

As we reached the tiny port, I heard the familiar snort of a camel and then the smell hit me. Waiting in the shade of a large colonial-looking building were the camels and the man I took to be Saeed.

The colonel turned and spoke as he had done each time we had seen him, in Arabic, "Major Dickenson, you and I need to talk to the commander of this small outpost. Saeed, show these men how to saddle, load and mount the camels." He nodded at Richardson and Kemp, "Do so slowly for these lumps." He said the words slowly and I saw the hands of both men clench. They had understood that much.

I nodded to the camels, "Right lads, let's get our gear stowed away, eh? The cruise is over and it is down to work now."

We hefted our bags and followed Saeed who beckoned us with his hand. He was wearing khaki but with no sign of rank. He also had a keffiyeh and a sword. That told me he had been an officer.

Saeed was a good teacher because he was patient. He told us the names of our camels as he allocated them. Mine was called Aisha and she was a female. I never had the affinity for a camel as I did a horse. They were fine beasts to ride and fast but they were not likeable. He made his own animal rise and then showed us how to saddle them. They were bigger than horses and it took longer to do. There was a scabbard for the carbine. I realised that I needed a second for my Martini-Henry. The carbine might be a useful weapon for a horseman but I liked the extra range my rifle would give me. An advantage of a camel was that being so much bigger, they could carry more. When we were on patrol, they would not need to be so laden. We managed to store all that we had brought on the camels and Saeed even taught us how to make the animals stand and, more importantly, sit. The sitting side seemed perilous.

The colonel and the major arrived just as Saeed was about to have us mount. He had taught us how to make the camel sit so that we could mount and then the command we were all dreading, how to rise. He was a good teacher and he advised us how to do this. He explained how the motion of the camel as it

stood would sway us first one way and then the other. Everyone
was an experienced horseman and understood that. When you
went up a slope you leaned forward and when you descended,
you leaned back. Although I was the least experienced, I was
determined not to fall and I did not do so.

Colonel Kitchener nodded his approval and waving his riding
crop led us south. Saeed took the halter of the spare camel and as
the three officers rode at the front I rode at the rear with Saeed.
"Corporal Dunn, place yourself behind Lieutenant Hardy."

"Yes, Sergeant Major."

"You were an officer, Saeed?"

He gave me a sharp look, "A lieutenant. Very astute of you,
Sergeant Major."

"And I am guessing that you are still paid as one."

"Of course."

"Good."

"Good?"

"It means that you are used to command and if the rest of us
falls then you will take command and these lads will survive."

He laughed, "So your challenge to the colonel was not merely
political, you do care for your men."

"Any officer who does not is doomed to die. Is that not so?"

"It is."

"How far to our camp?"

"It will take us three days to reach it. There is an old,
abandoned fort. The walls will afford some shelter and it can be
defended. More importantly, it is rumoured by the Dervish to be
haunted and they fear it. We can travel from there to explore the
land."

"Do you know the land?"

He shook his head, "I am Egyptian. The rest of the men in my
regiment were slaughtered when they were ambushed. We
followed Pasha Baker. He survived, as did I but the rest of the
men were butchered and their bodies mutilated."

"And that is why you serve with Colonel Kitchener."

He nodded, "We have the chance to hurt the Dervish. The
colonel is a clever man, Sergeant Major. This handful of men is a
secret but if you succeed then when he becomes a general and
leads men to retake Khartoum, he can use the lessons learned to

defeat the Mahdists. He knows that fighting in a desert is not like fighting as the British Army is used to. You have to live with the desert. He will make a good general."

"General?"

"Colonel Kitchener is ambitious. I was an officer and I can see the signs but he is good." He looked over at me, "You are riding as though the queen is watching. Relax and use your crop to encourage Aisha now and then. Camels are lazy."

As the miles were eaten up by the loping camels I talked with Saeed about the land and how we might survive. "The problem will be the sheer number of men who we will have to avoid. At the moment we stand out as foreigners. We need to blend in."

I nodded, "I know, keffiyeh and cloaks."

"Yes, and the beards you are growing will help." He nodded at Johnson who was drinking from his canteen, "And your men must ration their need for water."

He was right, "Johnson, put your canteen away. You drink when I say and not when you feel like it."

"Sorry, Sergeant Major. My throat did not get that order."

"No comedians if you please. We will all drink at the same time and the same amount." I turned to Saeed, "We need equipment that we did not bring. Water skins, cloaks and the like."

"We will have to forage for them but do not worry. I know where we can get them."

He was enigmatic but, for some reason, I trusted him. Losing all your friends would either give you a death wish or make you determined to best your enemy. I knew that in Saeed's case it was the latter.

We were all ready for a rest when we reached the camp. There was a puddle of water that seemed to satisfy the camels. We unsaddled and saw to the animals before we began to organise ourselves. I saw the look of approval on the face of the colonel as I gave commands. "Corporal, get a fire on the go. I am assuming that we are still in Egypt and should be safe tonight. We will risk hot food and a brew. Poulter and Fielding, you will be on the first watch. You will be relieved in two hours."

"Sergeant Major."

"Eliot and Smith, second stag. Dunn and Coupe third. I will take the fourth and the last one will be Richardson and Kemp." It was not the worst duty, that was mine, but they both knew that it was a punishment. More importantly, the colonel knew it was too.

Major Dickenson came over, "The lieutenant and I should take a watch too, Sergeant Major."

"Yes sir, and tomorrow you will but I need to see how these lads cope. You and the lieutenant are more than welcome to get up in the middle of the night and have a shufti."

We ate a bully beef stew. There was no bread and no vegetables. It was just something warm and filling. While the days were hot, I knew that the nights were cold. The three officers sat apart and spoke, I do not doubt, about the strategic importance of our job. I was more concerned with the welfare of all of us. The voyage had been so pleasant that I knew the first night in the desert would be a shock to the system. I wrapped myself in my blanket and lay on a bed made of my greatcoat and camel blanket. It was smelly but softer than sleeping on the ground. Corporal Dunn shook me awake and the air vaporised before me. It was cold.

"Thanks, Middy. Anything?"

I saw his eyes widen, "There are snakes, Sergeant Major, and other creatures crawling about."

I smiled, "They don't have those on ships, do they?" He shook his head. "Shake out your blanket and greatcoat. Make sure there are none within."

He and Coupe did as I suggested. While they prepared their beds, I made water and then walked to the tethered camels. All were asleep and secure. I walked around the edge of the oasis and seeing nothing stood still to listen and to smell. I sensed nothing and I leaned against a palm tree after first checking that there were no spiders.

I smelled Saeed before I saw him. He did not know where I was and when I stepped out his hand went to his knife. I held up my hand. He smiled, "You are good. I thought you might want company."

"Very good of you, Saeed. I take it there are no enemy warriors close by."

"It is only when we near Sudan tomorrow night that we need to be wary although they have been quiet in this area for a while. You can smoke your pipe if you like." He wafted a hand, "It may keep the spawn of the devils from annoying me." The insects were attracted to the water. I smoked and it was quite pleasant.

"You gave the men a short duty, why?"

"If I gave them a normal four-hour duty then not all would be used and some would be tired tomorrow. This way we have all lost sleep. I want no brooding resentment."

The pipe went out and I checked my watch. Soon it would be dawn and a new day would start.

I shook awake Richardson, "All quiet. Wake me in two hours."

"Yes, Sergeant Major."

The faces as the men saddled their camels told me that the first night in the desert and their first duty had been a shock to the system. Their rumps, unlike mine, had been hardened by horses for many years but we all suffered the same from the camels. The different gait and saddle meant pain in different areas. The second and third nights were slightly easier as the two officers took a duty too and we each had a shorter watch. The deserted fort had a name but we, as all soldiers do, renamed it Fort Desolation as a joke. As billets go it was not the worst but I knew, as we tethered the camels, that it would take work. That work had to wait until Colonel Kitchener had spoken to us. He was not one for encouraging words and his message was stark.

"You have managed quite well but tomorrow your real work begins. You have three months to discover where the Dervishes are gathering. Some of you may not survive. That is in the nature of war but know that you do this for your queen and country. Make them both proud of you."

Saeed left with him but he promised me he would return with the skins and cloaks I had asked for. I did not like Colonel Kitchener but he was an officer who planned well. There were six tents waiting for us to erect. Two were large ones that the troopers would share and there were four others. I knew that Saeed would need one.

As the men unpacked them, I said, "We can share one if you wish, Middy.

190

He shook his head, "I do not yet feel like a corporal and the rank was unexpected. I know that you did it to protect me a little but I am made of a stronger character than you know. I will share with the other troopers."

I nodded and then laid out the tents. There was plenty of room in the old, deserted fort and I left space between them. We erected the officers' first, then mine and the spare. We all pitched in, including the officers and they soon went up.

Middy said, "We can do the rest, sir."

I nodded and turned to the major, "I will go and examine the buildings, sir, and see what we can reuse. I will sort my tent out later."

We had just tethered the camels, after unsaddling them and my first priority was to find somewhere secure. There was an old granary and the doors, whilst not perfect could be repaired. I knew that locals might wish to steal such a valuable animal. There was another building that looked like it had been a headquarters building and there was a repairable door as well as some furniture. Major Dickenson might like it. There was a bread oven situated close to one of the stone walls and a kitchen although there were no pans. The treasure I found was the old barracks. The roof had gone at one end and the beds had been scavenged for wood but there was a table and it would make a good mess. That and the well which, so far as I could tell, still functioned, were necessary for a comfortable life. I headed back to the major with the news.

"So, sir, if we are all happy about messing together there is a good mess hall, an office for you and we can secure the camels. If we have flour then we can make bread."

"Excellent Roberts. Roger and I are not precious about eating apart. This unit will be one that will succeed or fail based upon us getting on."

"I will go and unpack and then get the lads to make repairs and we can start the evening meal."

"I would like to send out a patrol tomorrow, Sergeant Major. The sooner we start the sooner the colonel will have the information he needs."

I nodded, "Might I suggest just half of the section, sir? We will still have plenty of work to do and Saeed will not be returned."

"Good idea." He looked at the lieutenant, "Perhaps it might be an opportunity for you to get to know the desert. Sergeant Major Roberts is an old hand."

I have found that soldiers are very clean and like order. They were all happy to work in making a mess, repairing the granary gates and ensuring that we had a kitchen. The colonel, or more likely Saeed, had ensured that there was food for the camels and for us. Sam Smith nodded at the sacks, "If we get the bread oven in working order, Sergeant Major, then we can make fresh bread. Some of the oats meant for the camels will liven up the bread."

"Good idea. That is your task for the morning." I did not just supervise. Colour Sergeant Bourne and Sergeant Windridge had happily lifted mealie bags at the mission station and I knew that while I could do as the two officers did and watch men work, we would all eat sooner if I pitched in.

"When you have emptied the corned beef cans, we will wash them and use them as cooking pans."

I also found that soldiers were good at improvising. Old nails were found and reused. We discovered a broken chest of old and rusted tools but some were salvable. We swept the mess and found as many benches and chairs as we could. It felt like a feast when we sat down to eat. All that was missing was the odd bottle of beer. We made do with tea sweetened with tinned milk.

After we had eaten and the mess tins cleaned, we sat around the table. I gave out the duty rota for the fort. It would be back to the four-hour duty rota but the ones who would be on patrol the next day were given early duties so that they could enjoy uninterrupted sleep. The major listed those on the patrol. Along with the lieutenant would be Kemp, Richardson. Fielding, Coupe, and Eliot. I had experience and I had the novice. They were all happy.

I had the first duty along with Coup and Kemp. The fighting platform had been damaged in places but it still made a good, if somewhat precarious place to watch. We had barred the entrance with the broken doors. Leaving Kemp to have the first stint at the

192

gate I took Coupe around the rest of the fighting platform. It was just to get to know him better.

"Your name, Coupe, is an unusual one. Where does it come from?"

"France, Sergeant Major. My father served in the Crimea and fell in love with an English nurse. They came back to nurse my grandmother. He was a Chasseur and it seemed natural for me to join the cavalry. I envied him his action. He was in the Charge of the Light Brigade. His regiment helped to rescue the survivors. He said that they were brave soldiers but badly led."

That confirmed what Trooper had told me. I was amazed by the links in my life. "And you are named James after your father?"

He shook his head, "No, Sergeant Major, my Scottish grandfather. At home, I get called Jamie."

"Then tell the others." I had heard them call him James but that was because that was how he had been introduced to them.

"I don't like to make a fuss."

"It isn't about making a fuss. Your name is your identity. Don't let others dictate the way you are called."

It was a quiet duty. The purpose of the fort evaded me. There was neither a village nor an oasis close by. I knew that there had to be a reason for its erection but I could not fathom it.

The next morning I was up before dawn. I had asked Middy to wake me an hour well before the sun rose. I roused the troopers on duty and then the lieutenant. I planned on using the cool of the morning to enable us to ride further. We could come back after the searing heat of the sun. Malik had been a good teacher. I did not bother with my helmet but, instead, used my keffiyeh. I also took my Martini-Henry rather than the carbine. We still had the problem of water. I took two canteens. Until Saeed returned, we were a little vulnerable.

We ate and then mounted. The sun was still a faint glow in the east. When I had studied the map, I found that the fort was just outside the Dervish-controlled land. If we headed south along the road, then we would find whatever settlements there were. I intended to use the road at first just to get our bearings but later we would go across country. That was where Corporal Dunn would come into his own.

I briefed them from the back of the camel. I included the lieutenant. He was a virgin in terms of active service. I could not risk the men, "We ride south. Kemp and Richardson you will be at the back. You have both seen action and have the most experience. I will ride with Lieutenant Hardy at the front. Fielding, you ride next to Coupe... Jamie." I patted my rifle. "I have a bullet up the spout but I hope we do not need to use our guns today. Until Saeed returns with the gear to make us look like Arabs, we are all marked out as soldiers of the queen, even wearing khaki. When we return each of us will tell the corporal what we have seen. Lieutenant Hardy will keep a sketch of our route. This land must become as familiar to us as our own home. Watch for my signals. If I reach for my rifle then you do the same. If I whirl my arm around then fall back. Any questions?"

There were none. Even the two old hands looked worried and that suited me. The greatest danger lay in overconfidence.

We left the fort and headed on the barely recognisable road south. It was when the sun rose that I saw the purpose of the position of the fort. It lay on a slightly higher piece of ground and we crossed the caravan trail that led from the east to the west. Artillery could rain death on any trying to travel in either direction. That itch scratched I continued south. As the day grew hotter so the pace grew slower. We saw no one but the piles of dried camel dung told me that camels used the road. In itself that was not sinister. It could be merchants and did not necessarily mean Dervishes. I spied some green in the distance.

"Lieutenant that may be an oasis. If so, there could be water and shade."

"Right, Sarn't Major. I think we are all ready for a rest and a drink of water."

"Yes sir, but, equally, it could be somewhere we might be ambushed. When we get close enough, I will take a look-see and you be ready to come to my aid if I need it."

"Shouldn't you send one of the other troopers?"

"Meaning that I am more important than they are? It doesn't work that way, Lieutenant. I am going because I have served in the desert before. I will happily let a trooper scout out when I am confident that they can."

I smacked Aisha with the crop.

"Then by that token, you will have to be on patrol tomorrow."

I nodded, "Yes sir, and the day after too until all the men have been on patrol. If Saeed was here then he can share the load but the desert is not the place for a novice. I know that some of the lads want action. I will be happy for a fortnight of boredom."

When we were half a mile from what was clearly a piece of vegetation, I held up my hand to stop the patrol. "If I open fire then come running and if not then wait for my signal." I encouraged Aisha to move quickly and she began to run towards the stunted trees. I drew my pistol rather than my rifle and, as I neared the greenery, I wheeled her around. It was clearly uninhabited. I slowed her to a walk and headed to the centre. There was a patch of damp mud. It was an oasis but not one that could be relied upon. I went to the northern edge and beckoned the lieutenant. Aisha grazed on the foliage.

The troopers were disappointed when they arrived. Kemp snorted, "I thought the oases over here were places to get water and shade."

Shaking my head I pointed up, "This is shade and as for water, Lieutenant Hardy will mark this on his map and one day when we come here, there might be water. See to your animals. Have one drink from your canteen and then rest. I will take the first watch. Richardson, you will be next up. How long should we rest, Lieutenant, two hours?"

He took the hint and nodded, "Two hours is fine and, Kemp, this will be marked as Kemp's oasis." He smiled, "Potentially useful but possibly barren."

The others laughed and I think that Kemp was flattered that his name would be on a map. Having already tethered Aisha, I walked around the perimeter of the occasional oasis. I saw that it had once been bigger; there were signs of trees that had died further from the mud hole. Malik had told me that oases were not a guarantee of water. It would depend upon the season and who had used it. I saw no signs of recent occupation and deemed that the Dervish knew the waterhole was dry and would use other oases.

I had deliberately not taken a drink so that when I returned and nodded to Richardson for his watch, I was ready for it. The lukewarm water tasted like nectar. I took a sip and washed it around my mouth before letting it slip down. I took, in all, six sips. I saw that Fielding was smoking his pipe, "Harry, I am not saying you shouldn't smoke your pipe but if you do it will make you thirstier."

He took the pipe from his mouth and looked at it, "You are right, Sergeant Major. I should have realised that myself." He put the pipe away. "It takes some getting used to this place. Why would anyone want to live here?"

I sat with my back to a tree. Lieutenant Hardy said, "People were born here and brought up in this land. For them it is home and they are used to it. They have no choice but they are making the best of it. I suspect that they can endure the conditions easier than we can and when it rains then it might well become a Garden of Eden."

I did not contradict the lieutenant but I doubted that Sudan would ever be a Garden of Eden.

We continued south for two hours, marking on the map the signs of habitation. They were mainly abandoned mud houses. Some had been deserted for some time and the land was reclaiming the mud used to build the dwellings. I saw signs of other camels but there was no way of knowing if their riders were peaceful or belligerent.

It was getting on to dark when we neared Fort Desolation. The smell of the fires told us that they were cooking. It would also tell any Dervish scouts that it was now occupied. We rode in and the lieutenant went to report. As Coupe took the lieutenant's camel's reins the officer said, "Thank you for the lesson today, Sergeant Major. You stopped me from making a fool of myself."

"You were fine, sir."

He shook his head, "You led me like a toddler taking his first steps and I appreciate it. I would have run and fallen flat on my face."

"Yes sir, and that is always a good lesson for you rarely do it a second time." I led Aisha to the granary, "Right lads, see to your animals first and then have a good drink. You did well today." I went to my tent and took off my tunic. We did not have water to waste on washing and so I beat the tunic with my hand, outside my tent. Clouds of dust rose. When I had removed most of it, I hung it over the chair I had found and repaired. I took my spare uniform. It felt and smelt clean. I took a cloth and wiped the worst of the dust from my boots. They were not shining but they looked better than they had. When I was off duty, I would polish them until they shone. I donned my forage cap and tucked my swagger stick under my arm.

I headed for the mess. The rest of the section, Middy apart, were in the mess. I looked at Major Dickenson, "Who is on duty, sir?"

"Corporal Dunn volunteered to keep watch while we ate."

The smell from the stew was appetising but it was not right to leave the young midshipman on duty.

"I shall join him. Poulter, you and Smith can relieve us when you have finished." I looked at the major, "My fault, sir, I should have organised a rota."

Lieutenant Hardy shook his head, "No, Sarn't Major, I am adjutant and that is my job. I will create one."

"As you wish sir. We are all learning, eh? This is new to us all."

As I walked to the wall, I reflected that we were a battalion in miniature. The difference was that in a battalion there were specialists to do particular tasks. Here we had to be jacks of all trades. As far as I knew I was the only one who had tended wounds and that made me MO. Lieutenant Hardy was right, as adjutant, he was the one responsible for the duty rota but in a battalion, he would have had a sergeant and corporal to help. When we left Sudan, we would all be better soldiers.

"Who goes there?"

I was pleased with the challenge, "Sergeant Major Roberts, corporal."

"Advance and be recognised." He had his carbine in his hands.

"Anything?"

"Quiet as the grave."

I sniffed the air, "The smell of woodsmoke and food will carry across the desert. If the Dervish have any scouts out then they will soon know there are British soldiers here."

He nodded, "How did it go today, Sergeant Major?"

"We found a dry oasis and deserted homes but then we did not go far. In a week or so we will have to spend the night in the desert. That will be after we are familiar with the land thirty miles all around us."

We sat in silence except that the land was not silent. There were creatures out there and as we were not speaking, we heard them. Far out in the desert, there was the scream of an animal taken by a predator. It was a warning of the dangers of the desert. Our reliefs came and the two of us headed for the mess. Those who would be riding on the next day's patrol were already preparing having spoken to the men I had led. Every trooper was now a teacher. The major and lieutenant sat at one end of the table and Middy and I at the other. Saeed brought his tea over and joined us.

"Did you manage to fill our shopping list?"

He grinned, "The colonel was quite happy to authorise the payments. This," he waved his arm around the mess, "is the only sign of British occupation. He wishes it to succeed. What you do here, Sergeant Major, is important."

"Good."

He looked at the corporal, "And tomorrow you go on your first patrol."

Middy used a spoon to finish the last of the stew and nodded, "I am excited and fearful at the same time."

Saeed nodded, "That is good. Had you just been excited then I would have been worried." He turned to me, "I issued the water skins, keffiyeh and cloaks to the men. They filled them from the well. Yours is empty but the well will have more water now."

I had finished and I stood. There was water, somewhat greasy now, for me to wash up my mess tin. I cleaned it as best I could and dried it on the now grubby cloth. Lieutenant Hardy would need to organise that too.

I went to the two officers, "Sir, I am going off duty now. I shall need to prepare for tomorrow."

Major Dickenson said, "You needn't come tomorrow, Sergeant Major, we have Saeed now."

"I know sir, and he is a good man, nonetheless, for the first week, I will be with the men." My words left them in no doubt that argument was futile.

# Chapter 16

With Saeed and the corporal, we had two more men on the patrol that second day and I pushed the patrol harder. Once again, we had left in the cool of pre-dawn. This time it was the corporal who was making the map and he rode next to the major. I rode at the fore with Saeed and we took the road that led west. It was a better-travelled road and was the main caravan route. Saeed warned me that we might find Dervish patrols for they would rob any that was taking supplies to the Egyptians or the English. As we rode, he noticed that I had my rifle rather than my carbine. He had brought a spare scabbard for me but I had not yet had the chance to fit it. "Why do you bring the rifle, Sergeant Major? Surely it is harder to use from the back of a saddle."

I nodded, "I do not intend to use it from the back of the camel." I patted the Remington revolver. "This will do for me at the moment. I am a rifleman, Saeed and I am comfortable with my weapon."

He patted his own pistol, "I prefer a pistol and a sword but I was an officer. I wish I had the skill to use such a weapon."

We came across the first village just ten miles from the fort. Saeed said, as we approached the village, that they were unlikely to be rebels as they were too close to the Egyptian border. This was a true oasis and there were trees and tended fields. The villagers looked up fearfully as we rode into the village. Major Dickenson spoke to them while I scanned their faces for signs of danger. There appeared to be none. He told them that we were British soldiers and were there to protect them.

"They know that the British will offer protection while the Dervishes," he shrugged, "their actions are determined by whoever leads them."

As we rested and drank from our new water skins I could not help but notice that the villagers seemed happy. The families all worked in the fields but the children did so happily. There were squeals of laughter. These people had lived like this for centuries. They grew just enough to live and no more. If they ran out of food they starved and if the oasis dried up they would have to move. I thought back to England. Life was hard there but if you worked as hard as these people did then you would not starve.

We did not take their precious water and I think that made them warm to us. Certainly, as we left, there were waves from the children.

"They were afraid when we rode in for even though we do not wear Dervish clothes we could be taken for Arab raiders."

"Arab raiders?"

"Yes, slavers. The Dervishes are not the only enemy in this part of the world. There are those who prey on such places. They are Arabs, who take slaves from here and then sell them in the east. They care not to whom they sell slaves. They have been taking slaves…" he spread his right arm, "since the beginning of time. I dare say they sold them to the Romans."

"Then we should stop it."

I was indignant. We had outlawed slavery more than fifty years earlier and I hated the idea of people being taken from their homes and made to work for another. Life in England was never easy but at least we had a choice and we were paid.

"It is like trying to stop sand running through your hands, Sergeant Major. The desert is like a sea and we cannot be everywhere. With the Mahdi and his men controlling the land, there is little we can do about it."

"That does not stop us from trying though. I will speak to the major later." At the back of my mind was the thought that stopping the slavers would make the Sudanese more likely to welcome us as friends.

"They have weapons and they will defend themselves."

"I saw no guns."

"That is because they kept them hidden but they would be to hand. That village is quite a large one in comparison to some of the others we will find. The smaller ones are easier for the slavers. They do not like to fight."

We found another two villages on our journey west although the first one had been the largest. We used the shelter of the trees of the last village to eat and stay out of the sun for a while. I wandered over to watch Corporal Dunn making his map. I noticed it was far neater and more precise than Lieutenant

Hardy's. He had not written the names of the villages but instead marked them as Village 1, Village 2 and so on. I understood why. When Saeed had told us the names of the villages it had been their Arabic names. While we had been taught to speak the language, we had not been taught to write it. Lieutenant Hardy, without the aid of Saeed, had done the same. With the exception of Kemp's oasis, the others had all been designated a number.

While we ate our rations Major Dickenson came over to Saeed and me, "Saeed, we will have to do it some time, how about we leave the road for the journey back?" He pointed to the north east, "We could get back more quickly and explore some of the desert. Corporal Dunn seems quite good at navigation."

I nodded, "I think even I could get back to the fort from here sir, but there may be dangers we cannot anticipate."

"You mean enemies?"

"Saeed has told me of slavers in the region. I do not think that they would take kindly to a British presence and we are a small enough section to make them risk an attack. We have camels and good weapons."

The major had made up his mind. It was his first independent command and I think he wanted to impress the colonel, "Then it will be a good test for the men. It will keep them alert."

I stood, "I will go and warn them."

Middy was seated with the rest of the section under the shade of an old tree. "The major has decided that we will travel back a different way. We will not be taking the road. That means, Corporal we will be in your hands and for the rest of you we will have to be doubly alert."

Middy grinned at me. I could see he was relishing his task. It was something in which he had a skill, "For my part, Sergeant Major, I am confident about the navigation part but we have yet to endure action."

Sam Smith nodded, "Don't worry about that, Corporal. We all joined up for a bit of action."

In the event, it was an anti-climax. We reached the fort in a shorter time than we expected and it was still daylight. We saw nothing except for a couple of vultures circling to the south of us when we neared the fort. The major seemed happy that his risk had paid off.

As soon as we reached the fort and after we had tended to our camels, Sam went back to the bread oven. He was determined to get it up and running so that we could enjoy fresh bread. Jake went with him and I was pleased that the men were acting on their own initiative. I knew that would have been far harder in a troop or a battalion. Lieutenant Hardy had been busy in our absence. The gates were repaired and he had a notice board. The duty rota for the next fortnight was there and I saw that he had divided the duties equitably. The two officers invited Saeed and me to join them for a brew and a smoke. Middy was happily adding details to the map. Lieutenant Hardy had recognised his own deficiencies and from now on Middy would be the mapmaker.

The major must have been brooding from what he saw on the patrol, "Those vultures we saw this afternoon, I don't like it."

Saeed and I nodded but the lieutenant asked, "It is just vultures sir, what can they possibly signify?"

"Perhaps nothing but something was dead and it looked, from their position, to be close to the road. It may be an animal in which case when you head there tomorrow, you will find the bones of the beast that was killed. I want the corporal to go with you tomorrow. He is more use there with you, lieutenant. I will try to get the fort in a better shape to defend. As soon as it is I intend to leave two men here and take the rest to make a two-day ride and head deeper into Dervish territory."

I knew he was right but it was a risk. I stood, "Very well, sir. I shall go and sort out my new scabbard."

I used rope to secure it to the saddle. It did not look pretty but it was functional and it meant I now had two long-range weapons. I had never heard any soldier complain about too much firepower.

The lieutenant's new rota meant that it was not exactly the same group of men who rode on that third patrol. Jake and Tom now rode with Jamie and Syd. It would do them no harm and meant that the lieutenant had the experience of Kemp with him. With Jamie, we had a bugle. I could not see why we would need it but it was a comfort, somehow. Sam was happy to be left behind and, as we left the fort in darkness, promised us fresh bread when we returned. I admired his optimism.

We found where the vultures had been hovering. It was the first village, Middy's Village 1. When we rode in, we saw the two fresh mounds of earth. I nodded to Saeed who went to the south to check for tracks while I went north. "Take out your carbines and keep your eyes peeled." The lieutenant dismounted to speak to the villagers who, recognising us, emerged from their houses.

The advantage of dawn when you are looking for tracks is that in the sharply angled light from the rising sun, they stand out more clearly. In this case, there were none. I spied the tracks of snakes and other creatures but nothing suggesting either hoofed animals or men. I rode back to the village.

Lieutenant Hardy had remounted and Saeed returned from speaking to the men. He said, "Slavers. They rode in yesterday afternoon. The two who were killed tried to stop them from taking their families. Although the men managed to drive them off the slavers managed to get two girls and a young boy who were weeding the far field." He looked at me and added, quietly, "Children."

"No tracks to the north, sir."

"And none to the south, effendi."

Lieutenant Hardy pointed west, "They headed for the next village."

Corporal Dunn asked, "Do we need the rest of the men, sir?"

"We might need them but we can't afford the time. We shall be on our own. Saeed, Sergeant Major, you two lead off." The lieutenant was showing confidence and that was a good thing but I hoped we had not bitten off more than we could chew.

I knew that time was not on our side and I rode Aisha harder than I had hitherto. It felt like a wild ride but in reality, it was not. A racing camel can cover great tracts of land very quickly and once you worked out where to position yourself it was as easy as riding a horse. The vultures circling and swooping over Village 2 told us the story before we arrived. It was a smaller village than the first one and the slavers had spent the night there. The vultures scattered as we rode in, "Richardson, Coupe, ride to the far end of the village and look for tracks. Keep watch. Corporal, take the other men and look in the huts."

"Sir."

Saeed dismounted and turned over the partially scavenged bodies, "It is the headman and his son." He stood and looked west. "A well thought out slave raid although they failed at the other village, they were able to take this one." He put his hand over the coals. "The ash is still warm. They left this morning and I know where they will be."

Lieutenant Hardy looked at Middy's map and nodded, "The third village. Sarn't Major."

"Corporal." Middy and the other two came out of the huts. "Anything?"

"No, Sergeant Major."

"Remount."

"Saeed, what will they do? Keep heading west?"

"Perhaps but there were twelve others in this village. Added to the ones they took from the first village and the ones they will take from the last then that is enough. They will head for Abyssinia and make their way to the coast. They will have a holding pen there and ships to take the slaves away."

"Then we must stop them."

I knew that Lieutenant Hardy was angry but we needed caution, "Sir, we can't just gallop into the last village."

"I know, Roberts, what do you suggest?"

"I will take Richardson and we will work our way around to the far side of the village. If you bring the other lads in, we can cut off their retreat and fire on them from two sides."

Middy said, "Sergeant Major, what about the slaves and villagers, don't we risk hitting them?"

"I trust the men, Middy." I looked around at the faces of the others, "Just like on the range eh, mark your targets and squeeze the trigger."

"Yes, Sergeant Major."

I wheeled Aisha and Richardson and I headed north to ride around the village. I knew that we were riding the camels hard and there would be a price to pay but these were children. I thought of Griff and baby Jack and my resolve hardened.

With just two of us, it was easier to ride close together and I spoke to the veteran who, despite all his experience, had never fought in the desert or against Arabs. "This will be new for both of us. We dismount and use the camels for cover. Our job is to get their attention and allow the lieutenant and the others to surprise them. We mark our targets and go for the kill." He nodded. In my head, I was trying to remember the layout of the small village which had less than a dozen huts. They were mainly concentrated around the green area. Their tended fields were spread out. As I remembered it there was a small paddock at the west end of the settlement where they kept their goats. We would use that as cover. The village was to the south of us and I knew where it was when we heard the firing. The old muskets that the slavers used had a distinctive pop. They had not yet taken the village. It was inevitable that they would but it gave Richardson and me a chance to get into position while the attention of the slavers was elsewhere. We rode for a mile beyond the firing and then I led us south, at a walk so as not to raise dust and the road.

We reached the road and dismounted. I took out the Martini-Henry and chambered a bullet. "We walk. I am hoping that, if we are unlucky enough to be seen, they might take us for merchants." We had not seen many merchants on our way to Fort Desolation but the ones we had led their laden camels.

"How many do you reckon, Sergeant Major?"

"I have no idea. Saeed said that this is all about profit and I am guessing that there won't be a huge number but whatever there is we kill."

He turned to look at me, "We don't take prisoners?"

"If they surrender then yes, of course, we do. Richardson, we are few in number. A wounded man can still hurt us. The corporal and Coupe are young lads. Do you want their deaths on your conscience?"

"You are right, Sergeant Major."

The firing had stopped and as we neared the village I was grateful, once more, to Saeed for procuring the cloaks and keffiyeh. From a distance, we looked like Arabs. We were just one hundred yards from the village and the goat pens when we were spotted. I saw that there were at least twelve men with guns. We had not seen any guns in the village the previous day. Our appearance must have confused them for they did not react immediately. I saw them talking and that gave us time.

"Aisha, down." My camel obeyed. Richardson's beast was a little more unresponsive but eventually obeyed. I rested the rifle on the saddle and aimed at the nearest slaver. The slavers now knew we represented danger and moved towards us with their weapons aimed at the new threat. I squeezed the trigger and he fell. With luck, Lieutenant Hardy would be leading the rest of the patrol to attack the rear of the wall of warriors racing at us. It would be a real test for the young officer. This would be like Rorke's Drift all over again. I had to keep loading and firing. The difference was that this time I had no bayonet on the end of my rifle. Richardson's carbine made a different sound. We had practised with them but the men were not yet used to the unfamiliar weapon. His first bullet merely wounded the Arab slaver. I was using a familiar friend and each one of my bullets found flesh. I was aided by the fact that they were running towards me but I was calm inside. I trusted my rifle and my skill. Richardson soon got the hang of the carbine and the last man he killed was just ten feet from us. We did not rise. Both of us were too experienced for such an error. I saw Lieutenant Hardy and Saeed on their camels in the village. I raised my rifle in the air and Saeed acknowledged it. It was at that moment that one of the dead warriors rose like Lazarus and ran at us with his sword. Richardson fired from the hip and his .45 bullet smacked into the man's chest. It made a hole as big as my fist. This time he was dead.

I stood, "Up, Aisha."

Walking our camels in to the village we stopped at each body. It was partly to ensure that they were not feigning death but also to remove their weapons and search their bodies. I hung the muskets, rifles and swords from my saddle and stuck the daggers in my belt. I collected the coins and slipped them into my tunic pocket.

"Well done, Sergeant Major, Trooper Richardson. You made our job easier." Lieutenant Hardy waved his hand at the other dead slavers. There were six in addition to the twelve we had killed. "No prisoners I am afraid, but there were no casualties amongst the villagers."

I pointed to our laden saddles, "Sir, we have the weapons we took. We might as well give them to the men here, keep a couple for the ones in the first village. Better if they can protect themselves."

"You are right."

We left to trek back along the road to the abandoned village in the early afternoon escorting the survivors of the attack. There were too many of them to ride but the three taken from the first village were seated with Saeed, Corporal Dunn and myself. The little boy before me was silent. I spoke to him as I would Griff. By the time we approached their village, he had begun to respond and even laughed at a weak joke I had told. We would be arriving back at Fort Desolation in the dark but none of us minded. For the first time, we had done something worthwhile, something Christian. We had saved more than thirty Sudanese from slavery and eliminated a gang of slavers. No matter what Colonel Kitchener wanted us to do we would sleep easier that night and our food would taste better. We would have earned it.

As we neared the fort Richardson said, "The carbine is all right but your Martini-Henry is a cracking weapon, Sergeant Major."

"I have used other weapons but this rifle was with me in Natal and it has served me well."

"Aye, that is what is important isn't it? A soldier likes a weapon he can rely on."

There was a buzz of excitement that night. We had been in our first action and not suffered any loss. We had done something worthwhile. The slavers' supplies had been divided up and shared between the villages and ourselves. It meant we had something different to add to our corned beef stews. Sam had the bread oven and while the bread was not the best the smell and the taste were welcome.

I handed the purses we had taken over to the major. He shook his head, "This is a different war out here, Roberts. It isn't a war where rules can be obeyed. You and Richardson can have them, spoils of war."

Of course, that was not in either of our natures and what we had was shared amongst the others.

After we had eaten and while the dixies were cleaned and dough prepared for the next day's bread I sat with the officers, Saeed and the corporal. The major was in an ebullient mood.

One of the things we had taken from the dead leader was a box of cigars we found in his saddlebags. He and the lieutenant smoked them. I heard the banter from the kitchen as those making the bread argued about the proportions of flour, oats and rye that should be used. It was a healthy sign.

"We have proved that we can survive in the desert and I think we can range further afield."

I looked at Saeed who gave a slight shake of his head. I nodded, "I agree, sir, that we did well today but it took its toll on Aisha and, if truth be told, the fort is still not defensible. If we go on a longer patrol, we need to know that the men we leave here can defend it."

"You may be right. What say we have tomorrow as a day of rest for the animals and we all set to with a will and finish off the fort?"

I was relieved and saw that the others were too.

The major was still deliberating as he smoked a cigar and he spoke his thoughts aloud, "When we leave for the longer patrol who should I detail to stay and watch the fort?"

I knew who I would choose but it would be up to the major. I fiddled with my pipe to give the major the time to think. He sucked on his cigar. "Let us be logical. We need the Sarn't Major, the corporal and Saeed as each of them has the skills we need to make maps and survive." I saw him glance at the lieutenant and then back at me. "Roberts, you know the troopers better than anyone. Who stays?"

"You need two men who have experience and are not easily rattled. There are only two, Kemp and Richardson. Syd showed today that he does not get rattled easily and I think Kemp is cut from the same cloth. Neither will like it but they are good soldiers and if they come on the next patrol then they will be happy."

He nodded and looked at the lieutenant, "And by the same token, Roger, I have to lead. I cannot in all conscience send a subordinate to lead the first overnight patrol. You can lead the next time."

"Yes, sir, I cannot lie, I am disappointed but you are right."

The men were all happy with the decision to finish off the fort. Soldiers do not like a mess and although we had made improvements it was still not a satisfactory place to either live or to defend. Everyone set to and the ones who were not happy were the ones designated to keep watch. It was just two men each hour but when their duty was over the sentries worked harder than anyone. I thought back to the two redcoat regiments to which I had belonged. In both cases, there were slackers and skivers. The major had done well and we had none of those. We were a small section but that, in many ways, made for a better and more efficient unit.

The night before the long patrol saw all those who would be going packing what they would need. That meant all but three. We were not taking either tents or the spare camel and we had to take everything we needed on our own animals. I ensured that every man had at least fifty rounds. I had expended twenty in our first fight. It was a sign of what was needed. We each took a full waterskin, filled from the well, as well as our canteens. If we did not find an oasis then the water would have to last us and our camels for two days. We took food and that included leftover bread as well as fresh bread. Finally, we took our greatcoats and blankets. The three men we left would have to share the night watch between them. That meant the lieutenant being on his own for at least two hours. It would be as hard a test for him as leading the section to charge into slavers.

We left the fort at dawn and, having finished repairing the gates, their slamming had an ominous sound.

# Chapter 17

The major wanted to get closer to Khartoum. We were following the caravan route across the Nubian Desert towards the town of Berber. Berber had been held by the Anglo-Egyptian army. When it had fallen the guns had been captured. The major wanted to know what forces Colonel Kitchener would face. The colonel had the governorship of East Sudan but, in reality, that meant just the port of Suakim and a tiny garrison. It would be a year, at least, before he could start to retake this part of Sudan and to do so he would have to take Berber. That would be the first conquest he would need to make, and until we investigated it he would be blind.

Saeed suggested that we ride in single file. It was the way the Arabs travelled but the troopers were used to riding in companionable pairs. The major liked the idea. Saeed led, he rode behind Saeed and I brought up the rear. I did not mind although I had to endure more dust. The puggaree and the keffiyeh were wrapped around my face so that only my eyes peered out from what looked like the bandage of a mummy such as I had seen in Cairo. Riding at the back enabled me to see all the men and to reflect that we looked nothing like British soldiers. We looked more like the slavers we had fought. Sir Garnet Wolsey would not be happy. We defenders of Rorke's Drift had been castigated by him for not standing in red lines and fighting like men. Had we done so then the disaster at Isandlwana would have been repeated.

That first day we also endured our first sandstorm. Had we been without Saeed it might have been a disaster but he recognised its approach and he had us stop, dismount, form a circle and hunker down behind our camels. When it struck, I was terrified for we entered a world of swirling sand. It was worse than any snowstorm I had endured in Wales. Had we not sheltered behind the camels then we might have been buried by the sand. It took an hour to blow itself out and when Saeed said it was safe to do so, we rose like sandy wraiths to shake away the sand. The road had disappeared and we were in a sea of sand once more.

Middy and Saeed were the ones who were the least worried about the storm. Middy took out his compass and pointed the direction we should take and Saeed found the road again. We could not see it but the ground was a little firmer on the caravan route that had lasted for centuries. We drank some water and then carried on west. We caught up with a caravan travelling in the same direction. It was going to Berber too and that meant that, even though we had overtaken it, the garrison there would eventually know that there were British soldiers in the neighbourhood. If we had tried to avoid them then the result would have been the same. In the desert travellers only avoided each other if one was a band intent on mischief. We stopped and the major spoke to the leader of the caravan. He asked about water and oases. We left and headed west towards a sun that was starting to set. We had not managed to travel as far as we would have wished. The storm had seen to that. We found an oasis, or what had been an oasis and camped there. The sandstorm had buried the water making it more like a mud bath than an oasis. Saeed assured us that by morning there would be water again. It might not be clear but the camels could drink it.

I asked about the caravan, "Saeed won't that caravan catch up with us and try to use this oasis too?"

He shook his head, "They will know that it is here and they can use its water in the morning after we have left. You might be British but that does not mean that they will trust you."

We camped with sentries and before my watch, I sat with the major and Saeed, "Tomorrow, Sarn't Major, we should near Berber. We have to get close to assess the potential danger when the colonel begins to reclaim this part of Sudan."

I gestured behind me with my thumb, "And we will have to be quick, sir. That caravan will be right behind us. How about we break camp early and leave the road? If we disguise our trail then we buy time. The caravan won't know where we have gone and even if they tell the garrison that they met British soldiers we have a chance of evading them."

The major looked at Saeed who nodded, "The Sergeant Major has a good plan. The road will be closely watched and may even be patrolled. The desert is not the place you seek British soldiers."

"Corporal."

"Yes sir,"

"If we leave the road and head into the desert how confident are you that you can find Berber?"

He took out the map we had been given. It was neither as good nor as detailed as the one he was making but it showed Berber, Khartoum and Suakim. "Fairly confident, sir. It won't be like trying to find an oasis. There will be buildings that will stand out from a distance and I am now getting used to the desert. It is easier to navigate than at sea."

"Good, then that is our plan. We leave an hour before dawn."

I stood and walked over to the men and detailed their watches, "Smith, I will take the last watch, you can do the second. Middy you can do the first one now. Johnson, the third, wake me promptly."

"Yes, Sergeant Major."

I lit a fire when I was woken and put on a brew. British soldiers are always better when they have hot tea. In a perfect world, it would be cow's milk laced with sugar but the cans of condensed milk we used were a reasonable substitute. I toasted a piece of the stale bread. I would smear some condensed milk on it in lieu of butter. We were all good at improvising. The sound of the crackling fire I kindled woke Saeed and I roused the corporal. By the time the tea was brewed, it was time to wake the others. We shook them awake.

"Jamie, cut down some fronds from the palm tree."

As I was the one at the end of the column, I would sweep clear the trail. The caravan would see where we had lit the fire and assume we had headed along the road to Berber. While the others breakfasted, I walked Aisha along the road. I walked her for half a mile and then, after mounting her rode south until I found a rocky outcrop. I headed back to the oasis and dismounted to tighten her girths.

"What were you up to, Sergeant Major?"

"If the caravan leader doesn't see tracks, he will be suspicious. I have laid a trail that suggests we are heading south. It may confuse him." I shrugged, "Every little helps, sir."

We walked our animals from the oasis. It made it easier for me to sweep the sand with the palm frond. A mile from our camp and satisfied that our trail was disguised, we mounted and headed into the unforgiving Nubian desert. I had the men load their carbines for if danger came, we would need to react and react quickly. Corporal Dunn had grown into his role as navigator. He was no longer the diffident young man who was afraid of being sick before the troopers. He was now confident and offered suggestions to the major with all the aplomb of a veteran. When they held their hands up and we stopped, well before the noon break, I knew that we were close to Berber. There was a long abandoned and crumbling building that offered a little piece of shade and some cover.

I rode through the troopers. "Sir?"

He pointed to the west and there I saw a shimmering shape that had to be Berber, "We don't need all of us to get close. I will take Saeed and we will close with the walls."

"Sir, are you sure? I can leave Dunn in command here. This is a handy little place to defend. You might need me." What I was really saying was that it should be Saeed and me who scouted but he was the officer and I saw him debating.

"Are you sure?"

"He found Berber, didn't he?"

He waved over the Corporal, "Are you happy to take command of the men here, Corporal?"

"Yes, sir, I have watched Sergeant Major Roberts and I am learning."

"Very well, Sarn't Major. Get the men sorted and we will give the camels some water."

If we had to run then we needed camels that would be able to travel quickly and that meant they should be watered and rested.

I waved the men over, "Use these ruins for cover." I pointed the way we had come. "One of you will need to watch that way. Keep your weapons loaded and your eyes peeled. If all goes well then we should be back in a couple of hours and we can head back to the fort. On the other hand, we may come in like the light brigade. You need to be ready to give us covering fire and then mount and head back the way we came. Stay under cover. Have the camels lying down and hopefully you will all be invisible." I looked at Corporal Dunn, "Today could be your coming of age."

He smiled, "We won't let you down."

I liked that he said we.

We left it in single file. It was the wrong time of day to travel for the sun was at its height but that meant the garrison might be less observant. You saw what you expected to see. When we were close enough to see the gates of the fort and that they were open, we dismounted and led the camels. The Dervish flag flew from the fort. Around it, a sprawl of buildings showed where the people lived. There were tended fields between us and them. I hoped that they would disguise us. We stopped and Major Dickenson took out his binoculars. There was a danger in using them as light might reflect off them. The sun was directly overhead and I shaded the end with my hands.

He spoke to me as he scanned the defences, "They have Krupp guns on the walls. It looks to me like there are four on each wall and smaller armaments." He moved the binoculars slowly, "I count just half a dozen guards on each wall."

I could see that there were four towers and that one, the one with the flag, was taller than the others. That would be the one which had the best vantage point. Even without binoculars, I could see that it was unmanned. That did not surprise me as it would be the most exposed and the hottest. "There is no one in the high tower."

Saeed grunted, "It is noon. The ones on duty are being punished. The rest will be in the shade."

The major put down his binoculars, "Do we go closer or have we seen enough?"

Just then Saeed, who had not been looking at the fort but at the road said, "Major, the caravan we passed is approaching the fort."

I frowned. The only reason why a caravan would travel in the heat was if there was danger. In this case, I suspect the danger was us. We had fooled them but in that fooling, we had piqued their curiosity. The caravan master would not risk angering the Mahdists and he would tell them that they had seen British soldiers to the east of them.

"Well, that puts the cat amongst the pigeons."

"Sir, if we turn and walk away, slowly, they might not notice us. As soon as the caravan master reports to the garrison commander then noon or not, he will have them stand to and they will see us."

"Right, lead on Saeed."

We walked our animals back the way we had come. To all the world we looked like Arabs but anyone who saw us would wonder why we were travelling away from water and shelter. It could not be helped. Even as we walked, I realised that night was our best ally. We could travel better and more comfortably at night and we would be hidden. Our secret weapon was the midshipman. He could navigate by the stars and the one thing you could almost guarantee in the desert was a cloudless night. We had risked being seen by doing what we had done in daylight. We could have approached closer and not risked being seen had we come at night. We were learning all the time.

We had travelled just half a mile when we heard the bugle in the fort. Saeed said, "It is their version of boots and saddles, effendi. They are mounting men."

The major was a risk taker, "We walk for another half a mile and then mount. We are not on the road and they may not look to the north."

I was not convinced and I knew that by mounting we would become a larger target. We walked and each step took us closer to the section whose waiting carbines offered us some salvation. I turned and looked. A column of horsemen had left Berber and was heading along the road. Perhaps the major had made the right decision. I turned and looked in the other direction. Another, smaller column of a dozen or so horsemen had left the town from another gate and these were heading towards us, "Sir, I think we have been spotted."

He turned and said, "Mount."

I made Aisha kneel. That was the problem with mounting a camel. It was never fast. In the time it took to make her kneel the horsemen were two hundred yards closer. As we encouraged our animals to run, I glanced over my shoulder and saw that they were another hundred yards closer. Once they got into their stride then the camels would be able to go faster than the horses but until then we were vulnerable. When the guns behind us cracked it confirmed that we had been identified. It also told me of the calibre of the men who chased us. They were not disciplined. I could have risked pulling my carbine and firing one handed but that was a waste of a bullet and I had been trained too well for that.

As we neared the ruins, I saw that I could not see the section. They had done well and the horsemen were in for a shock, "Sir, ride past the ruins and our lads can hit them in the flank."

"Right, Sarn't Major."

I slid the carbine from its scabbard. I would have to fire from the back of the camel and the shorter weapon would be my gun of choice. Glancing over my shoulder I was able to see that they were now just two hundred yards from us. Some waved rifles and muskets, presumably empty while others had swords and spears. All wore the distinctive garb of the Dervish, the white jibbahs covered with the coloured squares of material. A couple had shields hanging from their saddles.

It was as we passed the ruins that I saw the carbines of the section. As soon as Middy shouted, "Fire!" I wheeled Aisha and transferred the carbine to my right hand. The camel obligingly stopped and I rested my forearm on the saddle. It was not a rifle but I wanted to hit that at which I aimed. As the carbines of the section emptied saddles, I aimed at a rider to my left whose body and horse were protected by horsemen to his left. The carbine bucked and the rider clutched his shoulder. I chambered another bullet and this time shot his horse. He tumbled from its back. Although the men had emptied saddles the Dervish still wished to get at us whilst, in the distance, I heard the bugle of the horsemen on the road. They would soon come to the aid of their comrades. We needed to end this. I drew my pistol. I had not had the opportunity to fire the Remington pistol much but it had six bullets. I fired at the nearest men and in their eagerness to get at us, they made easy targets. All the saddles were emptied and the surviving horses wandered around the dead Dervish.

"Well done, lads, now mount your camels."

"Yes Sergeant Major."

"Corporal Dunn."

"Yes sir."

"You and Saeed take the lead. Head north."

"Sir."

The major rode next to me, "Well Sarn't Major, we have the information that the colonel wants but it begs the question can we outrun these horsemen?"

"Just keep it steady, sir. I will ride at the rear with a couple of lads. If we get the chance, I will try to discourage them. Don't wait for us, sir."

"Are you sure?"

"Yes sir. Fielding and Eliot, with me."

While the men mounted, I reloaded my weapons and put them in their holster and scabbard respectively. The two troopers arrived as Saeed and Middy led the men north. I glanced behind. We had a lead of a mile and I hoped it would be enough. "We are the rearguard. If we get the chance, I want to hurt them and discourage them." We began to ride.

Eliot said, "Ambush is a good idea, Sergeant Major, but there is no cover here."

"There is more than you think. Make sure you have one up the spout and listen to my commands."

Eliot was right if you thought about trees and hedgerows but what we did have were shifting dunes, hollows and wadis not to mention monolithic rocks rising like sinister spectres from the sand.

Aisha began to suffer. Fielding and Eliot's camels had been rested while we had scouted. I was aware that I was going more slowly than they were. An hour into the chase and with the horses just half a mile behind us, I spied hope when the head of our column disappeared. They had to have dropped down into a wadi.

"You two be ready to stop when I say, turn and face the Dervish. Wait for my command."

It was a wadi, an old dry riverbed from some ancient and long dried-up waterway. Saeed was leading the column east along the wadi. I stopped at the bottom and turned Aisha around. I drew my Martini-Henry and rested my elbow on the saddle. My trusty redcoat rifle was a comfort. If nothing else the halt would allow Aisha to recover a little. The horsemen appeared on the top of the wadi and they halted presumably to ascertain which direction we had taken.

"Fire!" I fired, reloaded and fired again. The two carbines cracked next to me. It had an effect and the riders pulled back. We had emptied a couple of saddles but, more importantly, we had made them slow. "Follow me!" I turned Aisha and we headed down the wadi. We had lost sight of the others but that did not matter. I was not Midshipman Dunn but I knew that our fort lay to the northeast and that the wadi, which had been a former river, would eventually reach the coast. Besides that, we had little choice. Saeed had chosen this route and it had to be for a reason. I could not see a way out and had to trust the Egyptian's judgement. The hooves behind told me that the Dervish warriors were still following and they would now be warier. The afternoon wore on and I knew that Aisha needed rest and water soon. The wadi helped us in that it was relatively flat and there was little chance of us being outflanked but if we were to escape it then we would have to climb and therein lay the danger for as we climbed we would have to slow and invite a bullet in the back. We had to soldier on for there was no alternative.

Disaster came when we found that the wadi was blocked. Some flood had caused huge stones to fall into the dry riverbed and we had no other choice than to climb the sides. I turned and saw that the Dervish were just five hundred yards from us. Even with their lack of skill with firearms, the number of bullets that would come our way would surely hit us. We had to turn and fight.

"Dismount and shelter behind your camels."

"Yes Sergeant Major." There was no dissent in their voices. We were going to die but they would die well.

I made Aisha sit and rested my Martini-Henry across her saddle. I had a better range and my rifle barked and sent the leading rider over the back of his horse. The carbines fired next to me and I chambered another .303. This was Rorke's Drift all over again. I would only survive if I could kill the enemy faster than they could travel. Their bullets were wide and wasted but they had swords and spears. Once they closed with us, we would be butchered for their weapons would be more use in close combat than ours. The wadi was narrow but the Dervish had spread out to try to get around us. I estimated that there were more than twenty of them. When they were just forty yards from me, I drew my carbine which had a bullet in the chamber and fired before dropping it and pulling out my revolver. I fired almost blindly at the wall of men and horses.

Suddenly a barrage of bullets came from the right. The carbines of the rest of the section opened fire and tore through the Dervish who had, until that moment, been anticipating victory. Barely six escaped and they galloped off back down the wadi. I stood, "Are you two alright?"

Tom shook his head, "We are but I don't know how."

I reloaded my revolver and pointed to the major, "They came back for us."

We searched the dead and made certain that none were feigning before smashing their ancient weapons and taking swords and purses from them. We even found four horses and they were taken too.

We left the dead to the circling vultures and headed north and east. I rode next to the major, "Thank you for coming back for us, sir, but it was a risk."

He shook his head, "We had to stop anyway after climbing the wadi and I realised that with you attracting their attention we could make a flank attack. Saeed reckons that there is an oasis not far from here."

"It will have to be, sir. Aisha is all in."

"As is mine. Perhaps we might have to take to the horses, eh?"

In the end, it was just a two-mile ride and darkness had fallen when we reached the tiny pool of water. It would have been foolish to risk a fire. It was not that we feared the Dervish, they would search for us but not until the next day, it was in case the flames showed other travellers where we were. From now on we would avoid contact with anyone.

# Chapter 18

We reached Fort Desolation in the middle of the morning. The ride down the wadi had shortened our journey back but we and our animals were weary. The smiles from the men we had left showed that they had worried about us and the horses invited many questions.

After we had seen to the animals Major Dickenson said, "The day after tomorrow Saeed, Corporal Dunn and I will ride to see Colonel Kitchener. We will stay overnight. Lieutenant Hardy, you will take four men on a patrol, at the same time. Backtrack along our route as it may well be that we have invited trouble from our Dervish friends."

"Sir."

I was not sure that it was a good idea especially as it tied me to the fort. I was not in command, the major was. I had learned over the years to make the best of things. I first fed Aisha. She needed the rest and the food. Then I went to see to the Dervish horses we had taken. They were smaller than the horses I had ridden in Natal but they were sturdy beasts. It was an option we had not enjoyed before. I also changed my uniform. I would do my dhobying the next day. That evening we enjoyed a hot meal and fresh bread. Kelvin and Syd had experimented and the bread they had made was delicious. One of the things we had taken from the slavers was a clay pot of honey. The Arab to whom it had belonged obviously had a sweet tooth. That and the sesame seeds we had taken made delicious bread and the meal that night was like a feast.

I also enjoyed a smoke. Whilst we had been on long patrol, I had forfeited that pleasure for fear of giving us away but in the safety of Fort Desolation, I could enjoy it. Lieutenant Hardy had produced a new rota in our absence and Coupe and I were the first on duty. I would have the luxury of uninterrupted sleep. The gates were now secure and I enjoyed a good night of sleep. The major left before dawn to take advantage of the cool of night to travel. The lieutenant waited until dawn to leave. He took with him Kemp, Richardson, Fielding and Eliot. The first two were keen for action and the last two knew our route.

We all enjoyed the day in the fort. Little jobs like dhobying were a pleasure after being so close to death. The animals all appreciated the rest and this was the main reason that the major did not ride back to Suakim sooner. I hauled water from the well and did my washing, Mindful of waste after I had hung my clothes to dry, I shouted to the others that there was water for dhobying. As I had drawn and heated the water, they were not about to worry about the less-than-clean colour. By noon, our uniforms were drying and the bread was baking. I organised my tent. I liked order. Even the afternoon duty seemed almost pleasurable. I was able to survey the land around the fort and see, in the distance, the land we had recently explored.

The next morning, after waving off the two officers and their men and assigning Smith and Coupe to watch the gates, I set the other two off on mundane but necessary tasks. I walked around the fort to see that all was well. Shipshape and Bristol fashion came to mind. I smiled, Perhaps Middy's presence had given me a new vocabulary. The sun began to climb into the sky. I would not say I was used to the heat but I could now bear it a little better although once it came to noon then I took shelter.

I checked the supplies. The major had not taken a list of what we needed and that was an oversight. We had used ammunition and that needed to be replaced. We had used a quarter of the bully beef. I wondered if we could hunt to augment our supplies. I dismissed the idea. I had not seen anything worth hunting. I went to the latrine and then headed back to the office. I was just about to organise food when we heard the sound of gunshots. The distinctive bark of the Monkey Tailed carbine told me that the lieutenant had run into trouble. I was in command and I had to make a decision quickly. I could not leave the fort undefended but there were just four of us. Smith was an experienced man. His attitude had shown me that I could make him, with the major's approval, a lance corporal.

"Coupe, go and saddle two horses." Horses would be quicker. "Fetch your bugle, carbine and waterskin. Smith, you are in command until I return." I went to my tent and grabbed a medical kit as well as my weapons.

"Will two be enough Sergeant Major?" Poulter seemed genuinely worried.

"It will have to be. If we are not back by dark... well it means we have bought it and you have to hold the fort until the major returns."

Smith had his weapon in his hand, "The fact that we can hear the firing, sir, well it means that they are close."

"Sound travels a long way, Smith. Bar the gates when we have gone and stand to."

"Right, Sergeant Major."

I grabbed the carbine and slung it over my back. I had no scabbard on the saddle and it would mean I could just take one lot of ammo. I put the bandolier across my chest. I knew I looked like some sort of bandit but we had no choice. Jamie brought the horses and I hung my water skin and canteen from the saddle. We mounted and as we left the gates were slammed ominously behind us.

The desert could deceive and so I followed the tracks of the camels. I knew the route in any case. The horses were good ones and responsive to the touch. I saw that Jamie was happier with the horse than he had been with the camel. That confidence would help. The firing was sporadic and did not appear to move. That led me to believe that the patrol was not moving. It reassured me. The men who had followed the lieutenant were solid chaps. They had fifty rounds of ammunition and they would know that if they could hold an enemy off until dark, they had a chance. We travelled four or five miles. As we neared the firing and I saw smoke rising in the air from the Arab muskets, I slowed. As much as I wanted to get to the patrol as soon as possible I did not want to rush in and get young Coupe killed.

The Dervish must have been using muskets for I saw the smoke in the distance. Black powder did that. I could not see camels or the men. I tried to remember the land ahead. When we had travelled back, I had been so concerned that I had not taken as much notice of it as I could. It came as a flash of inspiration. There had been a jumble of rocks and some scrubby bushes six miles from the fort. By my estimation, we were now about that distance from the fort. I wondered why the attack had taken place so close to the first and then dismissed it. The reason mattered not. The sounds of the Webley pistol and the Monkey-

Tailed carbine were reason enough to get to the aid of the beleaguered patrol.

"Coupe, I think I know where they are. I intend to sweep around and take the Dervish in the rear. Follow my lead and stay close. Have your carbine ready with a bullet up the spout and if I open fire then you keep firing as fast as you can. We need them to think that we are a relief column. Your bugle will come in handy."

I thought it unlikely that they would fall for such a simple trick but Coupe needed confidence. He had craved action but this was more than he had bargained for. We headed away from the firing and then I turned and looked towards the firing. I spied something I had not seen the previous day, there was a rock that was higher than the ground around it. It looked to me to be unoccupied. I wheeled my horse and led Coupe towards it. We reached its base and I realised that the firing was very close to us. By my estimate, it was on the other side of the monolithic rock. "Coupe, stay mounted. I have an idea." I handed him the reins of my horse and with my carbine cocked made my way up the rock. It only rose twenty or thirty feet but it was relatively smooth. Close to the top I lay down and bellied my way across. The rock was only slighter higher than the rocks around but it gave me a good view. I saw when I peered over the top that the patrol was trapped four hundred paces from me. The Dervish were between me and the patrol. I saw two dead camels and the body of Tom Eliot. The huge pool of blood told me that he was dead. I saw the flashes from the muzzles of at least three weapons and that told me that at least three had survived. I could not see the other camels. Between us were at least twenty Dervishes. There might have been more hidden in the rocks. They had two men holding the reins of their horses. Four bodies told me that the patrol had exacted revenge for Eliot's death. They were just one hundred and twenty yards from me. If they bothered to look around then they would see me. I knew that the Dervishes were just trying to keep the patrol pinned down. Nightfall would see an end to the standoff and it would be a bloody one.

I slithered back down. "Jamie," I pointed to the north, the direction of Fort Desolation, "Ride back half a mile and then turn around and sound the charge. Sound it for a hundred yards and then head to the west for a hundred yards. Do the same and then ride as fast as you can back here and join me." I wanted to confuse the Dervishes.

"Right, Sergeant Major." He trusted me, that was clear from his face but I wondered if I had bitten off more than I could chew. On the bright side if I failed then there might be one survivor to ride back to the fort. I tethered the horse to a rock and then clambered back up. I wished I had brought my Martini-Henri but it was too late for that. I made my way back up to the crest and hid below it. I opened the flap on my revolver and then placed six bullets for the carbine on a flat piece of rock. Taking a deep breath I moved to the crest. The duel was still going on. The dead camels told the Dervish that the patrol could not flee and they were being patient. They only fired at the muzzle flashes. A ball ricocheting off a stone could send splinters that could blind. I waited until I heard Jamie's bugle. I heard a cheer from our men and the Dervish looked around. I had their attention. I hoped that my trick might make them flee but I was not going to take any chances. I aimed at one of the horse holders. I heard a conversation between the Dervish. They were a long way off but I made out the words, "Finish" and "off". When the second bugle call sounded, I saw them all load their weapons as they prepared to attack in force. I shot one of the horse holders and then after reloading took aim at the second. The horses were well trained for they did not move at first but when I hit the second horse holder then two of the horses ran and the others started to follow. It was then that they realised they had an attacker in their rear for the horse holders were protected by rocks and bushes. I managed one shot before a fusillade of musket balls and bullets smashed into the rocks. Splinters shot into the air and I ducked. I reloaded and risked taking a second shot. I managed to hit one Dervish in the arm. Shooting the horse holders might have been a mistake on my part as the horses had fled and the Dervish had no choice other than to kill us and take our animals.

The patrol must have realised that help had arrived for they began a fusillade of their own. I only heard three weapons and that confirmed that another had been wounded or killed. I raised my head and fired again. This time a shard of stone gouged a line along my cheek but I wounded another Dervish and I saw another spread his arms as he was shot in the back from the other side.

"Coming, Sergeant Major."

I heard Jamie making his way up. I fired my carbine again and then, to give him a chance to get in position I drew my revolver and fired almost blindly into the Dervishes. I was rewarded with one scream of pain. Then I heard the voice of Lieutenant Hardy, "They are coming to flank you." He could see what I could not.

Grabbing the bullets I had not used I said, "Back down to the horses." I wondered why the lieutenant was not taking advantage of their splitting their forces and coming to our aid. There had to be a reason. As we reached the bottom and the two animals, Dervishes appeared from both sides. I had no time to count. I fired my carbine from the hip. I regretted emptying my pistol. Jamie fired his carbine and the closest Dervish to him fell. He had heeded my orders and had reloaded and fired before me. The problem I had was that in the time it took to reload they could close with me. Even worse was the fact that they were armed with swords and once they closed with us, we would be mincemeat. When I shot the next one his companion was so close that I had no chance to reload. Instead, I blocked the blow with the carbine. I stopped the blow but the carbine was ruined. As he lifted his sword for another strike, I smacked him in the face with the butt of the carbine. He reeled and I grabbed the barrel to use it like a club. It was searingly hot and I felt my palms burning. I gritted my teeth and swung it as he swung the sword. The two weapons collided. I saw, out of the corner of my eye another Dervish coming at me with a spear. He would skewer me. I drew my bayonet as I threw the ruined carbine at my swordsman. I ran at him for he, quite naturally, ducked when the carbine came at him. Would I reach him with the bayonet before I was speared by the spearman? Fate intervened and my foot slipped in the puddled blood from one of my earlier victims. The sword swung over my head. Falling forward my bayonet drove into his thigh. He screamed as the sword bayonet sliced into flesh before ending his pain as it severed his femoral artery.

I twisted as I fell and that was just enough to put off the spearman. The spear still struck me but it hit the leather of my holster first. It scored a line across my side but the holster had saved me from a worse wound. I felt it slice into flesh but it did not seem to incapacitate me. I grabbed the haft of the spear and pulled. His natural momentum brought him close and I whipped the edge of the bayonet across his throat. Grabbing the fallen sword I ran at the two men who were trying to end Jamie's life. He was using his bayonet like a sword but, like me, he was wounded. I drove the sword left-handed into the back of one of his assailants and then slashed at the leg of the other. I struck flesh and that allowed Jamie to end the Dervishes' life.

I put my bayonet back into its scabbard and laid the sword on the ground. I could still hear firing from the other side. I reloaded my pistol.

"Coupe, can you load your gun?" He nodded, "Then reload it and stay here. Watch the horses."

"Sergeant Major, you are wounded."

I put the back of my hand to my cheek, "Looks worse than it is and it is not my first wound." I picked up the sword in my left hand and then made my way back around stepping warily over the bodies of the dead in case any had feigned death. As I came around the other side, I saw that there were still eight Dervishes left alive. I did not hesitate and I fired into the back of the nearest one. The sound of my rifle told them where I was and they whirled around. A bullet from the patrol struck one man in the back and my bullet hit another. I saw the ancient musket rising as a Dervish took aim while another ran at me with a sword. My revolver cracked and I just had time to sweep aside the sword with my own. I managed to cock the revolver and I fired it at the Dervish whose body was so close to me that the force of the gun threw him back. Even as I cocked the pistol, I knew that one of the two remaining Dervishes would end my life. I raised the Remington to aim at the nearest one when the second one's head disappeared as Jamie blasted him. My bullet hit the other a heartbeat later. They were all dead.

I reloaded the revolver and said, "Thanks, Coupe, you saved my life."

He grinned, "Just paying back the favour."

"Watch my back. Lieutenant Hardy, Sergeant Major Roberts coming in."

"Come ahead."

I walked carefully, making sure that the dead were dead. When I reached the rocks, I saw that Harry Fielding was dead and Kelvin Kemp was in Syd Richardson's lap. Blood oozed from the side of his mouth, "I knew you would come. I told you, didn't I, Syd? I said, for an Englishman, he was a good 'un"

"Aye, you did, Kempy, now keep quiet while we tend to your wound."

Shaking his head he removed his hand from his stomach. He had been holding in his entrails, "I am a dead man." His eyes rolled back into his head, and he died.

"The lieutenant is hurt too."

"Coupe, find bandages." We were a mess. The lieutenant had taken a bullet to the leg and I saw that Richardson also had a wound to his leg. I took my bayonet and cut the lieutenant's breeches. I put my hand around the back. The bullet or the ball had gone clean through. Jamie handed me a bandage. We had powder to disinfect and I took it from the kit and doused the wound. The young officer winced. I smiled, "It is in the wrong place to impress the ladies sir." I wrapped the bandage around the wound and put the safety pin through it. "Right, Richardson, let's have a look at you and then I will deal with Coupe's."

"I am alright Sergeant Major."

"Let me be the one who decides that eh?" In his case, the bullet had scored a line along his knee. It would hurt and when it had healed would react badly to cold weather but it would not end either his life or his career. Jamie's looked awful for the sword had sliced through to the bone and would hurt like blazes but the former Dragoon Guard had tied a tourniquet and he would not lose the arm. His wound took longer to tend but I was happy with the result.

"You are the one who can walk. Fetch the horses and the camels. I want us back in the fort before dark."

Lieutenant Hardy shook his head, "This is all my fault. Three men are dead because of me."

I used some of the water from Fielding's canteen to clean the worst of the blood from my face. I would have to leave the cut to my side until we reached the fort. My burnt hands did not help me. The skin had already tightened. I was just grateful that the cut to my side was giving me no trouble although I felt a tiny trickle of blood. I could tend to that back at the fort. "The Dervishes killed these three men, sir. They died doing their duty and facing the enemy."

I stood and felt a little dizzy as I did so. I guessed that was the loss of blood. I steadied myself and looked around at the ambush. One horse forlornly wandered around. I walked over to it, clucking and it came to me. I took its reins and led it back.

"Here you are, Lieutenant, this will be easier to mount than a camel." Syd used his carbine like a stick and pushed himself up. I took the lieutenant's hands and lifted him to his feet as gently as I could. He winced. "Just take it steady, sir."

Jamie brought the other animals over and helped Syd to the back of one of the horses. The lieutenant could not mount alone and I had to help him. My dizziness returned. The hardest part was loading the three bodies on to the backs of the camels. Neither Jamie nor I were whole and it took it out of me. I winced.

"You alright, Sergeant Major?"

"Thanks, Coupe, you are a good lad. I am fine and a nice brew back at the fort will have me as right as rain."

I mounted the horse I had ridden to the rescue and Jamie mounted a camel. The two of us took the reins of the camels with the bodies and we headed back to the fort.

The lieutenant insisted upon leading and I rode at the rear with Syd, "What happened, Richardson?"

He kept his voice low, "A mixture of bad luck and bad decision making. We rode a few miles south of where you found us and stopped where the major organised the ambush. Tom told us. We were tootling about looking for tracks when a snake came out. The lieutenant shot it. We should have turned and headed back then but the lieutenant decided to have an early water and food break. Harry was the one who saw the Dervishes. He shouted a warning and we mounted and tried to leg it. That was when he was wounded but he soldiered on. It became a running fight. We were lucky that the Dervishes were such poor shots but they had men waiting for us at that big rock where you found us.

They fired a volley and got lucky. Tom Eliot and two camels bought it straight away. Kelvin broke his leg when he fell. The lieutenant went to help him and he was hit. I was helping Kemp to the rocks when we were both hit. A Dervish ran from nowhere and slashed at Kempy while he lay there. His wound must have been worse than mine." He shrugged. "We had a good position and I knew that you would hear the sound of the fight. We just had to hold them off. We conserved our bullets. They tried to rush us a couple of times but with the lieutenant's pistol we held them off. As soon as we heard the bugle, I knew we were saved." He chuckled, "A clever trick that. You are a mad bugger, Sergeant Major Roberts, coming for us with just a lad like Jamie."

"He did more than alright. He fought two Dervishes who had swords with just his carbine."

Richardson nodded, "Aye, I never thought I would say it but a sword would be handy, and a pistol too."

"Jamie, sound recall so that the fort knows we are coming in."

As the notes echoed across the desert, I suddenly felt tired, like the only thing I wanted to do was to crawl into my bed and sleep for a week. I did not feel old but, as the fort hove into view, I felt weary beyond words. The sun was setting behind us and the fort was a dark shadow as we limped into the safety of its walls. I dismounted the horse and patted its neck, "I don't know your name but you are a game 'un." I put my nose next to his head and suddenly blackness overtook me. I seemed to be falling.

*I spied a light and then saw a face appear. Annie came to tend to me. She shook her head, "Always too brave, aren't you?" She mopped my brow with a cloth. The smell of her took me back to that one time in the room in Shrewsbury.*

*"Are you back now or am I dead?"*

*"You can't die, Jack, Griff needs you." She began to fade.*

*"Annie!"*

*The darkness came again and I found myself falling again. I tumbled around and around. This time there was no Annie to give me succour. I heard a man's voice say, "Fetch the fire. We have one chance to save him." There was a pain like I had never experienced in my life and I smelled burning flesh. Then all went black.*

# Epilogue

## Suakim

Someone held my wrist; their fingers were soft and I could smell disinfectant. "His pulse is stronger, doctor."

"Get the smelling salts and let us see if that will rouse him."

I forced my eyes open and tried to speak. It came out as a croak. "He is awake!" There was an Egyptian orderly and he waved over the doctor.

The doctor smiled, "Well, Sergeant Major Roberts, you had us worried. The Governor will be pleased you have not died." I tried to speak but failed. "Ismail, give him some water." The doctor patted my arm, "You are made of strong stock Sergeant Major."

As Ismail let me sip water he spoke to me, "We have tended you for four days since you were brought here." He shook his head, "Your burnt hands and slashed face were bad enough but it was the wound to your stomach that almost cost you your life. You have bled badly. Your Corporal saved your life. He saw the wound when others thought it was your head and he managed to stem the bleeding with fire. You were brought here more dead than alive. Your companions are recovering in another part of this hospital." He leaned in, "I think that there will be a leave." He smiled, "You cannot go to war again for a while, that is for certain." He stood, "Now lie back and I will fetch you some soup. It is too early for solid food."

"And a cup of tea."

He laughed, "Of course a cup of tea. Where would the British Empire be without tea?"

I was too weak to sit up unaided and so I stared at the ceiling. I had almost died. The dream of Annie told me that. It also made me think of the afterlife. Had it been a dream of my own making or were the spirits of the dead just waiting to come to our aid when we needed them? I had lapsed in my prayers and perhaps it was now time to begin them again in earnest.

The orderly helped me to sit up and that made me feel less like an invalid. The soup was adequate but the sweet tea really helped. Ismail told me that my companions had been discharged and were awaiting passage back to England. The last place I wanted to be was in a hospital bed and I determined to get out and join them as soon as possible. If nothing else an early discharge meant I would see Griff and my family sooner.

It was early evening when Colonel Kitchener came to see me. He shook his head, "You have steel in you, Roberts. You should be dead but you hung on beyond all hope." He nodded at my uniform hanging from a rail, "You will need time to recover. You are to be sent home as soon as possible and given a three month leave and you have been awarded a bar for your DSO. If it was in my power then it would have been more but...You and your companions proved my theory. British soldiers can survive behind enemy lines and beat the Dervish at their own game. There is now a troop at your fort," He chuckled, "Fort Desolation! I love the humour of the common soldier. Major Dickenson is training them. He sends his best as does that enterprising corporal. It will not be long before he is a sergeant."

"He should be an officer, sir."

A frown flickered on his face and then disappeared as he smiled, "Still trying to tell me how to run my affairs eh?"

"No sir but I recognise leaders and Dunn is a natural one."

"Perhaps. Now is there anything I can do for you?"

"Yes sir, get me on that transport home with the others. That will be the best medicine."

"I would say that is the doctor's decision but perhaps you are right. Certainly, you and the small band of brothers at Fort Desolation achieved far more through fighting for each other than many an army. I will see what I can do."

Three days later, with the other walking wounded, I watched the coast of Africa slip by as we headed north to the Suez Canal and home.

**The End**

# Glossary

Butty (pl butties) - 19th-century slang for close friends
en banderole – worn diagonally across the body
Dhobi (n)– washing (from the Indian) dhobying (v)
Fellah- An Egyptian soldier, the equivalent of a private in a British regiment
Half a crown - two shillings and sixpence (20 shillings to the pound, 12 pennies to a shilling)
Laager- an improvised fort made of wagons
Lunger - nickname for the sword bayonet
Puggaree – a cloth tied around a helmet

# Historical Background

Like many people my age I first came to know about Rorke's Drift through the superb film Zulu. It inspired Keith Floyd to join the Guards! That too came alongside a British disaster, Isandlwana. Both the charge of the Light Brigade and the disaster at Isandlwana have much in common. Whilst the leadership and planning were appalling the behaviour and courage of the ordinary rank and file could not be questioned.

This book is about life as soldiers, ordinary soldiers. The soldiers of the Queen did not care who they were fighting they just knew they were fighting for their Queen and country. That idea may seem a little old-fashioned now but I am not rewriting history, I am trying to show what it might have been like to live in 19th Century Britain. The British Army saluted with their left hand until the First World War. The weapons used are, according to my research (see book list) the ones used in the period.

Many men joined the army as a softer option than the incredibly hard and dangerous work in the factories. I worked in an iron gang in the 1970s and I can attest to the hard work even then. I tended presses that reached 3000 degrees and needed the consumption of gallons of squash during each shift. How much harder would it have been a hundred years earlier? I was working an eight-hour shift while ten and twelve-hour days were the norm a hundred years earlier.

Anyone who has researched their family history in the nineteenth century and looked at the census records will know how even relatively well-off factory workers rented or boarded. Four and five to a bed was the norm. We take so much for granted today but even in the 1950s life was hard and had a pattern. With coal fires, no bathroom, an outside toilet, no carpets and little money for food then it was closer to life in the 1870s. Offal was often on the menu and you ate what was there. Nothing was wasted. Drinking beer and smoking were not considered unhealthy pastimes. There was a teetotal movement but it was only in the latter part of the nineteenth century that the water the people drank became healthy. Until then it was small beer that was drunk.

This series will continue but unlike my British Ace Series and my WW2 one, I will not be working my way through wars. I intend to look at how British soldiers served this country and how their lives changed as Britain changed.

One reason why the attempt to relieve Khartoum failed, apart from the usual vacillations of the politicians, was that the main army travelled by boats which had to be unloaded and carried over the cataracts and the smaller, allegedly faster relief force led by General Stewart, marched in square and took ten days to cover one hundred miles.

The British NCOs who were recruited to retrain the Egyptian army were the Sergeant Whatsisnames made famous by Kipling. They did a good job. Every officer who volunteered was given the ranks of major so that no Egyptian officer could give them orders.

The skirmish at Kassassin was immortalised in a poem reminiscent of Tennyson's Charge of the Light Brigade.

AT KASSASSIN

Rained on all day by the sun,
Beating through helmet and head,
Through to the brain.
Inactive, no water, no bread,
We had stood on the desolate plain
Till evening shades drew on amain;
And we thought that our day's work was done,
When, lo! it had only begun.

'Charge!' And away through the night,
Toward the red flashes of light
Spurting in fire on our sight,
Swifter and swifter we sped.
'Charge!' At that word of command,
On through the loose-holding sand,
On through the hot, folding sand,
Through hailstorms of iron and lead,
Swifter and swifter we sped.

Thud! fell a friend at my hand;
No halt, ne'er a stay, nor a stand.
What though a comrade fell dead?
Swifter and swifter we sped.

# Redcoat's Rifle

Only the red, flashing light
Guided our purpose aright;
For night was upon us, around,
Deceptive in sight as in sound.
We knew not the enemy's ground,
We knew not his force;
But on, gaining pace at each bound,
Flew man and horse.

Burst on the enemy's flank,
On through his gunners and guns,
Swifter and swifter we sped;
Over each bayonet-ranged rank,
Earthward their dusky waves sank,
Scattered and fled.
They ran as a startled flock runs;
But still we pursued o'er the plain,
Till the rising moon counted the slain,
And some hundred Egyptians lay dead.

Oh! 'twas a glorious ride,
And I rode on the crest of the tide.
We dashed them aside like the mud of the street,
We threshed them away like the chaff from the
 wheat,
We trod out their victory under our feet,
And charged them again and again;
For demons were loose on the hot-breathing wind,
And entered the souls of our men.
A feverish delight filled our bones,
Heightened by curses and groans—
The mind taking hold of the body, the body reacting on mind.

Ha! 'twas a glorious ride,
Though I miss an old friend from my side,
And sadness is mingled with pride.
Still, 'twas a glorious ride—
That race through the darkness, the straining, the
 shock,
The struggle, and slaughter by Kassassin lock

**Arthur Clark Kennedy 1891**

Books used in the research:

- The Oxford Illustrated History of the British Army- David Chandler
- The Thin Red Line- Fosten and Fosten
- The Zulu War- Angus McBride
- Rorke's Drift- Michael Glover
- British Forces in Zululand 1879- Knight and Scollins
- The Sudan Campaign 1881-1898 -Wilkinson-Lathom

*Griff Hosker January 2023*

# Other books by Griff Hosker

If you enjoyed reading this book, then why not read another
one by the author?

## Ancient History

### The Sword of Cartimandua Series
(Germania and Britannia 50 A.D. – 128 A.D.)
Ulpius Felix- Roman Warrior (prequel)
The Sword of Cartimandua
The Horse Warriors
Invasion Caledonia
Roman Retreat
Revolt of the Red Witch
Druid's Gold
Trajan's Hunters
The Last Frontier
Hero of Rome
Roman Hawk
Roman Treachery
Roman Wall
Roman Courage

### The Wolf Warrior series
(Britain in the late 6th Century)
Saxon Dawn
Saxon Revenge
Saxon England
Saxon Blood
Saxon Slayer
Saxon Slaughter
Saxon Bane
Saxon Fall: Rise of the Warlord
Saxon Throne
Saxon Sword

# Medieval History

## The Dragon Heart Series
Viking Slave
Viking Warrior
Viking Jarl
Viking Kingdom
Viking Wolf
Viking War
Viking Sword
Viking Wrath
Viking Raid
Viking Legend
Viking Vengeance
Viking Dragon
Viking Treasure
Viking Enemy
Viking Witch
Viking Blood
Viking Weregeld
Viking Storm
Viking Warband
Viking Shadow
Viking Legacy
Viking Clan
Viking Bravery

## The Norman Genesis Series
Hrolf the Viking
Horseman
The Battle for a Home
Revenge of the Franks
The Land of the Northmen
Ragnvald Hrolfsson
Brothers in Blood
Lord of Rouen
Drekar in the Seine
Duke of Normandy
The Duke and the King

**Danelaw**
(England and Denmark in the 11<sup>th</sup> Century)
Dragon Sword
Oathsword
Bloodsword
Danish Sword

**New World Series**
Blood on the Blade
Across the Seas
The Savage Wilderness
The Bear and the Wolf
Erik The Navigator
Erik's Clan

The Vengeance Trail

**The Reconquista Chronicles**
Castilian Knight
El Campeador
The Lord of Valencia

**The Aelfraed Series**
(Britain and Byzantium 1050 A.D. - 1085 A.D.)
Housecarl
Outlaw
Varangian

**The Anarchy Series England**
**1120-1180**
English Knight
Knight of the Empress
Northern Knight
Baron of the North
Earl
King Henry's Champion
The King is Dead
Warlord of the North

Enemy at the Gate
The Fallen Crown
Warlord's War
Kingmaker
Henry II
Crusader
The Welsh Marches
Irish War
Poisonous Plots
The Princes' Revolt
Earl Marshal
The Perfect Knight

**Border Knight
1182-1300**
Sword for Hire
Return of the Knight
Baron's War
Magna Carta
Welsh Wars
Henry III
The Bloody Border
Baron's Crusade
Sentinel of the North
War in the West
Debt of Honour
The Blood of the Warlord
The Fettered King

**Sir John Hawkwood Series
France and Italy 1339- 1387**
Crécy: The Age of the Archer
Man At Arms
The White Company
Leader of Men
Tuscan Warlord

**Lord Edward's Archer**
Lord Edward's Archer

Redcoat's Rifle

King in Waiting
An Archer's Crusade
Targets of Treachery
The Great Cause
Wallace's War

**Struggle for a Crown
1360- 1485**
Blood on the Crown
To Murder a King
The Throne
King Henry IV
The Road to Agincourt
St Crispin's Day
The Battle for France
The Last Knight
Queen's Knight

Tales from the Sword I
(Short stories from the Medieval period)

**Tudor Warrior series
England and Scotland in the late 14th and early 15th
century**
Tudor Warrior
Tudor Spy

**Conquistador
England and America in the 16th Century**
Conquistador
The English Adventurer

# Modern History

**The Napoleonic Horseman Series**
Chasseur à Cheval
Napoleon's Guard
British Light Dragoon
Soldier Spy

1808: The Road to Coruña
Talavera
The Lines of Torres Vedras
Bloody Badajoz
The Road to France
Waterloo

**The Lucky Jack American Civil War series**
Rebel Raiders
Confederate Rangers
The Road to Gettysburg

**Soldier of the Queen series**
Soldier of the Queen
Redcoat's Rifle

**The British Ace Series**
1914
1915 Fokker Scourge
1916 Angels over the Somme
1917 Eagles Fall
1918 We will remember them
From Arctic Snow to Desert Sand
Wings over Persia

**Combined Operations series**
**1940-1945**
Commando
Raider
Behind Enemy Lines
Dieppe
Toehold in Europe
Sword Beach
Breakout
The Battle for Antwerp
King Tiger
Beyond the Rhine
Korea
Korean Winter

Tales from the Sword II
(Short stories from the Modern period)

**Other Books**
Great Granny's Ghost (Aimed at 9-14-year-old young people)

For more information on all of the books then please visit the author's website at www.griffhosker.com where there is a link to contact him or visit his Facebook page: GriffHosker at Sword Books

Printed in Great Britain
by Amazon

18081395R00142